The Sociolinguistics Reader

M

P
V

A member of the Hodder Headline Group

First published in Great Britain in 1998 by
Arnold, a member of the Hodder Headline Group
338 Euston Road, London NW1 3BH

Co-published in the United States of America by
Oxford University Press Inc.,
198 Madison Avenue, New York, NY 10016

British Library Cataloguing in Publication Data
A catalogue record for this book is available from the British Library

Library of Congress Cataloging-in-Publication Data
A catalog record for this book is available from the Library of Congress

ISBN 0 340 65206 3 (pb)

2 3 4 5 6 7 8 9 10

Publisher: Naomi Meredith
Production Editor: James Rabson
Production Controller: Rose James
Cover designer: Chris Halls

Composition by J&L Composition Ltd, Filey, North Yorkshire

Contents

Introduction

Sociolinguistics has changed almost out of all recognition since the 1960s, when the first readers in the subject were published. At that time the dominant branch of linguistics was generative syntax, and practising linguists could sit in their armchairs consulting their intuitions about language structure. Sociolinguistics was a peripheral, hybrid subject, a rebel discipline attracting a relatively small number of scholars who refused to consider language divorced from the social context of which it is inevitably a part. Its roots lay in the disciplines that had traditionally investigated people, society and culture, especially anthropology; and much of the emphasis in research was on the different forms and uses of language that could be observed in different cultures around the world.

Since that time a very large amount of research has been carried out on language in its social context and there have been huge advances in our understanding of how language is used, in European-type cultures as well as in those cultures more traditionally studied by anthropologists. Sociolinguistics has developed a research methodology of its own that is every bit as rigorous and scientific as that of mainstream linguistics, though it is, of course, different. It has become recognized as simply another, equally valid, way of doing linguistics, and is routinely taught as part of a wide range of degree courses, at all levels. Its coming of age has been marked by the publication of several excellent textbooks designed for teaching. There have been related developments in other branches of linguistics too, such as pragmatics, discourse analysis and corpus linguistics, all of which analyse different aspects of language in context. All these fields of linguistics – and others – now overlap with sociolinguistics in their subject-matter, both informed by it and informing it themselves.

The proliferation of interest in language and society is welcome, and has made it possible to approach the analysis of language in its social context from several different standpoints. Each approach and perspective has its own specialized journals which provide outlets for research, and the enthusiasm with which researchers investigate their subject is leading to an ever-increasing number of these specialized journals. However, while the increase in research outlets is beneficial for the development of the discipline as a whole, it makes learning about sociolinguistics more difficult for students and their teachers. The textbooks tend to discuss the same classic pieces of research, which are necessary as a first step for students, providing an overall view of the way that the subject has developed over the years. But students – and their teachers, not all of whom are specialists in sociolinguistics – also need to read more recent research reports if they are to gain an idea of the excitement of current research questions, and the interest of the controversies that inspire sociolinguists to constantly try to discover more and more about language. They need to read about more up-to-date research than they will find in their textbooks, and to read the work of leading researchers in its original form. Since the number of research journals is now so large, the task of finding relevant papers for students is daunting, even for the experts in the field. The aim of this two-volume reader is therefore to make available for students and their teachers some of the most important research papers that have appeared since 1986 in those areas of sociolinguistics where the greatest amount of research has been concentrated.

We selected 1986 as our cut-off point because, although the main purpose of the reader is to serve as a teaching resource, a secondary aim is to allow it to stand as a state-of-the-art account of the discipline of sociolinguistics in the closing years of the twentieth century. Some of the papers will stand the test of time and become classics; others may be refuted or outdated by future work. It is not possible at this stage to determine which will remain important, although in our view all the papers make valuable and timely points.

A certain amount of subjectivity is probably inevitable when choosing papers to be included in a reader, but we did not wish the volumes to represent merely our own personal favourites. In order to guard against this we carried out a survey amongst colleagues in Europe, Australasia and North America, asking them to tell us which papers they recommend most often to their students. This survey informed our eventual decision to focus on four areas within sociolinguistics where there has been a particularly large amount of influential research since 1986, to such an extent that the results have affected the development of the discipline as a whole. Although our informal survey revealed considerable variation in the papers that teachers choose to use, there were some that were mentioned again and again by the specialists in the field. These are all included in these volumes, together with some that were mentioned less often but that nevertheless seem to us to be useful in a collection of this kind. We would like to thank colleagues who replied to our questions, and especially those who sent us copies of the reading lists for their courses. While apologizing in advance to anyone whose names we have forgotten to mention, we would like to place on record our thanks to the following teachers and researchers for their suggestions and comments: Ulrich Ammon, Lars Gunnar Andersson, Allan Bell, David Britain, Jennifer Coates, Ralph Fasold, Elizabeth Gordon, David Lee, Janet Holmes, Dick Hudson, Brit Maehlum, Sharon Millar, Lesley Milroy, Dennis Preston, John Rickford, Michael Stubbs, Renee van Bezooijen, Keith Walters, Geirr Wiggen, John Wilson and Ruth Wodak.

Obviously the responsibility for the final choice rests with us. We also take responsibility for the decision only to make cuts in the papers where this seemed absolutely necessary, in accordance with our aim of providing easy access to research papers in their original form. Students will find, therefore, that some of the papers in these volumes refer to previous research with which they may not always be familiar, and that some of the papers are easier to follow than others. We make no apologies for this, since it reflects the state of the original research literature, of which these volumes provide a flavour.

Further reading

After each of the four sections in these volumes we recommend some specialized textbooks and list the main journals that are outlets for research in that area of sociolinguistics. The main general textbooks in sociolinguistics are:

Holmes, Janet (1992) *An Introduction to Sociolinguistics*, Harlow: Longman.

Hudson, R. A. (1996) *Sociolinguistics*, 2nd edn, Cambridge: Cambridge University Press.

Romaine, Suzanne (1994) *Language in Society: An Introduction to Sociolinguistics*, Oxford: Oxford University Press.

Trudgill, Peter (1995) *Sociolinguistics: An Introduction to Language and Society*, 3rd edn, Harmondsworth: Penguin.

Wardhaugh, Ronald (1992) *An Introduction to Sociolinguistics*, 2nd edn, Oxford: Blackwell.

A textbook written at a more advanced level is:

Fasold, Ralph (1984 and 1990) *The Sociolinguistics of Language: Introduction to Sociolinguistics*, 2 vols.

Section I

Multilingualism and language contact

Most communities in the world are multilingual. In these communities there is more than one language that plays an important role, and many or all of the individuals in such communities are at least bilingual. It is difficult for people who have grown up in monolingual communities – in many European countries, for example – to appreciate the extent to which this is true, but in most parts of the world monolingual people are the exception rather than the rule.

One of the most obvious problems associated with newly formed multilingual communities – for example in countries such as Australia and Canada which have seen considerable immigration from different parts of the world – is that of cross-cultural communication. Socio-linguistic research has made it clear that to communicate successfully in a language other than your own, it is not enough to learn the phonology, grammar and vocabulary of that language. You also have to learn how to use it appropriately in particular social situations according to the norms employed and accepted by its native speakers. One has to acquire *communicative competence* as well as straight linguistic knowledge.

The paper by **Christine Béal** in this section deals with a particular set of cross-cultural communication problems, namely those that may occur in interaction between French-speakers and English-speakers, particularly insofar as the linguistic activity of asking questions is concerned. One particular problem is associated with *indirectness*. In normal human societies, nobody says exactly what they believe, want or mean at all times. We all of us use indirectness as a strategy from time to time – we use hints and suggestions and vagueness and other ways of toning down what we say so as to reduce the amount of friction that can arise in face-to-face interaction with other human beings. Sociolinguistic research has revealed, however, that human societies differ in the extent to which they use indirectness as a communication strategy – and this can cause misunderstanding if, in communication between speakers from different language or cultural

1

backgrounds, hints are not noticed or, conversely, if a hint is perceived where none was intended. Asking a question is a particularly *face-threatening act.* To ask somebody for information which they may be unable or unwilling to give, or to ask them to do something that they may not want to do, is potentially an imposition. Questions are often therefore associated with a degree of indirectness. It emerges from this paper, however, that misunderstandings can occur here even in conversation between speakers from two relatively similar linguistic-cultural backgrounds, however high their actual language proficiency may be. The paper by **Cynthia Roberts** and **Pete Sayers** deals with a similar set of problems, although this time in situations where there is more of an imbalance of power between interactants. In both cases there is the very clear implication that there is scope here for the application of the results and findings of sociolinguistic research to the application of a particular real world problem – we may call this *Applied Sociolinguistics.* If people can be made aware of this type of communication problem, they can take steps to overcome it.

We also include material in this section on the linguistic behaviour of bilingual individuals. One of the most interesting aspects of bilingual behaviour goes by the name of *code-switching.* This refers, in conversations between bilingual people, to the practice of switching backwards and forwards between one of their languages and another. Sociolinguists are interested in two main aspects of this kind of phenomenon. First, they want to know what speakers' motivations are for switching in this way when there is no obvious communicative need to do so, given that all parties know both languages. Second, they are interested to learn whether there are grammatical or other linguistic rules or norms according to which switching is done. Can you switch from one language to another wherever and whenever you like, or is it more complicated than that? The paper by **Shana Poplack** deals with this issue, and compares the norms of one community with those of another.

In multilingual communities, a number of interesting phenomena occur which are of particular importance for sociolinguistics. One such phenomenon is the linguistic influence that one language can exercise on another. This is the focus of studies of *language contact,* which a number of papers in this section are concerned with. The paper by the senior and influential British sociolinguist **Robert Le Page** is one such, although he makes the very important point that notions such as 'bilingualism' and 'language contact' presuppose that languages are unproblematic, given entities when in fact this is very far from being the case. Languages are social constructs. It is true that some languages and language communities – French and English, for example – are relatively *focused;* speakers of these languages have very strong and clear ideas about the names of such languages, and about boundaries between them and other languages. Other communities, on the other hand, are relatively *diffuse,* in that it may not be particularly important to them what their language is called or that it be rigidly distinguished from, or kept separate from, some other language. Terms such as 'code-switching' are of course typical of an attitude to languages which regards them as being focused, separate identities. Le Page has been particularly interested in his work in languages known as creole languages. These are languages which have arisen out of interaction between two or more languages. Many people in the Caribbean, for example, speak English-based or French-based creoles which developed as a result of the Atlantic slave trade out of interaction between Europeans and speakers of West African languages. The bulk of the vocabulary of English-based creoles – although by no means all of it – is derived from English, hence the description 'English-based'; but the grammatical structures are very different from English, and demonstrate both West African features and some (maybe universal) features of regularization as a result of their genesis. Creole languages develop out of limited, simplified *pidgin* languages with no native speakers that grow up in trading and other contact situations. Since creole languages have native speakers, however, and they are used for the full range of purposes that any native speaker would require of their language, there is nothing limited or reduced about them at all.

Language contact is also one of the themes of the paper by **Barbara Horvath**. This urban dialect study looks at the variability (see Volume II, Section II) to be found in the English spoken in Sydney, and amongst other things compares the pronunciation of the English spoken by Australians of Anglo-Celtic ancestry (from the British Isles) and that spoken by more recent immigrants. Horvath's study of the different social dialects or *sociolects* spoken in Sydney relies on the statistical technique of principal components analysis, which it is not necessary to understand to appreciate her results. In her research in Sydney she has shown that some speakers who are deeply integrated into the speech community can be referred to as *core* members of the community, while others can be labelled members of the *periphery*. This has implications for their linguistic characteristics.

The paper by **Peter Trudgill** is also concerned with language contact, although this time in a historical context. Indeed, this paper can be labelled an essay in *sociohistorical linguistics*. He too is concerned with immigration, and attempts to explain one particular feature of an English dialect in terms of the role of bilingual speakers. The Whinnom model of pidginization which he mentions is a reference to an important paper by Keith Whinnom, who argues that pidgin languages (see above) develop only if at least three languages are involved in a contact situation, so that the *source language* (English, in the case of English-based pidgins) comes to be used in a reduced and simplified form by the speakers of the other two languages in the absence of speakers of the source language.

Multilingual societies are also interesting because of the different social, cultural and political relationships which may exist between their different languages, and because of social, political and educational problems which may arise because of these relationships. Our final paper in this section, by **Susan Gal**, is a case study of a particular

1

Keeping the peace: a cross-cultural comparison of questions and requests in Australian English and French

Christine Béal

Originally published in *Multilingua*, 13(1–2) (1994).

Introduction

Linguistic politeness
In their famous work on politeness, Brown and Levinson (1987) set out to investigate universal principles of language use. While recent work shows that not all the concepts they developed were applicable across cultures (Matsumoto 1988; Watts, Ide and Ehlich 1992; Kerbrat-Orecchioni 1992b), they did provide a useful analytical framework for the study of politeness phenomena. They showed very convincingly that requests are in essence 'Face-Threatening Acts' (1987: 59), and that all cultures share at least some common strategies to solve this problem.

The search for language universals, however, is not always the most useful approach when dealing with cross-cultural communication, because, as Ide (1988: 372) points out, 'if such universals of linguistic politeness exist, how can we account for the differences in different languages . . . ?' Brown and Levinson (1987: 36) themselves point out that 'even minor differences in interpretive strategies carried over from a first to a second language . . . can lead to misunderstanding and cross-group stereotyping of interactional style'.

When exploring problems of cross-cultural communication it is those minor differences – and their sometimes devastating consequences – which inevitably become the focus of the research. It is the case with this paper, which sets out to analyze the differences in requesting strategies between native speakers of Australian English and a group of French native speakers using English as a second language while working for the Australian branch of a French-based multinational.

Working hypotheses
The working hypothesis developed for this investigation assumes that a systematic comparison of the performance of L2 speakers in English with

5

their performance in their own language (French) and with the performance of native speakers in English (English-speaking Australians) would:

1. provide some insights into the areas of greatest discrepancies between the languages through specific, and wherever possible, quantified linguistic examples;

2. provide a better understanding of the nature of these specific differences in linguistic behaviour (some may be purely linguistic, for example, while others may reflect diverging cultural values);

3. facilitate the task of L2 teachers by identifying problems of cross-cultural communication clearly and putting them in a context of understanding rather than judging. This should in turn make it easier to sensitize L2 learners to such problems.

Data collection

The present work on requests is part of a larger project on aspects of cross-cultural communication between French and Australian-English speakers.

Because the differences which can cause trouble are indeed very minor sometimes, and rather subtle, it was assumed that they could not be safely elicited from memory or speaker's intuition. Even those linguists who gained remarkable insights from the Cross-Cultural Speech Act Realisation Project (CCSARP) questionnaires (Blum-Kulka, House and Kasper 1989b) bemoan the 'inadequacy of native speakers' intuition' and the fact that 'there is a difference between their perceived speech behaviour and their actual speech production' (Wolfson, Marmor and Jones 1989: 181). Therefore all language samples were recorded in 'on the job' situations in an effort to guarantee 'speech acts produced by native speakers in context' (Blum-Kulka, House and Kasper 1989: 3).

A large French company agreed to let willing employees be interviewed and taped. Many visits were paid over a period of nearly two years. About thirty people were interviewed, some of them twice and several hours of office conversation were recorded. Some data were collected in a large 'open-space' office area and some in the offices of two 'heads of section', one Australian[1] and one French. Therefore there were examples of interaction with all the possible combinations of French/French, Australian/Australian, and French/Australian. Examples of misunderstandings or uncomfortable moments verbally reported were also collected.

Data analysis: requests

French people when speaking English often come across as blunt or arrogant. This fairly widespread stereotype was confirmed in a series of initial interviews with the Australian colleagues of the particular group under study. On the other hand, the French speakers in question were coming up with comments about their Australian colleagues amounting to saying that they were 'wishy-washy', 'kept beating around the bush' or even were 'hypocritical'. The two series of comments did in a sense match each other and pointed towards some clashing concept of politeness. Looking in detail at request strategies used by both sides therefore seemed an obvious starting point, since requests, as we have already pointed out, are essentially face-threatening acts calling for redressive action.

In the literature on the subject, 'request' usually means 'getting somebody to do something'. Because of the nature of the data, there were actually many requests for information, as well as for approval and permission, which needed to be investigated as well. An initial distinction was made between questions (a *verbal* answer is expected) and requests (some *action* is expected). When put together, they are referred to as 'asking'.

'Asking' was divided into three categories, asking by Australians speaking English, by French speakers speaking English as a second language, and by French speakers speaking French.

Within each of those categories the questions/requests were then subdivided into three groups:

1. The first group contained all utterances which did not make use of any politeness strategy whatsoever (i.e., what Brown and Levinson [1987: 94] would call 'Bald on record'. There is no redressive action. In other words the asking takes the form of a direct interrogative form, or of an imperative or 'want' statement, as in the following examples taken from the Australian speakers' data:

(1) Any messages for me?
(2) That's not acceptable . . . Where's my stationery form?
(3) Typewrite the form, I don't want hand-written notes through here.

These utterances will be referred to in this paper as 'asking without a softener'.

2. The second group contained questions/requests which displayed the use of at least one type of politeness strategy, be it positive or negative: it could be face-threatening act minimalization or enhancement of the addressee's positive face. We used the term 'softener' to include all those devices which can somehow tone down the illocutionary force of the speech act: from starting the sentence with 'so' or a 'false start' stutter to modalization or an offer of justification. These were later broken down into several categories for finer analysis (see tables below).

3. The third group contained questions/requests with two or more 'softeners'. Here are some examples of asking taken from the Australian data and containing softeners:

(4) One softener:
   Sally, do you know where Linda is?
(5) Two softeners:
   Can you ring me a cab, *please*?
(6) Several softeners:
   Nicole, there's one more thing that *would* be great *if* you *could* do it before you go.

The initial findings: overall tendencies

The results were quite striking: only about 40% of Australian asking did not contain any kind of softening device, while 60% had at least one or more. The figures were the opposite for French speakers speaking English: 60% of direct asking, 40% only with some sort of redressive action. Furthermore, 25% of Australian asking contained two or more softeners against only 14% of asking by French people speaking English. When speaking French, the tendency to *not* soften up the asking was even stronger: nearly 75% of direct asking, and only 7.5% containing more than one softener. Table 1.1a sums up these results while Table 1.1b displays the breakdown of the same results into questions, requests and offers.

When one separates the questions for information from the requests, the picture becomes even clearer: although the French tend to be more direct in all speech acts, it is when they are asking for information that they differ most from Australians, with nearly 70% of direct questions versus only 45% for Australians.

Finally, it is worth noting the extremely low percentage of direct *requests*

Table 1.1a Overall tendencies

	Australians speaking English	%	French speaking English	%	French speaking French	%
Asking with no softener	108	39	211	62	73	71
Asking with one softener	95	35	78	23	21	20
Asking with two or more softeners	72	25	51	15	9	9
Total	275	100	340	100	103	100

Table 1.1b Details of speech acts requesting an answer: questions (Q), requests, (R) and offers (O)

		Australians speaking English	%	French speaking English	%	French speaking French	%
Asking with no softener	Q	103	39	195	62	68	71
	R	5		15		3	
	O	0		1		2	
Asking with one softener	Q	75	35	62	23	16	20
	R	15		16		5	
	O	4		0		0	
Asking with two or more softeners	Q	44	26	22	15	4	9
	R	29		26		5	
	O	0		3		0	
Total		275	100	340	100	103	100

among Australians (about 10%). These results match those of the Cross-Cultural Speech Act Realisation Project which compared five languages (Blum-Kulka and House 1989: 133). Tables 1.2a and 1.2b show these results.

It is easy to infer from these results that, through the cumulative process of daily encounters, French people would indeed come across as blunt from an English speaker's perspective. But should one conclude that the French are simply less polite or can this linguistic behavior be explained in some other way? The following analysis, which takes a closer look at individual utterances, suggests that when analyzing the performance of the French in English, one comes across three types of phenomena: some of the discrepancies seem clearly linked to the mastery of L2, some are linked to pragmalinguistic transfer and some, finally, tie in with cultural values and different concepts of face and face-threatening acts.

Mastery of L2

The group of French people under study had all learned English at school. Some had followed an intensive refresher course before being sent to Australia: at the time of the study, they had been in Melbourne for a period of between six months and two years. Others had migrated voluntarily years ago. Yet all retained a distinctive 'frenchness' in their way of expressing themselves, which suggested that, while not necessarily speaking incorrectly, they were using the English language selectively, favoring certain syntactic turns and shying away from others. In relation to requests,

Table 1.2a True requests (asking the person to *do* something)

	Australians speaking English	%	French speaking English	%	French speaking French	%
No softener	5	10	15	26	3	23
With softeners	44	90	42	74	10	77
Total	49	100	57	100	13	100

Table 1.2b Asking for information and offers (asking the person to *say* something – 'Yes', 'No', explanation)

	Australians speaking English	%	French speaking English	%	French speaking French	%
No softener	103	46	195	69	68	76
With softeners	123	54	88	31	22	24
Total number of requests	226	100	283	100	90	100

it seemed particularly relevant to assess which kinds of 'softeners' they predominantly used.

The various strategies used to soften up the requests were broken down into six categories adapted from the Coding Manual of the Cross-cultural Speech Act Realization Project. The performance of French speakers in English was compared to that of native speakers of Australian English, as Tables 1.3 and 1.4 show.

The results show that overall the French speakers favored those softeners which were easy for them to use, in other words, those which either consisted of a single lexical item (for example: 'so') or which had a syntactic equivalent in French (for example: 'could'). They especially avoided those which have no equivalent syntactic structure in French (for example: question tags) presumably because they were feeling unsure about using them. When they did try to use those, they often made mistakes, as will be shown further on. If one looks at the results in greater detail, it seems particularly relevant to note that:

1. Where there was only one softener in the request, that softener was 'minimal' in 50% of French utterances versus 30% of Australian utterances.

Table 1.3 Type of softeners used by native speakers of French in questions/requests containing one softener only

	Australians	%	French	%
Minimal (*so and* a first name)	29	31	40	50
Verbal (e.g., modal)	25	26	10	13
Tag	13	14	3	4
Minimalizer (hedge, downtoner, understater)	12	13	0	0
Justification	0	0	2	3
False start	9	9	10	13
Other	7	7	13	17
Total	95	100	78	100

Table 1.4 Type of softeners used in the overall number of questions/requests

	Australians	%	French	%
Minimal (*so and* a first name)	38	35	69	53
Verbal (e.g., modal)	45	27	33	41
Tag	21	13	5	6
Minimalizer (hedge, downtoner, understater)	36	22	5	6
Justification	7	4	10	8
False start	21	22	22	17
Total number of questions/requests with softeners*	167		129	

* It must be remembered that two or more softeners can occur in the same speech act, causing the overall number of questions/requests to be less than the total number of softeners.

This, added to the 62% of French requests already containing no softener at all would further contribute to the impression of 'bluntness'.

2. Verbal choices contributed greatly to politeness distinctions among Australians (about 25%) but showed an interesting pattern among French speakers: it was present in only 13% of sentences containing one softener only but in 41% of overall requests (this means including those containing several politeness devices). If one also takes into account that in 70% of those cases the form chosen was 'can' or 'could', a likely explanation is the following: where French speakers did not feel that a great deal of politeness was required (one softener), they tended not to use a modal, but when they felt very polite behavior was required (two or more softeners), then they would translate the syntactic form which would automatically be used in French under such circumstances, that is, the 'conditionnel de politesse' – they would use 'could' systematically, where their Australian counterparts might choose among a variety of other options, such as 'would you', 'do you mind', etc., or even tags or hedges. It seems appropriate here to quote Thomas (1983: 103) about expressing obligation in English, because it would also apply to requests:

> Foreign learners, bewildered by the large number of possible ways of expressing obligation in English (must – ought – should – have to etc.) often select one which they then use in all contexts.

3. Tags and minimalizers were hardly ever used by French speakers for the above mentioned reason that they have no syntactic equivalent in French, and therefore do not come 'naturally' to French speakers. For example, one of the few attempts at using a tag resulted in an incorrect sentence: '*So, this is the top of the painting, it is?*' Similarly, hedges such as 'kind of' or 'sort of' in introducing a verb do not translate into French. An example from the Australian data is: 'Oh, O.K., and, and . . . if you sort of highlight that in some way (etc.)'. These were hardly ever used by French speakers.

4. Justification was used in comparable proportions by both Australian and French speakers.

5. False starts were also comparable at first sight, although careful analysis of the data seems to show that French speakers' false starts were often 'genuine' – meaning they were actually struggling with the wording – whereas the Australian ones were more often a kind of polite stutter, and therefore a softening device. The French did not use a false start if they could avoid it:

(7) Australian false start:
     What, what did you do then? What Uni?
(8) French speaker's utterance:
     Which kind of study have you done?
(9) French false start:
     Try to to . . . to give it to Mark and join [sic] Mark and then send it.

6. The six categories of softeners covered most of the devices used by Australians (90%) whereas there were still a substantial number of other devices being used by the French speakers. This is because they tended to

translate a number of expressions from French into English (see below, 'pragmalinguistic transfer'), often inappropriately.

7. Above all, French speakers did not seem to know how to combine several softening devices appropriately. The Cross-cultural Speech Act Realization Project, in which hundreds of utterances were compared across four languages, provides some very interesting statistical results. The speakers of Australian English, apart from using twice as many down-graders with conventional indirectness as the speakers of the other languages under scrutiny, were most noted for their tendency to combine several downgraders in the same request. This leads the author to comment that 'the accumulated effect of deferential politeness created by the use of a number of downgraders in one utterance is typically English' (Blum-Kulka 1989: 62). Examples of this tendency abound in our Australian data:

(10) Australian speaker:
Can you just give Barbara a bit of a hand on sorting out the memory on that machine? You wouldn't mind?

(11) Australian speaker:
Oh, O.K. and and if you sort of highlight that in some way, and perhaps underline it, I don't know . . .

French speakers' attempt at reproducing the same kind of politeness were often clumsy and long-winded, a characteristic typical, it seems, of L2 speakers. According to researchers in the field of non-native language use 'one specific interlanguage phenomenon revealed in speech act realization is that of verbosity': Blum-Kulka and Olshtain (1986) found that learners' requests are realized systematically by longer utterances than those of native speakers.

(12) French speaker:
Anthony, I was wondering if you would have the book of financial receipts, because the other day we . . . I suggested you . . . that you have a look. We don't find it now. Would you have it?

These efforts could in turn 'backfire', giving the impression that the speaker was 'over the top', and possibly insincere.

As can be seen from the above, part of the problem can clearly be linked to difficulties in mastering some parts of the English morphosyntax and in the fossilization which results from the systematic circumnavigation of these perceived linguistic obstacles. When Lado, as quoted in Riley (1989: 233) writes that 'the student who comes in contact with a foreign language will find some features of it quite easy and others extremely difficult. Those elements that are similar to his native language will be simple for him, and those elements that are different will be difficult', it is tempting to point out the obvious limitations of this observation alongside Riley (1989) and other contrastive linguists (Loveday 1982, 1983; Thomas 1983).

Our own data are certainly proof enough that this 'hypothesis' in itself cannot account for all L2 learners' problems and that many interlanguage errors are best explained in terms of pragmatics. There is, nevertheless, an element of truth in it, and some mistakes *are* simply related to differences in linguistic systems. When a whole group of L2 speakers consistently shy away from using certain parts of the target language, or make mistakes when trying to use those parts (as was the case with modals, question tags, hedges and the combination of downgraders in our data) and when it so happens that there is no linguistic equivalent in their own language, then surely the problem *is* a purely linguistic one, at least as far as the learner is concerned. The fact that these particular usages also have social implications is something only the L2 teacher can highlight and reinforce through practice in the classroom. Unfortunately, many L2 speakers are still left to choose the easier route and therefore never develop a complete mastery of the second language.

Pragmalinguistic transfer

Speakers of a second language tend unconsciously to transfer utterances and speech acts from their native tongue into the target language. Often this transfer is inappropriate because, despite a surface similarity on the syntactic or even semantic level, the illocutionary force of a given utterance varies from language to language. This results in what Thomas (1983) describes as 'pragmalinguistic failure'. It also corresponds to the 'formal categories of politeness (pragmalinguistic level of analysis)' defined by Haverkate (1988: 386).

In the case of requests, pragmalinguistic failure occurred when the French speakers transferred French linguistic strategies or translated French 'softeners' into English. The main ones are dealt with in the following sections.

Territorial breach apology
There was a tendency to translate literally the standard French apology *Excusez-moi de vous déranger* into English as in the following example:

> (13) On the telephone.
> French speaker: Ann? Sorry for disturbing you. It's Béatrice. Could you check something for me?

As one Australian informant who does not speak any French pointed out, this sounds 'over the top' and 'neurotic' because 'it's the sort of thing you'd say if you were waking somebody up at three o'clock in the morning'. Although not all informants were as uncompromising, all agreed that this was an odd turn of phrase and that the standard apology was: 'Excuse me, have you got a moment?'

In the same way, many French people used 'sorry' as a translation of the French *pardon*, therefore inappropriately:

> (14) French speaker: Sorry Ann! At what time do you leave?

Impersonal verbs
One frequent way in which requests are mitigated in French is through the use of impersonal verbs such as *il faut* ('it must be'), *il suffit* ('all that has to be done'), *il vaut/vaudrait mieux* ('it is/would be better to') etc., as in the following exchange:

(15) *Est-ce qu'il faut taper ce rapport?* ('Should this report be typed?')
(16) *Il vaudrait mieux d'abord que tu fasses relire l'anglais* ('You had better get your English checked first.')

In French, this strategy takes the emphasis away from the will of the person issuing the order and dilutes it into a kind of abstract obligation. This is what Haverkate (1988: 405) calls 'defocalization' which he defines as 'the strategy which enables the speakers to suppress the identity of the agent by making use of constituents and constructions which express non-specific or implicit reference'. When it gets translated into 'this has to be done', it can result in a serious falling out as was reported in a previous article (Béal 1990: 20).

Use of future tense
The future tense is often used in French as a softer option to the imperative.

(15) *Bon parfait. Je crois qu'il faudra remplacer par X Pacific (nom de la compagnie).* ('Very well, I think this will have to be changed to X Pacific [name of firm].')
(16) *Ah oui bon, tu les attacheras, c'est c'est . . . quand tu auras des feuilles séparées, il suffira de les numéroter etc.* ('O,K, you will staple them together. It's it's . . . when you get separate sheets, all you'll have to do is number them.')

This strategy, when applied to English, results in sentences sounding awkward and not very polite as in the following recorded examples:

(17) French speaker:
And when you'll be O.K. [*sic*], you'll give it to Laurence for her to issue the ticket.
(18) I will need to see you about the BHP report, if it is convenient now?

'Intonation' questions
An extremely common way of asking questions in French is through the exclusive use of intonation. In such cases the rising pattern at the end of a sentence is the sole indication that it is indeed a question, but the actual syntax of the sentence remains that of a statement. This is basically the normal way to ask yes/no questions (Kerbrat-Orecchioni 1992a: 89) and it accounted for more than 60% of all questions/requests asked in French (see Table 5). While fulfilling a number of various purposes, there is no doubt that in a lot of cases these intonation questions clearly have a mitigation function (cf. Blum-Kulka and House 1989: 281). This is especially clear when the 'question' is in fact a request (a different speech act).

(19) On the telephone:
Vous voulez venir chez John là? On a un point de détail sur une lettre d'offre. ('You want to come to John's room? We need to sort out a detail in a letter of offer.')

Recent research in French verbal interactions points towards the existence of a continuum from question to assertion with many utterances having an intermediate status (Kerbrat-Orecchioni 1992a). This ambiguity between statement and question also makes real questions (vs requests) less confrontational than they might otherwise be. For example, the question *Vous avez rangé des choses?* ('You put away a few things?') while looking for a file is half way between 'Did you put away a few things?' and 'It seems to me you have put away a few things': this removes any risk of the hearer interpreting the utterance as tinged with reproach.

The same ambiguity can also protect the speaker's own face: the request comes across as double-checking and anticipating rather than asking out of ignorance.

(20) *Je l'donne à Aileen?*
'(I assume) I give it to Aileen?'
(21) *. . . et euh je peux pas attendre de l'avoir?*
'. . . and er I couldn't wait until I receive it (could I)?'

When speaking English, French native speakers tend to transfer this strategy, they used it in 26% of all questions/requests while Australians only used it in 7.5% of cases.[2]

In English however, the interrogative is not necessarily perceived as a syntactic downgrader, and the lack of conventional indirectness ('could you', 'would you') is what is more likely to be felt. See examples below:

(22) French speaker:
You let me know when you have it?
(23) French speaker:
If you come in, come and bring it to me?
(24) French speaker:
You can finish it with him?

Because in English the favored politeness strategy is to use conventional indirectness, English speakers on the whole would not see the rationale behind these other forms and would find the speaker at best 'awkward', at worst 'rude' or 'blunt'.

When it is pointed out to L2 learners that a particular wording is unlikely to be interpreted as they intended, they are usually keen to try and improve. This is not an easy task given the spontaneous, 'automatic' character of most utterances: this fact accounts for some awkward turns of phrase when the speaker is obviously trying to repair after the event. This is the case with one of the examples previously mentioned: 'I will need to see you about the BHP report, if it is convenient now?', in which the speaker tries to 'patch it up' after he has 'slipped'. On the whole, however, pragmalinguistic errors are willingly acknowledged by L2 speakers. Such is not the case for sociopragmatic failure, which ties in closely with cultural values.

Socio-pragmatic conflict: the presentation of self and interpersonal dynamics

The perception of face-threatening acts

Brown and Levinson (1987: 247) point out the importance of taking into consideration 'the extent to which all interactional acts in a culture are considered FTAs, and the different kinds of acts that are so considered'.

Not all requests are assessed in the same way by French and Australian English speakers. In a number of cases, there seems to be a suspension of face concerns amongst the French. This is particularly the case:

1. When asking for information rather than service, where Australians would put in a downgrader, or a tag, or at least the person's name, the French often asked the question without any kind of redress:

> (25) French speaker:
> When can you find out?
> (26) French speaker:
> Which [*sic*] kind of study have you done?

2. When making a general announcement, the collective 'face' was not taken into consideration:

> (27) French speaker:
> Does anyone have my stapler?
> (28) French speaker:
> I want euh. I want an extraordinary meeting of secretariat. We meet just here. Laurence, Yan, Ann, Frédérique, come quickly here!

3. Conversely, when asking for advice or permission, the French employees did not seem very concerned about protecting their own face. It seemed as if acceptance of the hierarchical position somehow 'neutralized' the face-threatening act of admitting that one is in a one-down position. Australians, on the contrary, seemed more prone to use strategies that diffused the potential threat to their own face, like 'fishing' for permission rather than asking up front and risking rejection. The two examples below in parallel situations illustrate rather well the difference in approach:

> (29) French speaker: Now, it's about company X. Do you remember?
> Australian speaker: Yes.
> French speaker: You are aware I was preparing something on it? I finished my telex, draft, and I just received a memo 'call report' from Robert adding a lot of things, changing a lot of things. Do you think I . . .
> Australian speaker: Which one, X?
> French speaker: Yeah, X.
> Australian speaker: Yeah.

French speaker: Do you think I can just add one at the end and say something about question to be raised? or . . . latest information? *Or I have to change everything?*

Australian speaker: No . . . Just add 'latest information'.

French speaker: *Yes? I can do it?*

Australian speaker: Yeah. So latest . . . later 'a call was made to that company (laughter) on that day'.

French speaker: (laughter) Thank you.

(30) The following example took place between Australians. A typist was asking her superior for permission to correct a mistake with correction fluid rather than have to fix it on the word-processor and re-print the whole page.

Typist: *Ann, is there any way of correcting that?* I'm not sure how that happened there. I was typing, I wonder where it is . . . (looking at the page) . . . Six French francs and it's meant to be one Australian dollar for four French francs?

Ann: Mmm mmm . . . (looks) . . . Tippex . . . (laughter)

Typist: Thanks.

The content-oriented focus

House (1984: 253), when summing up the results of contrastive analyses between English and German speakers in which 'both sets of subjects acted out a controlled and structured range of culturally parallel situations in their native tongues', points out that 'the English native speakers operate more strongly on an other-directed, interpersonal level resorting to more routinized, formulaic conversational behaviour while the German subjects behave in both more self-directed and content oriented ways'.

The French speakers observed also had a tendency to focus on the topic rather than on the interactant. This linguistic habit, very obvious when they spoke French, was often transferred into English. It was expressed in at least two ways:

1. On the syntactic level, by the frequency of a particular structure in which the topic is first mentioned by a pronoun, then fully mentioned by its name at the end of the clause.

(31) Examples in French:
   a. *Tu l'as vú*, le telex Bertolli?
        ('Have you seen it, the Bertolli telex?')
   b. Il *aurait été envoyé quand, ce chèque là?*
        ('It would have been sent when, this cheque, here?')

(32) Example in English:
   Has it been already transmitted to Paris, that telex?

In the same circumstances, Australians would be more likely to say something focusing on the interactant as in 'would you know'?'/'have you seen . . . by any chance?' etc.

2. Affect, including negative affect, towards the task at hand was frequently expressed. It was *not* directed at the interactant. For example, somebody going on holiday gave a colleague a file with some work to follow up. The colleague exclaimed:

(33) *Bon alors, c'est moi qui hérite de ça pour tout le mois de mars, n'est-ce pas merveilleux?*
('Right, so I am the one inheriting this stuff for the whole month of March, isn't that wonderful?')
[The other person laughed.]

Australians, however, are often disconcerted by this show of 'negative feelings'. One French interviewee commented:

Ça m'a même amené, moi, à faire attention, à modifier mon comportement parce que je me suis rendu compte effectivement que parfois le fait de manifester mon irritation sur quelque chose, sur un dossier, sur euh . . . sur une letter, etc . . . s'il y avait quelqeu'un en face de moi euh . . . ça le mettait mal à l'aise parce que j'avais bien l'impression qu'il prenait ça pour lui, hein!
[This led me to be more careful, to change my behavior, because I realized that sometimes if I expressed some irritability towards a task, a file, a letter, etc . . . if there was someone else present, he felt uncomfortable, because I got the very clear impression that he thought it was directed at him!]

Self-assertion versus self-effacement
There seems to be a positive value attached to self-assertion for the French speakers. In our data this was reflected in a number of ways:

1. While both Australians and French people used about the same number of imperative and 'want' verbs, Australians usually mitigated the impact with a downgrader or a politeness marker such as 'please'. French people did not (see Table 1.5):

(34) Australian speaker:
   a. Here's the deal! *Please* run through the deal, *all right?*
   b. *Just* put 'security' *if you don't mind*, leave that there, put the asterisk here and include that paragraph there.
(35) French speakers:
   a. No, no! I want an explanation before!
   b. Anyway, start on it tomorrow, Prue, because I want to discuss it with Jack.
   c. This is your masterpiece. I want you to have a look at it before I send it to Sydney.

As was pointed out in one of the interviews, French people actually expect orders to be given in a relatively direct fashion. 'Giving instructions' is felt to be distinct from 'asking a favor' and too much conventional indirectness is equated with a lack of confidence and leadership. The interviewee was a high-ranking executive in the company. The following extract is particularly revealing:

C'est que même quand il s'agit de tâches régulières, de tâches normales, il y aura une précaution oratoire que n'emploiera pas un Français. A la limite, le Français s'il l'emploie, il le fera, il prendra cette précaution oratoire si c'est justement en dehors des tâches normales et régulières de la personne à qui il s'adresse. Mais autrement, non, ça sera, bon, 'Faites-moi ci'. 'Allez me chercher ça, s'il vous- plaît', mais 'Would you mind?' euh . . . non. A la limite, à la limite si on fait ça en France, on remet en cause son autorité, ça a l'air de dire qu'on n'est pas capable de donner un ordre, de donner une instruction. [Even in the case of normal regular tasks, they [Australians] use oratory precautions that a French person would not use. Actually, if a French person does use such precaution, it will be because he is requesting a favor outside the normal job definition of the person he is asking. Otherwise, he will simply say 'Do this, fetch that, please' but 'Would you mind? . . .'certainly not . . . Actually, to do that in France is like sabotaging one's own authority. It gives the impression that one is incapable of giving an order or a directive.]

This rationale was not shared by the Australian employees. One of them commented:

It comes across as sort of well, er . . . especially on the management level, euh, 'You!', you know 'You will do this' type of scene, without sort of saying to you 'Oh Gary, listen, I wouldn't mind if you had a look at that because we need to do . . . to do this' but it's more 'I need this, you will do this' end of story.

Note also the use of the future in the reported speech 'you will do this' which was obviously felt to be offensive, as was already mentioned above.

2. Another way in which French 'self-assertion' was expressed was through direct, assertive questions versus the more tentative approach of the Australians. The following examples, relating to a similar type of situation, will illustrate the case. The person speaking had just finished a job for somebody else:

(36) Australian speaker:
I've done it. I hope everyone is happy.
(37) French speaker:
Voilà! Ça vous convient, comme ça?
('Here you are! Does it suit you, like this?')

In (36) it is possible for the addressee to simply answer 'Thank you' while in (37) s/he has to say 'Yes' or 'No'. The approach can therefore be seen as more confrontational.

3. Self-assertion could also be observed in the number of questions starting with 'but' amongst the French speakers (see Table 5). In conversation amongst French people, a new turn is often introduced by *mais*. *Mais* does not necessarily signal disagreement: it merely defines what is about to be said as distinct from what has previously been said (Béal 1993: 98). In some circumstances, *'mais a une valeur d'introduction du dire plus que d'opposition stricte'* ('the function of *mais* is to introduce a new utterance rather than a contradiction') according to Cadiot et al. (1979: 97). It is frequently used to add a complementary piece of information, to introduce a personal point of view or to check that one's understanding of the previous statement is correct. It is functionally very close to the Italian *ma* as described by Testa (1988). It is, however, a way of asserting one's opinion rather than playing it down, while the English 'well' which also introduces many utterances is more consensus oriented. Therefore the tendency to overuse 'but' gives belligerent overtones to the conversational style of French people speaking English, as the following examples show:

(38) French speaker:
    a. But do we really need to put that in a letter of offer?
    b. No, but what do you prefer?
    c. Yes, but it was in Sydney?

4. Self-assertion was also expressed in the number of questions using 'or' and an alternative (see Table 5) as in the following examples.

(39) French speaker:
    a. We already have it on hand or not?
    b. Do you think I can just add one at the end and say something about question to be raised or do I have to change everything?
    c. Did you send that telex to X [name of company] or to Paris?

By offering the alternative, the French speaker wants to make sure that the interactant knows he/she is aware of the situation and not asking out of ignorance. It is part of projecting an efficient and competent image. In English, however, it may come across as impatience.

5. Finally, French native speakers often used a tone of joky mild provocation towards people they were working with. Other people were expected to pick up the challenge and stand up for their choices and opinions. Australians would often decline to play the game.

(40) An abstract painting bought by the management was about to be hung on the wall. A French person walked past it and said to an Australian colleague who happened to be nearby:
    French: Are they going to put this horror up?
    Australian: They're coming this afternoon.

While the French person is angling for an opinion (be it reinforcement of his/her own or controversy) the Australian prefers to stay non-committal.

The different perception of what constitutes FTAs, the focus on content rather than interactant, and the emphasis on self-assertion vs self-effacement, though realized in the language by choices which may sometimes be directly translated from L1, (as in the case of 'but' and 'or'), are basically social attitudes and expectations towards the situation at hand. They are different from pragmalinguistic transfer (see above) in which the speaker is unaware that this 'translation' does not carry the same illocutionary force as in his/her native language. When pragmalinguistic errors are pointed out, speakers are easily willing to correct them. But socio-pragmatic 'errors' are not easily recognized as such, because they have as much to do with cultural values as with language skills. Speakers are therefore often unwilling to change their ways, because they feel that their very identity is under threat. As Brindley (1986: 35) points out:

> If teachers explicitly set out to teach socio-cultural competence, are learners being asked to give up their own personality by taking on a different communicative style?

Table 1.5 sums up the different points discussed so far.

Table 1.5 French speaking English: some unfortunate habits

	Australians speaking English (No. = 275)		French speaking English (No. = 340)		French speaking French (No. = 103)	
	No.	%	No.	%	No.	%
Asking as direct expression of will without softener	5	1.8	19	5.6*	9	9
Asking introduced by *but*	4	1.5	21	6?	3	3
Asking presenting an alternative 'this or that?'	4	1.5	18	5#	6	5.5
Asking by intonation only	21	7.5	92	26!	61.5	
Total questions/requests that could possibly antagonise (direct expression of will with softener excluded)	15	12.3	151	42.6	82	79

Possible impressions conveyed to Australians
* authoritarianism   # impatience
? disagreement   ! bluntness

Conclusion: relevance of these findings for cross-cultural communication in the workplace

This analysis has demonstrated marked differences in the strategies used by L1s and L2s when requesting. The L2 speakers displayed a number of weak points in their mastery of L2 and transferred a number of linguistic and pragmatic habits from French into English. This could convey an impression of impatience, bluntness, or flippancy.

The most striking fact was how little thought the company as an institution had ever given to the role of language in communication. They seemed to consider language as a neutral tool which had nothing to do with the specific society and culture it represented and was somehow 'transparent' for everyone. Top ranking French executives were 'packed off' to Australia after a quick refresher course in England. As for the native speakers of Australian English, nothing was done to prepare them to work with French people, let alone in some cases, have them as their bosses. Predictably, the result was a fair amount of negative stereotyping and resentment on both sides.

In a multicultural society like Australia, there is clearly a great need to bring to the consciousness of all parties involved some of the problems of cross-cultural communication.

L2 speakers
As far as L2 speakers are concerned, the analysis shows that an important number of interlanguage errors can be traced to poor linguistic training (as was seen especially in the case of modal, question-tag and downgrader

usage in English for native speakers of French) and pragmalinguistic transfer. Company training courses should focus on these errors which can be corrected reasonably easily once speakers are made aware of them. The same courses should also sensitize L2 learners to socio-pragmatic differences and train them to practise those linguistic realizations of politeness specific to L2 which are different from their own language.

The formulation of requests obviously constitutes a particularly sensitive area, but research shows that turn-taking (Béal 1993; Clyne, Ball and Neil 1991) and patterns of routinized speech (Béal 1992) can also play an important part in giving an overall impression of either politeness or flippancy. Ideally specific programs should be designed for specific situations/workplaces with a two-pronged approach of analysis followed by linguistic input involving all parties concerned (i.e., L2 learners and their native speaker colleagues). The 'Developing successful communication with recently arrived migrants in industry' project currently under way at the Language and Society centre at Monash University, Melbourne, is a good example of such a project.

Native speakers
While the onus is obviously on L2 learners to eventually improve their skills to near native competence, companies such as the one discussed above would be well advised to give their native speakers interacting with L2 speakers some preparation and some awareness of the pragmatic rules of their own language.

In Australia many native speakers of English have never studied any foreign language at school, because it was not compulsory until recently, and are therefore 'monolingual' in the narrowest sense of the term. The saddest example reported to us of this lack of awareness is that of an ESL (English as a Second Language) teacher who became annoyed when her students from mainland China called her 'teacher, teacher!' In retaliation, she started to call them 'student, student!' Clearly it had not crossed her mind that the students were simply 'translating' a respectful form of address.

In our case study, many Australians also had no idea that, say, the same 'good' intention might produce different formulations in different languages. And yet, our findings point towards Australian English having some very specific features. They are in agreement with those of the Crosscultural Speech Act Realization Project, which compared five languages. According to these results Australian English speakers are 'the least direct: less than 10% of the Australian English requests are phrased as impositives, more than 80% are phrased as conventionally indirect'.

Furthermore, 'English speakers of Australian English use twice as many downgraders with conventional indirectness as the speakers of Canadian French and Hebrew' (Blum-Kulka and House 1989: 62).

Another important finding about Australian English was that 'the high level of indirectness combines with a very low degree of intrasituational variability' (Blum-Kulka and House 1989: 133). In other words – and this is peculiar to Australian English – most requests in most situations with most types of participants tend to be formulated in the same way. It was certainly the case in our data, in which Australian superiors, for example, never gave 'orders' or 'instructions', but always requested work to be done as a service.

From this vantage point, what emerges are actually the peculiarities of Australian English speech habits. The relative directness of the French, or the fact they may establish finer distinctions of hierarchy or degree of imposition in the formulation of a request stops appearing as an oddity. It is the Australians who seem unduly tentative, self-effacing and 'egalitarian'. The term 'whimperatives' has even been coined by some linguists (Wierzbicka 1991) to describe this type of indirect requests.

It is not suggested, of course, that Australian speakers should change their ways. Fundamentally, different cultural backgrounds and different value systems underlie the speaker's linguistic performance. The point is that when several different nationalities rub shoulders together, as was the case in the above company, it is important to bring out some of these differences into the open. It is the chance for everyone to understand a little more about the relationship between intention, formulation, and interpretation and to avoid kneejerk reactions.

It seems a pity that in the case studied – as in many other workplaces, no doubt – no attempt was made to bring things into perspective and to avoid some of the most basic misunderstandings.

Notes

1. The term 'Australian' denotes in this context a person who is a first language or native speaker of Australian English. Conversely 'French' in this context refers to a native speaker of French.
2. Australians seemed to use 'intonation only' for questions which were marked, for example in order to express surprise or to tease:
   (1) Australian speaker to French expatriate:
       You pay tax here? At the Australian rate?
   (2) You said your basket was empty? . . . [and the person puts a whole batch of files to process in it].

References

Béal, C. (1990) 'It's all in the asking: A perspective on problems of cross-cultural communication between native speakers of French and native speakers of Australian English in the workplace', in *Australian Review of Applied Linguistics* Series S,7: 16–32.

—— (1992) 'Did you have a good week-end?': Why there is no such thing as a simple question in cross-cultural encounters. *Australian Review of Applied Linguistics* 15(1), 23–52.

—— (1993) 'Les stratégies conversationnelles en français et en anglais: conventions ou reflet de divergences culturelles profondes?' *Langue Française* 98, 79–106.

Blum-Kulka, S. (1987) 'Indirectness and politeness in requests: same or different?' *Journal of Pragmatics* 11, 131–146.

—— (1989) 'Playing it safe: the role of conventionality in indirectness' in Blum-Kulka, Shoshana, Juliane House and Gabriele Kasper (eds.), 37–68.

24 *Christine Béal*

Blum-Kulka, S. and House, J. (1989) 'Cross-cultural and situational variation in requesting behavior' in Blum-Kulka, S., House, J and Kasper, G. (eds.), 123–153.
Blum-Kulka, S. and Olshtain, E. (1986) 'Too many words: Length of utterance and pragmatic failure' *Studies in Second Language Acquisition* 8, pp. 47–61.
Blum-Kulka, S., House, J. and Kasper, G. (1989a) 'Investigating cross-cultural pragmatics: an introductory overview' in Blum-Kulka, S., House, J. and Kasper, G. (eds.), pp. 1–29.
Blum-Kulka, S., House, J. and Kasper, G. (eds.) (1989b) *Cross-cultural Pragmatics: Requests and Apologies*, Norwood, New Jersey: Ablex.
Brindley, G. (1986) 'Semantic approaches to learner language' *Australian Review of Applied Linguistics* Series S(3), 1–43.
Brown, P. and Levinson, S. (1987) *Politeness: Some Universals in Language Usage.* Cambridge: Cambridge University Press.
Cadiot, A., Chevalier, J., Delesalle, S. et al. (1979) 'Oui mais non mais ou: Il y a dialogue et dialogue', *Langue Française* 42, pp. 95–102.
Clyne, M., Ball, M. and Neil, D (1991) 'Intercultural communication at work in Australia: Complaints and apologies in turns' *Multilingua* 10(3), pp. 251–273.
Haverkate, H. (1988) 'Toward a typology of politeness strategies in communicative interaction' *Multilingua* 7(4), pp. 385–409.
House, J. (1984) 'Some methodological problems and perspectives in contrastive discourse analysis' *Applied Linguistics* 5(3), pp. 245–254.
Ide, S. (1988) 'Introduction: Linguistic politeness' *Multilingua* 7(4), pp. 371–374.
Kerbrat-Orecchioni, C. (1992a) 'L'acte de question et l'acte d'assertion: opposition discrète ou continuum?' in Kerbrat-Orecchioni, Catherine (ed.) *La question.* Lyon: Presses Universitaires de Lyon, pp. 87–111.
—— (1992b) 'Limites de la théorie de la politesse comme ménagement des faces' in *Les interactions verbales*, Paris: Armand, C.: pp. 253–269.
Lado, R. (1957) *Linguistics across Cultures*, Ann Arbor: University of Michigan Press.
Loveday, L. (1982) 'Communicative interference: A framework for contrastively analysing L2 communicative competence exemplified with the linguistic behaviour of Japanese performing in English', *International Review of Applied Linguistics* 20(1), pp. 1–16. (1983) *The Sociolinguistics of Learning and Using a Non-native Language*, Oxford: Pergamon.
Matsumoto, Y. (1988) 'Reexamination of the universality of face: Politeness phenomena in Japanese', *Journal of Pragmatics* 12, 403–426.
Riley, P. (1989) 'Well, don't blame me!: On the interpretation of pragmatic errors' in Olesky, W. (ed.), *Contrastive Pragmatics*, Amsterdam: Benjamins, J. pp. 23–249.
Testa, R. (1988) 'Interrupting strategies in English and Italian conversation: smooth versus contrastive linguistic preferences', *Multilingua* 7(4), pp. 285–312.
Thomas, J. (1983) 'Cross-cultural pragmatic failure', *Applied Linguistics* 4(2), pp. 91–112.
Watts, R. (1992) 'Linguistic politeness and politic verbal behaviour: Reconsidering claims for universality' in Watts, R., Sachiko, I. and Konrad, E. (eds.), *Politeness in Language: Studies in its History, Theory and Practice*, Berlin/New York: Mouton de Gruyter, pp. 43–69.
Wierzbicka, A. (1991) *Cross-cultural Pragmatics*, Berlin: Mouton de Gruyter.
Wolfson, N., Marmor, T. and Jones, S. (1989) 'Problems in the comparison of speech acts across cultures' in Blum-Kulka, S., House, J. and Kasper, G. (eds.), pp. 174–195.

2

Keeping the gate: how judgements are made in interethnic interviews

Celia Roberts and Pete Sayers

Originally published in K. Knapp, W. Enninger and A. Knapp-Potthoff, eds, *Analyzing Intercultural Communication* (Mouton de Gruyter, 1987).

> Everyone complains of his memory, but no one complains of his judgement.
> Duc de la Rochefoucauld, *Les Maximes*, 89

Interpretative processes in the gatekeeping interview

This paper analyzes the interpretative processes in interethnic interviews from the perspective of trainers working in the field of equal opportunities at work.[1] There is a growing demand in Britain for cross-cultural training to ensure equal opportunities and to develop antiracist strategies. This demand reflects a deepening concern for a more racially just society in which there is equal access to opportunities and public resources.

In our increasingly bureaucratized society, there are large numbers of people who hold certain resources, facilities or opportunities, and who decide, within the constraints of the organisation they represent, who should have them – who should be allowed through "the gate". These people have been described as "the gatekeepers" (Erickson/Shultz 1982). An important element of training for equal opportunities focuses on the gatekeeping interview.

Our approach, as trainers, has been to work cooperatively with anthropologists, sociolinguists and ethnomethodologists, with John Gumperz in particular, in the *collection* and *analysis* of interview data. The aim of this data collection is to examine how the processes of interpretation used in interethnic interviews lead to judgements about individual clients and applicants. Using ethnographic techniques, we have adopted a case study, problem solving approach typical of the work of conversational analysts as described by Steven Levinson (Levinson 1983). The data collected forms the beginning of a data base from which hypotheses about the nature of cultural difference in formal interethnic encounters can be made (Gumperz 1982). The data is also used as training material and the perceptions and

25

reactions of the "gatekeepers", as trainees, serves to authenticate the material and add to our understanding of the data.

Our methodology[2] consists of collecting authentic interview data in institutionalized settings. The data, where possible, is of both *intra*ethnic and *inter*ethnic interviews. The participants are, subsequently, asked to comment on their overall impression of how the interview went and the decisions or likely outcomes from it. In some cases, as in the interview described in the second part of this paper, participants view the data and are asked to comment on it section by section. The empirical analysis of the data by researchers follows the approach of ethnomethodologists[3] in assuming that the data, unless it can be proved otherwise, consists of utterances and responses which are meaningful to the participants. The contrast between intraethnic and interethnic materials serves to highlight how in certain crucial sequences mutual understanding has not been satisfactorily negotiated. That is to say, from the evidence of the data itself and from *post hoc* analysis by participants, speakers' questions and responses which are meaningful to them are not perceived as meaningful in the same way by their interlocutors.

Training alone cannot achieve equal opportunities. Systems and policies must also be introduced or changed. However, organizations are held together by people interacting with each other. And in such service organizations as health, social services, housing and education, the organization is judged, by the public it is there to serve, at the point of interaction between "gatekeeper" and client.

The point of interaction – the "gatekeeping" interview – is, therefore, a significant point of intervention for training. It is the point at which the bald facts of institutionalized discrimination can be related to individuals' attitude and behavior. Also, by focusing on what is a typical and essential aspect of "the gatekeepers"' job, trainees can be helped to see that traditional professional skills and goodwill are not enough. Trainees need to be disturbed into broadening their interpretative framework so that they question their own behavior and means of evaluating others.

Making judgements

Gatekeepers bring to training a set of assumptions and responses which are on a cline between an essentially "normative" approach and a questioning one. There are trainees who take for granted that the way they interview clients and make decisions about and for them is the right and the only way. There are, however, many others who express concern and goodwill but feel they lack specific knowledge in dealing with interethnic encounters or feel vaguely dissatisfied with the process and outcomes of interethnic interviews. Although rarely articulated as such, it is a lack of certainty about how to make judgements which can make them feel anxious or inadequate. Alton Becker (Becker 1979) suggests that learning a foreign language is like being temporarily insane because of the great gap between what you say and what you want to mean. This gap undermines your feeling of coherence in the world. Similarly, for gatekeepers in interethnic encounters, uncertainties about interpretation of intent can undermine their sense of reality and natural justice in making decisions.

Trainees, whatever goodwill they express, are often unwilling or unable to locate their judgements of individuals in specific evidence from the interaction. They tend to rely on what we might term a general and diffuse optimism or pessimism about the client. They may have a generalized commitment to trying to ensure equal opportunities and therefore make a positive judgement about an individual's worth or competence. More commonly, any awkward moments or misunderstandings often lead to a generally negative impression of the applicant.[4] While the latter more negative approach serves more obviously to reinforce and rationalize the disadvantaged position of minority ethnic groups, the former may be equally damaging in the long term. This is because continued uncertainty about whether a judgement was right can put into question the fairness of both institutional and individual practices. Ultimately, individuals on both sides of the interview need to be convinced that the judgements made are both fair and sound.

For the interviewee perceived discrimination is as damaging as actual discrimination. The interviewers, therefore, must be able to back up their decisions from evidence from the interview and, of course, that interview must be conducted in a culturally sensitive way.

Interview data, as well as being easy for trainees to relate to, is the focus of our training for "gatekeepers" for a number of reasons. Interviews are absolutely critical in creating or denying equal opportunities. Also as a defined "speech activity" (Levinson 1979), they provide conditions for the distillation of individual judgement in interaction. And, as such, inevitably, particularly in job interviews, they capture culture in interaction. There are a range of "gatekeeping" interviews from the selection interview, where the goals are apparently clear and shared, through to the advice and counseling interview where the overall goal may not be explicitly agreed upon. But they are all complex and learned by a gradual process of acculturation that interactants find difficult to articulate or analyze. Because they are so complex, organizations and individuals often find it easier not to think or talk about them at all. Or, alternatively, they are reduced to manageable proportions in short courses on interviewing techniques and "how to be objective" which do not take account of the reality of how people make judgements.

The job interview
The job interview is one of the most culture-specific speech events we all have to face. Certainly, the British interview is a highly conventionalized routine demanding a great degree of shared knowledge and experience. The very nature of this routine inhibits either side from undertaking the kind of "procedural work" (Widdowson 1983) which allows interactants to find a shared basis for interpreting each other. For example, judgements at interviews are based on how comfortable the interviewee makes the interviewer feel. If the interviewee requires a high level of reformulation of interviewers' questions in order to establish intent, the interviewer may evaluate the candidate as awkward or obtuse.

In addition to the conventions of the interview, there is a built-in paradox in which it is necessary to try to be fair and yet selection entails discrimination between candidates. The result is an event whose peculiarity is well illustrated if Gricean maxims of conversational cooperation (Grice 1975) are applied. These maxims of quantity, quality, relation and manner can only apply to an interview if they are interpreted in a particular way according to the "rules" of the British interview "game". These general maxims could all be systematically "flouted" and yet the interview could be considered essentially a cooperative activity and a highly successful one. For example, the injunction "Be truthful" (the maxim of quality) is usually interpreted in an interview as presenting that part of the truth which will help you get the job! In interethnic encounters what constitutes cooperativeness will be even more difficult to tie down since principles of cooperation will be encoded differently in different languages and cultures. It follows from this that in an interethnic interview there may be "flouts" of the cooperative principle on two levels.

Firstly, there are the difficulties which may arise in any interview where assumptions about what constitutes cooperativeness may not be entirely shared. Secondly, there are the more readily perceived flouts of the general cooperative principle because it is an interethnic conversation. Such flouts are regularly interpreted negatively in terms of wrong attitude, incompetence or inadequate socialization into the white majority culture (Gumperz/Jupp/Roberts 1979 and Gumperz 1982).

Schema and frame
Before illustrating these points, it is important to relate them to a theory of language use which accounts for the relationship between ongoing interaction and personal judgements. We mentioned the shared knowledge and experience necessary for the successful negotiation of an interview. The accumulation of knowledge and experience into a set of knowledge and belief structures can be defined as schemata. This term originally described by F. C. Bartlett (Bartlett 1932) has become widely used both in discourse analysis and in artificial intelligence. Schemata include knowledge and beliefs about objects, events and situations but they also include assumptions about how we expect to get things done, our notions of roles, responsibilities and relationships and what is relevant, significant and typical in our world.

The conventions of the British interview and the notions of conversational cooperation are examples of schemata which help people to set up "structures of expectation" (Tannen 1979) which will make sense of a particular interaction for them. For example, a typical schema in a British interview is "interviews are an opportunity to sell yourself". This schema is what most interviewers and interviewees socialized into a white British culture will bring to the encounter. It will help to determine but will not account for the progress of the interview. In other words, schemata operate at the level above the actual ongoing processes of the interaction.

We also need to take account of what happens moment by moment in an interaction and how to interpret speaker intent at the level of utterance. Here the notion of interactive frame first explored by Gregory Bateson (Bateson 1972) and developed in a particularly relevant way by Deborah Tannen and Cynthia Wallat (Tannen/Wallat 1982) is useful. The interactive frame alerts the listener to what is going on at each stage of the interaction. For example, the schema "Interviews are an opportunity to sell yourself" may be partially realized by a typical set of questions in the interview which are hypothetical questions about handling people. In this context the particular frame[5] "OFFER TO DISPLAY UNDERSTANDING OF PEOPLE" for example, would be inferred from a question like "If you found yourself in such and such a situation, how would you react?"

When interviewees understand the speakers' intention, the response is relevant and the interview proceeds smoothly. Such a successful negotiation is illustrated in example 1 (below), in which a South Asian candidate is interviewed for a junior administrative post in a manufacturing company. One of the interviewers is concerned with how the applicant might react to angry workers querying their payslip:

EXAMPLE 1

Interviewer: *How do you think, Mr S., you'd cope with what may undoubtedly happen which is that amongst the insults that are thrown at you, as an administrative worker, there will be racial insults . . . ?*

In this instance, Mr S.'s reply indicates that he understands the interviewer's frame and he responds accordingly:

Mr S.: *. . . as you say there may be some isolated cases which will prove very very hostile towards me – the possibility is there but I believe to understand the difficulty of the worker and explain him properly and with patience – I believe I can persuade him and solve that problem – that is a genuine problem. I will take up with the foreman – as er – that gentleman has he worked full time – and this sort of discrepancies in wage packet I will check the record – right and I will satisfy him.*

Here Mr S. demonstrates that he is both capable of defusing a potential, fraught situation and of dealing with problems in a practical way.

There is in addition a dynamic in the interaction in which schemata and frame are operating together all the time. In other words, the inidivdual's assumptions and knowledge of his or her particular world (schema) interact with what is perceived to be happening at the moment in the interaction (frame) (Tannen/Wallat 1982). If people do not share the same schema or do not agree on what frame they are in, the lack of understanding in one can easily make the other go wrong. In interethnic encounters where people have different contexts within which they have been socialized, there tend to be fewer shared schemata and more opportunity for misinterpretation of frame. In the job interview referred to above the following sequence occurred:

EXAMPLE 2

Int: *What are your feelings, Mr S., because we do have some complaints from time to time about the extended leave system – um – and certainly some of the white workers do feel that this is abused sometimes by black workers – particularly Indian and Pakistani workers. What are your feelings about somebody who perhaps chronically overstays an extended leave?*

Mr S.:   er . . .

Int: *You said you've done it once with, if you like, forward permission – you warned the superiors and you haven't got a bad record for punctuality on returning. But what are your feelings about the worker who perhaps every time he goes on extended leave, comes back late with no form of warning to the staff?*

Mr S.:   *Well, during my stay most of the immigrants, particularly Indian and Pakistanis, they started after me and we are quite friendly with each other, we know about each other. Well so far as I'm concerned I've got no problem whenever I wanted to go, there is no doubt about that. So I know the other – my friends, but there are some isolated cases where there is a possibility that those gentlemen might have abused this system or this facility. There is a possibility, but as I know some cases they are genuinely in difficulty as their families are living there – they have to go after a year or two and they are in problem. I have got one case – now from the last year that gentleman is with . . . (– Company) for the last 12, 13 years. He lived in England, he got citizenship, everything – now he has got a problem with the immigration authorities, well this is not your ultimate family some children are not yours, we don't issue you an entry certificate. So, such – that gentleman has to go at least year or after two years and as some gentlemen abuse the system it reflects on such cases – gives wrong impression to the management and due to poor communications I believe there may be some misunderstanding between the employers and the management.*

Int: *I think that particular problem wouldn't be a great difficulty in the post that you're applying for at –. I think you might have noticed from the job description that at the plant where this vacancy is that the workforce is 98% white. I think, in fact, you'd find that was far less of a problem than in – plant. However it does lead on to another problem which one has to face when you're applying for this type of job. You'd be dealing with people's queries about wages, obviously from the job details and you were an hourly paid worker yourself – so you know how annoyed people get when there's something not right with their pay packet.*

Mr S.   *Oh yes.*

Although, here, the interviewers are still concerned with how Mr S. will handle people in the frame "OFFER TO DISPLAY UNDERSTANDING OF PEOPLE", there is another frame operating here which is an "OFFER TO DISPLAY A BALANCED VIEW". However, the applicant's schema, as far as we can retrieve it from the data appears to be: "People expect me to explain Asian behavior". And he interprets the interviewer's frame as "REQUEST TO JUSTIFY HIMSELF AND THE GROUP HE REPRESENTS". There is no evidence from the interviewers' reply that they consider he has responded to the frame "OFFER TO DISPLAY A BALANCED VIEW". Instead, they reply to the surface message of his stretch of talk. The implied criticism in this shifting to matters of content is hidden by the long turn of the interviewer which could be interpreted by the interviewee as a signal that all is going well.

In a different section of the interview, the interviewers again get locked into long turns of description and explanation. Here Mr S. suggests that he saw a change in attitude among some foremen once he had started to apply for jobs at foreman level himself. The interviewers fail to elicit what they would see as a satisfactory response as to why this change had taken place and so switch from probing questions to simply "ELICIT AGREEMENT". The frame "ELICIT AGREEMENT" involves long stretches of what Frederick Erickson (Erickson/Shultz 1982) has called 'hyperexplanation' in which the interviewer talks in ever longer turns and at increasingly lower levels of abstraction.

EXAMPLE 3

Int: *Were these – were these – were some of these people who were not staff – colleagues of yours who might object?*
Mr S.:   *Yes.*
Int: *Not necessarily people you were working for but other people who were working with you as a Grade B or Grade C operative – who were resenting the – er – maybe a bit jealousy – what that – erm – er – you said – thought that possibly – could be – er – envious – that the difficulty perhaps – working for you – this is – the – er – perhaps was it – putting words into your mouth – a possibility thought that – that you were looking for something above yourself – or looking for something – above what you should be going for – you're not . . .* (not audible) *country – er – I don't want to put words in your mouth – this is the impression I'm getting – tell me if I've got this wrong.*

In this example, the cumulative effect of misunderstanding, despite the goodwill of the interviewers, led to a judgement that the interviewee lacked competence. This negative judgement was clear from the post-interview discussions during which the interviewers expressed doubts, in particular, about whether Mr S. had the communicative abilities required for the job. Erickson and Shultz have also shown that where there was less sharedness and more uncomfortable moments in interviews counselors asked more general questions which were difficult to answer and did more checking up (which was unhelpful) as opposed to advising (which would have been helpful). So in both the job interviews and the counseling interviews misunderstandings and awkward moments trigger a routine of questioning which serves to confirm, in the interviewers' eyes, the lesser competence of the interviewees.

Where the interviewers' schemata about minority ethnic group candidates are much more negative then the schema/frame mismatches are much more obviously damaging. For example, impressions rapidly formed and conforming to negative ethnic stereotypes (schemata) lead to interactive frames which will help to reinforce this impression. Questions which start "So you haven't . . . " are typical of questions which shape and diminish the candidate and which, as we have already suggested, are almost impossible to negotiate around.

Conversational style

In interethnic encounters, in addition to schema and frame mismatch, there are differences in communicative style and, at the formal level of language, in syntax, lexis and prosody which will affect the interaction. Again, Erickson and Shultz's work has shown that a lack of shared styles of conversation among interactants can lead to asymmetry, awkward moments and a less favourable outcome for the interviewee. The interviewer feels uncomfortable, often at a deeply unconscious level because of a lack of rhythmic coordination and so judges the candidate in a negative way without having any evidence for doing this. In the example shown there is some schema/frame mismatch and this is compounded by Mr S.'s discourse style which is clearly different from the style of a speaker of a standard variety of English. His opening utterances in example 2 do not appear to be a direct response at all. In fact, he gradually builds up a line of argument through description and anecdote and finally makes his point at the end. By this time, as far as the interviewers are concerned, Mr S. has flouted both the general Gricean maxims, as they operate in any kind of talk, and their specific interpretation in the interview context: he has said too much, not been clear or relevant and appears to have avoided giving a straight answer.

The question that non-standard varieties of discourse style raise is the extent to which in interethnic encounters, judgements, and specifically negative judgements, are related to language difficulty and difference. What seems to be a typical phenomenon, which is illustrated in the extended example below, is that interactants have considerably more difficulty in making sense of surface utterances when there are schema and frame mismatches. There are many instances in the interaction where schema and frame are shared, and where difficulties of interpreting speaker intent do not occur or are minimal, but when difficulties do arise they are usually not attributed to language differences as such but to attitudes, personal attributes or level of general competence or intelligence. Our concern as trainers is to be able to point out to interviewers the occasions in their interviewing where language difficulties do arise and to compare our judgements and analysis of what is happening with theirs.

Analysis of a gatekeeping interview for training purposes

In this section we relate the general points made in the first part to the analysis of a particular gatekeeping interview between a South Asian and a white British interviewer. Because the analysis is for training purposes, we concentrate on those features which trainees could relate to and which are susceptible to change. As we said, our objective in training is to broaden the interpretative framework of the gatekeeper, to prise open the gate so that a wider cross-section of the population is allowed through.

In order to do this, we focus on blockages in attitude and behavior and on that group which we have characterized as questioning of their professional role and individual knowledge and skills when faced with an interethnic interview. One of the key characteristics of this group is often embarrassment. This relates both to their discomfort about how far to take positive action to ensure equal access and opportunity, and to their anxiety not to appear out of control in the interaction when interpreting the intent of a second language speaker of English. This embarrassment can lead to a major blockage and inhibit the interviewer's use of questions for clarification and other repair strategies. The cumulative effect of these blockages can result, as we have suggested above, in a chronic undermining of one's sense of judgement.

In this section, therefore, we will illustrate:

i. the relationship between schema/frame mismatch and language difference and how this affects judgement, and (relating to this superordinate problem)
ii. the question of topic control and how this relates to the interviewer's perception of controlling the interview
iii. the relationship between topic control and clarification and repair strategies
iv. how the gatekeeping judgement was made in one interview analyzed in detail.

Obtaining data for research is difficult. A real job selection interview between applicant and employer is a very sensitive encounter to allow non-participant observation and recording. In reality, it has proved virtually impossible to gain such totally "live" data. However, it has not proved so difficult to get both interviewers and interviewees to perform on video tape in training exercises where, although there is no job immediately on offer, both parties act themselves and confirm afterwards that their performance is realistic. Interviewees (usually students on language courses for the unemployed) are as keen to present themselves at their best in the simulation interviews as they would be at a real interview, and interviewers find themselves making exactly the same type of judgements about candidates as in a real interview. This can be confirmed by participants' own reactions to their performance on video. Any tension removed from this type of encounter because it is not a real interview is more than replaced by the tension produced by the presence of the video recording equipment.

In all, we think we can fairly say that the data we have obtained is worthy of serious attention, and that the findings of analysis of such data is relevant to the training needs of both interviewers and interviewees.

Schema and frame mismatch and language difference
In the examples quoted above (1 and 2) we showed how complex interviewers' questions can become in an "OFFER TO DISPLAY UNDERSTANDING OF PEOPLE" frame and how complex interviewees' answers can become in a "REQUEST TO JUSTIFY ONESELF" frame. We have suggested that the interpretation of the other person's frame and schema is essential to good understanding and fair assessment, and also that this

process can be further complicated if the interviewee is a second language speaker.

In the following example we shall show how schema/frame mismatches can radically affect the interviewer's judgement of the candidate in relatively uncomplex exchanges such as the one here typical of a selection interview for a government skills training course where the interviewer's frame is one that should be relatively straightforward "ELICITING THE QUALITY OF THE APPLICANT'S MATHS":

EXAMPLE 4

Int: *How's your maths?*
App: *(silence)   (the applicant is a non-native speaker of South Asian origin)*
Int: *Not so good, eh?*
App: *No.*

The schema underlying the interviewer's question *How's your maths?* goes roughly like this. 'Interviewees are not often up to standard in maths and are also embarrassed by their inabilities. Paper qualifications are not reliable indications of actual ability, many of our applicants don't have any at all, so direct questions about exams taken are not as useful as a general indirect question such as "How's your maths?"'

If we ask native speakers of English how they would expect to answer such a question they offer things such as:

a) *Well, I've got* **X or Y** *(qualifications)* or
b) *Not bad, All right* (and similar) **said with confidence**

It is the second type of answer (b) that we find most interesting. The propositional content of the answer (e.g. *not bad* or *all right*) does not seem as meaningful to the interviewer as the absence of embarrassment which must also be perceived in the answer if it is to be successful. Somewhere also in the interviewer's schema is the idea that the question *How's your maths?* is a trap which, if triggered, will reveal the applicant's embarrassment about the poor quality of his/her maths.

The applicant's silence after the question *How's your maths?* is perceived by the interviewer as embarrassment caused by the poor quality of the applicant's maths, and this interpretation is articulated in the follow-up question by the interviewer, *Not so good, eh?* The applicant's reply confirms this for the interviewer. The interviewer is now convinced that he has elicited the facts about the applicant's maths and no further questions on the subject are asked. From a monocultural native speaker perspective no other interpretation is possible.

From a crosscultural perspective, and from a second language learner's perspective, another equally valid interpretation is also possible. *How's your maths?* is a difficult question for the applicant to process. There has been no prior introduction to the topic of maths. Things like *and now I'm going to ask you about your maths* (or similar) are not usually part of the standard British interview format. *How's your maths?* is deceptively similar in structure to social questions such as *How's your family?* or *How's your cough?*. The format *How's your maths?* makes it difficult to focus on the new topic. Even if the applicant understands that the question counts as an introduction to the topic of maths, the force of the question or the schema behind it is difficult to work out.

The result is an embarrassed silence from the applicant. But this silence is not an embarrassment caused by the applicant's feelings about his maths but one brought about by the difficulty of the second language learner's task in processing the language of the interviewer. The rest of the exchange is interpretable in a variety of ways. *Not so good, eh?* may imply to the interviewee that the standard expected is higher than he thought. *No* as an answer fits any deference schema the applicant may have, i.e. it is not fitting for the applicant to deny what the interviewer has asserted. This deference schema also prevents the applicant independently introducing the topic of his own educational qualifications which in many cases like the one above are well above the minimum required by the interviewer.

By analyzing exchanges like the one above interviewers on training courses can be encouraged to

i. be more aware, i.e. be aware how interviewees' responses to questions are typically interpreted and how other interpretations may be equally possible and valid, and
ii. to develop new interview skills such as introducing topics explicitly and using direct questions when indirect ones do not produce unequivocal responses from interviewees.

Topic control

In example 4 (above) the applicant is either silent or produces only a one word response. However, simply getting this candidate to talk more is not the solution. Problems of interpretation in schema mismatch can be compounded when interviewers as a positive strategy encourage interviewees to talk. Unfortunately, this can lead to long stretches of seemingly purposeless interaction because neither side has worked out explicitly the specific goals of this stretch of the interview. They find themselves operating with schemata which are not shared but with no explicit realization that they are not shared. In addition, with a second language speaker, long chunks of narrative may be misinterpreted or lead to severe information loss on the part of the interviewer. The question for the interviewer to consider is, therefore, how much to retain or relax control of the interview.

One of the features that differentiates an interview from a conversation is the fact that one party to the conversation (the interviewer) controls the topic. Controlling the topic in a job interview is a matter of skill. Too much control can cause the interview to become like an interrogation where the interviewer ends up doing far more of the talk than the interviewee. Such a distribution of talk does not make for a good interview.[6]

Skilled personnel interviewers agree that in a good job selection interview the candidate should do about sixty percent of the talking with the interviewer doing no more than forty percent. Critical of the style of interviewing that produces 'interrogation' interviews (in which there is tight control of topic on the part of the interviewer) one interviewer we videoed went to a lot of trouble to encourage the candidate to talk and was, in fact, successful in getting both the non-native speakers he interviewed to respond very fully to his questions. One of these interviews has been analyzed in detail in Sayers (1983b). To get the candidate to talk the interviewer relaxed his control of topic and deliberately became less controlling within the interview. This is one aspect of the relationship between power and social distance in interethnic communication which Ron and Suzanne Scollon discuss (Scollon/Scollon 1983). The interviewer opened the interview by saying:

EXAMPLE 5

Int: *What I'd like to do this afternoon is to talk to you a little bit about yourself and about what perhaps you'd like to do in the future, so I've got some questions I'd like to ask you. It might also be that you can ask me questions either towards the end or perhaps, if you feel you want to do so, just ask me the question straight out. So what I'd like to do is for us to have a discussion and feel free to be as open as you can.*

The interviewer gives a double invitation to ask questions, giving the candidate prior permission to take control of topic if he wants to. The net effect of a relaxation of topic control is that the candidate talks very freely in answer to the interviewer's questions. Problems in the interaction in this interview then occurred when chunks of the candidate's talk were not understood by the interviewer. Where both schema/frame mismatches and second language surface structure (syntax, lexis and prosody) interact, it is very easy for both parties to be talking past each other. This is, however, not necessarily immediately recognizable by the interactants. There is a good example of this in the interview under discussion. The candidate has been talking at length about his skills as a do-it-yourself gas appliance installer, when the interviewer asks:

EXAMPLE 6

Int: *I mean, how did you find out how to do it, did somebody show you?*
Cand: *Well, er, I saw somebody when they're working you know, that's why I know.*
Int: *So, you found out from them?*
Cand: *Yeah, everything is no hard the people try, because the people when's done nothing don't know anything, but when after learn and see they use the brain, you know, if the somebody can do it, why I can't, I can easy you know if I try, so that's why I know.*

The interviewer's purpose in asking *How did you find out how to do it?* was to ask specifically about learning and training. His frame is "ELICIT HOW SKILLS WERE ACQUIRED" and his schema is that training (however informal), and more importantly trainability, is an important criterion for assessment in a selection interview for a job of which the candidate has no previous experience (the case in this interview). Checking with the interviewer afterwards (i.e. after the interview was over) the interviewer admitted to us that he had not understood the candidate's reply to his follow-up question (the second question in example 6). One reason for this might be the surface quality (here syntax and prosody) of the candidate's English. There are certain points of difference between the candidate's English and standard English, but there are many other passages of similar surface structure elsewhere in the interview which the interviewer has no difficulty understanding. A more satisfactory reason is that the candidate's reply here is based on a different schema and its purpose is not perceived by the interviewer because it does not meet the expectations of the frame of his question.

The interviewer is listening for something specific on the topic of training, how skills were acquired and learnt and to what level, according to his schema about the importance of trainability. The candidate, however, is talking about something broader and more general – his philosophy of life in relation to people learning new skills, and how he applies that philosophy to himself. The interviewee's frame could be described as "EXPLAIN (MY) GENERAL PHILOSOPHY OF LIFE". His schema is that a general (non-specific) explanation of his philosophy of life is the best way to answer the interviewer's question about how he learns new things. This frame produces an utterance which is difficult for the interviewer to interpret as a reply to his question the frame of which was substantially different, namely "ELICIT HOW SKILLS WERE ACQUIRED". The interviewer's schema was that trainability would be best deduced by the candidate giving specific examples of how new skills were acquired.

This schema difference is not unbridgeable. The interviewee's reply could, for example, have formed an adequate introduction to how specific skills were acquired, but because the surface form of the utterance was also difficult for the interviewer to interpret it was not possible for him to see the relevance of the candidate's reply or to capture its intended meaning. The interviewer fails to make sense of the candidate's reply because he is trying to fit the surface structure of the reply into his, the interviewer's, schema. Once the schema/frame difference was pointed out to the interviewer upon replay of the video recording of the interview, the surface structure of the reply became (suddenly) interpretable.

The interviewer is now caught in a dilemma. If he asserts his control of topic and responds to the candidate's reply by explicitly directing the candidate's attention to what he (the interviewer) wanted to talk about, there is a danger that the candidate will become inhibited, his talk dry up and the interview become the undesired interrogation type. If he does nothing, there is a danger that the interviewer will not get the information he needs to build up a satisfactory picture of the candidate. The less powerful style of interviewing, as advocated by skilled personnel officers, involves the interviewer in controlling topic gently – gently enough to enable the candidate also to incorporate his own topics in the discourse.[7] In fact, it is just this ability to allow the candidate to incorporate his own topics into his replies that enables the interviewer under scrutiny in this interview to succeed in finding out a great deal more about this candidate than other more powerful interviewers managed under similar circumstances with other candidates. In a crosscultural interview, however, the less powerful, more gentle control of topic becomes increasingly more difficult as problems such as those originating from schema mismatch together with non-standard surface structure introduce themselves into the interaction, and make it more difficult for the interviewer to process the amount of talk generated in the candidate's contributions.

Clarification and repair strategies
The strategy our less powerful interviewer uses is to allow the candidate to carry on talking in the hope that given enough time the situation may become clearer. This is how the interviewer articulated his own strategy reflecting on his own performance while watching the video recording. Unfortunately, this clarification does not happen of itself, and in a goal-orientated activity such as a selection interview this lack of clarification leads to a negative assessment of the candidate's suitability for the job. The interviewer felt that the candidate "wouldn't fit in" to the organization he represented, and this assessment was largely based on the part of the interview that dealt with the candidate's do-it-yourself skills – the section we have been looking at.

This is a revealing example of the way in which the candidate gets blamed for the interviewer's discomfort and lack of skills. (We come back to the interviewer's assessment of the candidate in the next section.)

In attempting to let the candidate carry on talking in the hope that understanding will become clearer in time, the interviewer is relying on what Schegloff/Jefferson/Sacks (1977) have called the preference for "self-initiated self-repair" in conversation. The interviewer, in letting the candidate carry on speaking, hopes that the speaker (in this case the candidate) will realize that he is not being understood and initiate some sort of repair strategy such as "do you understand what I mean?". Unfortunately, such meta-pragmatic utterances do not occur in the candidate's discourse and our more general experience tells us they are not common in the English of non-native speakers in interaction where there is an institutional power difference (e.g. in gatekeeping encounters). Such utterances would appear to pose a face threat (Brown/Levinson 1978) and are not uttered at all unless the speaker is either in a position of power or the social distance between speaker and hearer is small (see Scollon/Scollon 1983 for discussion). A job selection interview, even a relatively informal one, does not allow this. So self-initiated self-repair is not a real option. For the interviewer to clarify the situation he would have to initiate a repair sequence himself, but such "other initiated repairs" (Schegloff/Jefferson/Sacks 1977) are not conversationalists' first preference; they are "dispreferred" and as such must also pose a face threat to a user.

However, we would expect an interviewer (even a less powerful interviewer) to be able to do such a face threatening act if clarification was obviously called for. Our interviewer, however, does not initiate any repair or clarification strategy (other than letting the candidate carry on talking) at the key section in the interview where the candidate's trainability is being assessed (during the discussion of do-it-yourself gas repair skills).

There are many places in this interview and others we have videoed where there is an absence of repair initiation at moments which were crucial for the assessment of the candidate by the interviewer. It is our theory that such repair initiation fails to occur because it would pose a face threat to the interviewer and the interviewer at that time does not feel confident enough to take the risk. Another way of looking at this phenomenon in interviews is to say that the loss of topic control at key moments in the interaction causes the interviewer embarrassment, and that feelings of embarrassment cause further loss of control over the interview. A certain amount of control does need to be shed by interviewers if minority ethnic candidates are to be able to contribute well to the interview, but interviewers then need to develop compensatory skills to regain control at key moments, and this means primarily, initiating repair sequences.

There are additional factors in crosscultural interviews, and interviews with second language learners as candidates, which may also contribute to the feelings of embarrassment the interviewer suffers at moments of non-comprehension. One of these is the interviewer's feelings about the race and immigration issue. In his wish to avoid any prejudice or paternalism he treats the candidate as equally as possible. In other words he affects to be "colour-blind" and "deaf to language difference", on the wrong assumption that to treat everyone the same is to treat everyone equally.

The effect of this wish is to inhibit any moves by the interviewer to compensate for the fact that the candidate is a minority ethnic second language learner. In addition, he fails to acknowledge that, if the candidate is to be treated equally, special skills (in repair initiation and topic control, for example) are needed by the interviewer to overcome the disadvantage caused by the interviewer's own inexperience of second language learners or learning.[8] The wish to treat the candidate as equal will also lead the interviewer to underplay, while listening to the candidate, any difficulties caused by the learner's interlanguage and hence not search there for reasons to account for the intuitions upon which his judgement of the candidate will be based. Judgements will be given non-linguistic rationales.

In other cases where interviewers have recognized second language difficulties as playing a role within the interview, there is a tendency to use the language factor as a reason for not clarifying misunderstandings. They assume that any of the candidate's talk which they did not understand was therefore meaningless, i.e. not meaningful for the candidate. Instead of clarifying such utterances, interviewers choose to ignore them. In this way they often fail to grasp where key points for the candidate are occurring, and the whole interaction starts to go wrong. As a case in point, see example 7. Here, an unemployed Bangladeshi worker was afraid that the amount of money he had managed to save was near the limit for supplementary benefit.[9] He was persuaded to ask a supplementary benefits officer on one of our training courses. It was a risky thing to ask and he put the question indirectly by first stating how he was unemployed and living as best he could on little money but still managing to save small amounts.

EXAMPLE 7

> Int: *What's your enquiry please, Mr A.?*
> Mr A.:   *Enquiry?*
> Int: *What's your enquiry? What's your problem?*
> Mr A.:   *Me? Not problem, you know. Yes. Me, after three years, been three*
>   *years, you know, unemployed.*
> Int: *Three years unemployed, yes.*
> Mr A.:   *Unemployed, no money, you know.*
> Int: *Not enough money.*
> →Mr A.: *Yes, if I saving next time any money, you know, ten pound, five pound,*
>   *I keeping bank and building society.*
> Int: *Yeah, I see. What sort of money do you have coming in at the moment?*

The interviewer then goes on to ask a long series of questions to check whether Mr A. is getting all the benefit he might be entitled to, and Mr A. is never given the opportunity to ask his question about savings. The interviewer was quite happy at the end of the interview that Mr A. had come to check that he was receiving the correct benefit and was very surprised when we (the trainers) told him of Mr A.'s intended question. The key part of Mr A.'s introduction (marked by a → on the transcript above) where he begins to mention savings is also the place where the surface structure of his English deviates most from standard. It is also the only part of Mr A.'s introduction where the interviewer does not repeat back what Mr A. said. The interviewer had failed to understand the surface structure (here syntax and prosody) of what Mr A. said,[10] and consequently disregarded its content and did not seek to clarify it. The interviewer confirmed this for us afterwards on viewing the video recording of this interview.

Making the gatekeeping judgements
Formal analysis of an interaction can only take the analyst so far down the road to understanding what factors in an interview affect gatekeeping judgements. The main source of information about how judgements are made is the gatekeeper himself.

In the training exercise that produced the interview data in examples 5 and 6 the interviewer was himself interviewed immediately after the simulated job interview by a trainer who had not himself witnessed the interaction. The aim of this post-interview was to capture the interviewer's impression and assessment of the job interview, without contamination from the trainer's own view of the event. This was done before the interviewer himself had had a chance to watch the video recording. Interestingly, his initial impressions are significantly different from his considered impressions when watching the video.

Firstly, at the time of the post-interview (immediately after the job interview) the interviewer commented that he had not had difficulty with the candidate's English and he felt he had understood what was said. Secondly, although he was "happy" with the interviewee as a candidate and with what the candidate had said, he was not sure he (the candidate) would "fit in" to the organization. Hence it was unlikely, on balance, that the candidate would have been offered a job had there been one to offer. The combination of these two findings is both revealing and worrying. It is worrying because terms like "wouldn't fit in" seem sufficient for the interviewer not to open the gate. It is a judgement based on feeling or intuition rather than on specific evidence such as experience or qualifications or what the candidate actually said.[11] If the interviewer had been able to identify specific language difference and difficulty, the issue could have been tackled explicitly. Because the interviewer chose to be "deaf" in this respect, he was not able to assess the trainability potential of the candidate and the candidate might well interpret his lack of success as racial discrimination. Interestingly, (and an important point in training) the interviewer could easily recognize the second language phenomenon when he reviewed his and the candidate's performance on video.

In another part of this job interview there is a section where the candidate and the interviewer were in open disagreement. The interviewer was describing the likely pay rates available in the organization he represented and the candidate was openly saying that this would not be enough to meet his needs. In the post-interview however, this discrepancy between available and desirable remuneration did not worry the interviewer as much as the candidate's attitude to his do-it-yourself skills. It was the issue of trainability and whether the candidate would be sufficiently safety conscious that led to the negative evaluation "I'm not sure he would fit in" and the decision not to open the gate. So it is not overt differences of view that lead to interviewer discomfort and refusal of the candidate, but lack of clarity and certainty.

This type of post-interview evaluation forms part of the data used in training. Together with the interviews themselves the post hoc evaluations are significant in raising awareness in trainees of three crucial areas:

i. how easy it is to either overestimate or underestimate language difference and difficulty.
ii. how readily interviewers will make sweeping judgements which are not located in the actual evidence of the interaction or can only be located in evidence which has been constructed by the interviewer locked into a negative dynamic or purposeless exchange
iii. how ambiguity about the issues of power and control can create a communicative environment in which little or no explicitly goal-orientated exchange of meaning is possible.

Authentic video for training
The issues discussed in this paper are raised through using authentic video material in the training room. Some of this video is of naturally occurring real time sequences. Other material is made with participants acting themselves, as we describe above. The video material can be used to establish global differences between, for example, Asian/Asian and white/white interviews. Or it can be used to analyze discrete moments in the interaction where uncomfortable moments occur.

The aim is to help trainees to monitor their own behavior, locate their judgements in actual evidence and satisfy themselves that they are not assessing the evidence in an ethnocentric way. The training is the beginning of a process which the trainees themselves must develop over time.

We are not trying to teach people how to talk to a particular ethnic group. We are trying to help people to be more flexible and sensitive in dealing with all individuals. We are helping people to look into themselves and use resources which are in each one of us but which previous training, experience and systems have prevented us from using. There is no set style to switch between, rather a developing sensitivity which helps us to question our own behavior and not judge others by our own culture.

So, to sum up, we need to build on the strengths and skills of the trainees as professional people; disturb without threatening and show that new skills and sensitivities can be developed. In this way the gatekeepers can be helped to make sound judgements, of which they are confident, which "open the gate" to those who so often have it slammed in their face.

Notes

1. The training discussed in the paper is undertaken by the Industrial Language Training (ILT) Service in Britain. ILT is funded by the Government's Manpower Services Commission. Its aim is to train minority ethnic group workers and white majority managers, trade unionists and professionals to improve communications and help implement equal opportunity policies at the level of individual behavior and action. ILT works in manufacturing and service industries, with central and local government and with the health services.
2. The methodology described here has been developed and used by anthropologists and sociologists (Gumperz 1982; Cicourel 1969; Erickson/Shultz 1982) and is widely used by the Industrial Language Training Service in Britain in analyzing authentic data for training purposes.
3. A useful summary of the work of ethnomethodologists in conversation analysis is to be found in *Recent Developments in Conversation Analysis*, John Heritage, 1984, Warwick Working Papers in Sociology, University of Warwick.
4. Erickson/Shultz's work (1982) shows a clear causal connection between the number of awkward moments and the overall "emotional tone" of the counseling interview as evaluated both by participants and non-participant analysts of the videos.
5. Capital letters will be used throughout to name a particular frame.
6. See Thorpe (1981) and Sayers (1983a) for analysis of crosscultural interviews that go wrong because of this.
7. See Keenan/Schieffelin (1976) for the term "incorporation of topic".
8. Very few of the interviewers we train have any direct experience of operating in a second language.
9. Under a 1983 change in the regulations, if a claimant has over a certain amount in savings he loses entitlement to supplementary benefit.
10. The utterance *Yeah, I see* (final line of example 7) should not be taken as a sign of comprehension. Sayers (1983a) has many similar examples of *I see* indicating non comprehension. It signals a move to next topic or sub-topic, not necessarily that the previous topic has been understood.
11. As Erickson/Shultz (1982) illustrate, this vague feeling or discomfort can be rooted in something as imperceptible as arhythmia in interaction.

References

Bartlett, F.C. (1982) *Remembering*, Cambridge: Cambridge University Press.

Bateson, G. (1972) 'A theory of plan and phantasy' in G. Bateson (ed.) *Steps to an ecology of mind*, New York: Chandler, pp. 150–167.

Becker, A. (1979) 'Text-building, epistemology and aesthetics in Javenese shadow theatre' in A. Becker and A.A. Yengoyan (eds.) *The imagination of reality: Essays in South Asian coherence systems*, Norwood, N.J.: Ablex, pp. 133–149.

Brown, P. and Levinson, S. (1978) 'Universals in language usage: Politeness phenomena' in E. Goody (ed.) *Questions and politeness: Strategies in social interaction*, Cambridge: Cambridge University Press, pp. 56–289.

Erickson, F. and Schultz, J. (1982) *The counselor as gatekeeper: Social interaction in interviews*, New York: Academic Press.

Grice, H.P. (1975) 'Logic and conversation' in P. Cole and J. Morgan (eds.) *Syntax and semantics III: Speech acts*, New York: Academic Press, pp. 43–58.

Gumperz, J.J. (1982a) *Discourse strategies*, Cambridge: Cambridge University Press.

Gumperz, J.J (1982b) (ed.) *Language and social identity*, Cambridge: Cambridge University Press.

Gumperz, J.J., Jupp, T.C. and Roberts, C. (1979) *Crosstalk*, London: National Centre for Industrial Language Training.

Keenan, E.O. and Schieffelin, B.B. (1976) 'Topic as a discourse notion' in C.N.Li (ed.) *Subject and topic*, New York: Academic Press, pp. 335–385.

Levinson, S.C. (1979) 'Activity types and language', *Linguistics 17*, pp. 365–369.

Levinson, S.C. (1983) *Pragmatics*, Cambridge: Cambridge University Press.

Sayers, P. (1983a) *What the manager learnt*. Applied Linguistics Project for M.A. in Linguistics for ELT, Lancaster University.

Sayers, P. (1983b) *Topic collaboration and interview skills*, M.A. Dissertation, Lancaster University.

Schegloff, E.A., Jefferson, G. and Sacks, H. (1977) 'The preference for self-correction in the organization of repair in conversation', *Language 53: 2*, pp. 361–383.

Scollon, R. and Scollon, S.B.K. (1983) 'Face in inter-ethnic communication' in J.C. Richards and R.W. Schmidt, (eds.) *Language and communication*, Longman: London, pp. 156–190.

Tannen, D. (1979) 'Whats in a frame?' in R.O. Freedle, (ed.) *New directions in discourse processing*, Norwood, N.J.: Ablex, Vol. II, pp. 137–183.

Tannen, D. and Wallat, C. (1982) *Interactive frames and knowledge structure schemas in interaction: Examples from a pediatric examination*. Paper presented for the U.S.–France Joint Seminar on Natural Language Comprehension, St. Paul, Les Durances, France.

Thorpe, D. (1981) *Cross-cultural communication in an industrial job interview*. Applied Linguistics Project for M.A. in Linguistics for ELT, Lancaster University.

Widdowson, H.G. (1983) *Learning purpose and language use*, London: Oxford University Press.

3

Contrasting patterns of code-switching in two communities

Shana Poplack

Originally published in M. Heller, ed., *Codeswitching: Anthropological and Sociolinguistic Perspectives* (Mouton de Gruyter, 1988).

Recent interests in the constraints on bilingual behavior, and in particular, code-switching, show trends which seem to have come full circle.[1] By early accounts (e.g. Labov 1971), the behavior embodied in code-switching was the exception to the systematic and rule-governed nature of language variation. Researchers such as Gumperz and his students subsequently showed convincingly that code-switching was at least subject to pragmatic and/or interactional conditioning, was highly sensitive to the characteristics of the participants, and could be used for a variety of conversational functions (e.g. Gumperz and Hernandez-Chavez 1971; Blom and Gumperz 1972; Gumperz 1976/82). The issue of purely linguistic, or syntactic, constraints on code-switching was either not addressed or dismissed with the claim that there were none (e.g. Lance 1975). Empirical studies of actual speech behavior by, among others, Gumperz (1976/82), Hasselmo (1970, 1972), Pfaff (1979), and McClure (1981) revealed regularities which soon caused linguists to reject this view and even to adopt the opposite extreme, leading to a proliferation of particularistic and often poorly motivated statements of precisely where in the sentence a bilingual may or may not switch. It was soon seen that such ad hoc constraints, though they might hold in a majority or even all instances, were not generalizable from one language pair to another or even across different studies of the same pair in different contexts. Later, the view that some more general constraints might hold, constraints based on a universal compromise strategy of some sort, and predictable on the basis of the grammatical properties of the two languages involved in the alternation, gained currency. We return to this view below. More recent papers have contested this universalistic approach (e.g. Bentahila and Davies 1983), or have situated constraints at other than the syntagmatic level (e.g. Joshi 1983; Prince and Pintzuk 1983), or have rejected all but some language-specific conditions, reminiscent of the positions of the earlier work cited above.

In reviewing this and other current work, two issues become obvious. One is that researchers often confound different bilingual behaviors, including code-switching, but also borrowing on the community and individual levels, incomplete language acquisition, interference, and even acceptability judgements, and use them all as evidence about code-switching patterns. In this paper we stress that these linguistic manifestations of language contact are fundamentally different, both in their constitution and in their implications for the structures of the languages. Thus it is illogical to use a datum which may in fact be a fully integrated loanword, like *attorney general* in English, as evidence about word order violations in French-English code-switching. The second issue also pertains to the nature of appropriate data: attempts at assessing the true status of these different bilingual phenomena are futile unless they first distinguish community-wide from individual, and perhaps idiosyncratic, behavior. Conditions elucidated on borrowing and code-switching should in the first instance be community-wide, or part of the bilingual *langue*, since individual manifestations can only be understood against the background of the community norms. Too many variables which are crucial determinants of this behavior cannot be inferred without detailed knowledge of:

1. the bilingual ability of the informant in each of the languages,
2. the detailed nature of the two monolingual codes in question as they are actually used in some bilingual community, and as distinct from the "standard" varieties of either, and
3. the existence of particular community-specific or "compromise" solutions to the problem of reconciling two codes with conflicting rules within the same utterance, solutions which may be ungrammatical and/or unacceptable in other communities.

The nature of an utterance involving elements from more than one language may be predictable from a particular combination of these factors. Yet there is no way of inferring this information from any but systematic examination of the languages as used in the speech community. Thus use of informants of unspecified bilingual competences or linguistic backgrounds, or of isolated or exceptional examples, without situating them within patterns of community usage, is simply not relevant evidence for the existence of norms of bilingual behavior. A sufficient understanding of an individual's bilingual behavior seems beyond the reach of any but systematic corpus-based research carried out within her or his community.

We illustrate the role of the speech community in understanding bilingual behavior with a series of studies of two bilingual communities, which are superficially similar from both sociological and linguistic points of view, but use very different strategies for handling incorporations from English. In so doing, we return to the issue of distinguishing different contact phenomena. Early on, Haugen (1956) proposed that bilingual phenomena be located along a continuum of code distinctiveness, with switching representing maximal distinctness, integration (or borrowing) representing maximal levelling of distinctions, and interference referring to an overlapping of two codes, contrary to contemporary norms. While theoretically, these categories are eminently reasonable, in real life, bilingual behavior is not so easily classified. Indeed, as Hasselmo (1970) observed, although the intention of the speaker may be to choose either to switch or to use an integrated loanword, the constructions actually produced are often ambiguous.

Spanish/English contact among Puerto Ricans in New York

A first series of studies was carried out in a stable bilingual Puerto Rican community in East Harlem, New York (e.g. Language Policy Task Force 1980; Poplack 1980, 1981). Analysis of data collected by Pedro Pedraza, a group member, as part of a program of long-term participant observation of language distribution and use in the neighborhood, revealed that code-switching between English and Spanish was such an integral part of the community linguistic repertoire that it could be said to function as a mode of interaction similar to monolingual language use. An example of the sort of code-switching frequently heard in this community may be seen in (1), where in the course of a single utterance the language of the discourse oscillates from English to Spanish and back to English; and during each stretch in one language there are switches of smaller constituents to the other.

(1)   But I used to eat the **bofe**, the brain. And then they stopped selling it because   **tenían, este, le encontraron que tenía** worms. I used to make some **bofe! Después yo hacía uno d'esos** concoctions: the garlic **con cebolla, y hacía un mojo, y yo dejaba que se curara eso** for a couple of hours. (04/601)[2]
'But I used to eat the **bofe**, the brain. And then they uh, stopped selling it because they had, uh, they found out that it had worms. I used to make some **bofe!** Then I would make a sauce, and I'd let that sit for a couple of hours.'

We examined a large number of these switches to find out how they functioned in discourse (Poplack 1980). One of the characteristics of this kind of "skilled" or fluent code-switching (as opposed to switching for lack of lexical or syntactic availability, and as opposed to the "flagged" switches we discuss below) is a smooth transition between L_1 and L_2 elements, unmarked by false starts, hesitations or lengthy pauses. And in fact, these data showed smooth transitions between the switched item and adjacent sentence elements in 97% of the cases. Other characteristics include an apparent "unawareness" of the particular alternations between languages (despite a general awareness of using both codes in the discourse), insofar as the switched item is not accompanied by metalinguistic commentary, does not constitute a repetition of an adjacent segment, is made up of larger constituents than just a single noun inserted into an otherwise L_2 sentence, and is used for purposes other than that of conveying untranslatable or ethnically bound items. Again, only about 5% of the Spanish/English switches were used in one of these ways (ibid.).

Now, there are two purely linguistic problems that have to be solved in the course of alternating between two languages without the benefit of pausing, retracting, repeating, or otherwise indicating that you are about to pass from one language to the other. One is the resolution of eventual conflict between the word orders of the two languages involved in the alternation. In the case of Spanish and English adjective placement, for example, where the basic Spanish order is NA and the basic English order is AN, a switch to English after N means forfeiting the opportunity to produce A in Spanish while never having had the chance to say it in English. The second problem is local morphophonological conflict between the two languages, as when an English verb used in a Spanish context must be inflected for tense and mood.

Detailed analysis of the Spanish/English code-switching data revealed that there were only two general syntactic constraints on where intrasentential switching could occur (Poplack 1980, 1981; Sankoff and Poplack 1981): the free morpheme constraint, which prohibits mixing morphologies within the confines of the word, and the equivalence constraint, which requires that the surface word order of the two languages be homologous in the vicinity of the switch point.

As a result of the operation of these constraints, sentences containing switches turned out to be locally grammatical by standards of both Spanish and English simultaneously, suggesting highly developed linguistic skill in both. Indeed, there were only 11 violations of the equivalence constraint, or well under 1% of the 1,835 switches studies, though the switches had been produced by both balanced bilinguals and non-fluent speakers (Poplack 1980).

In considering how these latter were able to code-switch frequently and still maintain grammaticality in both languages, we found that the Puerto Rican community in East Harlem could be characterized by three switch types: tag, sentential and intrasentential, each requiring increasingly greater control of both languages to produce. These were distributed across the community according to bilingual ability, with the most highly bilingual speakers switching mainly within the bounds of the sentence.

Code-switching vs. borrowing

Now the majority of the material involved in the code-switching studies cited above consisted of switches of sentences or constituents of sentences which were unambiguously Spanish or English. But the smaller the switched constituent, and particularly at the level of the lone lexical item, the more difficult it is to resolve the question of whether we are dealing with a code-switch or a loanword. Since a code-switch, by Haugen's definition, is maximally distinct from the surrounding discourse, while a loanword should be identical to recipient-language material on the basis of synchronic considerations alone, differentiating the two might seem to be an easy matter. However, superficially the two may be indistinguishable in appearance. Phonological integration, an oft-cited diagnostic, may not provide a clue if the speaker pronounces all his English words, whether borrowed or not, according to Spanish patterns (i.e. with a Spanish "accent"). Morphology may also be irrelevant if the form requires no affixation, as in the case of a singular noun. Similarly, because of "interlinguistic coincidence" between English and Spanish, syntactic stretches in the two languages are often homologous. The co-occurrence of forms from two languages may also be due to interference or incomplete second language acquisition.

In seeking a way to identify full-fledged loanwords, a number of indices measuring various aspects of the linguistic and social integration of borrowed words were developed (Poplack and Sankoff 1984). These were abstracted from the types of criteria used implicitly or explicitly by scholars of bilingualism (e.g. Bloomfield 1933; Fries and Pike 1949; Weinreich 1953; Mackey 1970; Hasselmo 1970, etc.) to characterize loanwords, and included measures of frequency of use, native language synonym displacement, morphophonemic and/or syntactic integration, and acceptability to native speakers.

The frequency of use and phonological integration indices were found to measure phenomena which are closely related and proceed concurrently, a result which provides solid confirmation of the claims in the literature that borrowed words which are frequently used are made to conform with recipient language linguistic patterns.[3] English-origin material integrated into Puerto Rican Spanish, i.e. established loanwords,[4] could thus be defined as those concepts for which the identical, phonologically adapted designation was used by many or all speakers.

In summary, in the bilingual behavior of the Puerto Rican community in East Harlem there exists a mode of discourse characterized by frequent switching in a smoother and "unflagged" way between stretches of grammatical English and stretches of grammatical Spanish, the stretches consisting of words, phrases, sentences or larger discourse units. In addition, there are English lexical contributions to Spanish, manifested in terms of loanwords, which follow a well-defined linguistic and social trajectory.

Moreover, there is an operationalizable dichotomy between loanwords and switches. In the ideal case, a word or sequence of words which remains phonologically, morphologically and syntactically unadapted to Spanish could be considered English, i.e. a code-switch from Spanish, while one which is integrated with Spanish patterns could be considered Spanish. Though these criteria could not always be applied, for the reasons detailed above, we also had recourse to the empirical findings that 1) virtually all of the eligible Spanish-English code-switches respected the equivalence constraint, and 2) English-origin words which are used frequently are integrated into Spanish phonological and morphological patterns. Thus, given any single English-origin word in Puerto Rican Spanish discourse, if the same word was used by many speakers and hence uttered with Spanish phonology and morphology, and if in non-equivalent Spanish-English structures (e.g. adjective placement), it followed Spanish rules, then we could consider it a loanword and not a code-switch.

French/English contact in Ottawa-Hull

A second series of studies forms part of an ongoing research project investigating the French spoken in Ottawa-Hull – the national capital region of

Canada – and the effects on it of close and sustained contact with English (Poplack 1983a). The Ottawa-Hull urban complex is divided by a river which is both a geographic and linguistic border: on the Quebec side (Hull), French is the majority and sole official language, while on the Ontario side (Ottawa) it has minority status. One goal of this project is to characterize and compare the French spoken in the area in both its status as official language and in its minority guise. Five neighborhoods were selected on both sides of the border, each with a different proportion of English mother-tongue claimants, in order to test the hypothesis that influence from another language is a function of the recipient language's status in both the immediate and wider environment.

Each was sampled according to strict random sampling procedures, resulting in a fully representative sample of 120 francophones native to Ottawa or Hull respectively, stratified according to age and sex. Lengthy, informal interviews were carried out with informants by local francophone interviewers.

As in the Puerto Rican case, negative stereotypes of the French of the region and notably of that spoken on the Ontario side are widespread, particularly as regards the effects on it of coexistence with English. Our ongoing investigation of speakers' own attitudes toward the language(s) they speak reveals a complex system of linguistic values, not too dissimilar from those obtaining in the Puerto Rican (and other minority) communities (Poplack and Miller 1985). First the French language itself, though endowed with affective import, is widely seen as having less instrumental value than English, with the inverse assessments made of English. On the other hand, speakers commented freely on the "unfairness' of having to learn English when anglophones rarely make the effort to learn French. The use of English in largely French contexts which we will examine below can therefore not be simply ascribed to prestige factors or "impression management". Second, linguistic insecurity vis-à-vis European French *(le français de France)* is generally admitted, although Canadian varieties (with the notable exception of informants' own dialects) are imbued with some covert prestige. Not surprisingly then, the majority of informants on both sides of the border feel that they personally do not speak "good French", characterizing it most frequently as anglicized and *joual* 'slang'. Descriptions of "anglicized French" include the metaphor of mixing, which we interpret to refer to the widespread use of borrowing in the area as well as to code-switching, and another evoking "true" or intrasentential code-switching. Interestingly enough, the latter was limited to Ottawa residents, who, as we shall see, in fact engage in this type of switching somewhat more than the Hull speakers. Indeed, Ottawa speakers showed far greater familiarity with code-switching in general, in terms of overtly recognizing its existence, admitting to engaging in it personally, showing neutral rather than negative affect towards it, and even correctly identifying their own reasons for doing it: they claim that the English way of saying it is often shorter, more succinct, and more apt or expressive.

The French speakers' attitudes contrast sharply with those of the Puerto Ricans in the previous study. Though the Puerto Ricans were also fully cognizant of the prevalence of code-switching in their community and saw nothing wrong with it, their reason for switching was in essence because they "were bilingual" and this mode of discourse was appropriate to their dual identity (Attinasi 1979; also Zentella 1982). As a rule, they did not consider that one language was better for specific interactional or conversational purposes, or that certain concepts could be more felicitously expressed in one language than the other. We shall see below how this difference in attitudes is consistent with dramatically different code-switching behaviors in the two communities.

Code-switching in Ottawa-Hull

Turning now to the actual speech patterns of the Ottawa-Hull informants, exhaustive examination of their incorporations from English in approximately 290 hours of tape-recorded French conversation,[5] revealed some 1766 sequences which could be unambiguously identified as code-switches. Note that though it was largely possible to distinguish code-switching from borrowing in the Puerto Rican Spanish-English data, this is by no means always the case. In Ottawa-Hull (as in many other bilingual communities), French discourses may contain liberal amounts of English incorporations whose status as loanword or code-switch is at first blush unclear, as they may be consistent with both French and English morphology or syntax, as in the examples in bold type in (2):

(2)   a. Il y avait une **band** là qui jouait de la musique **steady**, pis il y avait des games de **ball**, pis . . . ils vendaient de l'**ice cream**, pis il y avait une grosse **beach**, le monde se baignait. (M.L./888)
'There was a band there that played music all the time and there were ball games, and . . . they sold ice cream, and there was a big beach where people could go swimming.'
b. Il y avait toutes sortes de chambres là, tu sais là, un **dining room, living room** un **den**, un **family room**, un **rec room** mais . . . mille neuf cent quatre-vingt dix-neuf par mois. (L.M./174)
'There were all kinds of rooms there, you know, a dining room, living room, a den, a family room, a rec room, but . . . $ 1999 a month'.

In the Ottawa-Hull region a large number of other bilingual phenomena also intervene to further complicate identification, to which we return below. One thing seems clear, however. When we exclude the problem category of uninflected single words (or compounds functioning as single words), other sequences can be identified as to their language membership on morphological and syntactic grounds. Thus the English-origin material in bold type below is being handled like French and not like English, receiving French affixation in (3) and French word order in (4).

(3)   Sont **spoilés** rotten. (JR,'1528) 'They're spoiled rotten.'
(4)   A côté il y en a un autre gros **building high-rise**. 'Next door there's another big high-rise building.'

Determination of the status of such forms is treated elsewhere (Poplack and Sankoff 1984; Sankoff and Poplack 1984; Sankoff, Poplack and Vanniarajan 1985); the discussion which follows is limited to the treatment of unambiguously English sequences in otherwise French discourse, i.e. to code-switches, as opposed to borrowing, as in the bold-face portions in (5).[6]

(5) a. On va avoir une dépression là que **we'll be rationed if we don't all die**. (JB/756)
     'We're going to have such a depression that . . .'
  b. Les français apprennent l'allemand parce que **they have to deal with them** économiquement là. (PX/1084)
     'The French learn German because they have to deal with them economically.'

Table 3.1 depicts the distribution of code-switches across the five neighborhoods sampled in Ottawa and in Hull. We note first that in the Ottawa communities, people tend to switch three or four times as frequently as in Hull, bearing out the prediction of our hypothesis

Table 3.1 Functions of code-switching in five Ottawa-Hull neighborhoods

	Ottawa (Ontario)			Hull (Quebec)	
	Vanier	Basse-Ville	West-End	Vieux-Hull	Mont-Bleu
No. of Speakers	23[a]	23[a]	22[a]	24	24
Function of code-switch: expression/"mot juste"	19	18	22	20	13
Meta-linguistic commentary	9	18	9	24	36
English bracketing	10	17[b]	8	15	12
Repetition translation, explanation	8	8	7	10	7
Reported speech	10	13	14	16	18
Proper name	4	3	4	5	7
Changed interlocuter	18	4	17	2	7
False start	5	7*	4	0.7	0.7
At turn boundary	2	0.7	0.7	0	0
Sentential	13	6	12	2	4
Intra-sentential	3	5	2	6	1
TOTALS[c]	552	423	514	148	136

[a] Four sample members whose use of English greatly exceeded that of the other informants and whose status as French L$_1$ speakers is not clear, were excluded from this study.
[b] Asterisks indicate that the effect is essentially due to that number of individuals.
[c] Percentages may not add up to 100 due to rounding.

regarding the influence of English in the environment. It is striking however, that in all of the neighborhoods, on both sides of the border, at least half of all the switches (and considerably more in Quebec) fall into the same four major types: a) when the switch provides the apt expression or what I will call the *mot juste*, as exemplified in (6), b) the switch occurs while discussing language or engaging in metalinguistic commentary, as in (7), c) where the switch calls attention to or brackets the English intervention by the use of expressions such as those in (8), and finally, d) in the context of explaining, specifying or translating as in (9).[7]

(6) a. C'est un – **a hard-boiled killer.** (CD/1955) 'He's a hard-boiled killer.'
    b. Il dit, "je veux pas avoir des **dishpan hands**." (IM/14445) 'He says, "I don't want to have dishpan hands".'
    c. Ça aurait été probablement le pays communiste idéal là. **Quote unquote** là. (PX/882) 'It probably would have been the ideal communist country'.

(7) a. Je m'adresse en français, pis s'il dit "**I'm sorry**", ben là je recommence en anglais. (MMR/3254) 'I begin in French and if he says, "I'm sorry", well then I start over in English'.
    b. Mais il dit, "c'est dur pour nous-autres: *le, la les*, vois-tu? Eux-autres, c'est rien que **the**". (RM/2538) 'But he says, "it's hard for us: *le, la les*, They only have *the*."'

(8) a. Mais je te gage par exemple que . . . excuse mon anglais, mais les **odds** sont là. (CD/716) 'But I bet you that . . . excuse my English, but the odds are there.'
    b. J'ai accepté le Seigneur là, ben . . . j'étais comme sur un . . . **cloud nine, cloud nine** qu'ils appellent. (MC/2476) 'I accepted the Lord then, well . . . I was like on a . . . cloud nine, cloud nine, as they say'.

(9) a. Je suis un peu trop anglicisé, anglifié, **anglicized**. (GF/1361) 'I'm a little too anglicized, anglified, anglicized.'
    b. J'ai été quissi pour **acupuncture**. Connais-tu ça de l'*acupuncture*? 'I also went for acupuncture. Do you know what acupuncture is?'
    c. J'ai acheté une roulotte, un **mobile home** là, une maison mobile. (GF/83) 'I bought a trailer, a mobile home, mobile home.'

Use of English fulfills other functions as well, however on a more individual basis. Thus English may be used to report speech as in (10), but this is mainly limited to one or two speakers in each neighborhood. Similarly, a few speakers opt to designate proper names having both English and French designations in English, as in (11). Informants of course switched to English when addressing interlocutors other than the interviewer, although the opportunity only rarely arose, even in the Ottawa neighborhoods, despite the fact that there is more chance there to use and hear English. Even here, the effects are inflated by the presence, during a small number of interviews, of individuals the informants generally address in English. Finally, switching to another language may of course be used to fill lexical gaps. This is how we interpret the behavior we have classed under the category of false starts, self-corrections and disfluencies (12).

(10) Pis il nous a appelé des grenouilles, hein? Bon, des **frogs**. Ben, j'ai dit, j'ai dit "Jess", j'ai dit, "**maybe we're a frog, but we're not dumb**." Pis il dit, "**what**

do you mean?" J'ai dit, "**we learn to swim**." Ben, j'ai dit, "**you never seen a frog who don't swim**, hein?" Ben, il dit, "**no**". Ben j'ai dit, "**you're too stupid**." J'ai dit, "**you don't swim**." Il dit, "**sure**" il dit, "**I can swim**."Il dit "**sure**." "**Well, I says** – j'ai dit, "**show it to me**." (RM/2462)
'And he called us frogs, you know? Well, frogs (Engl.). Well, I said, "Jess", I said, "maybe we're a frog, but we're not dumb." And he says, "what do you mean?" I said, "we learn to swim". Well, I said, "you never seen a frog who don't swim, eh?" Well, he says "no." Well, I said, "you're too stupid." I said, "you don't swim." He says, "sure", he says, "I can swim." He says "sure". Well, I says – I said, "show it to me".

(11) a. Il avait le choix soit d'aller dans l'armée, dans **Navy** ou dans l'**Air Force**. (AB/2179) 'He had the choice either to go into the Army, the Navy or the Air Force'.

    b. Montreal   [m ntrijal – mõreal]
       Ontario   [anteriou – õtarjo]
       IGA   [aiɟiej – iʒea]

(12) a. Le- le- le- spontanéité de- de- de- **the spunk** de le faire, (RC/84) 'The- the- the- spontaneity of- of- of- of-the spunk to do it.'

    b. C'est- c'est pas distor – tu sais, **it's not distorted**. (GF/2222) 'It's- it's not distor – you know . . .'"

Even this use is quite rare, and almost non-existent in the Quebec neighborhoods. However, switching to English for any one of the latter functions is only sporadic in comparison to the first four. Indeed, wherever any one of them appears to have a meaningful effect, this is invariably due to one or two individuals with a particular predilection for the type in question, as indicated by the asterisks on the Table.

Comparison of behavior in the Quebec and Ontario neighborhoods reveals subtle differences in the uses to which code-switching is put beyond the frequences noted above, as can be appreciated graphically in Fig. 3.1.

Here we see that in the three Ottawa neighborhoods code-switching to English tends to be done to provide what is perceived to be the best way of saying a thing, or the *mot juste*, a finding which is consistent with Ottawa speakers' description of their reasons for switching: to designate items for which the French equivalent has already been displaced (Poplack and Miller 1985). This use generally far outweighs the others. In Quebec, on the other hand, switches to English are largely restricted to metalinguistic commentary, a device having the effect of showing full awareness on the part of the speaker in using English. In the upper-middle class Mont-Bleu neighborhood of Hull, this strategy accounts for more than 1/3 of all the data, whereas the working-class Vieux Hull shows an intermediate pattern.[8] The Hull speakers' linguistic behavior is also consistent with their own favorable attitudes towards proper speech, their belief that interventions from English are due to momentary lapses, as well as their attitude that good French must of necessity exclude anglicisms.

Now the use of code-switching to fulfill particular discourse functions, and especially functions such as the ones we have outlined here, is hardly new. This functional or "semantic" approach was introduced by Gumperz over a decade ago (e.g. Gumperz 1976/82; Blom and Gumperz 1972) and has proliferated amongst students of the school of "interactionist

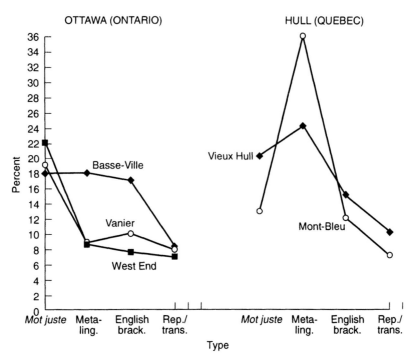

Fig. 3.1 Distribution of favoured code-switching types by neighbourhood

sociolinguistics" ever since (e.g. Elías-Olivares 1976; Huerta 1978; Auer 1981; Valdes 1981; di Luzio 1984; Heller 1982; among many others).

The aim here is not to enter into the interpretation of the "meaning" of these individual switches; indeed it is still unclear that each has a stateable meaning beyond the rough labels assigned them. Rather, I want to focus on the global function all of these code-switches fulfill in the discourse: that of flagging, or breaking up the speech flow, and the consequences of this for the investigation of purely linguistic constraints on code-switching. Perhaps the most noteworthy feature of Table 3.1 is the dramatically reduced frequency in all neighborhoods of spontaneous code-switches at a turn boundary within the same interaction, as in (13), switches of full sentences or independent clauses, as in (14), and especially, intra-sentential switches as in (15).

(13) Interviewer: C'est juste un petit micro, il y a une clip tu peux mettre sur ton gilet là. 'It's just a small mike, there's a clip you can put on your sweater. Informant: **I'm a star!**

(14) Parce que **I was there and** la seule raison c'était parce que je voulais oublier toute. (JB/996) 'Because I was there and the only reason was because I wanted to forget everything.'

(15) a) Tu sais, les condamner à chaise électrique **or** que c'est qu'ils- qu'ils voudraient. (CD/1909) 'You know, condemn them to the electric chair or whatever they want.'

b) Faut que tu **pack your own** au Basics. (KC/336) 'You have to pack your own at Basics.'

c) Le gouvernement de l'Ontario **is an equal opportunity employer.** (CN/832) 'The government of Ontario . . .'

Thus the kind of behavior we had designated as "true" code-switching (i.e. in which individual switches cannot be attributed to stylistic or discourse functions) in the study of the Puerto Rican community, where it was largely confined to skilled bilinguals in appropriate, in-group interactions, is but a minor phenomenon in the Ottawa-Hull French study. Table 3.1 shows it does not exceed a small percentage in any of the communities studied. This despite the fact that the participant constellation, mode of interaction and bilingual situation appear to be largely similar to those in the Puerto Rican study.

To recapitulate, where the Puerto Ricans code-switched in a way which minimized the salience of the switch points, and where the switches formed part of an overall discourse strategy to use both languages, rather than to achieve any specific local discursive effects, the Ottawa-Hull speakers do the contrary. They draw attention to their code-switches by repetition, hesitation, intonational highlighting, explicit metalinguistic commentary, etc. and use the contrast between the codes to underline the rhetorical appropriateness of their speech. We saw from Fig. 3.1 that this is an overt strategy in the Quebec communities, covert in Ontario. In contrast, the impossibility of systematically interpreting code-switches in terms of any conversational function in the Puerto Rican materials has already been demonstrated (Poplack 1980).

Now the *mot juste* is most frequently a noun phrase or an idiomatic expression. The equivalence constraint on intra-sentential code-switching is thus satisfied trivially or is not pertinent, either because the conditions for placement of this form are homologous in French and English, or because of the devices the speaker uses to deliberately interrupt his or her sentence at a code-switch boundary, as in (16), where a potential grammatical violation is remedied in just this way.

(16) Fait que là ben, je paye un peu moins en- comme on dirait en anglais, **according** à que c'est que je fais. (DM/132) 'So, well, I pay a little less in- as they say in English, according to (Fr. *selon*) what I make.

Thus the data provide few "interesting" tokens which could be used for or against the validity of the equivalence or other purely linguistic constraints on intra-sentential code-switching.

Code-switching differences between communities

To what should the differences in code-switching patterns between the Ottawa-Hull and New York Puerto Rican bilingual communities be ascribed? They cannot be due to linguistic (i.e. typological) differences between the two languages as compared with English, as these are minor and relatively few in number. It is more likely that at least part of the divergence between the two studies is due to differences in data collection techniques: the random sampling methodology used in the Ottawa-Hull study required that the interviewers, though of French Canadian ethnicity and local origin, *not* be group members in the strict sense, as opposed to the participant observation technique employed in the Puerto Rican research. For the same reasons, the large number of speakers interviewed in five separate neighborhoods precluded establishment of the familiarity resulting from years of observing and interacting with the same group of informants on a single city block. Moreover, though interventions in English from the Ottawa-Hull informants were never actively discouraged, they were not overtly encouraged either (by interviewer participation in the code-switching mode). The approach in these interviews was basically French, in keeping with our original goal of studying the French in the region. Since the optimal conditions for code-switching arise when all factors, the setting, participant constellation and situation are considered appropriate, this may account for the preponderance of "special-purpose" code-switching in Ottawa-Hull, as opposed to its virtual absence in the Puerto Rican study. Attractive as this explanation may be, however, it should be pointed out that we have no non-anecdotal evidence, either from the interviews or from systematic ethnographic observation, that there exist situations or domains, untapped by us, where intrasentential code-switching is the norm.

Until such evidence can be found, therefore, we cannot reject out of hand the possibility that these results may represent a true difference in communicative patterns, albeit one which has no simple explanation based on a summary comparison of the characteristics of the two bilingual contexts. The situations of French in Canada and Spanish in the United States share superficial similarities as minority languages, though French has been in contact with English longer than Puerto Rican Spanish has; it has the status of official national language in Canada while Spanish enjoys no such prestige in the United States, and French Canadian ethnics are neither as visible nor as highly stigmatized as are Puerto Ricans in New York. Yet none of these observations seem directly relevant to the code-switching patterns discussed above. Indirectly, however, the different social, historical and political factors have led to differences in attitudes towards use of English in the two situations, which themselves may be partly determinant of the contrasting code-switching patterns. These attitudes may reflect the fact that bilingualism is seen to be emblematic of New York Puerto Rican identity (as compared both with Island Puerto Ricans and non-Puerto Rican anglophones) whereas in the Ottawa-Hull situation, knowledge of English does not appear to be associated with any emergent ethnic grouping. Indeed, bilingualism among francophones (rather than anglophones) has traditionally been the outcome of contact throughout Canada (e.g. Lieberson 1970). Differences in professed affect toward English and toward switching may also play a role.

Moreover, although there is evidence that different methods of data collection may lead to quantitative differences in code-switching behavior even on the part of the same speaker (Poplack 1981), we have no reason to believe that this should result in the nearly categorical qualitative differences observed here: the sum of sentential, intrasentential and spontaneous switches at a turn boundary does not reach 4% of all of the Ottawa-Hull data, while the proportion of flagged or special-purpose switching in Puerto Rican Spanish does not exceed 5%.[9]

If the differences between the two communities are indeed due to true differences in communicative strategies, then this shows a much greater awareness on the part of Ottawa-Hull francophones of their usage of English during French discourse than most casual observers would have expected. But even if the result is an artefact of our methodology, i.e. is due to perceived inappropriateness (because of social distance along the axis of familiarity), we have the striking result that this reaction is neither idiosyncratic nor the property of a small group, but is a community-wide pattern. Its interpretation would then be that in situations where ("true") code-switching is perceived to be inappropriate or has not been negotiated, the response is not necessarily to eschew usage of English altogether, but to use it in ways that show full speaker awareness. Such usage corresponds well with both Ottawa and Hull speaker perceptions mentioned above regarding the role and value of English.

This finding raises other questions concerning the background assumptions of the French speakers in our study. As Gumperz (1982) has pointed out, bilinguals do not ordinarily engage in code-switching before they know whether the listener's background and attitudes will render it feasible or acceptable. Rather they begin interactions with a series of probes aiming to establish shared presuppositions. In addition, the most favorable conditions for code-switching according to him are ones where speakers' ethnic identities and social backgrounds are not matters of common agreement. The situation amongst the Ottawa-Hull speakers is somewhat different. Shared ethnic identity is established before the onset of the interaction.[10] No "probing" as to language knowledge appears in these interviews. Instead, members appear to equate French Canadian ethnicity with knowledge of both English and French, an assessment which is not always correct, as can be seen in the exchange in (17), which recurred not infrequently between interviewer and informant.

(17) Informant: Il y avait de la **wrestling** pis de la boxe pis . . .
     Interviewer: Le **wrestling**, c'était quoi ça?
     Informant: Le **wrestling**, quand les- les **wrestlers** là, comment-ce que
                   . . .?
     Interviewer: Ah ouais, ouais, okay.
     Informant: There was wrestling, and boxing and . . .
     Interviewer: Wrestling, what was that?
     Informant: Wrestling, when the- the wrestlers, how do you . . . ?
     Interviewer: Oh yeah, yeah, okay.
     Informant: Wrestling (Fr.)

Thus in the Ottawa-Hull region, members' implicit ascription of bilingual competence to each other (cf. Auer 1981) includes the (founded or unfounded) presupposition of competence in English. On the other hand their usage of English is calculated to demonstrate their own full awareness of doing so.

Code-switching vs. other bilingual phenomena

The discussion in the previous sections was based on some 1700 stretches of English-origin material which could be unambiguously identified as code-switches. However, there are thousands more which cannot be so identified in a clearcut way. In an earlier pilot study involving 44 of these same speakers (Poplack 1983b), we extracted some 2,300 English-origin forms consisting of a single word (or a compound functioning as a single word) from an exhaustive search of their recorded interviews. These were the words operationally excluded from the code-switching data base, as described in the previous section, although some may in fact be code-switches.

Recall that in the Puerto Rican case we were largely able to distinguish borrowing from code-switching even for lone lexical items. How can we ascertain the status of the English-origin words in Ottawa-Hull French discourse?

The straightforward case is that of certain high-frequency forms which are integrated into local French. These forms tend to recur across speakers, to have a single French phonological rendition, and to behave like bonafide loanwords in Ottawa-Hull French. It should come as no surprise that most are also attested nation-wide in other varieties of Canadian French (e.g. *chum, gang*).

In other cases, forms may seem equally linguistically integrated into French as in (18), but the frequency criterion is unclear or non-existent.

(18) Je serais pas capable de **coper** avec. (LM/1086) 'I couldn't cope with it.'

Indeed, with studies of the spoken language, even in a data base of this size, most borrowed words are relatively rare, such that those that occur tend to do so only once. Even in the lengthy recorded conversations with our subsample of 44 individuals, we were only able to identify about 500 English-origin words, or about 20%, which were used by at least two different people. This renders the status of words like *coper* indeterminate for the time being.

The situation is further complicated by the fact that "momentary" or nonce borrowings[11] coexist with the integrated loanwords, and the distinction between them is not necessarily recoverable from the structural form of the word. Occasionally the free morpheme constraint, which prohibits mixing phonologies within the (code-switched) word, can be circumvented through the mechanism of momentary borrowing. The examples in (19) show unadapted English morphemes conjoined with French verbal and participial affixes.

(19) quiter   [kwɪ́te]
     enjoyer   [ɛnjɔ́ˈje]
     traveler   [trævˈle]
     grower   [gɾoˈwe]
     polishait   [pʰaləˈʃɛ]
     shockés   [ʃaː ˈkʰe]
     drowné   [dɾawˈne]

This is in contrast with the Puerto Rican usage, which permitted no English root with Spanish affixes unless this root was first integrated into Spanish phonologically and sociologically, but seems to be at variance with the usual French Canadian treatment of integrated loanwords as well.

The Ottawa-Hull francophones also make use of several other strategies which allow them to combine the lexicons, word-formation rules and phonological rules from both languages. Aside from the fully integrated loanwords, synchronically indistinguishable from native French lexical items, we find other words (of greater or lesser frequency) which do not appear constrained to take on the same phonological forms, even when uttered by the same speaker (see also Mougeon et al. 1984). Thus we find coexisting examples such as the ones in (20) (Miller 1984):

(20) meetings   [ˈmiD iŋ] ~ [miˈtiŋ]
     tough   [tɔv] ~ [tʰ f] ~ [tøf]
     anyway(s)   [ɛnəwèz] ~ [ɛnɛwé]
     whoever   [uɛ̀vɔ́ʀ] ~ [uɛ́vʀ]

Alternatively, and more surprisingly, the French affixes are occasionally rendered in an anglicized way, so that the entire word will have English phonology but French morphology.

(21) afforder   [əˈfɾDe] for [aftˈde]
     relaxés   [rəˈlækse] for [rəlakˈse]

(This situation is further complicated by the fact that English retroflex [r] has penetrated the French phonological system and presently co-varies with apical [r] and velar [ʁ] even in French-origin words.) And in many other cases where the phonological systems differ minimally, only the affixes can be identified as to language (e.g. *mover* 'to move' [muˈve]). In addition, a wide range of English items may be borrowed "momentarily" by means of a strategy which is also widespread in other French-speaking communities in Canada. This is a distinctive stress pattern applied to English-origin words in predominantly French discourse, but never to French words, and never in English discourse by the same speakers if they are fluent bilinguals. (Among speakers less fluent in English, it forms part of the stereotypical "French Canadian accent", but the interesting fact here is its use by fluent bilinguals in the restricted context of nonce borrowing.)

Briefly, the main word stress rule shifts the heaviest stress to the right-most syllable within the word in French, and to the leftmost syllable in

English. The two languages also differ as to their rules for assigning syllable stress, or beats. A compromise between English and French stress assignment patterns appears to be taking place in polysyllabic words (and even frozen expressions) of English origin occurring occasionally in French discourse, as in (22):

(22) des **alcoholics**   [ælkəhʌlɪ́k]
      les **neighbors**   [néybə̀R]
      des **arguments**   [ʌ́rgjumə́nt]
      J'aime avoir du **peace and quiet** [pʰiys æn kwʌ́jə̀t]
      'I like having peace and quiet.'

Here we find main word stress assigned according to English rules, shifting stress to the left, while syllable stress is assigned according to French patterns. Final syllables which would normally be unstressed schwas in English thus receive secondary stress.

The resulting word-structures have no counterpart in English or in French, and constitute an example of the innovative solutions which evolve in given speech communities. Their particular function here appears to be to allow nonce borrowing of an English word without "switching" to English (i.e. producing it in English), while still informing the interlocutor that one is attending to the fact of uttering an English word. (These forms may also be accompanied by one or both of rising intonation and the punctuant *là*, which have the further function of bracketing these words.)

Discussion

What are the implications of these results for a general theory of bilingualism? The striking contrasts between the patterns of English influence in just two not very dissimilar communities do not augur well for any simple deterministic view of bilingual behavior. Nor are they promising for attempts to impose global restrictions on the purely linguistic level.

However, the development of any kind of discourse based on more than one code must eventually come to terms with the structural differences between them. For Puerto Ricans, code-switching *per se* is emblematic of their dual identity, and smooth, skilled switching is the domain of highly fluent bilinguals. The use of individual code-switches for particular effects or functions is relatively rare in intra-group communication, consistent with the perceived ability of either language to fulfill any communicative need. The equivalence and free morpheme constraints are simple and natural strategies to achieve this kind of discourse.

The French-English case presented made clear another point: evaluation of the equivalence or any syntactic constraint is a fruitless pursuit in situations where "smooth" code-switching is not a community-wide discourse mode. Here, English use as well as speaker attitudes towards it are consistent with highlighting, flagging or otherwise calling attention to the switch. Indeed, in order for the switch to accomplish its purpose – be it metalinguistic commentary, finding the *mot juste*, providing an explanation and so on – it must be salient, and should not pass unnoticed. One byproduct of this is the interruption of the speech flow at the switch point, effectively circumventing a grammaticality requirement or rendering one unnecessary.

On the other hand, the high rate of use of borrowed material, integrated or not, well-established or momentary, appears to be serving largely referential purposes, so that these should occur without fanfare in the flow of discourse. This explains to some extent the wide range of strategies current in this community to handle English-origin material, in addition to code-switching and fully integrated borrowing. From the brief description of some of these given in the previous section, it should be evident that they do not necessarily show the same regularities or restrictions as the other phenomena, and must be studied in their own right. Moreover, none of the characteristics of the languages involved in the alternation, the contact situations or other aspects of the bilingual context would have permitted us to infer or predict the differences in code-switching patterns outlined here.

In concluding, I have been using the term "code-switching" here to refer to the alternate use of two codes in a fully grammatical way, in the same discourse, and even in the same sentence. Others use "code-mixing", "code-shifting" or other terms for the same purpose, and this poses no problem. What is important is that this phenomenon be clearly distinguished, first conceptually, and then operationally as much as possible, from all the other consequences of bilingualism which involve not alternate use, but the truly *simultaneous* use of elements from both codes. And within this latter category, lexical borrowing on the community level should be kept distinct from "momentary" or nonce borrowing by individuals, on the one hand, and on the other, from incomplete acquisition and language loss. Not least important, all of these phenomena should be distinguished from speech errors which involve elements of both languages, and which may be properly considered "interference". Of course these distinctions are easier to label than to operationalize. In practice, one type of behavior may fade into another. And given a simple utterance containing words from two codes there is not necessarily any *a priori* way of distinguishing a switch from a loanword from one of the other results of language contact discussed here. What appears to be the same phenomenon may have a different status from one bilingual community to another.

This leads to my final point. What data are appropriate to the study and categorization of these phenomena? Clearly, if we are presented with a sentence of unknown pedigree containing elements from two codes, we cannot be sure of anything. We need to know the community patterns, both monolingual and bilingual, the bilingual abilities of the individual, and whether the context is likely to have produced speech in the code-switching mode or not.

Similarly, an acceptability or grammaticality judgement does not reveal whether the item in question is a grammatical code-switch, and established loanword, or a commonly heard speech error among L2 learners. And if the linguist has such difficulty making these analytical distinctions, it is unlikely that the informant should know the answers intuitively.

For an understanding of language contact phenomena, even more than in monolingual studies, corpus-based research on language use in well-documented contexts is indispensable. Subjective reactions, acceptability judgements and intuition all have their place, but they must be tied to knowledge of the community.

Notes

1. We gratefully acknowledge the support of the Social Science and Humanities Research Council of Canada who funded the project of which this research forms part. Earlier versions of this material were presented at the fourth Scandinavian Symposium on Bilingualism, and the fifth International Conference on Methods in Dialectology, and this paper appears in their Proceedings (*Methods V: Papers from the V International Conference on Methods in Dialectology*, ed. by H.J. Warkentyne (1985), Victoria, B.C.: University of Victoria, pp. 363–386, and *Aspects of Multilingualism*, ed. by E. Wande et al. (1987). Uppsala: Borgströms, pp. 51–77). The term "community" is used in this paper to refer variously to the New York Puerto Rican speech community, Ottawa-Hull francophones and the particular neighborhoods in which they live. This is ordinary language usage; we do not impute to each the ensemble of connotations sometimes associated with the notion of "speech community". Thanks to François Grosjean, Raymond Mougeon, Edouard Béniak and Daniel Valois who read and commented on this paper.
2. The code identifies the speaker and example number.
3. See Mougeon et al. (1984) for an opposing point of view in a situation of language shift.
4. As opposed to nonce borrowing and other types of language mixture discussed below.
5. The systematic combing of such a large data base was made possible by automated manipulation of the computerized Ottawa-Hull French corpus to extract English sequences which had been identified as code-switches during transcription (see Poplack 1983a).
6. Our basic procedure was to operationally exclude single nouns (or compounds functioning as single nouns) unless there was contextual evidence to indicate they were being treated as code-switches (as in the examples in (8)). Incorporations of single English elements from other grammatical categories were retained as code-switches, with the exception of those which are either well-documented as loanwords (e.g. *so*; Roy 1979. Mougeon et al. 1983), or which in the Ottawa-Hull corpus satisfy the frequency criterion for loanwords.
7. These categories and the others which follow are rough labels for discourse behavior rather than analytical constructs, and include discourse strategies along with linguistic categories. The former will obviously show some overlap, as a single utterance can accomplish more than one function in discourse. Since our concern here is to assess the amount of attention called to or motivation for an English intervention, switches were classed preferentially into categories most clearly reflecting this. Thus bracketing of a switch took precedence over its function to provide the *mot juste*, etc.
8. In fact both the largely monolingual French Vieux Hull and the highly bilingual Basse-Ville of Ottawa show intermediate patterns; in each neighborhood some people behave more like Ottawa speakers and others more like Hull speakers. This is not surprising – code-switching patterns could not possibly be determined solely by neighborhood of residence, being dependent on so many other

factors as well. More surprising is the regularity which does obtain here. We focus then on the gross differences between Ottawa and Hull.

9. Indeed, a pilot study of code-switching in Ottawa carried out by a group member using participant observation techniques (Trudel 1985) gave strikingly similar results to the ones reported here.

10. By the response of the potential informant to the interviewer's quest for a "francophone born and raised in the region" and by the interviewer's assessment of the "nativeness" of his French.

11. Grosjean (1982) refers to these as "speech" borrowings.

References

Attinasi, J. (1979) 'Language Attitudes in a New York Puerto Rican Community' in Padilla, R. (ed.), *Ethnoperspectives in Bilingual Education Research*, Ypsilanti, MI: Eastern Michigan University.

Auer, J.C.P. (1981) 'Bilingualism as a member's concept: language choice and language alternation in their relation to lay assessments of competence', Sonderforschungsbereich 99. Department of Linguistics, University of Konstanz.

—— (1984) "On the meaning of conversational code-switching". Ms.

Bentahila, A. and Davies, E. (1983) 'The syntax of Arabic-French code-switching', *Lingua* 59: pp. 301–330.

Blom, J.P. and Gumperz, J. (1972) 'Social meaning in linguistic structures', in Gumperz, J. and Hymes, D. (eds.), *Directions in Sociolinguistics*, New York: Holt, Rinehart and Winston, pp. 407–434.

Bloomfield, L. (1933) *Language History*, H. Hoijer (ed.), New York: Holt, Rinehart and Winston.

Duran, R. (ed.) (1981) *Latino Language and Communicative Behavior*, Norwood, New Jersey: Ablex.

Elías-Olivares, L. (1976) 'Ways of Speaking in a Chicano Community: a Sociolinguistic Approach', Ph.D. dissertation, The University of Texas at Austin.

Fries, C. and Pike, K. (1949) 'Coexistent phonemic systems', *Language* 25: pp. 29–50.

Grosjean, F. (1982) *Life with Two Languages*, Cambridge: Harvard University Press.

Gumperz, J. (1976/1982) 'Conversational code-switching' in: J. Gumperz, *Discourse Strategies*, Cambridge: Cambridge University Press, pp. 59–99.

Gumperz, J. and Hernandez-Chavez, E. (1971) 'Bilingualism and bidialectalism in classroom interaction' in Cazden, C. et al. (eds.), *The Functions of Language in the Classroom*, New York: Teachers College Press.

Hasselmo, N. (1970) 'Code-switching and modes of speaking' in Gilbert, G. (ed.), *Texas Studies in Bilingualism*, Berlin: Walter de Gruyter and Co., pp. 179–210.

Haugen, E. (1956) *Bilingualism in the Americas*, Publication of the American Dialect society no. 26, University of Alabama Press.

Heller, M. (1982) "Bonjour, hello?": 'Negotiations of language choice in Montreal' in Gumperz, J. (ed.), *Language and Social Identity*, Cambridge: Cambridge University Press.

Huerta, A. (1978) 'Code-switching among Spanish-English bilinguals: a sociolinguistic perspective', Ph.D. dissertation, The University of Texas at Austin.

Joshi, A. (1983) 'Processing of sentences with intra-sentential code-switching', to appear in Dowty, D. et al. (eds.), *Natural Language Processing: Psycholinguistic, Computational and Theoretical Perspectives*, Cambridge: Cambridge University Press.

Labov, W. (1971) 'The notion of "system" in creole languages' in Hymes, D. (ed.),

Pidginization and Creolization of Languages, Cambridge: Cambridge University Press, pp. 447–472.

Lance, D. (1975) 'Spanish-English code-switching' in Hernandez-Chavez et al. (eds.), *El lenguaje de los chicanos*, Arlington: Center for Applied Linguistics, pp. 138–154.

Language Policy Task Force (1980) 'Social dimensions of Language Use in East Harlem', Working paper no. 7, New York: Center for Puerto Rican Studies.

Lieberson, S. (1970) *Language and Ethnic Relations in Canada*, New York: Wiley and Sons.

di Luzio, A. (1984) On the meaning of language choice for the sociocultural identity of bilingual migrant children. Ms.

Mackey, W. (1970) 'Interference, integration and the synchronic fallacy' in Alatis, J. (ed.), *Georgetown University Roundtable on Languages and Linguistics*, 23, Washington, D.C.: Georgetown University Press, pp. 195–223.

McClure, E. (1981) 'Formal and functional aspects of the code-switched discourse of bilingual children' in Duran R. (ed.), *op. cit.*, pp. 69–94.

Miller, C. (1984) Phonetic criteria for loanword integration in Ottawa-Hull French, University of Ottawa class paper.

Mougeon, R., Valois, D. and Béniak, E. (1983) For a quantitative study of linguistic borrowing. Paper presented at the Canadian Linguistics Association.

—— (1984) Variation in the phonological treatment of lexical borrowings from English by speakers of a minority language. Paper presented at the XIII conference on New Ways of Analyzing Variation. University of Pennsylvania.

Pfaff, C. (1979) Constraints on language mixing, *Language* 55: pp. 291–318.

Poplack, S. (1980) "Sometimes I'll start a sentence in English *y termino en español*": 'Toward a typology of code-switching', *Linguistics* 18: 581–618.

—— (1981) 'Syntactic structure and social function of code-switching' in Duran, R. (ed.), *op. cit.*, pp. 169–184.

—— (1983a) 'The care and handling of a mega-corpus: the Ottawa-Hull French project', to appear in Fasold, R. and Schiffrin, D. (eds.), *Language Variation and Change*, Amsterdam: Benjamins.

—— (1983b) 'The propagation of loanwords within a speech community'. Paper presented at the XII Conference on New Ways of Analyzing Variation, Université de Montréal.

Poplack, S. and Sankoff, D. (1984) 'Borrowing: the synchrony of integration', *Linguistics* 22.1: pp. 99–135.

Poplack, S. and Miller, C. (1985) 'Political and interactional consequences of linguistic insecurity'. Paper presented at the XIV Conference on New Ways of Analyzing Variation, Georgetown University.

Prince, E. and Pintzuk, S. (1983) Code-switching and the open/closed class distinction. Ms.

Roy, M.-M. (1979) Les conjonctions anglaises 'but' et 'so' dans le français de Moncton. M.A. Thesis, Université du Québec à Montréal.

Sankoff, D. and Poplack, S. (1981) 'A formal grammar for code-switching', *Papers in Linguistics* 14.1: pp. 3–46.

Sankoff, D. and Poplack, S. (1984) 'Code-switching constraints in functional and typological perspective'. Paper presented at the XIII Conference on New Ways of Analyzing Variation, University of Pennsylvania.

Sankoff, D., Poplack, S. and Vanniarajan, S. (1985) 'The case of the nonce loan in Tamil'. Paper presented at the XIV Conference on New Ways of Analyzing Variation, Georgetown University.

Trudel, M. (1985) 'Une analyse préliminaire de l'alternance de code intra-groupe à Ottawa', University of Ottawa class paper.

Valdes, G. (1981) "Code-switching as a deliberate verbal strategy: a micro-analysis of direct and indirect requests," in Duran, R. (ed.), *op cit.*, pp. 95–107.
Weinreich, U. (1953) *Languages in Contact*, The Hague: Mouton.
Zentella, A. (1982) Spanish and English in contact in the United States: the Puerto Rican experience, *Word*, 33.1–2: pp. 41–57.

4

'You can never tell where a word comes from': language contact in a diffuse setting

Robert B. Le Page

Originally published in E. H. Jahr (ed.), *Language Contact: Theoretical and Empirical Studies* (Mouton de Gruyter, 1992).

Introduction

This paper is divided into three parts: in Part 1, I discuss some of the problems which orthodox linguistic theories present to variationists and creolists like myself, and I sketch the conceptual framework which our Caribbean data forced upon me.

In Part 2, I outline the case-histories of Belize, in Central America, and of the island of St Lucia in the Windward Antilles, relating each to the various cultural pressures operating on their linguistic evolution. Andrée Tabouret-Keller and I have dealt with these two cases in detail in our book *Acts of identity* (1985). There we illustrate the processes of diffusion and incipient re-focusing from our fieldwork data of 1970 and 1978. We also list and illustrate the four headings under which the psychological and social constraints which operate on the individual's creation of linguistic systems can be grouped.

In Part 3, I return to and explore the use of metaphors for the multi-dimensional "galactic" framework, indebted to quantum theory and to images drawn from astrophysics, within which one can envisage the kinds of "languages" for which we have stereotypical concepts actually coming into existence and then disappearing again in our multilingual universe. I try to project the universe of "languages in contact" as nearly forty years of work on creole and contact varieties have brought me to see it.

As a preliminary however I give some brief excerpts from our fieldwork data from Cayo District, Belize, to illustrate how our informants themselves saw their society and its languages. The conversations were recorded in 1978.

Recollections of the past
First, an old man, JW of Bullet Tree Falls. He said he had been born in 1898 in nearby San Ignacio. Thus he was eighty years old. He said that his

66

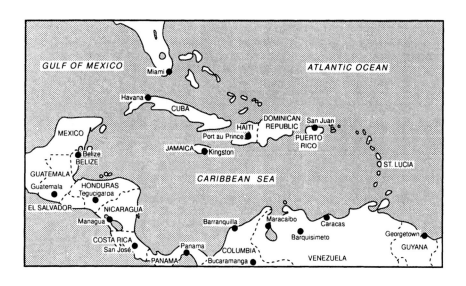

Map 4.1 The Caribbean, showing Belize and St Lucia

"grandfather" was English and his "grandmother" an Indian woman from Guatemala – but did not say which grandfather and grandmother:

> *My mother used to talk in Spanish to we and my father talk in English. My father never talk a half a half one word . . in Spanish . . mia mada yes my mother used to talk pure [= only] May . . the Spanish and Maya. The majority of me children-dem talk Maya . . Carib . . They go amongst them an' they learn the language you see.*

He claimed to have ninety grandchildren in the District.

It was clear from JW's memories of his childhood that he felt there had been quite clearly distinguished "races" in what was then the colony of British Honduras, and that each had had its language. His own "English" to me had quite a number of Creole and some Spanish features, evidence above – for example, the Creole pluralising suffix *-dem* (after an already-plural *children*), and the use of *mia mada* (*mi madre*) then corrected to *my mother*. As we shall see, it is really not possible to ascribe all linguistic features to any particular named system.

The present – 1978
Secondly, a young woman MB, sixty years younger than JW, told us that she used "Spanish, English and English Creole" but that the essence of

being "Belizean" – that is, a citizen of the newly independent state – was to be "mixed", and that went for the language too:

> *Even from Belize* [City] *to San Ignacio we have a difference in the language, right? Because here it's . . be more Spanish. Still it's Creole, right? but just a bit more Spanish words an' in Corozal they speak Spanish with a lot of Creole words i' . . . Ours is English, Spanish, Carib, everything . . Everything mixed up . . you can never tell where a word comes from.*

Two more short excerpts from young (early twenties) informants. EA said:

> *The languages of this country is something mixed specially the Creole . . and with Spanish also 'cause sometimes we find weselves talking Spanish and notice now and again you put in a bit of Creole or a bit of English.*

and AT said:

> *Well there is change because the older people used to speak broad Creole as we call it, but the younger ones coming up now don't speak it like that any more you know? . . Some of the Maya Indians even they speak the English, they don't speak the Creole.*

Part 1.   A general framework for contact situations

Theoretical problems

Suzanne Romaine starts her recent book, *Bilingualism* (1989), by saying that it would be odd to read a book with the title *Monolingualism*, and yet monolingualism is the underlying construct on which most linguistic theory and description is based. She ends the book (1989: 287) by quoting from the late Peter Strevens ("The localized forms of English" in Kachru 1982: 23) as follows:

> . . a central problem of linguistic study is how to reconcile a convenient and necessary fiction with a great mass of inconvenient facts. The fiction is the notion of a 'language' – English, Chinese, Navajo, Kashmiri. The facts reside in the mass of diversity exhibited in the actual performance of individuals when *they use a given language.* [my emphasis – Le P]

She then concludes: "This serves to remind us that linguistic theory is still a long way from being able to deal analytically with performance and what people do *when they use 'language', rather than a 'given' language.*" [my emphasis – Le P]

In between this beginning and this ending Romaine herself uses such terms as "English" and "Punjabi" and other language names (as I shall have to) as a convenient way of referring to abstractions from the behavior of communities, and to stereotypes[1] about that behavior, while remaining aware that the referent in each case is very far from being the autonomous entity which both linguistis and laymen tend to have in mind when they talk about "languages" and when linguists use terms such as "code-switching" or "code-mixing" or "borrowing" or "interference". A recent article (1989) by Georges Lüdi on behalf of the European Science Foundation's Code-switching and Language Contact Network illustrates my point; he writes as if contact-phenomena were the outcome of "contact between 'pairs" of discrete languages: "The phenomenon of code-switching, to be properly understood, requires the analysis of *many pairs of languages in contact* . . . ." [my emphasis – Le P] (Lüdi 1989: 8).

Another fairly recent book I wish to refer to is Brian V. Street's *Literacy in theory and practice* (1984). Street is an anthropologist who did extensive fieldwork in the 1970s on literacy in rural villages in Iran. He makes a broad distinction between those theorists who write about literacy as if it were an autonomous and universally-valid aspect of human language, the transference of "the system" from spoken to written symbolism; that same bridge which all communities need to cross in a similar manner (implied quite strongly I think in the French term for becoming or making literate, *alphabétisation*) in order to achieve "development" and "objective science" and so on; and those theorists who, like Street himself, believe that we need rather to recognize the ideological nature of "becoming literate", and that it has different meanings and implications from one culture to another.

Both Romaine and Street are making the point, among others, that the way most linguists think about language is strongly conditioned by Western European and American ideologies, theories and practices relating to the functions of spoken and written languages, to the relationship between these, and to the nature of linguistic structure which itself is based mainly upon centuries of study of written texts. They, and I, and many of my colleagues who have worked with the often diffuse vernaculars of contact situations, wish and need to revise that conventional thinking. A somewhat similar challenge to it has been expressed in some recent papers by George W. Grace of the University of Hawaii (see, e.g., Grace 1989).

"Projection, focusing, and diffusion" as a contribution to a theoretical framework for contact situations, and hence for all linguists
It is fitting that in discussing languages in contact Andrée Tabouret-Keller should take a "highly focused" situation and I a "diffuse" one. Professor Tabouret-Keller is from a country in which the concept of a language called "French", its autonomy, its reification, totemization, and institutionalization are firmly fixed in the public and political ideology, whereas I come from a country whose main language has in turn spawned the many regional varieties known rather inelegantly as "The New Englishes" (or, in Loreto Todd's title, *Modern Englishes*). A project by the organisation AUPELF (Association des universités partiellement ou entièrement de langue française) to prepare a dictionary or dictionaries of African French has run into opposition on the grounds that nobody should be making dictionaries of bad French and if it is good French the dictionaries are already being made in Paris (Marcel Diki-Kidiri 1988). At the level of educated varieties therefore "French" is a very highly-focused concept, "English" more diffuse since we readily talk and write nowadays about American English, Canadian English, Jamaican English, Australian English, Indian English, Singaporean English, and so on, and about dialects within these supposed Englishes; both dictionaries and grammars are available or in preparation for these. The standardizing grammar of Quirk et al. (1972) attempts to define a "common core" of usage, with marked variants.

Even within the English-speaking world however the debate about the proper variety to prescribe for education is by no means over; within the Francophone world the walls of the Académie Française are only just beginning to show hairline cracks. In Mauritius the education system treats "French" as being in effect the local vernacular and denies this status to Mauritian Creole, even though all Mauritians speak Mauritian Creole, on the grounds that it is merely "bad French" (Philip Baker, in *Abstracts 1988*: 40–41). Mauritian Creole has the status of a "non-langue" on the basis of a specious categorization which establishes French as a "langue".

The categories "focused" and "diffuse" are key ingredients in an attempt to establish a theoretical framework for linguistics which is genuinely universal (see *Acts of Identity* p. 202), by reexamining the ontology of the concept "a language". Uriel Weinreich, in *Languages in contact* (1953), makes the point that contact only occurs in the mind of the individual. The one undoubted universal in language is the individual user of language. It is often taken for granted that the concept of a communal language is also universal and can in some way be defined so that, for example, we all know the difference between "a language" and "a dialect", or that such terms as "first language" and "second language" can be used scientifically.

But apart from the concept of "the individual", which is itself, of course, far from monolithic although a necessary prerequisite of language, all of these other beliefs are stereotypes which derive from our particular cultures. Within our culture "Ciceronian Latin" is an autonomous system precisely because it is an abstraction from the finite written texts of a single individual. "The English language", on the other hand, has always been an abstraction from the way the English people have used language from time to time, either a term of art with unspecifiable parameters, or a highly idealised stereotype, behavior reified, totemized, and institutionalized.

Outwards from the individual to groups
If one takes this view about the centrality of the individual to any scientific study of language then one has to build outwards from that to accommodate the indisputable fact that cultures tend to throw up various stereotypes about the autonomy of their languages; and that these (for example, the concept of "God-givenness", or doctrines of "correctness") sometimes exert a powerful influence on the community so that people defend their implications, talk about "language purity", or about "owning a language", and so on. (A British journalist reported recently that an Italian politician told him "The English have nothing to give to Europe except their language, and we've already stolen that.").

The Chomskyan mode of bridge-building, as everybody knows, was to create a hypothetical idealized speaker-listener with complete knowledge of the linguistic system of a homogeneous language community. Although our experience tells us that this concept is much at odds with some basic and observable properties of language-using individuals such as their built-in innovative and creative faculties, nevertheless similar assumptions underlie many of the ways in which people talk about language learning. There are, it is felt, discrete systems. Every human being has the capacity to "internalize" at least one of them, possibly more. Sometimes when they learn two or more systems they mix them in use, either intentionally, or in a covert but rule-governed way, or from a lack of proper control of the systems. We have such terms as "code-switching", "code-mixing", and "using a mixed code" which presuppose that we can ascribe linguistic features to one external code or another. Then, of course, we run into all sorts of problems of ascription and of writing rules for the constraints on switching and mixing which derive at least in part from our starting point, the idea of discrete external codes being internalized. Many of these problems are discussed in a recent book on Alsatian French by Professor Tabouret-Keller's former student, Penelope Gardner-Chloros (1990). They are touched upon also in Valdman (1989) with reference to the situation today in Haiti. As an English-speaker who has worked for many years in post-colonial countries, I came into contact with varieties of supposed Mandarin or Malay or Hindi or Urdu or Marathi or Yoruba within which so much "English" had been naturalised as to enable me frequently to pick up the gist of what was being said; and my colleague at York, Mahendra Verma, has recorded much of this macaronic usage from his Indian friends, within which it is impossible to assign clear degrees of indigenization of borrowed features or to write rules to do so.

But suppose we start, not from reified discrete systems like "English" and "French" but from observable human beings using language, is it possible to create and preserve a theoretical framework for talking about language, about "bilingualism" or "diglossia" or "languages in contact" which, while not denying the force of these cultural stereotypes, nevertheless preserves intact the fact that the individual is the sole existential locus of language, and that the only universal source of differentiation, of discreteness in linguistic systems, lies between one individual and another? Charles Ferguson's original (1959) definition and exemplification of "diglossia" stipulated that High and Low codes were in each case varieties of "the same language", and Haiti was one of the four cases cited; but the cultural bias among Creolists since then has shifted towards regarding "Haitian Creole" as one or more languages distinct from French. Andrée Tabouret-Keller has referred (in *Abstracts 1988*) to the fact that officially at least in Alsace "bilingual" means "using both French and German", rather than "French and Alsatian", since Alsatian is not officially a language. In relation to Mauritius. Philip Baker writes (*Abstracts 1988*, p. 40):

> One bias or misconception which outsiders tend to bring to the Mauritian situation is an assumption that each of its five major languages is a self-contained entity. Mauritians are aware, to the extent that they are familiar with two or more of them, that much of the vocabulary of English derives from French, that local French draws heavily on English, that most of M[auritian] C[reole]'s lexicon is shared with local French, that M[auritian] B[hojpuri]'s basic vocabulary is all but identical with Hindustani even though it draws massively on MC for other terms, etc. These relationships have obvious implications for the design of orthographies of MC and MB.

Clearly, what I am asking is difficult to carry through with consistency; to some extent at least it involves keeping the metalanguage which we use for the scientific study of linguistic phenomena distinct from everyday language or customary linguists' usage; it involves constantly putting one set of terms or the other into quotation marks. If however we can at least bear the need always in mind, it may be easier to avoid imposing the stereotypes about discrete languages and the nature of linguistic systems from our own cultures on to other cultures where they do not necessarily apply or apply even less. We can also avoid wasting our argumentation on difficulties caused by our own disparate frameworks for analysis. The International Group for the Study of Language Standardization and the Vernacularization of Literacy (IGLSVL) at its first Workshop in 1986 (see *Abstracts 1986*) spent a good deal of time discussing the way in which linguists, as well as laymen, have exported to multilingual countries in the postcolonial period the stereotypes of their own cultures about the nature of languages. In reference for example to the case of Papua-New Guinea, Peter Mühlhäusler questioned whether it was helpful at all to think about the communal communicative modes of that country in terms of "languages".

Acts of identification
The bridge between the individual and communal systems is provided in our work (Le Page and Tabouret-Keller) by the concepts of projection and focusing, a cinematic metaphor. Each individual is envisaged using the linguistic systems they themselves have created in order to project on to others the universe as they envisage it, including their own place in it. They each have to establish their own identity, and do this by relating themselves, positively or negatively, to the people or groups of people they discern around them, endowing these with linguistic characteristics. The attraction and repulsion are projected through language use. It is true that we are moving towards the day when genetic science will be capable of uniquely specifying each individual in terms of a very, very long DNA number, but we identify ourselves by creating an idiosyncratic mode of linguistic (and other) behavior, at the same time using it to relate to others. We then get feedback from others about the extent to which they in turn accept our universe, find it compatible or incompatible with their own. We may then adjust our behavior accordingly, the others likewise. In this way linguistic groups form in the real world which resemble those in the minds of the participants. People may become more like others in their behavior. This is the process we call "focusing". And since the language of each individual reflects their perception of the language of the group, somebody who succeeds in becoming a member of a focused group becomes similarly focused in their individual behavior. Conversely, where individuals distance themselves from each other that community as a whole is diffuse. It is possible – and is frequently the case in some kinds of multilingual societies – to be a member of one highly-focused group among a number of other also highly-focused groups which are nevertheless discrete from, and distanced from, each other, as in a ghetto society, where there is only limited contact, possibly in specific domains such as marketing, between the members of different groups. Lesley Milroy's social and linguistic networks (1980) have proved a useful analytical tool in conditions such as those of Ulster where

speakers of "the same language" are nevertheless grouped within religious and geographical boundaries and dialect usage.

If I am a member of a very tightly-knit homogeneous group with only limited access to other groups, my view of "languages" may be that of "my own language" vis-a-vis "all other language". This is a not uncommon chauvinist situation. If, on the other hand, I live in a community such as that of Cayo District in the 1970s, or Alsace, many groups, and many languages, may be accessible parts of my daily world, the boundaries between them much less clear, and "language" generally a more diffuse phenomenon.

Part 2. The sociolinguistic survey of multilingual communities

Cayo District, Belize: the social background
In our studies of the people of Cayo District, Belize, in Central America, we deliberately started with a community which as a whole was in a state of post-colonial flux, passing through a period of social and linguistic diffusion in the 1970s.

The 1950s. My first visit there had been nearly twenty years previously, in the early 1950s. It was then still part of the colony known as British Honduras. Internal communications in the colony were quite difficult. The Belize River provided the main route from the coast into the District, and I have recorded the reminiscences of a lady who had been to school near the river; when the regular steamer came up with supplies and sounded its hooter everybody in the little town of San Ignacio came down to the landing stage, and school was suspended. To get to one settlement, the logging camp at Gallon Jug, I started out by road, switched to a boat and finished the journey on a light logging railway to record the story-telling of the foreman, a Creole. Timber cut in the forests was still the main export, although the supply of trees was dwindling rapidly. Another major occupation in Cayo District and across the frontier into Guatemala was tapping the chicle trees for chicle, the gum which was the basis of chewing gum. Another, practised primarily by "Spanish", "Mestizos", and "Indians", was subsistence farming on little milpas. There were a few larger cattle ranches. The total population of the District was very small – about 10,000 people.

There were still rural villages of indigenous Amerindians – Maya and Kekchi – speaking their own well-focused "languages" or "dialects", and, as a second language if they had one, some variety of the Central American Spanish of Guatemala or Mexico. The small towns close to the Guatemalan frontier, of which Benque Viejo was the Cayo District example, were settlements of Spanish-speaking "Spanish" or "Mestizo" people whose grandparents had come in as refugees from Guatemala or Mexico, many of them still having relations across the frontier in Petén Province or Yucatan. The capital of the District, San Ignacio del Cayo, stood on the cayo or island formed by the two rivers which joined there to form the Belize River. It contained some Lebanese/Syrian businessmen who imported goods – flour, tinned food, dry goods, kerosene, and so on – up the river from the port of Belize to supply the loggers and the chicle tappers when they went off into the forest, and arranged for the export of chicle and timber products down the river. It also contained the administrative headquarters of the District – a District Commissioner/Magistrate who was British, and a small civil service consisting very largely of Creoles from the coastal District, people who had had an English-medium education and used English for administrative purposes but Creole in their homes. The schools in the District were run by various missions and used whatever medium they could through which to teach English; thus at Mount Carmel School in Benque Viejo there were German nuns teaching Maya children for English-language examinations and using Spanish as the medium of instruction.

Two further ingredients in this ethnic, cultural and linguistic complex were the Miskito Indians, always referred to patronisingly as "Waika", who came up from the coast to work in the forests, and the Garifuna or Black Caribs, always referred to simply as Caribs, many of whom were teachers or policemen.

Most of the groups I have so far referred to used language which was itself the product of comparatively recent contact situations. The story of the Black Caribs has been told by Douglas Taylor (1951) and by C. J. M. R. Gullick (1976). They were the descendants of West African slaves who had been shipwrecked on, or had escaped to, the island of St Vincent and had taken wives from among the indigenous Island Caribs. After the French Revolution, during which they fought with the French against the British, they were deported en masse to the Miskito Coast and Bay Islands of Central America. The Island Caribs whose women they had taken had themselves earlier invaded and occupied Arawak-inhabited islands in the Antilles and taken Arawak wives. The complex history of the Miskito Indians has been unravelled by John Holm in his sociolinguistic history of the Miskito Shore (1978). They had had close contact with both the Hispanic and the English and Creole English Caribbean settlers since the seventeenth century.

The Creole English of the port of Belize in the early 1950s was still that of a fairly focused community of Creoles living in a small town on a river delta and having in some respects closer trading contacts by sea with Jamaica, through which a good deal of their mahogany was exported and whose ships came in regularly, than they did with the interior of their own country. The reluctance of coastal, urban Creoles to move inland resulted among other things in about half of the teachers in the rural areas being Black Caribs (Douglas Taylor 1951). Their Creole language of course had its origins in the slave trade, and in contact over a period of three centuries between speakers of African languages, speakers of various dialects of English, speakers of Creole, and of Spanish, and the standard English of education, and of the churches.

It was not until a metalled road was built into Cayo District in the 1950s and 1960s (it was still in parts a pot-holed hazard in the 1970s) that Creoles began to take up land for farming in the District, encountering as they did so the "Spanish speakers" moving in from the other end of the road.

Multidimensional networks or galaxies
The picture I am drawing of linguistic diffusion and focusing in Cayo District requires a view of so-called "languages" as abstractions from more-or-less temporarily focused nodes in a multidimensional network, or galaxy, of relationships and identities. None of the nodes in this network is wholly stable. The basic process in the formation of a node is that of groups of individuals identifying with each other for common purposes. At the end of the last century Hugo Schuchardt, in relation to pidgins and Creoles but also with more general reference, wrote that languages come into being for common purposes and disappear when those purposes disappear. In the early 1950s British Honduras was one of the few British colonies in which the concepts of the Creoles as a readily-identifiable and closely-knit group, and of Creole as a language, were accepted, so that people would for example tell me stories in ['kri: a] as well as in Spanish and talk to me in "English" – as one eighty-year old said:

> *yu fu taak it in Spanish bot ai di trai brok ang iina kriia, nong?*
> 'You should say it in Spanish but I am trying to translate it into Creole, aren't I?'

In Jamaica and other islands, by contrast, the way people commonly spoke among themselves was not regarded as a language but simply as "broken talk" or "bad English", although very similar to Belize Creole. The Creoles of Belize said similar derogatory things about their language within the context of education, but nevertheless called it Creole and identified themselves, with pride and feelings of superiority, as Creoles. One of the reasons for this was their need to distinguish themselves politically and culturally from the Spanish in particular, and also from Caribs and Indians. They were "Bay-born", the culture of the Bay was theirs. They inherited three centuries of hostility between "Creoles" and "Spanish". This hostility was reflected still in both pre-independence and post-independence politics, in the formation of one predominantly Creole political party and one which tried to sublimate racial and ethnic antagonism in claims to a common "national" identity. We had a number of informants like JW who claimed a Creole father who did not speak Spanish to a "Spanish" mother. We had other, "Spanish" informants who could not conceal their distaste and regret at "Creole" replacing Spanish as the lingua franca of their District.

The discrete communities of the past in Cayo District
The past history of this separateness and antagonism is reflected in JW's account of some of the events of his childhood:

JW: *You see when we come in this part of the worl' there only was Maya . . an' my children gone amongst the Maya people-them, they never used to talk Spanish, nor even a word in English, pure [= only] May . . they [my children] coming with that Maya . .*
LeP: *But they don't talk it today?*
JW: *Yeh, they talk, talk it, yes . . . in Bullet [Tree Falls] . . the ol' set of Indian you see.*
LeP: *Yeh, but not these young people here?*
JW: *No! No! No! – not this young people.*
LeP: *Why did they stop talking Maya?*

JW: *Because . . . they got school and they brought the Spanish and the English and they*
       forget that [Maya] *. . .*
       When we come here the people . . they nearly was naked . . the Indians-them, yah.
       We have big revolution here with the Indians-them you know? . . That was 'bout –
       oh, nineteen-eight [1908]. *. . I will let you know it plain . . the country use to be*
       develop by the . . Guatemantican and the Mexican-them you know, because nine-
       teen-ten [1910] *Mexico got a revolution and by the thousand they used to come into*
       the colony . . I was a big boy already . . they used to go to the States and buy arms to
       continue fighting. They used to steal money. We have a next revolution here that . .
       they cramp, they cramp the colony . . They tief out [= steal] *the chicle-them, they*
       tief out your mule-dem and kill you behind that . .

Cayo District in the 1950s contained relatively isolated and relatively focused settlements in its rural parts, and in some of the small townships also. Benque Viejo then was "Spanish". The next villages along the river, Succotz and Bullet Tree Falls, were mostly "Maya". I was asked by the new District Commissioner to go with him in his launch up and down the river on a tour of inspection; we went from landing-stage to landing-stage often to be greeted by a Creole or Carib policeman in an otherwise wholly Indian village. The prestige language in these frontier villages was still Spanish. In one we were offered entertainment ashore, which the District Commissioner interpreted to me as "some native girls singing". I looked forward to hearing Maya songs; but instead we sat for nearly an hour listening to the Christmas liturgy sung in Latin and Spanish, the girls nasal "entuning" (very reminiscent of Chaucer's Prioresse) accompanied on a huge marimba.

The "Spanish" of Benque Viejo (laid out in the Spanish fashion with its own Alcalde or Mayor) maintained close contacts with friends and relations across the frontier in Petén Province. The frontier bisected the football pitch of one mission school, and some Guatemantican children came over each day to school. The townspeople were proud of their Spanishness and hostile to any thought of intermarriage with Creoles or Caribs. Some of them claimed "pure Spanish" descent and felt they had cultural links with Spain itself. In practice it was difficult to make any very clear ethnic distinction between Spanish, Mestizo and Indian.

The Lebanese or Syrian traders, known in the colony as *Los Turcos* 'The Turks' – their forebears having emigrated from what had been a Turkish province before the First World War – in the 1950s still tended to look back to the Levant for their wives, although it was acceptable also for them to marry light-skinned "Spanish" women. Some still claimed a command of Arabic, and in 1978 one of their descendants, one of our informants, still claimed that the family was 'Arab':

EE: [*my father*] *he's a half Arab. My mother is a Spanish but his father is . . was a full*
       Arab you know, and his mother was a Mex . . em Guatemantican. So he was a half
       Arab. Then my . . my grandfather by my mother's side used to be an Arab too, you
       know? an' our mother used to be a Spanish.

LeP: *But if somebody said to you, what do you reckon your family is, what would you*
       say?

EE: *I would say Arab.*

LeP: *Arab?*

EE: *Mmhm – Anybody ask me I would say an Arab.*

The changed picture in the 1970s: mixing

Our sociolinguistic survey of Cayo District started in 1970. By then, considerable changes were in progress, some of the effects of which can be illustrated by continuing the above excerpt from EE's discussion in 1978. Although she lived in Benque Viejo she claimed that at home they mostly spoke "English" except to her father, who didn't understand it. When I commented that the children around us were speaking Spanish among themselves she agreed that they usually did that "among themselves". She had been to school in Belize for a time:

EE: *up there it's more Creole people talk an 'that's why we got to talk the English over there. Bika' [the Creole form of 'because' – LeP] here most of the time lone [Creole, = 'only'] Spanish we used to talk at home. Only when we go [Creole, = 'went'] to school we used to talk English.*

LeP: *What sorts of people are living around you here?*

EE: *Pure [Creole, = 'only'] Spanish people.*

LeP: *So what language do they talk?*

EE: *The most of the people here talk English . . Unless some of them would talk Spanish . . Some of them can't talk English . . Most of the time they talk the two of them, Spanish an' English.*

LeP: *Do they mix them up at all?*

EE: *Yeh, sometime when they speaking they would talk Spanish and a little bit of English.*

LeP: *When you say English do you mean pure English? or . .*

EE: *No – Creole.*

The informant RQ, a young man in 1978, represented the transitional, post-independence generation among whom the "Spanish" were throwing in their lot with the Creoles. He distinguished "Creole" from "English":

AT-K: *When did you pick up your Creole? Because when you were a small child you spoke Spanish.*

RQ: *. . in school . . here.*

LeP: *The children round here spoke Creole at school, did they?*

RQ: *Yes – Creole and Spanish.*

LeP: *Which most?*

RQ: *The two of them we speak.*

LeP: *Mixed up?*

RQ: *Yeh – . . Our teacher was a Carib . . . he used to speak English, you know because he's a teacher he had to. An'Creole . . . Spanish he . . didn't speak. We speak Spanish with our friends. With our parents. With other grown-ups. [The teacher] he used to talk in English. But we . . understand the English but we usually . . speak Creole. Most useful . . the Creole.*

RQ's father's parents, he said, were "Spanish", his mother's, "Spanish" and "Creole". His father would have described their family as of "mixed" race, and he would describe himself as "mixed". Where RQ worked they usually spoke Creole, although there were a lot of Spanish people there and also Maya Indians from San Antonio.

In 1970 our informant GM, whom I had first recorded telling Anansi stories in 1966, (see Le Page 1968) told us this about her parents, their language use and that of her peer group, with a vivid analysis of the role of the latter:

GM: [My mother] *a Mexican . . my father is a . . Creole . . Belizean . .*

LeP: *When you say "Belizean" what does that mean?*

GM: *His mother was a Belizean from here an' his father is an Irishman but he grew up in Belize so . . they call him a Bay-born . . he was born in Belize anyhow.*

LeP: *So he spoke Creole and your mother spoke Spanish?*

GM: *Well she spoke both.*

LeP: *But with you she spoke Creole?*

GM: *No well she don't . . she doesn't exactly speak Creole to us you know but we . . by going to school an' hear other children well we pick it up . . No she tried to talk to us the proper way but . . you know children . . we want to go our own way . . we pick up Creole . . .*

LeP: *But she learnt English at school, did she?*

GM: *Mhm.*

LeP: *So she wanted you to speak proper English?*

GM: *. . Now whenever we'd say something out of the way like . . something funny like* [biˈrkaˑz] *and we don't say* [biˈkɔːz] *she'd put* [biˈkɔːz] *and we'd say* [biˈkaˑ] *because we heard that in school you know,* [bɪˈkaˑ] *that's the way it is, . . we never finish a word . . we always . . cut it short or put more to it.*

LeP: *That school you went to in Santa Elena . . did most of the children there speak Creole?*

GM: *Mhm. And Spanish . . but this . . broken-up Spanish you know . . we call it Creole Spanish too because that's not grammatical Spanish.*

LeP: *But most of the families round there speak Spanish at home, don't they?*

GM: *Mhm.*

LeP: *So what did they talk in the playground, the children?*

GM: *Some Spanish and some* [ˈkria].

LeP: *Which most?*

GM: *That's* [fʊ] *tell . . I guess it's both. Balance half of each!*

LeP: *Did they ever mix the two up?*

GM: *Mhm . . . Have a language spoken like . . for instance you would want to say like . . "catch the ball" . . they wouldn't say "aralami la bola" or something like that they would say "catchia la bola" you know an' . . . that's "catch" . .* [laughs].

LeP: *Did your mother ever do that kind of thing when she talked to you?*

GM: *HNG!* [i.e., No!] *. . She spoke good Spanish, yes, because she learned good Spanish from her father . . her father is a pure-bred Mexican.*

LeP: *And when you spoke Creole Spanish did she correct that?*

GM: *Always . . Daddy the same way, because daddy never spoke to us in . . broad Creole* [i.e., Creole English] *. . although he . . right from Belize . . he always . . try to correc' us an' . . . get us speak correctly but we never . . we never give up to them . . .* [laughs] *as we get to bear children . . there it is!*.

Social reasons for change

There seemed to be three main reasons for the changes noted. The colony was by 1970 well on its way to full independence. Secondly, Guatemala, which claimed Belize as part of its own territory which should have been inherited from Spain had it not been illegally occupied by the British, threated to annex the whole country as soon as it became independent; as a consequence, a small British defence force remained on the frontier not far from San Ignacio. Thirdly, the road-building programme I have mentioned was by now well under way. The north-south road to Stann Creek on the coast had already been completed, and the east-west road from the port of Belize to the frontier beyond Benque Viejo had been resurfaced and partly macadamised.

These three changes provided fresh opportunities and fresh motivation for the younger generation to regroup themselves. The adoption of the name Belize for the whole country instead of just the port – now called Belize City; the threat of annexation; the roads which greatly increased the mobility of the population and drew people in to settle and farm in what had previously been fairly empty country; a primitive bus service from Benque Viejo to Belize City; more Creole civil servants and policemen moving into the District – all these and more social factors shaped the direction of the search for new identities among the younger generation, and the linguistic attributes with which to project those new identities. These social factors can all be examined under one or other of the four sets of constraints on the main theoretical statement about individual acts of identity (see *Acts of Identity*, pp. 182–186): they identified (with the help of a great deal of supportive propaganda) a fresh overarching group, Belizeans; provided a powerful motive for people to draw closer together for their own defence and in antagonism to "Spanish" Guatemala; and provided for much greater access by young people to "English" in the classroom and "Creole" in the playground in villages where children of different ethnic groups were now mixed up. Education remained for some a step towards higher education in Guatemala, where generous scholarships were available for Spanish-speakers; but for far more now it had become a step towards higher education in Belize, in Jamaica, or in Britain or the United States, or a step towards a better job. One of our Spanish-speaking informants from Benque Viejo went on to higher education in Belize but resolutely refused to be creolised, keeping his eye on a scholarship to study medicine in Guatemala City; but far more were like EE above.

The 1970 evidence
In our 1970 survey we studied the language used by two hundred and eighty children – one in four of the required age-group on the Cayo District school rolls – when spoken to in English, in five modes of an extended recorded interview with each: early rather formal conversation about school subjects; telling both traditional and school-reader stories; later more relaxed informal conversation about, e.g., cooking, and ghosts; and reading. The children were between the ages of ten and sixteen. We were thus able to map the variation between their more formal and less formal linguistic behavior against the variables of their geographical provenance, ethnic provenance, age, sex, and educational level; in addition we talked at length with their families, and matched the children's claims about language use in their homes against what older members of the household claimed. Andrée Tabouret-Keller (1980) made a detailed study of the

differences between the claims – the perceptions of the language situation – of the children and of the older generations.

The 1978 evidence

In 1978 we made a follow-up study of forty members of our original sample, now mostly in their early twenties. We concerned ourselves to record the attitudes they expressed towards language and towards any identities they felt they and their neighbours and families and the community as a whole now had. We were thus able to compare what they now said, and how they said it, with what they and their families had said in 1970, and make a real-time longitudinal study of their attitudes. Pressure at this time from Guatemala had intensified, and not long before the Guatemalan army had caused a panic flight from farms and villages near the frontier by moving up to the frontier in a menacing way. The results of this study have been published in *Acts of Identity*. I do not want to refer to them in detail here, but rather to illustrate them from the 1978 data.

Many of our 1978 conversations illustrated now not only the effects of the school playground described by GM, but the effects of the workplace. Labour had become much more mobile. Government inducements had led to new enterprises in citrus farming, sugar cane growing, garment factories, tourist hotels, and so on. Two devastating hurricanes had led to some population shifts; the first of these, Hattie, had led to the building of the village of Hattieville on the Cayo-Belize road, but the second led to the building of a new capital for the country at Belmopan, near the junction of the north-south and east-west roads. Belmopan was drawing in labour, entrepreneurs, civil servants, medical staff, and politicians from other parts of the country (although many of the civil servants were reluctant to make the move out of Belize).

Some illustrative cases

"Spanish"/"Creole".   Informant EO was now working at the Government agricultural station, Central Farm. He had been brought up by his grandmother who only spoke Spanish. Both of his parents spoke Spanish to the grandmother, but his mother now working in Belize and his father now working "somewhere around those Jamaicans" on the Pine Ridge road, both had to use Creole at work.

> LeP: *At Central Farm, what languages do people use?*
> EO: *Creole.*
> LeP: *All the time?*
> EO: *Yes, mostly.*
> LeP: *No Spanish?*
> EO: *Well, you got a few fellows . . about ten person . .*
> LeP: *They talk Spanish?*
> EO: *Spanish.*

Informant DR's father was the fire look-out at St Augustine, in the Mountain Pine Ridge. His parents, DR said, were both Spanish. He himself had done quite well at school in San Ignacio, and had tried to earn a living as a pupil-teacher in Cayo but found he could earn twice as much in a cigarette factory in Belize City. But:

DR: *The city was a bit bright, noise . . . So I finally decide to come back here* [St Augustine] *an' have a job. The only available job at this time is hard labour . . That's throwing a machete and an axe . .*

LeP: *What sort of language do you need for that? What do they use?*

DR: *Well . . at the moment the language here at home and with the workers, we just use a slang, which is known as Creole, you know? Derived from the English, you know? So, that's our language, you know, we have . . a few Spanish . . that speak Spanish there, so, you know, when we would get together . . I would speak Spanish with them.*

"Maya"/"Spanish"/"Creole". Informant MM was a young woman of Maya descent from Bullet Tree Falls whose family illustrated well the double shift in three generations from Maya to Spanish to "Creole"; she had a Spanish-sounding name and at first described her parents as "Spanish"; she was doing domestic work in Belize:

MM: *Since I finished school I began to work here in Cayo, I stop working here .. and went back to Bullet Tree then I went to Belize working there.* (laughs).

LeP: *. . . with what family, Spanish or English?*

MM: *Yes – Spanish . . . Till right now I am working with her.*

LeP: *What language did they use in the house in Belize?*

MM: *Mixed. Well – Spanish, sometime they talk in English, too.*

LeP: *Can you speak Creole?*

MM: *Well, that is the language I speak* (laughs).

LeP: *But in your home in Bullet Tree Falls . . . ?*

MM: *Spanish – pure* [= only] *Spanish we talk there.*

LeP: *Where did you learn to speak Creole?*

MM: *Well . . . in school so an' when I come out from there I learn more here in Cayo and in Belize . . . so.*

LeP: *Did your parents know any Indian language?*

MM: *Well, my mother knows Maya so . . . Sometimes she talk it. But with us she did not teach us.*

LeP: *Was your father Maya?*

MM: *Yes . . . both of them talk the language . . they speak the both languages . . . Sometimes they talk in Maya sometimes in Spanish.*

LeP: *And to you children . . . ?*

MM: *Spanish . . .*

AT-K: *. . . in Bullet Tree Falls, when the children are taught Creole in the school* [as MM had said] *. . from whom do they pick it up?*

MM: *Well, from the teacher . . .*

LeP: *Creole rather than English? They use Creole to teach the children?*

MM: *Yes. Well sometimes/wan a dem fiks dea kriia gud nong/ – make it sound better.*

Clearly in her perception the boundaries between "Creole" and "English" were rather fuzzy; you could "fix your Creole good, no?"

"Maya"/"Spanish"/"Creole".   Informant SH told us that she felt herself to be a Creole; her mother too she said was "pure Creole" in spite of having had a grandmother who was "a full-blooded Maya Indian . . she spoke only Spanish and Maya . . my mother was raised with her . . "in the Maya village of Baking Pot. Her father was from the Bay Islands of Honduras:

SH: *A Creole is . . anyone . . that is mixed with Negro and any other . . if the race is white, Spanish, Indian, whatever, as long as . . you had a mixture of Negro then you're a Creole . . . If you go to a foreign country . . . you'd say you're a Belizean . .. they use the term "a Creole" right here in the country.*

For her, being a Creole had nothing to do with the language you spoke.

"Carib"/"Creole"/"Mixed"/"English".   Informant DL was of mixed Carib/Spanish descent and married now to a Carib policeman. She was a teacher, and claimed to speak English and Creole and a little Spanish. Ethnically she called herself "mixed", "a Belizean":

LeP: *. . . Do you ever use Spanish?*
DL: *To outside . . . But in school I don't use Spanish, only English.*
LeP: *Do any of the children come from Spanish homes?*
DL: *Oh, a lot.*
LeP: *Can you tell me any of the difficulties they have when you are teaching them?*
DL: *Well . . . we put them along with the children that know English, you know. After a while they can talk it.*
LeP: *Do they learn to talk English or Creole?*
DL: *Yes, English. There's mostly Spanish as long as they pick it up. Then the Creole would come right in.*
LeP: *. . . Why is that?*
DL: *Well, because most people talk Creole.*

"Creole"/"Creole".   Informant AH had left school soon after we had originally recorded her at Black Man Eddy, and had gone to work in a canning factory at Pomona, a twelve-hour day (at the age of thirteen) which she did for eighteen months. The factory was near Stann Creek, a largely Carib area of the coast on the southern part of the north-south highway. When it closed she moved to a garment factory in the new capital, Belmopan, where she now was:

LeP: *What language did they use in the canning factory?*
AH: *Just Creole.*
LeP: *. . . the people working there, were they all Creoles?*
AH: *No, some were but most were Caribs . . . and they could talk Carib but I can't.*
LeP: *Did they talk it among themselves?*
AH: *Yes, but then I don't understand what they said.*
LeP: *So you got your instructions in Creole, did you?*
AH: *Yes, sir.*
LeP: *And what about the garment factory? . . .*
AH: *Oh . . . they talk Creole there.*
LeP: *Are they all Creole people working there?*

AH: *Yes. All . . . all Creole . . . Maybe we have about a few Guatemanticans that speak Spanish but they can talk Creole too.*

"Spanish"/"Creole"/"English". Finally, informant SH, from a purely Spanish-speaking family in Benque Viejo, was now working in a wine shop in Santa Elena. Previously she had been with her grandmother cooking for the older males of the family who were working in forestry in the Mountain Pine Ridge. Up there, she said, they spoke Spanish and English; in the wine shop, some of the customers spoke Spanish, some Creole, some English and she would answer accordingly. She was living with her aunt nearby, who spoke Spanish because she could not speak English, but all her young cousins in the house (aged nineteen, seventeen and fourteen) used Creole among themselves; as for Spanish, "them can't speak it so good". When I asked her to tell me the difference between "Indian" people and "Spanish" people, she replied "I'd say they were the same thing".

St Lucia: background
The French-speaking and formerly-French-speaking islands of the Antilles and the mainland territories of Louisiana in the southern United States and Guyane (to be carefully distinguished from Creole-English-speaking Guyana almost next door) on the northeast coast of South America present us with a fascinating series of comparable case-histories of sociolinguistic processes in a multilinguistic, multidimensional framework.

We can mention only briefly in passing Louisiana, Haiti, Guadeloupe, Dominica, Martinique, St Lucia, St Vincent, Grenada, Trinidad, and Guyane (setting aside a number of smaller islands). In no case is it possible to assess the linguistic outcome to date in terms of "pairs of languages in contact". To begin with, the patterns of the slave trade and of plantation slavery were quite complex and changing in terms of the numbers and provenances of both slaves and French emigrants. The Creole French which resulted was the language of communities in continuing contact with speakers of various dialects of French, of English, of Portuguese, of Spanish, of Dutch and of African and Amerindian languages. The period of contact, the demographic and political and economic circumstances, varied from territory to territory. The linguistic outcome is unique in each case although, as in the Anglophone Caribbean, there are sufficient similarities to justify us speaking of "Caribbean Creole French".

There is today an intellectual movement "Mokwéyol", which has among its aims the establishment of a standardized written variety of Creole French (here called "Antillean"), which could be used in literacy campaigns and in education throughout the formerly-French Antilles and the still-French provinces of Guadeloupe and Martinique. One of the leaders of Mokwéyol is a member of IGLSVL, Lawrence Carrington. His report of December 1988, *Creole discourse and social development*, sets out his program for research and training. If successful, focusing would take place around "Antillean" norms. Some scepticism has been voiced at IGLSVL Workshops about the influence of Mokwéyol and the lack of awareness among the general population of any need for or movement towards literacy in Creole.

Parents want their children to become literate in the language that has most economic advantage. Carrington (1988: 46–47) himself comments:

> Antillean has had a folk-history and notwithstanding the progress made in Haiti and in particular in the Haitian diaspora, [e.g., among refugees in Florida etc. – LeP] it has not been the language of administrative, political, economic or technological change. In all four of these sectors, the direction of change and movement has been determined by speakers of English and French or by pressures from societies in which Antillean is not present. . . . For all their similarities the Antillean-speaking countries of the region have had sufficiently different experience of government, administration and technology that they have responded in the lexical domain in different ways. . . . The readiness of items from one dialect to another lies in the similarity of phonetics, stress patterns, syllable structure, and morphology of all the dialects of the language.

"The language" here is the abstraction being made, "Antillean". Carrington makes a strong case for its instrumentalization while recognizing the antagonism his proposals often raise.

Valdman's 1989 paper on Haiti explores the question of a standard form for Creole French in that country, where the metropolitan French of the urban élite exercises a constant pressure on the lexicon of both urban and rural Creole as used in education, but more so on the urban varieties. Valdman finds it necessary to speak of the multidimensional language space in which Haitian speakers move.

The survey
When we carried out our sociolinguistic study in St Lucia in the 1970s the population of that island was far more homogeneous than that of Belize. The former British Windward Islands were British colonies from the beginning of the nineteenth century but each of them had had some period of French domination in the eighteenth century. In St Vincent this was very short-lived, and when I did some exploratory fieldwork there in the 1950s I found only one old lady, who was, it was claimed, an Island Carib speaker, who in fact produced a few words of Creole French to support that claim. In contrast, at that time Creole French was the most common vernacular in Dominica (see Christie 1969) and St Lucia, common among the older generation in Grenada, and still known among the older generation in some parts of Trinidad. Recently P. G. Christie (personal communication) gained the impression that young people in Dominica responded to her as much in English as in Creole French, and certainly in Grenada the Creole French has all but disappeared. In St Lucia we were concerned to discover what kinds of English or Creole English would be used by the schoolchildren when they were spoken to in English, and to correlate as in Belize their social and economic circumstances, age, sex, level of education with certain linguistic variables. The details are in *Acts of Identity*.

Our survey showed that the English used by the schoolchildren, supposedly the English they had been taught at school, reflected in a number of morphological features (the level of analysis on which we concentrated) differing patterns of influence from both indigenous and external contacts, today and in the past. In contrast to Grenada, this equally mountainous island had a history of poor internal communications, so that the Creole French of the small villages in the interior was well-focused until recently through lack of external contacts.

Among the external influences however were: the geographical proximity of Martinique to the north, a Department of France still using Creole French and French; of St Vincent to the south, using Creole English and English; and of Barbados to the east, using what can best be labelled "Bajan" and English. The links with Barbados had been particularly important in and around the capital, Castries, in the past for reasons of the colonial administration and of trade. There has been in the past considerable movement of labour in the Eastern Caribbean, including building labour sent from Barbados to St Lucia. In addition the British administration established schools which used English as the medium of instruction, forbidding the use of Creole French, and these were staffed to some extent by expatriate Englishmen or Barbadians.

Although when I was first doing fieldwork in St Lucia in the 1950s the draconian ban on Creole French, or "patois", in schools had been relaxed a little, the older teachers still pretended to have no knowledge or understanding of it; nevertheless, even then what was supposed at official level to go on in the classrooms and what actually did go on were two very different things, and by the time we did our survey the distinctions formerly drawn so firmly between "English" and "patois" were not only being blurred, but blurred differentially among different sections of the population. St Lucia is probably on the same road towards the use of some variety of Creolized Eastern Caribbean English as Grenada and Dominica.

The Caribbean as a cultural network
Each one of the islands in what is called "the Commonwealth Caribbean", in fact, is a potential node in the networks of cultural relationship which link them – to each other, to North America, to Britain, to France, to Central America and Venezuela, to various parts of Africa, to India from which large numbers of indentured labourers came in the second half of the nineteenth century, to the Cantonese and the Syrian background of shopkeepers and so on. And within each island, groups and individuals are caught up in the post-colonial search for their identity, and are refocusing their linguistic behavior accordingly. Today the tourist industry has an enormous potential influence.

Part 3. Conclusion

Multiple inputs and the diffuseness and subsequent focusing of multiple outputs in multilingual contact situations
The kind of picture I am drawing of evolutionary linguistic processes in contact situations is anathema to some creolists, who dismiss it pejoratively with the term "the cafeteria principle". That is because they wish to invoke only concepts associated with "contact" between "pairs of languages" coupled with "universals" of grammar.

A cafeteria example.   From our St Lucian data it is clear that there are three ways of expressing habitual usage in the verb, in addition to Standard. These are illustrated, as being each one characteristic of the vernacular usage of one of the other islands, from the following replies from informants in Jamaica, St Vincent, and Grenada asked to turn the English sentence 'Good children go to heaven' into their own dialect:

Ø	Jamaica	*gud pikni ga-a hebm*
does	St Vincent	*gud pikni doz gu a hevn*
-ing	Grenada	*gud childrin go-in tu hevn*

(Acts of Identity 86)

In the following piece of narrative (from a ghost story) told by a St Lucian child all three occur together:

> 'They say he taking your hair and go with it . . . they [spirits] goes go with you . . . they say they does take you and kill you . . . they giving theyself to the devil and they does give them money.' (*Acts of Identity* 136)

The use of *does*, *-ing* and Ø as verb markers for habitual aspect was among the criteria we used to group the children. All three forms were available to them. If we take the Eastern Caribbean as a whole we find that the *does* constructions are most closely associated with Barbadian (Bajan) usage, the *-ing* forms with communities affected by contact with Creole French. In St Lucia the *does* constructions occurred most among children in or close to Castries, the *-ing* forms most frequently among the most rural children. Since urban speech has some prestige, if we then view the community as a whole we find an incipient system emerging from this multidimensional and at present diffuse use of "English" in the island within which the tokens available to signal "habitual aspect" are socially marked; and if St Lucia follows Dominica and Grenada in becoming more and more "English-using", focusing of group usage will take place around more frequent, more prestigious and less frequent, less prestigious selection of one of these forms. Similar considerations apply to the incipient social marking and consequent frequency of selection of many phonological, morphological, syntactic, and lexical items. In this way what may initially be regarded as loans from external sources all become absorbed into one indigenous system with stylistic and social variants and possibly also variations of semantic nuance.

Are Creole situations aberrant?

I see no reason why a sharp distinction should be made between the language of Creole communities and of any other language community. The differences are matters of degree. It is significant that attempts have been made to claim Middle English as a "Creole language", and as often refuted either on typological grounds or on the basis of social history: in the first case, for example, that no pidginizing situation preceded the reemergence of English writing in its "Middle English" form, and in the second case, that the Norman-French-speaking elite, far from enslaving the English-speaking population, ended the Saxon institution of slavery. But to take the typological case first: a Creole language is simply the language of a Creole – i.e., a locally born as opposed to expatriate – community; it does not appear overnight out of a contact situation, but develops initially with the first few generations of locally born children. Many similarities between Creoles in phonology, in syntactic structure, and in the lexicon have been pointed to as if they were defining characteristics of "Creole languages", but many of these can be shown to be properties of a common substrate or superstrate input or universal characteristics of contact languages such as a reduction of the redundancy or of the stylistic choice available in one of the source languages (see Le Page 1977, 1990). And in the second case, the master-slave relationship was for a great many African slaves only one part, perhaps a small part (because contact between field slaves and their masters on large plantations was extremely limited) of the overall language input for Creole children. (For a recent study bearing out the validity of a gradualist theory of creolization, see Arends 1989.) In all cases of intimate contact between different communities there is likely to be multiple linguistic input to the children's language systematization, and the children will produce for their peer groups initially at least a diffuse and varying output. What happens next is a transactional focusing among peer groups, agreement on the social marking of tokens being exchanged, the emergence within each generation of sets of linguistic attributes assigned to different groups within the community, the use of these differentially by individuals to mark their own identity within the community.

Such an approach seems to me to provide a way of reconciling a great many apparently very different kinds of contact situation with what Thomason–Kaufman (1988) refer to as cases of "normal genetic transmission" – to provide, that is, a valid common general framework for the study of the evolution and change of all "languages". Those of us who come from very stable and highly focused societies may find it difficult to distinguish stereotypes about "normal transmission" from the real facts about language use, variation, and change in use, since we are so accustomed to think in terms of idealized, reified, discrete systems; but it is essential to see all language questions in terms of activity between individuals as they form social groups, even in the most static and highly focused communities.

If we do use such a framework for talking about "languages" we can easily recognise that "codes", "code-switching", "code-mixing" and "mixed codes" are terms of convenience which can, and need, never be defined in absolute terms. We can talk about probabilities within clusters of concomitant circumstances; of the possibilities that individuals have available to them, of the significance of their choices. Code-switching between the customary usage of two highly focused communities – for example, of English and French academics – will have one kind of probable significance; between "Spanish" and "Creole" in Belize switching will be very much harder to define and may pass unnoticed, just another stage in the evolution of 'Belizean'.[2]

Notes

1. On "stereotypes" see, e.g., Walter Lippman (1922) and much sociological literature since. See also Le Page (1989).
2. Since writing this paper I have received the preliminary draft of Norman Denison's paper for the forthcoming European Science Foundation meeting in Basel
   (January 1990) "An alternative to the '(single homogeneous) code'-view of language in use". Examination over thirty years of the repertoire of the inhabitants
   of the village of Sauris in northeast Italy has brought him to express views very
   similar to my own.

References

Abstracts (1986) *Abstracts and transcripts of the York 1986 Workshop of the International
   Group for the study of language standardization and the vernacularization of literacy,*
   edited by R.B. Le Page.
Abstracts (1988) Idem, *1988 Workshop,* edited by R.B. Le Page. University of York,
   Department of Language and Linguistic Science, Heslington, York, GB.
Arends, J.T.G. (1989) *Syntactic developments in Sranan: creolization as a gradual process,*
   Doctoral diss., University of Nijmegen, Holland.
Baker, P. (1988) 'The major languages of Mauritius and their domains', *Abstracts
   1988:* pp. 40–41.
Carrington, L.D. (1988) *Creole discourse and social development,* Ottawa, Canada:
   International Development Research Centre MS Report 212e.
Chomsky, N. (1965) *Aspects of the theory of syntax,* Cambridge, Mass: MIT Press.
Christie, P.G. (1969) *A sociolinguistic study of some Dominican Creole-speakers,* Doctoral
   diss., University of York.
Denison, N. (1988) 'Language contact and language norm', *Folia Linguistica* 22: pp.
   11–35.
Diki-Kidiri, M. (1988) Discussant in *Abstracts 1988:* p. 110.
Ferguson, C.A. (1959) 'Diglossia', *Word* 15: pp. 325–340.
Gardner-Chloros, P. (1990) *Language selection and switching in Strasbourg,* Oxford:
   Oxford University Press.
Grace, G.W. (1989) 'The notion of "natural language"', *Ethnolinguistic Notes,*
   University of Hawaii 3, 38: pp. 567–581.
Gullick, C.M J.R. (1976) *Exiled from St Vincent: the development of Black Carib culture in
   Central America up to 1945,* Malta: Progress Press.
Holm, J. (1978) *The Creole English of Nicaragua's Miskito Coast: its sociolinguistic history
   and a coparative study of its lexicon and syntax,* Doctoral diss. University College,
   London. Ann Arbor: University Micro-films.
Kachru, B. (ed.), (1982) *The other tongue: English across cultures,* Oxford: Oxford
   University Press.
Le Page, R.B. (1968) 'Problems of description in multilingual communities'. *Transactions of the Philological Society* 1968: pp. 189–212. Oxford: Blackwell.
—— (1977) 'Processes of pidginization and creolization', in: Albert Valdman (ed.),
   Pidgin and creole linguistics, Bloomington: Indiana University Press, pp. 222–258.
—— (1989) 'What is a language?', *York Papers in Linguistics* 13: pp. 9–24. University
   of York, Department of Language and Linguistic Science.
—— (1990) 'What can we learn from the case of Pitcairnese?', in: Rosemarie Tracy
   (ed.), *Festschrift for David Reibel* (to appear).
Le Page, R.B. and Tabouret-Keller, A. (1985) *Acts of identity,* Cambridge: Cambridge
   University Press.

Lippman, W. (1922) *Public Opinion*, New York: Harcourt, Brace.
Lüdi, G. (1989) 'Code-switching and language contact', *Communications*, Strasbourg: European Science Foundation 21: pp. 8–9.
Milroy, L. (1980) *Language and social networks*, Oxford: Blackwell (second edition 1987).
Quirk, R., et al. (1972) *A grammar of contemporary English*, London: Longman.
Romaine, S. (1988) *Pidgin and creole languages*, London: Longman.
—— (1989) *Bilingualism*, Oxford: Blackwell.
Schuchardt, H. (1882–1889) *Kreolische Studien* (Wien, various publishers) edited and translated in part by G.G. Gilbert, *Pidgin and creole languages*, Cambridge: Cambridge University Press, 1980.
Stewart, W.A. (1965) 'Urban Negro speech: sociolinguistic factors affecting English teaching', in: R.W. Shuy et al. (eds.), *Social dialects and language learning*, Champaign, Illinois: National Council of Teachers of English, pp. 10–19.
Street, B.V. (1984) *Literacy in theory and practice*, Cambridge: Cambridge University Press.
Tabouret-Keller, A. (1980) 'They don't fool around with the Creole much, as with the Spanish: a family case in San Ignacio, Cayo District, (Belize)', *York Papers in Linguistics*, 9: pp. 241–259. University of York, Department of Language and Linguistic Science.
Taylor, D. (1951) *The Black Carib of British Honduras*, New York: Wenner-Gren Foundation.
Thomason, S.G. and Kaufman, T. (1988) *Language contact, creolization and genetic linguistics*, Berkeley: California University Press.
Todd, L. (1984) *Modern Englishes: Pidgins and Creoles*, Oxford: Blackwell.
Valdman, A. (1989) 'The elaboration of pedagogical norms for second language learners in a conflictual diglossia situation', in: S. Gass, C. Madden, D. Preston and L. Selinker (eds.), *Variation in second language acquisition*, Clevedon, Avon: Multilingual Matters, pp. 15–23.
Weinreich, U. (1953) *Languages in contact*, Publications of the Linguistic Circle of New York No. 1, New York.
Young, C. (1973) *Belize Creole . . . in its cultural and social setting*, Doctoral diss., University of York.

5

Finding a place in Sydney: migrants and language change

Barbara Horvath

Originally published in S. Romaine, ed., *Language in Australia* (Cambridge University Press, 1991).

Introduction

When migrants enter their new country, they are immediately faced with the sometimes daunting task of finding a place to live. Studies of urban settlement patterns record that migrants often are concentrated in certain parts of cities; Little Italy and Chinatown in New York City may be among the better-known ethnic communities in the world, but they are far from unique. Ethnic neighbourhoods give migrants a place in the new country where they can speak their own language and obtain the goods and services they need to maintain to some degree the way of life they grew up with.

Ethnic communities are not entirely separate entities, however, built on the edge of town. They are created within the confines of the host community, occupying areas once exclusively the domain of the host community or areas vacated by other, often more upwardly mobile ethnic minorities. Initially, the hosts may be attracted by some of the innovations brought in by the migrants, notably the food and the festivals, but it is rare for the hosts to hold the ethnic communities in high regard. Nevertheless, whether the host is attracted or repelled, in finding a place for themselves, migrants bring about quite often dramatic changes in the host community.

Equally as daunting for migrants, but not as consciously undertaken, is the task of finding a 'place to speak' within the host speech community. The ethnic neighbourhood can never totally recreate the conditions of the home country. Cultural patterns cannot remain unchanged, the migrants cannot fail to join the speech community of the host. It is not a matter of simply learning to speak the host's language; the migrant must find a sociolinguistic niche to occupy. In locating themselves sociolinguistically, they also have the same potential for changing the character of the speech community as they have for changing its social geography.

The role of migrants as agents of language change should be a particularly fascinating one for sociolinguistics. However, all too often migrants, particularly first-generation migrants, are defined out of the field of interest; they are not considered to be members of the speech community because they do not speak the language as native speakers. This approach to defining a speech community is reminiscent of the early dialect geographers who wanted to include only those members of the speech community who best represented the speakers of an earlier form of the dialect and accordingly choose primarily rural, elderly folk for their studies, for example, Kurath's study of English in the New England region of the US. Sociolinguists interested in language change in progress have concentrated on urban communities where the actual process of language change in progress can best be seen. It is not often, however, that the role of the migrant is focused upon. Too often only native speakers of the language are included in the study, and this may well overlook important sources of change within the speech community.

Sydney is a multilingual speech community, largely as a result of immigration since the end of the Second World War. The most numerous groups of migrants from non-English speaking backgrounds from the late forties and fifties are the Greeks and Italians, but many other European language groups came during this period. New languages are continually added to the speech community as Australia accepts migrants and refugees from countries suffering political upheaval, for example, Spanish from Latin America, Arabic from Lebanon, and Vietnamese and Chinese from Vietnam. All of the languages are replenished by speakers who enter under the family reunion scheme which is part of the current Australian immigration policy. Support for multilingualism and multiculturalism is the overt policy of the Government; the Government funds a radio station in Sydney, for instance, which broadcasts in 60 languages. English, as would be expected, occupies a privileged place in the multilingual policy. All speakers are encouraged to speak English and there is an extensive adult English as a Second Language programme sponsored by the Government. Few can choose to ignore English because it is the language of government, most of the media, education, and work.

In this chapter I will examine how migrants and their children enter into the English speech community, that is, how they begin to fit into the sociolinguistic patterns that are already well-established in the community, and what effect, if any, they have on those patterns.

Australian English: the 1940s

Fortunately we have available good descriptions of Australian English (AE) at the time just prior and during the early phase of the major migrations of non-English speaking people to Sydney and the rest of Australia. Although there are earlier writings to be found about AE, the academic study of AE began in the 1940s with the work of Mitchell (1946). Along with his colleague, Delbridge, he was responsible for the first major description and empirical study of AE (Mitchell and Delbridge 1965). Since the forties there has been a steady flow of research on AE, with studies of phonological and lexical variation accounting for the better part of the published work. From the very beginning of this research tradition, the variability within AE has been recognised as of major interest. Mitchell and Delbridge have found very little disagreement with their division of AE into three major types. Broad, General and Cultivated. Although one might quibble that the labels embody too much subjective evaluation, they do correctly suggest that Broad has the least overt prestige, Cultivated the most, and General occupies a middle position.

The focus of the study of AE from the start has been on the variable pronunciation of a subset of the vowels. Some descriptions of consonant variation exist and researchers usually associate particular variants of the consonants with the varieties of AE as described by Mitchell and Delbridge. However, variation in the vowels, (iy), (ey), (ow), (ay), (aw), and (uw) (see table 5.1 for their phonetic realisations) has traditionally been regarded as the main differentiators of the three varieties of AE.

Mitchell and Delbridge (1965: 15) reported the following distribution for the three varieties:

Broad   34%
General   55%
Cultivated 11%

Australian English: the present
The description here summarises some of the results of a sociolinguistic survey of the Sydney speech community more fully reported in Horvath (1985). In this survey linguistic data was collected from 177 speakers using the typical sociolinguistic interview developed by Labov and his associates; the social characteristics that were built into the sample included ethnicity (Anglo-Celtic; Italian; and Greek); social class (lower working class; upper working class; and middle class); age (teenagers and adults their parents' age); and sex.

Determining the sociolects. The Sydney speech community was divided into sociolects by using a principal components analysis of the vowel variables (iy), (ey), (ow), (ay) and (aw). Table 5.1 gives the phonetic description of the variants. The phonetic description basically follows that of Mitchell and Delbridge (1965: 80–4) and Bernard (1970), except that some additions had to be made for an adequate description of the variation found in this set of speakers.

Table 5.1 The phonetic variants of selected AE vowels

		Cultivated	General	Broad	Ethnic Broad
(iy)	*beat*	[ıi]	[əı]	[ə˘ı]	–
(ey)	*bait*	[ɛı]	[ʌı]	[ʌ˘ı]	[a ˆı]
(ow)	*boat*	[ʌ˘ɯ]	[a ˆɯ]	[aɯ]	[ă ɯ]
(ay)	*bite*	[aı]	[a ˃ı]	[ɒ ˂ı]	[ɒı]
(aw)	*bout*	[aɒ]	[æɒ]	[æ ˆɒ]	[ɛɒ]

An additional variety had to be identified and in keeping with the AE tradition in giving labels to varieties which give some sense of social interpretation, we have labelled this variety Ethnic Broad (EB). It is 'broader than broad' in two senses: (1) if one acknowledges a relationship among the variants of the vowels such that the direction of change is from the Cultivated to the Broad, then the EB variant represents a further step in the change pattern, and (2) it has even less prestige than Broad. In fact, whereas it could be argued that Broad AE enjoys covert though not overt prestige, Ethnic Broad enjoys neither. In addition, since many of the speakers spoke English with a decided accent, we needed to be able to distinguish those vowels which were clearly part of the AE system from those that were probably the product of interference from the first language. We therefore included a category called Accented to carry this distinction, but did not characterise it phonetically.

By using only linguistic data and excluding social information, we are able to identify groups of speakers who share similar patterns of variation in their pronunciation of the selected vowels. Once the patterns of variation have been determined, the social and linguistic distribution within each group can then be described; we define these groups as sociolects. Each sociolect, then, consists of patterns of linguistic variation and patterns of social variation.

The principal components analysis yields two major subdivisions among the speakers in the sample; these subdivisions have been labelled the core and the periphery of the speech community. Further subdivisions can then be made: two sociolects in the periphery and four in the core. The appropriateness of the labels will become apparent once the distribution of the vowels and speakers is described.

The periphery. Of the 177 speakers, 47 are identified as being in the periphery. The distribution of each of the variants for each of the vowels for the two sociolects are shown in the histograms in Fig. 5.1. The primary difference between the two peripheral sociolects is the degree of accented variants; Sociolect 1 is much less integrated into the AE speech community and Sociolect 2 is more integrated, where integration is a measure of the proportion of vowels in a peripheral sociolect which are clearly part of the AE system.

The social characteristics of these two sociolects is also of interest. All of these speakers are adults and are either Italian or Greek; it is not true, however, to say that all of the Italian or Greek adults are in the periphery. In fact, ten are in the core speech community. The major social characteristic separating the two sociolects is ethnicity: 62 per cent of Sociolect 1 are Greeks and 71 per cent of Sociolect 2 are Italians.

Mitchell and Delbridge categorised speakers to arrive at their determination of the numbers of speakers of the three varieties. For a number of reasons, however, we categorised individual occurrences of the vowels by the speakers. As we can see from the histograms, if we were to label Sociolect 1 'Accented' we would be failing to notice the occurrence of substantial numbers of variants that were not accented. However, in order to compare our study with the Mitchell and Delbridge study, all of the

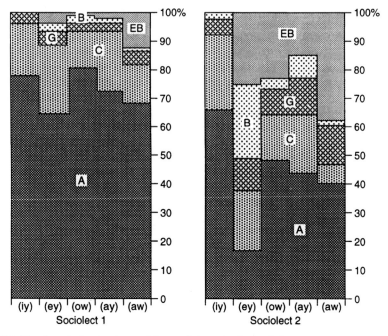

Fig. 5.1 The linguistic structure of the sociolects in the periphery

Table 5.2 Percent distribution of vowel variants in the peripheral sociolects

Vowel variant	Sociolect 1 (%)	Sociolect 2 (%)
Cultivated	18.32	17.89
General	3.82	11.33
Broad	1.04	7.83
Ethnic Broad	4.07	20.56
Accented	72.74	42.39

vowel data have been aggregated in Table 5.2 and the overall percentage of each variety for the two sociolects is shown.

Clearly the major differences between the two is not only in the amount of accented vowels but also the use of the Ethnic Broad, Broad and General variants. Notice that there is almost an equal amount of Cultivated variants in the two sociolects. We will return to discuss the interpretation of these differences after we have examined the core sociolects.

The core. The core consists of 130 speakers; the distribution of the variants for the five vowels is shown in histograms in Fig. 5.2. The most obvious differences between the core and the periphery are the absence in the core of any Accented variants; surprisingly there are no Ethnic Broad variants.

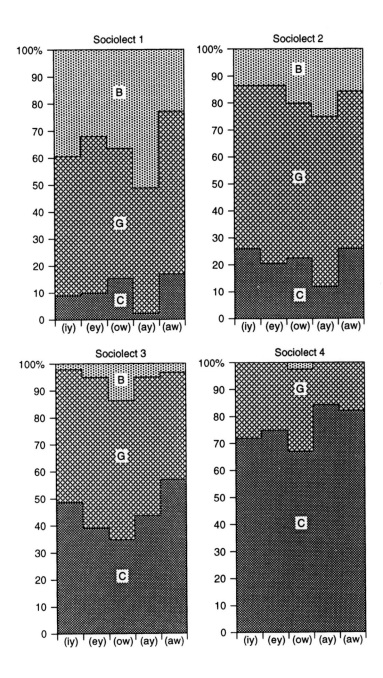

Fig. 5.2 The linguistic structure of the sociolects in the core

This principal components analysis shows this relationship between the core and the periphery as a definite split, hence the labels.

On the other hand, the relationship among the four sociolects is quite different; that these sociolects form a continuum rather than clearly defined separate dialects is shown in the decrease of the number of Broad variants as one goes from Sociolect 1 to 4 and the increase in the number of Cultivated variants from Sociolect 1 to 4. The General variants peak in Sociolect 2 and 3. Once again we see clearly that there is no variety in which only one of the variants is present and all the others absent. In fact, there was not a single speaker in the sample who used only one variant of any of the vowels studied.

The social characteristics of the four sociolects are quite complex. The graphs in Fig. 5.3 show the importance of sex differentiation. Sociolect 4 at the Cultivated end of the continuum consists entirely of females, and males dominate Sociolect 1 at the Broad end. I will examine the ethnic dimension of this variable further. Middle class speakers increase from the Broad to the Cultivated end and working class speakers decrease. However, it is age and ethnicity that are the most interesting variables in addressing the question of how it is that migrants find a place in the host speech community.

First of all, it is important to recognise that the core is over-represented by teenagers, despite the fact that we began with an evenly distributed sample, that is, 30 speakers each in three ethnic groups and two age groups.

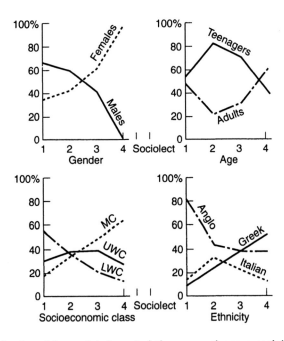

Fig. 5.3 Distribution of the social characteristics across the core sociolects

(In fact we ended up with only 27 Italian adults, which totals 177 speakers instead of the expected 180.) This accounts for the fact that teenagers dominate all core sociolects except for Sociolect 4. There are also more Anglo-Celtics among the 130 core speakers since all 60 are in the core and there are only 30 Italian and 30 Greek teenagers plus the seven Greek and three Italian adults. The most relevant patterns on the ethnicity graph are the dominance of Anglo-Celtics in the Broad sociolect and the Greeks in the Cultivated.

Let us begin to assess how migrants enter the speech community by examining each ethnic group in turn. First of all, let us compare the Anglo-Celtic group in the core with the Mitchell and Delbridge distribution across the three varieties, as shown in Table 5.3. The adult speakers in the Sydney study should be more or less from the same generation since Mitchell and Delbridge collected their data from teenagers in about 1960. For the sake of comparison, core Sociolects 2 and 3 have been combined.

We can take the distribution of Anglo-Celtic adults across the three varieties to be roughly equivalent to the patterns found by Mitchell and Delbridge. There are a number of differences in the way data was collected and analysed in the two studies so it would be a mistake to take such a comparison too seriously. The differences between the Sydney adults and teenagers is important; whereas two-thirds of the adults are in the General category, three-quarters of the teenagers are. Both the Broad and the Cultivated varieties would appear to be losing speakers from this ethnic group.

If we now add the Greek and Italian teenagers as well as the ten Greek and Italian adults who are in the core, as in Table 5.4, we can see whether the distribution patterns are the same as the Anglo teenagers. If so, this

Table 5.3 Percent distribution of Anglo-Celtic speakers over the three varieties of AE

| | Mitchell and Delbridge | Sydney | |
		Adults	Teenagers
Broad	34	27	20
General	55	67	76
Cultivated	11	7	3

Table 5.4 Percent distribution of Greek and Italian speakers over the three varieties of AE

| | Sydney | |
	Greeks	Italians
Broad	3	6
General	87	91
Cultivated	11	3

would indicate that once in the core the members of these ethnic groups are indistinguishable from the members of the host speech community.

The move toward the General variety is even more noticeable among the other two ethnic groups, with the Italians being almost entirely within the General sociolect. Quite interesting is the very low representation of both groups in the Broad category compared to the Anglo-Celtic teenagers. Also interesting is the number of speakers among the Greeks who are in the Cultivated variety; they represent the highest percentage in this variety of all the ethnic groups. In fact, the differences between the three ethnic groups can be shown to be even more distinctive when we separate the two sociolects which we combined to compare the results with the Mitchell and Delbridge findings, as in Table 5.5.

The Italians (which includes all the teenagers and three adults) and the Anglo-Celtic teenagers are alike in their patterning except that the Italians are not represented in Sociolect 1 to the same degree. However, the Greeks show themselves once again to be quite different; well over half of them are to be found at the Cultivated end of the continuum compared to only about a quarter of the Anglo-Celtic teenagers and just over one-third of the Italians. This pattern alone would be justification enough to claim that the Italians and the Greeks remain distinctive within the core community. However, when we examine once again the sex variable we see an even more striking difference. The male/female distinction is a very important one for the Anglo-Celtic speakers, for both adults and teenagers, but for the Greek and Italian teenagers, it is not.

Inter-generational variation
According to variationist accounts of language change such as Labov (1966)

a) language change proceeds quantitatively;
b) the process of change is linguistically and socially structured;
c) social evaluation is the motor of change;
d) inter-generational variation is a surrogate for change over time: each generation moves a change along 'one step'.

What needs further discussion within the variationist paradigm is the role of the host community in urban settings where there is a high influx of

Table 5.5 Percent distribution of all ethnic groups across the four core sociolects

| | Ethnic groups | | | |
| | Anglo-Celtic | | Greek | Italian |
Sociolect	Adults	Teens	(All)	(All)
1 (Broad)	27	20	3	6
2 (General)	30	53	38	58
3 (General)	37	23	49	33
4 (Cultivated)	7	3	11	3

migrants. It is possible to interpret the failure to include migrants in socio-linguistic studies as a presumption that it is the host community that sets the parameters for how a change will proceed. Migrants from non-English speaking backgrounds, or rather their children, become Aussies by losing their accents and falling in step linguistically with their social counterparts, that is, in this case with Anglo-Celtic Australians of similar sex and social class backgrounds.

As we have seen so far, the second-generation Italians and Greeks remain distinctive to some degree. One pattern that is definitely not followed is the distinction that Anglo-Celtics make between males and females which is a distinction long noted in AE studies (Horvath 1985; Mitchell and Delbridge 1965; McBurney quoted in Ellis 1887). Let us look at the inter-generational variation between the three ethnic groups and then take up the central question of how migrants enter into a speech community and what effect they have on that community's patterns of sociolinguistic variation.

The differences between the Anglo adults and teenagers is more or less the expected one; there is a gradual shifting away from the highly marked ends of the continuum and a movement toward General with the sex differences being maintained. One of the major differences between the Greek adults and teenagers, though dramatic, is expected: the teenagers do not speak with a Greek accent. The Greek adults are also very low on the use of either the Ethnic Broad or Broad variants of the vowels and so are the teenagers. The Greek adults, both in the periphery and in the core, have a distinct preference for the cultivated end of the continuum and so do the teenagers. These two ethnic groups, the Greeks and the Anglo-Celtics, demonstrate the expected linguistic patterns. The younger generation moves the pattern of vowel variation along 'one step'.

The Italian teenagers, however, do not meet the expected inter-genera-tional pattern, except that they too do not speak with an accent. Although the use of Ethnic Broad and Broad vowels make up over a quarter of the adults' linguistic behaviour and there is also a fair representation in the Cultivated variety, the teenagers move away from both of these varieties and are to be found entirely in the two General varieties. If we assume that the development of the Ethnic Broad variety moves the Australian English pattern along 'one step' (as I have argued elsewhere), then the Italian teenagers are taking two steps backwards and in so doing jump ahead of their Anglo counterparts.

We have already seen that the second-generation Greeks do not simply fall in line sociolinguistically with the supposed Anglo-Celtic trendsetters; the Anglo-Celtics are moving away from the Cultivated end of the con-tinuum and it is the Greeks who are breathing new life into it. I have identified three intergenerational patterns:

1) Anglos follow the previous generation as expected;
2) Greeks follow the previous generation but this is not expected because instead they should follow their Anglo counterparts;
3) Italians do not follow the previous generation nor do they behave like their Anglo-Celtic counterparts; instead they jump ahead of the

Anglo-Celtic teenagers by moving not one but two steps away from the ends of the continuum.

The speech community and change in progress
The two generational model of change that emerges from the analysis of the patterns of variation in the study of the Sydney speech community is shown in Fig. 5.4. In the first generation, migrants form satellite or peripheral speech communities which may be attached to the host speech communities at different places. Recognising that there is variation in the first generation migrants, nevertheless, we can say that by and large the Italians 'attached' themselves at the Broad end of the AE continuum and the Greeks at the Cultivated end. However, the Italian first generation can be described as being more integrated into the AE speech community than the Greeks for two reasons. Firstly, overall they use more vowels that are clearly part of the AE system. Secondly, they add a new variant to the AE vowel continuum. The first-generation Greeks, by contrast, use a very small proportion of AE vowels and the majority of the AE vowels are Cultivated.

In the second generation we see that all of the speakers are fully within the host speech community, that is there are no more accented vowels and, importantly, no EB variants of the vowels. Ethnicity, however, remains a distinctive social variable for this second generation. They do not, for instance, maintain the linguistic importance of the sex variable and they have a different distribution over the vowel continuum.

We can also see what impact this influx of the children of migrants has

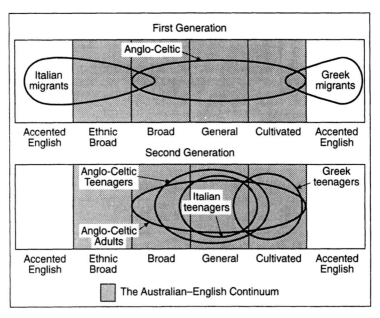

Fig. 5.4 The sociolinguistic relationship between migrants and their hosts: an intergenerational model

had on the host community. The very highly stigmatised variant EB is clearly avoided by the children of Italian migrants; the children move right away from the Broad end of the continuum. The development of the EB variant may well have acted as an impetus for the Anglo-Celtic teenagers to move away from the Broad end of the continuum as well. Although Broad has been overtly stigmatised almost from the beginning, it has been maintained largely as a male-dominated variety with covert prestige. The Cultivated end of the continuum appears always to have had a minority of speakers. Without the newcomers to this sociolect, the Greeks, it may well have withered away. This might be called the 'cultural cringe' variety. It is regarded by Australians to be the closest to British Received Pronunciation and therefore the most acceptable and the one with overt prestige. The rise of nationalism which is now flourishing in Australia, so that England is no longer regarded as 'home' as it was widely thought to be in the 1940s, has resulted in a more positive social evaluation of the General, though not the Broad, variety. The Greeks, however, having no particular associations, either positive or negative, with England, simply regarded the Cultivated end of the spectrum as the dialect of AE having prestige. The Australians, on the other hand, have redefined what it means to speak 'real Aussie English' as General.

In the discussion so far it is the speech community that has played a key role. In the past the notion of the speech community has not been particularly well theorised. Studies of New York City, Philadelphia, Washington, DC, Norwich and Belfast more or less assumed that the people living in the confines of the city could be regarded as members of the speech community, unless of course they were clearly a subculture within that city, such as the Blacks of Harlem or Washington, DC, where they were considered a separate speech community. In the study discussed here it was necessary to begin by questioning the assumption that everyone who lived in Sydney belonged to the same speech community. That questioning has led to a better understanding both of how migrants enter into a new speech community and of how they affect the patterns of variation and change in the host community.

I began this chapter with reference to how migrants situate themselves geographically in the host community. It is interesting to find in the geographical literature corroboration for the notion of integration into a speech community as well as specific corroboration for the notion that the Italians and the Greeks differ with respect to the degree of integration into the AE speech community. In the social atlas of Sydney Horvath and Tait (1984) use an index of residential segregation which measures the extent to which the geographical distribution of a subpopulation differs from that of the total population. An index of 0 means that the subpopulation is perfectly integrated and an index of 100 indicates total segregation. In Sydney the least integrated ethnic group is the Vietnamese, the most recent migrants, with an index of 79; third generation or greater Australians have an index of 19. The Greeks in Sydney have an index of 55 on this measure and the Italians 45. Sociolinguists may well have gone too far in drawing a distinction between themselves and dialect geographers. Perhaps it is time to reconsider the relationship between sociolinguistics and social geography; migrants trying to find a place in Sydney certainly ignore neither.

References

Bernard, J.R. (1970) 'Toward the acoustic specification of Australian English', *Zeitschrift fur phonetik sprachwissenschaft und kommunikationsforschung* 23: pp. 113–28.

Ellis, A.J. (1887) *On early English pronunciation*, London: Early English Text Society, V, pp. 236–48.

Horvath, B.M. (1985) *Variation in Australian English: the sociolects of Sydney*, Cambridge: Cambridge University Press.

Horvath, R.J. and Tait, D. (1984) *Sydney: a social atlas*, Canberra: Division of National Mapping.

Labov, W. (1966) *The social stratification of English in New York City*, Washington, DC: Center for Applied Linguistics.

Mitchell, A.G. (1946) *The pronunciation of English in Australia*, Sydney: Angus & Robertson.

Mitchell, A.G. and Delbridge, A. (1965) *The speech of Australian adolescents*, Sydney: Angus & Robertson.

Ozolins, U. (1991) 'National language policy and planning: migrant languages', in S. Romaine, (ed.), *Language in Australia*, Cambridge: Cambridge University Press, pp. 329–48.

6

Language contact and inherent variability: the absence of hypercorrection in East Anglian present-tense verb forms

Peter Trudgill

Originally published in J. Klemola, M. Kytö and M. Rissanen, eds, *Speech Past and Present: Studies in English Dialectology in Memory of Ossi Ihalainen* (Peter Lang).

Hyperadaptation

It is a matter of common linguistic knowledge that contact between different languages and different dialects not infrequently leads to relatively straightforward influence of one variety on another. Phenomena resulting from such influence are typically described by labels such as *interference, transfer* and *borrowing*. It has also been observed, however, that such contact also often results in more complex changes which cannot be explained straightforwardly in terms of influence, and which produce forms which were not originally present in any of the dialects or languages in contact. Labels used to describe such phenomena include *interlanguage* (Selinker, 1972) and *interdialect* (Trudgill, 1986). Interdialectal forms may include (a) forms which are phonetically or in some other way intermediate between forms used in the original dialects, and (b) hyperadaptations. Hyperadaptive forms result from speakers' faulty analysis of the structure of one dialect in relation to the structure of another, together with subsequent overgeneralisation. Such forms include both hypercorrections and hyperdialectisms (Trudgill, 1986).

In this paper, I examine a situation of apparent dialect contact which could have been expected to lead to the production of hypercorrect forms, but which has not in fact done so. I then attempt an explanation for this absence of hypercorrection.

East Anglian verb forms

It is well known that the Traditional Dialects of East Anglia lack third-person singular present tense -*s*. The publications of the Survey of English

Dialects show zero-marking for this verb form in northern Essex, all of Suffolk, and all of Norfolk except the Fens. According to David Britain (personal communication), who is an expert on the sociolinguistics of the area (see Britain, 1991), the non-Fenland Norfolk town of Downham Market has Ø, while the Cambridgeshire Fenland town of Wisbech has -s. Emneth, which is a suburb of Wisbech but is administratively in Norfolk, also has -s.

Local dialect literature confirms that 3rd-person zero is a typical feature of the Traditional Dialects. For example, Charles Benham's *Essex Ballads*, originally published in Colchester in 1895, contain verses such as:

> I loike to watch har in the Parson's pew
> A Sundays, me a-settin' in the choir;
> She *look* jest wholly be'tiful, she *do*.
> That fairly *seem* to set my heart a-fire.
>
> That *seem* ridic'lous nons'nse this, I doubt,
> A-tellin' on yer how she *make* me feel,
> But who's to help it when she *walk* about
> More like a angel than a gal a deal.
> *Miss Julia: The Parson's Daughter*

Similarly, the Norfolk dialect poet John Kett in more recent writings uses forms such as:

> That *seem* as though, whenever I sow seeds
> They fare t'come up slow, or not a'tall.
> An' them there hollahocks agin that wall
> In't haalf as big as them untidy weeds.
>
> But I'll say one thing, bor, an' that in't tew –
> Now Winter's come, an' that ole North wind *blow*,
> My garden's buried und'ra foot o' snow . . .
> That *look* like all the others now, that *dew*!
> *My Garden*

This zero-form also survives in the more modern dialects of at least the northern and central parts of the area, as in the urban dialects of Norwich, Great Yarmouth and Ipswich. However, it is clear that in these varieties the usage of zero-forms is variable. In the modern dialect of Norwich, forms with Ø alternate with forms with -s. This variability correlates with social class background, and with formality of style. Trudgill (1974) shows the following extent of Ø usage (Table 6.1). An obvious explanation for this variability would appear to lie in contact between the original Traditional Dialect forms, which lacked -s, and the prestigious Standard English of the education system and the media, which of course does have -s. This explanation also appears to be favoured by the strong and obvious correlation of percentage of usage of standard forms with social class and formality of situation.

Table 6.1

Speakers	% -s	
	Informal	Formal
Lower working class	3	13
Middle working class	19	36
Upper working class	25	62
Lower middle class	71	95
Upper middle class	100	100

Absence of hypercorrection

If contact between the local dialect and Standard English lies at the root of the variability we find in modern East Anglian English, we would then expect to find at least spasmodic, individual occurrences of hypercorrect forms on the part of East Anglian speakers, especially perhaps those with less education. We would imagine that, in attempting to speak in a more statusful or "correct" manner, they would employ standard -s but, because of a faulty analysis of the Standard English system, they would also from time to time add -s to persons other than the 3rd-person singular. There are many examples in the literature of similar forms of contact between standard and nonstandard varieties leading to instances of hypercorrection. For example, hypercorrect -s occurs in the speech of native speakers of forms of Caribbean English which lack 3rd-person -s in their basilectal form (see Edwards, 1979). Similar hypercorrect forms are reported in some varieties of AAVE (Schneider, 1983).

The focus of this paper is on the interesting and perplexing fact that in East Anglian English, hypercorrection in fact does not occur for this feature. It is always difficult to argue for the total absence of a phenomenon, and some sociolinguists will doubtless find this assertion difficult to accept. The absence does, however, seem to be genuinely total. There are, for example, no hypercorrect present-tense forms at all in the data from the Trudgill (1974) Norwich study; and in a lifetime of observation of speakers in the area, I have never heard a single example of -s being added to persons other than the 3rd singular. When East Anglian speakers use more standard or formal styles, it is true that they do variably add -s to 3rd-person singular forms, but they always get it right and never append it to other persons.

I argue here that the correct explanation for this rather surprising lack of hypercorrection in East Anglian English lies in the historical sociolinguistics of the area, and is intimately connected with the way in which the local dialects acquired zero-forms in the first place.

The history of -s in English

Any explanation for the absence of 3rd person singular -s from East Anglia must necessarily look at the history of the development of -s in modern

English itself. Middle English present-tense verb forms had a regional distribution as shown in Table 6.2, illustrated from the verb to *thank* (see Fisiak, 1968). The Midland plural form *-en* was borrowed from the subjunctive, and provided a singular/plural distinction not available in the other dialects. During the Middle English period, this form gradually spread to the other dialects, and the *-n* was increasingly lost. With the eventual loss of final /ə/, only the 2nd and 3rd-person singular forms retained inflectional endings. With the loss of the singular 2nd-person *thou* forms in favour of plural *you* forms, this left the 3rd-person singular forms as the only ones distinct from the base.

As can be seen, and as is well known, the 3rd-person singular ending in the South was *-(e)th*, in the North *-(e)s*. The origin of the Northern *-es* form is somewhat controversial. Hogg (1993, p. 306) writes:

> In Northumbrian only, final /θ/ in [the third-person singular and in the plural present indicative] is often spelled as <s> The morphological restriction on these forms indicates that the shift could take place only under favourable morphological conditions, but its spread to the plural shows that the stimulus cannot solely have been an analogy with Scandinavian.

Whatever its origins, the originally northern form spread gradually south. According to Brook (1958), "The forms in *-es* spread from the north to the East Midlands and the North-West Midlands in Middle English, and by the fifteenth century spread to London English". Baugh and Cable (1993) claim that the spread of *-es* forms to the south is "difficult to account for, since it is not easy to see how the Northern dialect, where they were normal, could have exerted so important an influence on the language of London and the South". Nevertheless, spread they did. The general consensus is that this spread was gradual and effected colloquial speech first, and that there was a long period in the London area when both forms were available to differing extents. It is often pointed out that Shakespeare, for instance, was able to use both *-th* and *-s* forms depending on the needs of style and metre. According to Baugh and Cable, *-s* forms predominated in the London area by 1600. The geographical spreading did not, of course, end in London, and forms in *-th* are known not to have been replaced by *-s* in Traditional Dialects in the far southwest of England (Devon and Cornwall) until the early years of this century (see Wakelin, 1972).

A number of 3rd-person zero forms occurred from the 15th century onward (Holmqvist, 1922), but these were very infrequent: Kytö (1993) reports 7 (= 1.5%) examples out of a total of 461 third-person singular present-tense verb forms in the Helsinki corpus for 1500–1570.

Table 6.2

	South	Midlands	North
1st sing.	thanke	thanke	thanke
2nd sing.	thankest	thankes(t)	thankes
3rd sing.	thanketh	thanketh/es	thankes
Plural	thanketh	thanken	thankes

Typology

Typologists are agreed (see Croft, 1990) that Standard English is unusual amongst the languages of the world in having marking in the present-tense only on the 3rd-person singular, which is typologically the form least likely to have person marking. It is therefore not at all surprising that many dialects of English do not share this characteristic of Standard English. Many dialects of British Isles English, for example, have a system in which present-tense -s occurs with all persons. In north of England dialects where it occurs, it is likely that this represents a survival of the original Middle English system. (There is, however, the further complication that many north of England varieties, like Scottish and northern Ireland varieties, have a subject agreement rule such that 3rd-person present-tense plural verb forms take -s unless they are governed by the pronoun *they*. This constraint has also been found in some American varieties (e.g. Wolfram and Christian, 1976) and elsewhere (Poplack and Tagliamonte, 1989), and has been argued by Bailey et al. (1989) to have been present at earlier periods at least in parts of the south of England also.) The generalised -s system, however, is also very prevalent in large areas of southwestern England and south Wales (see Hughes and Trudgill, 1995), where it must represent a more recent regularisation.

Conversely, there are many other varieties of English which have achieved regularisation by having no person marking at all for any person in the present tense. In Trudgill (1996), I argue that it is not a coincidence that all these varieties, such as Pitcairnese (Ross and Moverley, 1964) and Caribbean English, are forms of English which have been involved in language contact. I suggest that the loss of an irregular and typologically unusual form of personal marking is a typical example of the kind of simplification which takes place in contact situations involving adults. I also argue that East Anglian English is no exception, and that here too contact provides the correct explanation for the origins of zero forms.

Contact and change

Histories of the English language, having dealt with the influence of Norman French and Old Norse on English, rarely thereafter comment on language contact or multilingualism in England at all, with the possible exception of a brief mention of the shift from Cornish to English in Cornwall, which was completed in the 18th century. A consideration of the earlier history of English, however, suggests that language contact of different types has frequently occurred not just in Ireland, Scotland and Wales, but also in England. Consider the linguistic history of East Anglia itself.

After the gradual replacement between the 5th and 7th centuries of the ancestor of modern Welsh – and what little Latin there was – by the Anglo-Saxon spoken by the invading Angles and Frisians, East Anglia must have remained fairly monolingual for a century or so until the arrival of the Danes in the 9th century. For the next few hundred years, however, multilingualism must have been a frequent feature. After the Norman conquest, for instance, Norwich itself in the 12th century must have had, in addition to the original speakers of English and Danish, speakers of the newly arrived Norman French, as well as the Breton and Flemish spoken by many of the Normans' followers. Large numbers of Jews also arrived with the Normans, and they may have been speakers of Ladino (Judaeo-Spanish). Later, during the 14th century, there were also numerous Flemish-speaking weavers who arrived in the city. It is very unlikely, however, that these particular instances of language contact had any kind of effect on the present-tense verb system of East Anglian English.

Historical events which do appear to be relevant are the following. From 1348 onwards, the different provinces of the Low Countries, for the most part modern Belgium and the Netherlands, came gradually under the control of the Dukes of Burgundy. Mary, the daughter of Charles the Bold, Duke of Burgundy, married Emperor Maximilian of Austria. Their son Philip married Joanna, the daughter of Ferdinand of Aragon and Isabella of Castile, and thus control of the Low Countries ultimately passed to their son, who as Charles V was Holy Roman Emperor, as well as being King Charles I of Spain. When he abdicated in 1556, the imperial office went to his brother, emperor Ferdinand I. The crown of Spain, however, together with control over the Low Countries and other colonies such as Naples and Milan, went to his son, King Philip II.

Although Charles had been educated in the Low Countries, his son Philip had been brought up in Spain. Philip was also a devout Catholic, and most of his domestic, colonial and foreign policies were focussed on stamping out Protestantism. It was therefore inevitable that there would be friction in the Low Countries where, in the northern provinces (now The Netherlands) Calvinism had taken deep root. Under the control of Philip's sister, Margaret of Parma, the stationing of Spanish troops in the Low Countries, the prosecution of "heretics" and the Spanish Inquisition led to an insurrection against Spanish domination even in the mainly Catholic south (modern Belgium), where loss of autonomy was resented.

Dutch, Flemish and Walloon refugees fleeing to England from this Spanish persecution settled in Sandwich (Kent), London and Colchester, but the biggest group of refugees by far found its way to Norwich, probably attracted at least in part by an already etablished group of invited weavers. In 1565, the mayor and Alderman of Norwich had invited 30 "Dutchmen" and their families – no household was to exceed ten persons – to Norwich in an attempt to modernise the local textile industry, which was of great economic importance to the region, but which had been lagging behind in terms of technology, design and skills. In the event, 24 Flemish and 10 Walloon master textile makers arrived and settled in Norwich (Rickwood, 1984; Vane, 1984). The refugees themselves, although predominantly also textile workers, included ministers, doctors, teachers, merchants and crafts-men. They were mostly from Flanders and Brabant, but there were also many Walloons from Armentieres, Namur and Valenciennes (note that at this period, the border with France was further south than it is today), and even some German speakers from Lorraine. The very high proportion of "Strangers", as they were called, in the city did lead to a certain amount of friction, and there was at least one attempted revolt against them; but generally, the absorption of a very large number of refugees into the population, while it undoubtedly caused overcrowding, seems to have been relatively trouble-free. The economic benefits of the reinvigorated textile trade were plain for all to see.

By 1579, 37% of the population of Norwich, which at that time was 16,236, were native speakers of Dutch or French. Some of the Flemish community returned to the Low Countries, as a result of religious persecution, during the 1600s, but the foreign community was further strengthened by the arrival of some French Huguenots after the revocation of the edict of Nantes in 1685. According to Ketton-Cremer (1957), church services in Dutch and French were maintained in the churches that had been given over to the immigrant communities "for many decades", and the congregations seem to have remained vigorous until 1700 or so. The last French-language service in Norwich was in 1832, and the last in Dutch in the 1890s, but by then the languages had attained the status of liturgical languages only. Now only surnames survive, and most of those in anglicised form. It is clear, however, that Norwich remained a trilingual city for 200 years or so, well into the 18th century.

The argument is, then, that the zero form, typical of the kind of simplification that takes place in language-contact situations as a result of imperfect learning by adults, was introduced into Norwich English by the Strangers. This is not to say, however, that East Anglian English was or is as a whole a contact variety like, say Pitcairnese. Clearly it is not. The modern dialect of Norwich contains no other interlanguage features which can be described as the result of contact-induced simplification, nor indeed any phonological or grammatical features which appear to be the result of direct interference of or borrowing from Dutch or French. (There are, it is true, some probable lexical items, such as *lucam* 'attic window' from French *lucarne* 'skylight', and *dwile* 'floorcloth' from Dutch *dweil* 'floorcloth'.)

As far as crucial grammatical features are concerned, however, Norwich English, like other forms of East Anglian English, bears no resemblance to a creoloid, by which term is meant a variety which, when compared with some source variety, resembles a post-creole in that it shows some features of simplification as a result of the influence of imperfect learning by non-native-speaker adults, but which has maintained a continuous native-speaker tradition, unlike pidgin-derived creoles and post-creoles. Indeed, we would not expect Norwich English to resemble a creoloid like Afrikaans, for example, because the degree of language contact was not nearly so great nor as prolonged. At all times, in spite of the large numbers of foreigners in the city, native speakers outnumbered non-natives by at least two to one.

It is apparent (Trudgill, 1996) that, under normal circumstances, given that the Strangers were in a minority, albeit a large one, the zero form would never have won out. Circumstances were not normal, however. The point is that the Strangers must have arrived in Norwich from the Low Countries at more or less the same time as the new -s form arrived from the North and Midlands of England. It was in a situation of three-way competition between the older -*th* form, the newer -*s* form and the foreigners' -∅ form that the typologically simpler -∅ form was successful (see Trudgill, 1996), leading to the situation that we find in the dialect today.

Inherent variability

As far as the absence of hypercorrection is concerned, we can say the following. It had always seemed probable that the current social and stylistic variability involving -∅ and -s in the English of Norwich and other parts of East Anglia, as outlined above, was a relatively recent phenomenon resulting from 20th-century and perhaps 19th-century interaction between the local dialect, on the one hand, and Standard English, on the other. The absence of hypercorrection seems, however, to detract from the probable validity of this scenario. I now hypothesize that this variability, totally free from hyperadaptation as it is, may be the direct and continuing result of the way in which -∅ forms were introduced into Norwich English in the first place.

The zero ending, as we have seen, appeared in the English of Norwich, the capital city and central place of East Anglia, simultaneously with the new -s form which had spread geographically from the north of England. The two new forms, however, must have been differentially influential in replacing the original -th in different sections of the community. A large number of the Strangers, although they brought wealth to the city, remained amongst the poorer sections of the population, as is often the case with immigrants and refugees (Rickwood, 1984). It is probable, therefore, that their non-native English had a greater influence in the city on the developing English of the lower classes, of whom many of them became a part, than on that of the upper classes, who would have been subject to greater influence from the fashionable new -s form that was also taking over in London and elsewhere in the South. Alternation between zero and -s may therefore have been a permanent and continuing feature of Norwich English ever since the more-or-less simultaneous arrival in Norwich of (a) the Strangers, and (b) present-tense -s.

In my work on dialect contact (Trudgill, 1986), I have shown that, in a dialect mixture situation, it is usual, if new-dialect formation takes place, for only one variant of a given feature from the mixture to survive. However, where, unusually, more than one variant survives, it is usual for the two or more surviving variants to be subject to *reallocation*. A phonological example of this is provided by the fact that the modern Norwich dialect has three variant pronunciations of the vowel of words from the lexical set of *broom, room*: /ʊ/, /ʉ: / and /u: /. It is clear from rural dialect studies that each of these pronunciations is to be found in the immediate rural hinterland of Norwich, /ʊ/ to the south, /ʉ: / to the north and east, and /u: / to the west (see Trudgill, 1986, pp. 112–119). In the urban dialect, however, with the involvement of in-migration in the development of the urban dialect followed by dialect-mixture and reallocation, /u: / is now the middle-class variant, /ʊ/ the upper-working-class variant, and /ʉ: / the lower-working-class variant.

If we conceive of language contact in 16th-century Norwich as leading to a situation of contact between three dialects as far as 3rd-person verb forms were concerned – the older indigenous dialect with -*th*, the newer indigenous dialect with -*s*, and the Strangers' more regular but lower-status dialect with -∅– then we can see the current situation as resulting from a process of reallocation that took place four hundred years ago. The reallocation of variants in a dialect mixture may result in the redistribution of variants according to social class dialect, as with Norwich, *broom, room*, or formality of style (see examples in Trudgill, 1986). In the case of East Anglian -*s* versus -∅, however, the reallocation of variants was according to *both* style *and* social class. In the three-way competition between the different 3rd-person present-tense singular forms, -*th* was lost forever, but both -*s* and -∅ survived because they were allocated different functions in the local dialect. The ability of native-speakers of Norwich and East Anglian English generally to switch stylistically between -∅ and -*s* without hypercorrection may thus be the result of centuries of familiarity with a system that originated in language contact and dialect mixture, and which produced, as a result of reallocation of variants from different dialects – native -*s* and non-native -∅ – long-term and thus genuinely inherent variability.

Acknowledgements

I am very grateful to Ian Kirby, Janet Smith and Michael Greengrass for their help and advice on this paper.

References

Bailey, G., Maynor, N. and Cukor-Avila, P. (1989) 'Variation in subject-verb concord in Early Modern English', *Language variation and change 1*, pp. 285–300.
Baugh, A.C. and Cable, T. (1993) *A history of the English language*, London: Routledge.
Benham, C. (1960) *Essex ballads*, Colchester: Benham Newspapers.
Brook, G.L. (1958) *A history of the English language*, London: Deutsch.
Britain, D. (1991) *Dialect and space: a geolinguistic study of speech variables in the Fens*, Unpublished Ph.D. thesis: University of Essex.
Croft, W. (1990) *Typology and universals*, London: Cambridge University Press.
Edwards, V.K. (1979) *The West Indian language issue in British schools*, London: Routledge.
Fisiak, J. (1968) *A short grammar of Middle English*, Warsaw: Pan!stwowe Wydawnictwo Naukowe.
Forby, R. (1830) *The vocabulary of East Anglia*, London: Nichols.
Hogg, R. (1993) *A grammar of Old English I: Phonology*, Oxford: Blackwell.
Holmqvist, E. (1922) *On the history of English present inflections*, Heidelberg: Winter.
Hughes, A. and Trudgill, P. (1995) *English accents and dialects (3rd ed.)*, London: Edward Arnold.
Kett, J. (n.d.) *Tha's a rum'un; bor!* Woodbridge: Baron.
Ketton-Cremer, R.W. (1957) *Norfolk Assembly*, London: Faber.
Kytö, M. (1993) 'Third-person singular inflection in early British and American English,' *Language variation and change 5*, pp. 113–140.

Moens, W. (1888) *The Walloons and their church at Norwich 1565–1832*, London: Huguenot Society.

Poplack, S. and Tagliamonte, S. (1989) 'There's no tense like the present: verbal -s inflection in early Black English,' *Language variation and change 1*, pp. 47–84.

Rickwood, D. (1984) 'The Norwich Strangers, 1565–1643: a problem of control.' *Proceedings of the Huguenot Society 24*, pp. 119–128.

Ross, A.S.C. and Moverley, A. (1964) *The Pitcairnese language*, London: Deutsch.

Schneider, E. (1983) 'The origin of verbal -s in Black English,' *American speech 58*, pp. 99–113.

Selinker, L. (1972) 'Interlanguage,' *IRAL 10*, pp. 209–231.

Trudgill, P. (1974) *The social differentiation of English in Norwich*, Cambridge: Cambridge University Press.

—— (1986) *Dialects in contact*, Oxford: Blackwell.

—— (1996) 'Third-person singular zero: AAVE, East Anglian dialects, and Spanish persecution in the Low Countries', in E.H. Jahr (ed.), *Historical sociolinguistics*, Berlin: Mouton de Gruyter.

Vane, C. (1984) 'The Walloon community in Norwich: the first hundred years,' *Proceedings of the Huguenot Society 24*, pp. 129–140.

Wakelin, M. (1972) *English dialects: an introduction*, London: Athlone.

Wolfram, W. and Christian, D. (1976) *Appalachian speech*, Arlington: Center for Applied Linguistics.

7

Cultural bases of language-use among German-speakers in Hungary[1]

Susan Gal

Originally published in *International Journal of the Sociology of Language*, 111 (1995).

Introduction

Speakers' ideas about the languages they speak have played a central role in sociolinguistic explanations of language use. It is true that Bloomfield (1944) called such ideas 'secondary and tertiary responses' to language and advised linguists to attend instead to less conscious patterns. But later students of language use have found them indispensable in constructing theoretical models. Gumperz's (1982) notion of 'social meaning' in linguistic structures, the psychological concept of 'attitudes' (Ryan and Giles 1982), and Brown and Gilman's (1960) 'values' of status and solidarity all attempt to capture regularities in speakers' ideas and beliefs about the social significance of language. Each tries to link such ideas to a larger theory about social life. 'Values,' for instance, are borrowed from structural-functionalist sociology. More recently, anthropologists have argued that ideas about language should be viewed as parts of cultural systems, and as linguistic ideologies, thereby linking sociolinguistics to developments in cultural theory (Geertz 1973), as well as in social theories about the role of 'consciousness' in the maintenance of social formations (Roseberry 1988).

In these approaches, the evaluation of a language or linguistic variety as prestigious depends not only on the social structural fact that it enjoys state support in education and other high domains. Rather, a language is rendered prestigious within a system of ideas that has a discernable logic, and that is embedded in broader cultural discourses about the bases of social stratification and the nature of persons (Irvine 1985). Similarly, the ability of a linguistic variety to convey solidarity depends on a system of ideas and beliefs that provide a symbolic association between language and social group. Evidence from many parts of the world indicates that the association of one language with one culture and one people is neither natural nor necessary. Even in Europe, where this symbolic equation seems to have become axiomatic, historians remind us that it is a relatively recent development, associated with the rise of the nation-state. It is a cultural configuration created largely by elite theorizing of the last 200 years (Hobsbawm 1990).

As the role of elites in their formation suggests, cultural systems are rarely politically neutral. On the contrary, control of cultural representations is a crucial form of power. For instance, when speakers of minority languages accept the centralized state's often negative evaluation of their language, they denigrate the very language they call their own, while accepting the authority of a dominant, state-supported language that they often do not speak very well. This constitutes a form of symbolic domination (Bourdieu 1977), or, in Gramsci's conceptualization, it is the imposition of cultural hegemony. Since such hegemony is rarely total, sociolinguists have begun to look for 'folk theories,' or local ideologies that oppose, contradict, or subtly challenge dominant views disseminated through the schools, the press and other centralized institutions. Such divergent ideas are then interpreted by scholars as part of alternative worldviews, as oppositional cultural practices that 'resist' the incursions of state power (Woolard 1985; Gal 1989).

Building on this theoretical position, my aim is to call attention to the logic and heterogeneity of local cultural systems, to forms of innovation often ignored by students of 'resistance' and domination. I present a brief description of ideas about language that are part of local culture among bilinguals in a largely German-speaking town of southern Hungary. Analysis of the discussions, everyday opinions, and linguistic practices in this town suggests that, contrary to widespread assumption in much sociolinguistic research, in this case the status of the minority language is *not* firmly fixed relative to the language of the state; the languages' symbolic associations with social groups are currently matters of denial, disagreement, or dispute. The value of the minority language is constructed not only through solidarity, but by reaching for a novel kind of status – by recontextualizing the opposition between Hungarian and German to be a transnational, pan-European opposition rather than a local one.

My evidence is based on five months of participant observation and interviewing in the community of Bóly (before World War II Német-Bóly, in German: Bohl) in Baranya County, Hungary, begun in 1987 and continued in 1990. After a brief historical sketch of German-speakers in Hungary, I present ethnographic evidence about linguistic ideas in Bóly.

German-speakers in Hungary

Three historical experiences must briefly be mentioned in order to contextualize current ideas about language among German-speakers in Bóly. The first of these is the original arrival of German speakers into southern Transdanubia (Hungary). The ancestors of those now living in Bóly entered Hungary in the 1740s, toward the end of many centuries of German-speaking immigration to other parts of Hungary. Like the earlier waves of migration, they were simultaneously drawn by the promise of land grants and driven by the poverty and difficult economic conditions in their places of origin. The counties in which the eighteenth century migrants were concentrated – Baranya, Tolna, and Somogy in southern Transdanubia – were mockingly labelled *Schwäbische Türkei* 'Swabian Turkey' because the migrants often settled villages that had been depopulated during the Turkish wars, and because they were believed to come from Swabia.[2]

The second historical experience concerns the characteristic economic and sociopolitical features this population developed in the nineteenth and early twentieth centuries. By the nineteenth century, German-speakers in Hungary were wealthier than their Magyar and Serb counterparts; a greater percentage owned medium-sized farms, fewer were landless laborers (Bellér 1981: 146). In Bóly, an oral tradition maintains that German-speaking families entered Hungary in poverty and amassed land and other forms of wealth through hard work and judicious investment. Bóly's population, by 1910, was entirely German-speaking and Catholic. It included both artisans and agriculturalists, who prospered through participation in the expanding national and international market. Clubs, associations, and voluntary societies provided a rich social and cultural life that was the pride of Bóly's inhabitants (Kovács 1990). The memory of this cultural activity survives among all generations. Indeed, the image of Bóly as damaged by 40 years of Communism, but still a political and cultural center, constitutes one of the grounds on which people base their sense of dignity, pride, and self-respect. Another is the ethos of hard work, personal restraint, and respect for material accumulation that continues to be an organizing feature of daily life.[3] The town has been demographically stable for over a century (pop.: circa 3000) and relatively prosperous.

The third historical experience that shaped current language ideologies can be dated to the years leading up to the Second World War, when large numbers of German-speakers in Hungary joined the *Volksbund der Deutschen in Ungarn* [Association of Ethnic Germans in Hungary] and later were recruited into the German SS. The Volksbund was both an organization of ethnic-cultural revival and an organ of the Third Reich's foreign policy. Many of those who became members of the Volksbund fled with the retreating German army at the end of the war, others were later deported from Hungary – along with many nonmembers – for their participation in it. Subsequent Hungarian policy toward German speakers in the Communist era fluctuated greatly and is only now being discussed in detail, as Hungary's turn away from state socialism and toward closer ties to western Europe (including a newly unified Germany) makes fuller criticism of the last 40 years politically feasible (e.g. Tilkovszky 1989). Although severely stigmatized as kulaks and enemies of the state directly after the war, German-speakers in Hungary regained their rights of citizenship in the 1950s. But the use and teaching of German were at first suppressed, later neglected, and not actively supported until the 1970s. In that decade political dissidents in Budapest started to raise the issue of the Hungarian state's responsibility toward Hungarian ethnic groups beyond the borders of Hungary. Partially in response to such criticism, the policy toward internal minorities also began to change. By 1989, the final year of the Hungarian Communist party, the official policy's logic was clear: Hungarian state support for language maintenance among Hungary's internal minorities, support for their education and contact with their 'mother countries,' was to provide, on the international stage, the ethically unimpeachable model for what should be done for Hungarian minorities in Romania, Slovakia, and other neighboring states. The emphasis on the German minority in particular designated them, in addition, as a 'bridge' between Hungary and West Germany, with which closer ties were essential in attempts to rescue a failing economy (Magyar Szocialista Munkáspárt 1989).

Ethnographic evidence

At the time of my fieldwork in Bóly in 1987 and 1990 the results of these new policies could be felt at the local level. Only about half of Bóly's inhabitants were of German-speaking families, the rest were ethnic Hungarians, most expelled from Slovakia in the late 1940s – in the same political climate as many of Bóly's German-speakers had themselves been expelled – and resettled in Bóly. The president of the town council was a man of German background, a Communist Party member, a fluent speaker of German, and a politician agile in the ways of state-socialist bureaucracy, who insisted that it was the 'ethnic angle' that had allowed him to obtain investment for local schools by central planners. A home for German national minority children had also been built, an innovative special track for German-language instruction had been added to the conventional German track in the newly built elementary school, the kindergarten also had at least nominal German language instruction, and important West German diplomats on state visits to Hungary stopped at Bóly to be greeted by students speaking German dialect.

There are many aspects to the local response to new state policies and the larger political economic context of the 1980s and 1990s.[4] First, there is a marked attempt, especially by older people, to restrict the access of outsiders to information about local opinions, especially about language. This creates a veil of ambiguity that tries to repel the tentacles of the state bureaucracy from local or familiar affairs. Second, there is an attempt to deny, evade, or dismiss the link between language and minority nationality that forms the basis of dominant linguistic ideologies throughout Europe. But here I will discuss only the third major response, another form of resistance: the inner cultural logic of local opinions about the German and Hungarian languages. My examples are meant to suggest the several senses in which German and Hungarian are evaluated, how their relative status, power, and authority are conceptualized.

The general categorization of language in Bóly distinguishes between Hungarian on the one hand and German on the other, but within German there are further distinctions. Sometimes all of these are called, simply, *Deutsch*, or *német*, but at other times *schwäbisch* (H: *sváb* or the verb *svábolni*) is the term used for the local dialect as well as the many German dialects spoken in Hungary, and generally known to be quite diverse. These are distinguished from what is considered the more general standard learned in school in the two tracks specializing in German. Those who have traveled abroad also know that in Austria and Germany, speakers in different locales use somewhat different vocabularies and often quite different pronunciations of German. Since 1989, the installation in Bóly of satellite-transmitted German television has made these far-ranging differences even more obvious. Among those over 50 there is even developing a kind of folk comparative linguistics that distinguishes which stations (and thus regions) are 'easier to understand' and therefore 'closer to us.' Some linguistically astute older speakers have even developed comparative word lists, and for everyone who knows any German at all, access to satellite TV has meant an increase in passive vocabulary in many domains.

Nevertheless, despite this consciousness of great variation in German, there is still a conceptual distinction in Bóly between the local dialect and the school variety, in which the school German enjoys the classic form of hegemony: it is admired and is felt to be authoritative even by those who don't know it or don't fully control it. When one of the German teachers ran for town council as a national minority candidate in the multiparty elections of 1990, his campaign speech was delivered entirely in what I perceived as, and people called, faultless *Hochdeutsch*, utterly *nach Schrift* 'standard German'. There were many kinds of responses to this performance, including numerous admissions by people of all ages that they had not caught it all, and the contemptuous observation that probably no one in Bóly understood a thing he said. But everyone agreed that he spoke beautifully, persuasively, just as he ought to have, given the purpose and circumstances. Also typically, the local forms, while denigrated in some contexts, carried connotations of local solidarity among people over 50, and the substitution of TV-words or school pronunciation was remarked upon and criticized as putting on airs. But for those born after the war, the source of embarrassment and the general reluctance to speak German of any kind is not only due to the dialect/standard distinction but also to their sense that in comparison to their knowledge of Hungarian, they lack a complete vocabulary, cannot express themselves, and also have particular difficulties with the noun class system and the case system.

In contrast to this rather familiar story of dialect and standard in German, the evaluations of German with respect to Hungarian are more complex, less amenable to an analysis based on school authority vs. local solidarity, and more rooted in the particular historic experience of this population within a larger political economy. As elderly people told me stories of the Volksbund's division of the community into supporters and opposers – sometimes splitting families – and recounted painful memories of the subsequent resettlements, forced moves, confiscations of land and property, collectivization drives, the stigmatization of the well-to-do, and the public vilification of German-Hungarians, it became clear that many inhabitants of Bóly felt multiply wounded – shamed as well as enraged: *Letiportak, elvették a nyelvünket* 'They trampled us, and took away our language'. Stories of the deportations dwelt not so much on the loss of property *per se* as on the loss of the fruits of one's labor, the basis for human dignity as defined by the local culture. Yet this humiliation and rage coexisted with a bitter pride in the ability to survive through hard effort and even prosper, as in the often-repeated saying, if you throw a Schwab up into the air naked, he will come down fully dressed. Even for those born after World War II, an awareness of a version of this history, and a barely articulated sense of shame, have often formed the backdrop for local ideas about language. People born in the early 1950s remember their parents furtively telling them not to speak German on the street; even much younger men told me that, often on the basis of their surnames, they encountered anti-German taunts when they went to middle schools in other towns. And everyone tells the emblematic and pathetic story of the old Schwab woman, in the similarly emblematic '1950s,' who hardly knew a word of Hungarian but walked the street fearfully greeting everyone with *jó napot* – the Hungarian for 'good day', pronounced in exaggerated German-accented Hungarian.

Yet the deportation of family members and the ascendance of state socialism also had other effects on the linguistic evaluations of postwar generations, effects equally profound but contradictory. Since official histories elided the events, and some of those adults who remained were at first reluctant to talk about them, in many families it was through the visits of relatives resettled in West Germany – visits first allowed in the 1960s – that the postwar generations started to hear about the 1940s. Furthermore, their own trips to visit those same relatives gave young people in the 1970s an experience of Western wealth that was otherwise rare for Hungarians in that period and highlighted, for them, the relative poverty and economic frustrations of state-socialism. These trips and visits also made accessible to them the sort of Western goods that brought prestige and the envy of their neighbors, the resettled ethnic Hungarians who had no such relatives. Thus the political-economic division of the continent during the Cold War was quite immediately visible in Bóly, in the highly prized blue jeans sported by one set of apparently lucky children. The economic advantage and, equally important, the cultural cachet of contacts with West Germany have only increased as this contact has become easier in recent years and the economic situation of Hungary has deteriorated. Indeed, during the economic crisis of state-socialism in the 1980s, the possibility of temporary jobs in West Germany – either through family contacts or through other sorts of acquaintances – became very attractive, as did permanent migration on the basis of German origins.[5]

In all this, the instrumental, economic value of German has become increasingly salient. Thus, a great deal of the discussion about German and its value in Bóly, especially among those born after the war, is not readily interpretable as local or even ethnic solidarity, but rather as a veiled but powerful criticism of state-socialism. It involves a recontextualization of the opposition between Hungarian and German to a transnational, pan-European context rather than a national one. Although it is clear that Hungarian, as the language of the state and its educational institutions is indispensable – even the oldest Bólyi speakers know Hungarian and are pleased to be told how well – German is seen by many to represent a superior form of society and to open much-needed economic opportunities that are also seen as morally superior. One saying sums it up: 'Magyarral csak Hegyeshalomig lehet menni' [With Hungarian you can only go as far as Hegyeshalom] (for a long time the major border crossing to the West). This evokes the relative lack of economic and political power of Hungary on the continent, when compared to the demographic, cultural, economic, and political strength of German-speaking areas. It brings the political economic division of the continent right into people's linguistic evaluations. Since the people of Bóly who argue in this way about the value of German also often note that they feel culturally different, even alien from the Germans of Germany, this way of thinking need not always equate language and social group.

One can see this valorization of German as a version of the increasingly high value placed on all Western languages throughout Hungary in recent years as opportunities for tourism and trade have increased and the need for commerce with the West has become politically recognized. Clear indicators of such a reevaluation of German among at least some young adults in Bóly are the numerous German classes given yearly in the adult-education center, the insistence of a small set of parents on speaking German with their children explicitly in order to keep migration and work possibilities open to them in the future, and the high enrollment in the German track in elementary school.

The separation of this valuation of German from the one based on local solidarity is important. Most people over 50 explicitly state that the encouragement of German language instruction in Bóly is an *erőltetés*, a Hungarian term that implies the exertion of unnatural negative force, a compulsion or constraint to accomplish something against the general will. It is often accompanied by the judgment that these efforts came too late, because the postwar hostile atmosphere affected an entire generation and 'cut off the head of the minority' so that it can no longer be glued back. Some younger people agreed: when asked directly, some said the whole Schwab question means nothing any more, others that it is 'hopeless.' An engineer of about 35, running for public office in the multiparty elections of 1990, and himself of partially Schwab origins, told me with some irritation that it is only journalists and researchers – indeed, people like myself – who now instigate trouble by asking questions concerning language and nationality that no one really cares about anymore. These views could not be more antithetical to the efforts at ethnic revival and so-called 'bridge building' of the dominant state policy. This separation of German as a symbol of local identity, and its value as a transnational resource is perhaps most clearly evident in the fact that Bólyi adults of 30 and 40 simply do not use German at home; they quite deliberately restrict their sometimes considerable knowledge of the language to one situation: communication with monolingual German-speakers who come to visit or are encountered on trips abroad.

Conclusion

This has been a brief look at linguistic ideologies in a German-Hungarian town of Transdanubia. I have argued that ideas about language have a logic of their own as part of broader cultural systems. Moreover, they deserve to be interpreted in a larger sociopolitical context as the products of symbolic domination and the resistance that this often evokes. But the case of Bóly is more ambiguous and complex than many of the examples of linguistic resistance described so far. To understand it, one must explore the historic experience of this minority population and the current state policies that have constrained their lives, as well as their strategic position in Europe's political economic relations. Here I have focused on only one of the many ways that the inhabitants of Bóly attempt to resist dominant definitions of their languages and their minority identity. The evaluations of German evident in Bóly diverge from the usual status accorded to a minority language vis-à-vis the language of the state. Instead, these evaluations emerge from local images of the town's history, and Bóly's experience of Cold War social cleavages. In addition, the German-speakers of Bóly commonly refuse to take on the role of 'model minority' that state policies would exploit. Their linguistic ideologies offer, instead, a powerful yet veiled criticism of state-socialism, one that innovatively reevaluates the relative authority of German and Hungarian by recontextualizing the comparison between them to a pan-European political-economic field in which Hungarian, though the language of the state, is less powerful than German.

Notes

1. The research reported here is part of a larger project supported by a Fulbright Research Fellowship and a Fellowship from the American Council of Learned Societies, for which I am grateful. My thanks to Katalin Kovács for her great generosity in introducing me to Bóly and for many productive discussions. I also thank the people of Bóly who graciously consented to tell me about their lives.
2. In the eighteenth century, all German-speakers in Hungary came to be called H: *sváb* (G: *Schwaben*) 'Swabians'. This was at first offensive to settlers who had come from other regions. Today *magyarországi német* 'German-Hungarian' is the official designation, or sometimes simply *német*, but *sváb* is also widely used, certainly by German-Hungarians themselves. Several individuals in Bóly alerted me to the possibly derogatory connotation of *sváb*, but most emphatically dismissed this and found nothing objectionable in the general use of the term. As with any ethnic or nationality label, the connotations of the term are historically changing and sensitive to context.
3. Interestingly, the devotion to hard work and accumulation are also, sometimes, part of an explicit, ironic, mild self-stereotyping among the inhabitants of Bóly, while being condemned as offensive clichés by the Democratic Union of German-Hungarians, a government organization. The same characteristics are also part of the public lore of ethnic stereotypes in Hungary, common even among ethnographers.
4. For details about other forms of resistance to dominant ideologies in Bóly, as well a fuller discussion of what can be taken as 'dominant' in this ethnographic situation, see Gal (1993).
5. For a summary of similar processes among German-nationality groups in Romania, see the summary of the literature in Gal (1987). Migration itself might be seen as a form of resistance.

References

Bellér, B. (1981) *A magyarországi németek rövid története* [A short history of the German-Hungarians], Budapest: Magvető.

Bloomfield, L. (1944) 'Secondary and tertiary responses to language', *Language* 20, pp. 44–55.

Bourdieu, P. (1977) *Outline of a Theory of Practice*, New York: Cambridge University Press.

Brown, R. and Gilman, A. (1960) 'The pronouns of power and solidarity', in *Style in Language*, T.A. Sebeok (ed.), Cambridge, MA: Technology Press.

Gal, S. (1987) 'Codeswitching and consciousness in the European periphery', *American Ethnologist* 14, pp. 637–653.

—— (1989) 'Language and political economy', *Annual Review of Anthropology* 18, pp. 345–367.

—— (1993) 'Diversity and contestation in linguistic ideologies: German-speakers in Hungary', *Language in Society* 22, pp. 337–359.

Geertz, C. (1973) *The Interpretation of Cultures*, New York: Basic Books.

Gumperz, J.J. (1982) *Discourse Strategies*, New York: Cambridge University Press.

Hobsbawm, E. (1990) *Nations and nationalism since 1780*, New York: Cambridge University Press.

Irvine, J. (1985) Status and style in language, *Annual Review of Anthropology* 14, pp. 557–581.

Kovács, K. (1990) 'Polgárok egy sváb faluban' [The bourgeoisie of a German-Hungarian village], *Tér és Társadalom* 4(1), pp. 33–76.

Magyar Szocialista Munkáspárt (1989) 'Nemzet-nemzettudat-nemzetiség' [Nation-national consciousness-national minority], *Társadalmi Szemle* 2, pp. 3–13.

Roseberry, W. (1988) 'Political economy', *Annual Review of Anthropology* 17, pp. 161–185.

Ryan, E. and Giles, H. (eds.), (1982) *Attitudes Towards Language Variation*, London: Arnold.

Tilkovszky, L. (1989) *Hét évtized a magyarországi németek történetéből, 1919–1989* [Seven decades in the history of Hungary's Germans, 1919–1989], Budapest: Kossuth.

Woolard, K. (1985) 'Language variation and cultural hegemony'. *American Ethnologist* 12(4), pp. 379–394.

Section II

Linguistic variation and change

In this section we deal with the most obviously *linguistic* form of sociolinguistics, which is sometimes referred to as 'secular linguistics', i.e. linguistic research carried out in the real world, as opposed to offices or laboratories. Sociolinguistics of this type is 'linguistic' in the sense that it has goals which are indistinguishable from the goals of linguistics generally – the achievement of a greater understanding of the nature and structure of human language and languages. The papers in this section deal for the most part with one particular topic which is central to linguistics and which is of concern to all linguists, namely the mystery of linguistic change. All languages change through time, but linguists have as yet no very great understanding of why this is, or even of how it happens. What makes the papers in this section *socio*linguistic is the methodology on which they are based. It is perfectly possible to study linguistic change by, for example, analysing ancient texts. In this book, however, the problem of the fact that all languages change is tackled through empirical work carried out in a social context, in particular speech communities. That is, the research on which these papers is founded has been performed by linguists who, rather than working in the comfort of their universities, have gone out, recorded, investigated and analysed language of the type which is used by ordinary people for ordinary purposes in their everyday lives.

It is also axiomatic for the secular linguistic enterprise that all languages are internally variable. Not only do they consist of different regional and social accents and dialects, they also demonstrate variation within the speech of individual speakers. Many sociolinguists would agree that language change can be viewed as these types of linguistic variability 'writ large' – diachronic change is synchronic variability which has been given scope through time to move in a certain direction, with certain variant forms gradually winning out at the expense of others. Alternatively, we can say that variability represents the seeds of linguistic change, or the potential for linguistic change.

123

This section is therefore focused on the fact that the two issues of linguistic variability and linguistic change are intimately linked. This is clear in the first paper, by **Jenny Cheshire**, who examines the role of *never* as a negator in English sentences from the point of view both of its grammatical and semantic development through time in the history of the language and of differences between different social dialects in the modern language. This paper also provides a good link with the previous section, in that it also considers the role of conversational interaction in the development and usage of *never* as a negator.

J.K. Chambers also considers the twin themes of change through time and synchronic variation. He makes the point that, in modern societies, geographical mobility is very common, and many people have to adapt to new dialects of their native language during the course of their lifetimes. The sociolinguistic-theoretical importance of this paper lies in the fact that Chambers attempts to establish a set of principles which new arrivals in a speech community employ or adhere to in accommodating to the new dialect; and he illustrates these principles with data obtained as a result of empirical research with speakers of Canadian English who have moved to England. Chambers' paper contains many numbers and statistics.

Our third paper, by **James Milroy** and **Lesley Milroy** makes reference to the 'quantitative paradigm' of William Labov. Labov is the American linguist who remains by far the most influential figure in the development of empirical sociolinguistic research into linguistic variation and change, and his influence is apparent throughout this section, as well as elsewhere in this book. The term 'quantitative paradigm' simply refers to the way in which Labov has shown that variability in language is not chaotic, but patterned. This patterning, however, becomes apparent only if quantitative analyses of large amounts of data have been carried out. Milroy and Milroy discuss patterns of variation which emerge when language data is correlated with speakers' social class background and sex; the role of these features, together with that of speakers' membership of particular types of social network, in linguistic change; and their relative importance.

The paper by **Gregory Guy** and **Sally Boyd** is obviously also quantitative, and is indeed a classic of work in what is often referred to as 'variation theory'. It too looks at both synchronic and diachronic variation, in this case in the pronunciation of past tense verb forms such as *kept* and *left* which have final *-t* and a vowel different from that of the infinitive. Their work can be described as a study of linguistic change which focuses on 'age-grading', a term which refers to the way in which individual speakers may change their linguistic behaviour during the course of their lifetimes.

Care has to be taken to distinguish between age-grading, on the one hand, and linguistic change in *apparent time* (as opposed to real time), on the other. The study of linguistic change in apparent time as a sociolinguistic methodology was developed and refined by William Labov. The technique is based on the supposition that the way in which languages change through time can be studied by noting that ongoing changes will be reflected in differences between speakers of different age groups in particular communities, with younger speakers favouring newer forms. If the speech of younger members of a community differs as far as a particular feature is concerned from that of older members, it can often be assumed, especially if age-grading does not appear to be a factor, that this reflects the fact that a linguistic change involving this feature is currently in progress. The paper by **David Britain**, again using quantitative methodology, employs this technique to investigate a change which seems to be taking place in many parts of the English-speaking world more or less simultaneously. This change involves the increasingly frequent use, especially by younger people, of statements employing what at first sight might appear to be question intonation: Q. *Where are you going?* A. *I'm going to the cinema?* Britain, like Cheshire, explains this development, in part, in terms of conversational interaction. Britain also refers to the concept of the 'linguistic variable'. This, too, was a term originally employed by William Labov. It refers to linguistic forms (vowels, consonants, grammatical constructions) where there are alternative forms (variants) with the same linguistic function, such as the -*t* versus -Ø variants analysed by Guy and Boyd, or the alternation between -*ing* and -*in'* pronunciations in English words such as *walking, running*. Britain's paper is one of the first to extend the concept of the linguistic variable into the field of prosody (intonation).

Quantitative methodology is also apparent in the paper by **Guy Bailey** and **Natalie Mayor**. This paper, too, reflects the enormous pioneering influence of Labov, this time in the study of African-American Vernacular English (also known as Black English Vernacular). This is the variety or varieties of English spoken by many Americans of sub-Saharan African ancestry across the United States of America, and which differs in a number of interesting respects from the English spoken by White Americans. The historical origins of AAVE or BVE are fascinating and controversial. It has often been argued, for example, that AAVE/BVE is related to the Atlantic Ocean English-based Creole languages – language varieties spoken in the Caribbean and elsewhere which arose as a result of the slave trade, out of contact between English and West African languages (see Section I). The argument is that AAVE/BVE, while now clearly a variety of English, was historically a Creole language which has subsequently been and is continuing to be *decreolized*. In other words, influence from English, as a result of contact between the original Creole and English over the centuries, has led the Creole gradually to lose most of its Creole features. Current differences between Black and White varieties of American English may then simply be a reflection of the extent to which decreolization has not yet reached completion. Bailey and Maynor, however, suggest that, whatever the history of AAVE, decreolization is no longer taking place, and indeed that AAVE is currently moving away from White varieties of American English in terms of its linguistic characteristics. This is quite naturally a topic which arouses enormous interest in the USA: if White and Black varieties of

8

English negation from an interactional perspective

Jenny Cheshire

Originally published in L. Mondada, ed., *Formes linguistiques et dynamiques interactionnelles* (Cahiers de l'Institut de Linguistique et des Sciences du Langage de l'Université de Lausanne no. 7, 1995).

Introduction

This paper discusses the use of *never* as a negative marker in present-day English. I will argue that its importance has been overlooked because of the convention in linguistics of analysing forms in isolated sentences rather than in their conversational contexts. This practice forces us to rely on our intuitions about the role of a given form in the structure of a language, so that we risk unwittingly describing the internalised prescriptive norms concerning its use rather than the way in which it really functions. In the second section I briefly set out the history of English *never*, and in the third I describe the problems that linguists have encountered in its analysis. I then suggest the insights that can be gained if we consider *never* in the conversational contexts in which it is used.

A brief history of English *never*

Jespersen (1917: 4) sets out a common pattern for the evolution of negative expressions:

> The history of negative expressions in various languages makes us witness the following curious fluctuation. The original negative is first weakened, then found insufficient and therefore strengthened, generally through some additional word, and this in its turn may be felt as the negative proper and may then in due course of time be subject to the same development as the original word.

The history of the expression of negation in English fits into this pattern. Old English *ne* was too weak to survive unaccompanied, and by the Middle English period had been strengthened by the addition of *not*. Thus the earlier *ic ne secge*, 'I do not say', became in Middle English *ic ne seye not*,

127

with 'embracing negation (see Horn 1989: 454). Horn points out that amongst the world's languages negation is typically strengthened by minimizers (like the French *pas*, 'step') or by indefinites. Speakers of English seem to prefer the latter way of reinforcing a negative: our present-day *not* derives from *nowiht/nawiht*, 'nothing', itself from *no/ na+wiht*, 'not ever anything'. This 'negative existential pronoun' (Horn (1989: 455) was reanalysed as a simple adverb, presumably facilitated by contexts allowing both interpretations (such as *I sowed nought/I sowed not*) and then spreading into contexts where there were no semantic indefinites (Bossuyt 1988: 311–12).

From this point on most histories of English focus on *not*. The continuing development of the use of *not* conforms to Jespersen's NEG First principle, 'the natural tendency . . . for the sake of clearness, to place the negative first, or at any rate as soon as possible' (Jespersen 1917: 5). This was achieved by the introduction of DO-support, already attested in the fifteenth century and becoming standard by the seventeenth, so that *I seye not* became *I do not say*. With modal verbs and auxiliaries *not* remains after the verb (*I may not, cannot* and so on), but in ordinary main verb clauses the negative marker is before the main verb once again, as it was when the negative was expressed by the simple *ne*. The cycle has continued: in its turn *not* has now become phonetically weakened to the clitic *-nt*, first in spoken English and now, in present-day English, in some written texts too. *Not* became semantically weakened also, no longer interpreted as referring to universal time, but used as a simple negator to refer to a specific moment or period of past time. We can see from early texts how writers – and presumably speakers too – turned once more to the universal temporal negator to reinforce the expression of negation: examples (1) and (2) contain *naeure* and *neuer*, both from *ne aefre*, via *naefre*, literally 'not ever' or 'never', referring here not to all time but to past time:

(1) *ði moder was an hore, for nuste heo naeure ðene mon ðat ðe streonde hire on*
     (Lazamon's *Brut*, 1205)
     'Thy mother was a whore because she didn't know the man who begot thee'
(2) *He asked what that was and his wiff said she wost neuer*   (*The Book of the Knight of La Tour-Brandy*, 1450)
     'He asked what that was and his wife said that she didn't know'

In present-day English *never* continues to be used as a negative marker, sometimes with the possibility of the literal meaning of universal temporal negation, as in (3), where the utterance could be interpreted as 'on all occasions that Sally is offered meat, she will refuse it', and sometimes without universal temporal reference, as in (4) to (6), where the utterance refers to the past (unless otherwise specified, all examples in this paper are taken from my own recordings of spontaneous conversation: names given to speakers, such as "Benny" and "Nobby" in example (6) are pseudonyms):

(3) Sally's a vegetarian . . . she never eats meat
(4) You'll never catch that train tonight (Quirk *et al.*, 1985: 601)
(5) I never went to school today

(6) Benny: . . . we all went up there and jumped on him
    Nobby: you never . . . you you hit him with a stick and then booted him

If the process of standardisation had not intervened we could expect the cycle to have continued, with *never* eventually replacing *not* as the conventional marker of negation, just as *not* eventually replaced *ne*. *Never*, in its turn, would have become phonetically reduced through rapid speech processes, and would have lost its expressive force through frequent use. The spelling in example (1) suggests that the intervocalic consonant in forms resulting from *ne aefre* may already have been lost by the thirteenth century; and the spelling *ne'er* in the representation of speech in nineteenth-century novels indicates how *never* must have been pronounced at that time. With standardisation, however, came the desire for the speech of the educated to resemble the form of the written language. During the nineteenth century short forms such as *howe'er*, *e'er* – and presumably also *ne'er* – were branded as vulgar by schoolmasters (Jespersen (1982 [1905]: 219), presumably because they didn ot preserve the <v> of the written form and perhaps also because they were used by social groups from whom speakers who considered themselves to be educated wished to disassociate themselves. Today the shortened form of *never* has disappeared from most varieties of English, surviving only in some rural dialects.

Not surprisingly, prescriptivists objected not only to the reduced form of *never* but also to the restriction of its meaning from universal temporal negation to simple negation. Although there is no record until the mid-eighteenth century of a prescription involving *never* (see Sundby *et al.* 1991), guides to good usage published during the twentieth century virtually always comment disapprovingly on the use of a single form, *never*, with two meanings that are apparently incompatible (referring to universal time on the one hand and to one specific occasion on the other). The comments range from the severely prescriptive, as in Wood (1981), to the merely precautionary, as in Fowler (1965) or *Collins Dictionary of the English Language* (1981), and they tend to become more severe as time goes on:

Fowler 1965 (*Modern English Usage*): 'this use of *never*, however illogical, is idiomatic, at least colloquially.'

Collins Dictionary of the English Language (1981): 'In good usage, *never* is not used with simple past tenses to meant *not*'.

Wood 1981 (*Current English Usage*): *Never* means 'not ever, on no occasion'. It is common to hear sentences such as *I never saw you at the party*. It is, however, incorrect to use *never* when referring to one occasion. *Never* can only be used in continuous contexts:

  Bob: *I didn't see you at the party, Jim.*
  Jim: *I've never been to any of Sue's parties.'*

The cycle has been interrupted, then, by the process of prescription and codification that are part of the standardisation of language. The phonetic reduction of *never* has been reversed and its semantic restriction tends to be frowned on. Nevertheless, *never* does still occur with simple past tense tenses with the meaning 'not', both in nonstandard English and in what is usually considered to be standard English – in other words, in published written prose and in the speech of people who consider themselves to be educated (see Trudgill 1984). Examples (5) and (6) above were uttered by working-class adolescents who used many features of nonstandard English syntax, but examples (7) and (8) are from stretches of discourse that otherwise entirely conform to the norms of standard English:

(7)   He got ready to spring down from on high right among the spears of the goblins . . . But he never leaped   (J.R.R. Tolkien, *The Hobbit*, 4th edn (Allen & Unwin, 1978), 95).

(8)   Kay never went to Delft on Tuesday . . . she stayed with our friends in Rotterdam   (American university professor)

Prescriptivists tend not to comment on features that are in frequent use by the favoured sections of society, so the relative lack of comments in the eighteenth and nineteenth centuries presumably indicates that educated speakers used *never* more frequently in this way then than they do now. We do not know the extent to which educated speakers today use *never* to mean simply 'not', though this of course is an empirical question which could be answered by analysing a data base such as the Lund corpus. Cheshire (in press) discusses the acceptability of *never* in a range of linguistic contexts: it seems that educated speakers of British English find examples such as (7) more acceptable than examples such as (8), perhaps because in (7) the time reference is to an indeterminate period when the protagonist could have jumped, but didn't (whereas in (8) *Tuesday* clearly specifies a precise day to which *never* refers). Examples such as (6), above, where *never* stands alone, were found to be the least acceptable. This use of *never*, however, is very frequent in the nonstandardised varieties of English: it is reported in all the British urban centres surveyed by Cheshire *et al.* (1989), and it is used in many English-based creoles as a simple negator referring to past time (Holm 1988). For educated speakers, however, expressions such as *I never* or *he never* seem to have become a social marker of groups with whom they do not want to be associated.

Perhaps the most accurate statement, then, concerning the use of *never* in present-day English is that its development as an emphatic negative marker has been slowed down in standard English, so that this use is probably more widespread amongst speakers of the nonstandard varieties. This way of expressing negation in English has not, however, been given proper recognition by linguists, as we will see in the following section.

Linguistic descriptions of *never*

It is usual to distinguish between two types of non-affixal sentence negation in English: negation with *not* or *n't*; and negation with the negative words *never, neither, nobody, no, none, nor, nothing* and *nowhere*. Tottie (1991), for example, terms the first type *Not*-negation and the second type *No*-negation. Quirk *et al.*, (1985: 782) give a list of the negative words together with their corresponding 'non-assertive' forms, pointing out that there are two negative equivalents for a positive sentence containing an assertive form: thus *we've had some lunch* has the two negative forms *we haven't had any lunch* and *we've had no lunch*. In the same way, these authors tell us, *he sometimes visits us* has the two negative forms *he doesn't ever visit us* and *he never visits us*.

The inclusion of *never* in the *No*-negation category of negative words can be traced back to Klima's classic paper on negation in English (1964). Klima assumed that the same peculiarities of occurrence characterise *ever* as *any*: namely, *ever* occurs in negative, interrogative and restrictive sentences whose corresponding simple sentences do not permit its occurrence (Klima 1964: 280). Thus *we've had any lunch* and *he ever visits us* are both unacceptable. If we move beyond our intuitions, however, and examine the way that speakers actually use these forms, it becomes clear that *ever* occurs very rarely in negative utterances. For example, in the 53,000-word corpus of adolescent speech that I recorded in adventure playgrounds in Reading during the late 1970s there are 73 occurrences of *never*, but no occurrences whatsoever of *not* plus *ever*. The adolescents used a number of nonstandard linguistic features (analysed in Cheshire 1982), so it might be reasonable to wonder whether their linguistic behaviour is typical of other speakers of English. However, my figures correspond almost exactly with the results of Tottie's analysis of 50,000 words drawn from the London–Lund corpus of educated adult speech. Tottie found only one token of *not* plus *ever*, but 78 tokens of *never*. She also found that there were more tokens of *never* in her corpus than of the other negative words with which *never* is conventionally classed: she writes that she had originally intended to analyse the class of negative words together, but that there were so many occurrences of *never* that she was obliged to remove them to a separate data sample in order to avoid skewing the analysis. She was led to pose two questions that she hoped future research would address: why does *never* occur so frequently; and why does the *not ever* variant occur so rarely?

It seems to me that part of the answer, at least, is that *never* can be a marker of strong negation in English, as I outlined in the previous section. This means that it should be seen as a negative item in its own right rather than as equivalent to the words in the class of *No*-negation expressions with which it is conventionally classed. In fact, Quirk *et al.* (1985: 783) report a stylistic difference between *never* and the other negative words, saying that in all cases 'except possibly with *never*' the combination of *not* (*n't*) and the non-assertive word is more colloquial and idiomatic than the negative variant: this stylistic difference, presumably, is a reflection of the functional difference between *never* and the class of *No*-words.

Our failure to recognise the status of *never* as an independent marker of negation has left unresolved questions in other analyses, too. For example, Labov (1973) in his analysis of Hawaiian Creole English was puzzled by the occurrence of *never* in utterances such as (9) and (10):

(9) He never like throw first ('he didn't like to throw first')
(10) And that thing was coming and something black on top the horse never have head ('. . . something black on top of the horse didn't have a head')

Influenced by Klima's analysis, Labov assumed that *never* was the 'the same' as *not ever* and that it must therefore refer to 'universal' time, with a gloss 'not on any occasion'. This assumption led him to discuss at some length an apparently insoluble semantic problem, that of identifying the kind of cognitive process that could connect *never* as an indefinite item, with universal reference, to *never* as it is used in (9) and (10), where it refers to a single event that took place in the past.

As we saw in the previous section, however, the use of *never* with a time reference that is less than universal is not restricted to Hawaiian Creole English. We saw earlier that it occurs in 'standard' and 'nonstandard' English alike. Nevertheless sociolinguists and dialectologists have failed to observe this widespread use, labelling the use of *never* to refer to a single occasion in the past as 'nonstandard' or 'dialect' (see e.g., Cheshire 1982; Coupland 1988; Hughes and Trudgill 1979; Orton *et al.* 1963–9). All of us, like Klima and Labov, seem to have assumed that standard *never* corresponds to *not ever* and that it can be glossed as 'not on any occasion'. This assumption leads us then to classify other uses of *never* as 'nonstandard' or, in Labov's case, to conclude that although the limitation of *never* to a particular point in the past may be a possibility, albeit an 'extraordinary' one, he would be reluctant to include it in 'a general grammar of English' (Labov 1973: 59). This is obviously an unfortunate conclusion, given how widely this usage occurs.

Since the use of *never* to refer to a past occasion is more than just a possibility, then, linguists need to decide how to analyse it. Should we assume that we are dealing here with polysemy? This would lead us to propose that there are two *never* forms in present-day English: one meaning 'not ever' and one simply meaning 'not', expressing emphatic negation. Or should we decide instead that present-day English has a single form, *never*, whose meaning varies from referring to universal time to referring to a single point of time, depending on the context in which it is used? The question has important implications for variationist analyses, for the answer determines the forms that are considered to constitute the linguistic variable. For example, when I analysed the nonstandard English of adolescents in Reading I considered only variation between *never* and *didn't* with reference to a single past occasion in both cases (Cheshire 1982). Tottie (1991), on the other hand, analysed only variation between *never* and *not ever*, disregarding, therefore, those tokens of *never* where it referred to a single occasion. Each of us performed a different analysis, and each of us failed to obtain a full picture of the way in which *never* functions in present-day English. I will attempt to provide a fuller picture in the following sections. My argument will be that it makes more sense to consider *never* as a single form: as an emphatic negator, whose time reference is determined by the linguistic context in which it occurs.

Never in interaction

It makes good sense to consider the function of *never* in conversational contexts rather than on the basis of our intuitions, for negation, in spoken language at least, often relates to a previous utterance. In order to understand how negation is expressed in a language, therefore, it seems obvious that it should be analysed within the context in which it occurs.

In the examples that follow we see how speakers use negation to ensure that addressees have the same orientation to the topic as they have themselves, in terms either of shared background knowledge or of their personal stance. In (11), for example, Jacky corrects my presupposition that she has two parents, explaining in her negative clause why it is her mother who scolds her most.

(11) Jenny: Who is it who tells you off in your family . . . your mother or your father?
Jacky: Well my mum 'cos I haven't got a dad now . . . so it's my mum worse luck

Example (12) is from a conversation where Wendy and I were discussing indoor fireworks and, in particular, whether or not an indoor rocket was dangerous. Wendy's negative clause responds to the meaning that she infers from my *oh yes* uttered with rising intonation on *oh* and a fall–rise on *yes*. The intonation suggests that I am not convinced by Wendy's previous account of the safety of the rocket, as is shown by her response, which aims to reassure me:

(12) Wendy: but you know you just put it in the bo in the bottle and em . . . you know it kind of it . . . only it goes round the room
Jenny: oh yes
→ Wendy: it don't hit the ceiling it just goes round and round
Jenny: good job
Wendy: you have to mind your head mind you 'cos it goes up and round and round

These two examples show speakers using *not* to form a negative clause in order to ensure that their interlocutor's orientation to the topic is in tune with their own, by negating an implicit inference that they draw from their interlocutor's contribution, and that their negation then makes explicit (in 11), that Jacky has two parents; in (12), that an indoor rocket could shoot up into the air and hit the ceiling). Speakers use *never* in exactly the same way. Example (13) is from a conversation during which Nobby and his friend had been telling me about three other boys that they 'went around' with sometimes, even though they disliked them. I was trying to obtain details of this 'going around', and asked a question which presupposes that a group of boys from another playground, at Shinfield, sometimes comes to Nobby's part of town. Nobby's negative clause negates this presupposition:

(13) Jenny: What about when there's a real big fight like with the Shinfield lot or something like that . . . would you sort of join in on their side?
→ Nobby: Shinfield never come down here . . . they're scared of us

In (14) we see my earlier example (5) in its wider discourse context. In the same way as Nobby does in (13), Marie corrects my presupposition – this time that she had been to school that day:

> (14) Marie   I had to do a lot of banging and my n my hands as you can see
>   took quite a long time . . . about three or four hours just to do it
>   Jenny: Was that at school you made that?
> → Marie: No I never went to school today

In (13) *never* has the meaning of universal temporal quantification, referring to all possible occasions when I might have expected the 'Shinfield lot' to come down to the playground where we were talking. In (14), on the other hand, *never* has a more restricted time reference, to the day in question: this is the 'problematic' use of *never* discussed earlier. I will discuss this use in more detail below; for the time being, I want to stress that negation generally, whether expressed by *not* or by *never*, has an interactional role in ensuring the coherence of the emerging discourse. In other words, it can link the current turn to the previous one, by negating a presupposition that has just been expressed, whilst simultaneously ensuring that the interlocutors have a shared orientation to the topic that they are pursuing, so that the subsequent turn is felicitous. This cohesive function is perhaps one reason why negation occurs more frequently in spoken than in written discourse: Tottie (1991) found twice as much negation in her sample of spoken English as in the sample of written English. We can relate this discourse function of negation to the further function of creating interpersonal involvement in discourse (Chafe 1982; 1986), for Tottie also found that negation tended to occur in speaker turns that clearly testified to the cooperative effort that is necessary for conversation to be successful, such as in tag questions seeking corroboration from interlocutors (Tottie 1991: 43). In her sample, negation also showed a correlation with mental state verbs such as *know* or *think* which, as Chafe (1982) has pointed out, indicate the involvement of speakers in what they are saying and occur more frequently in spoken English than in written English.

The concept of involvement is very relevant to an understanding of why the universal temporal quantifier has been a favoured negative strategy throughout the history of English. Although different writers use the term 'involvement' in somewhat different ways, it stems in all cases from the assumption that spoken discourse is a collaborative production, with speakers and addressees working together to produce meaning as the discourse unfolds (see Chafe 1982; Gumperz 1982; Tannen 1989). Quantifiers have an important role in securing interpersonal involvement, since they require the addressee to determine their scope and their precise interpretation. In (15), for example, the universal quantifier *all* is in construction with *his hand* in the first clause and *head* in the second; it is unlikely, however, that *all* refers to Nobby's brother's entire hand and still less likely that it refers to his entire head. Instead, addressees determine the extent of the quantification on the basis of their knowledge of the world: by using *all*, Nobby alerts his addressees to the need to interpret *bashed up* as referring to the widest possible extent of his brother's hand, given the context:

(15) Nobby: My brother had all his hand bashed up . . . all his head was bleeding

All therefore functions as a very effective intensifying device, as has been pointed out by Labov (1984) and Cheshire (1989). We can think of quantifiers in terms of scalar implicatures – as members of an implicational set, such that an utterance containing one item from the scalar set entails the items lower down on the scale. Just as *excellent* entails 'good', so that *this is an excellent meal* entails 'this is a good meal', so *all* entails 'most', 'many' or 'some'. *Never* can similarly be seen as the high point on a scale containing *never, often, sometimes* and *once*. Thus when speakers use *never*, they invite the addressee to fix as wide a time-reference as is possible in that context. Sometimes the time-reference will be all possible occasions, as in (13) – *Shinfield never come down here* – where my previous turn had specified the time reference as indefinite, with *what about* . . . and where the immediate context in which Nobby uses *never* specifies 'all possible occasions' through the use of the 'timeless' present tense. In other utterances the tense of the verb or the presence of a time adverbial specify a time-reference that cannot be to all possible occasions: thus in (16) the verb is in the present perfect tense, indicating that the period in question is past time up to and including the present:

(16) You've never read Cold Comfort Farm have you? (Svartvik and Quirk 1980: 626)

In exactly the same way, the tense of the verb and the adverbial *today* specify the time reference of *never* in example (5), above (*I never went to school today*). In the case of example (7) (now 17)), when *never* occurs alone, we need to look beyond the current turn to the previous one, considering its function across speaker turns:

(17) Benny: we all went up there and jumped on him
→ Nobby: you never . . . you you hit him with a stick then booted him and then I had to do the rest

Nobby's *you never* follows on from – and negates – Benny's *we all jumped on him*, with the time reference of *never* specified by the tense of the verbs in Benny's utterance. We see here, then, how syntax can be constructed jointly, across speaker turns (see Jeanneret, 1992); we also see how important it is to consider a form in its conversational context in order to understand its syntactic function. In (17) the interlocutors also have to use their knowledge of the world in order to understand that the reference is to one specific past occasion (you jump on someone once only, of course, as the first stage in a fight).

We can now recognize, then, that the different uses of *never* discussed in the third section are essentially the same: in each case, interlocutors can fix the time to which the utterance refers by scanning the context in which *never* occurs, and by bringing into play their knowledge of the world. Sometimes the time-reference can be to all possible occasions, in which case *never* can be said to be acting as the universal temporal negator; but sometimes the time-reference is restricted by other linguistic forms in the utterance, or by the knowledge on which we draw in order to interpret the utterance. Variationist analyses that investigate the use of only one of the meanings of *never*, then, have given only a partial account of its functions.

It is worth stressing that the uses commonly considered to be nonstandard are no different from the other uses of *never*. In each of the examples just discussed, an alternative clause is possible using *not*, as can be seen by considering the pairs of sentences below. The difference is simply that using *never* invites the addressee to fix the time-reference of the quantifier and it can be said, therefore, to involve them actively in constructing the meaning of the emerging discourse:

> Shinfield never come down hee
> Shinfield don't come down here

> you've never read *Cold Comfort Farm* have you?
> you haven't read *Cold Comfort Farm* have you?

> I never went to school today
> I didn't go to school today

> you never
> you didn't

If, as I have argued, quantifiers can facilitate the creation of interpesonal involvement, it is hardly surprising if speakers turn to the universal temporal negator as a way of reinforcing a weakened negative.[1] In time, as the sense of quantification becomes lost and as phonetic changes make the form semantically opaque (as has happened with English *not*), the one-time quantifier becomes a simple non-emphatic negative marker, no longer recognised as a quantifier and no longer, therefore, actively involving the addressee in fixing the time reference of the form. *Never* does not seem to have reached this stage yet, and it may well never become fully opaque: we saw in the second section that the contracted form *ne'er* is rarely used today, so that *ever* remains as part of its form, as a reminder of its etymology (see further Cheshire, in press). In my recordings of conversational English there are many stretches of discourse where *never* co-occurs with other features that express interpersonal involvement, suggesting that it can be one way, amongst others, of involving the interlocutor. In the extract below, for example, *never* co-occurs with a cluster of addressee-oriented forms: several occurrences of *see*, the deictic *that* accompanying a gesture, and the quantifier *all* (the addressee-oriented forms are in italics):

(18) Jacky: The other day . . . when we was up Ridgeway . . . when we was at primary school . . . she always used to get me in trouble . . . and I used to hate *that* . . . I didn't mind getting in trouble . . . but her . . . she kept on getting me in trouble . . . and one day I was sitting in class . . . and a student was reading us a story . . . I wasn't listening anyway . . . but she kept on fiddling with my bracelet . . . and trying to pull if off me . . . and I went like *that* . . . *see* . . . and she sent me outside the door . . . but it was her *see* . . .

and when the teacher come . . . Mr Mayhews . . . he come in and told me off . . . *see* . . . and he blamed everything onto me . . . so I told him what happened and when he asked Wendy . . . Wendy said that she *never* . . . and they *all* agreed with her *see*.

Note that Jacky's use of *never* requires the addressee to refer back to the previous clause in order to fix its time-reference, like Nobby's *you never* in example (6) (later (18)).

If *never* does function as a way of securing the involvement of the addressee, we would expect it to occur in conversational contexts where addressee involvement is particularly important. It is no surprise, therefore, to find that *never* is frequently used in friendly arguments, as one of a cluster of addressee-oriented features which together can be interpreted as positive politeness devices, allowing the interlocutors to attend to each other's positive face as they disagree with each other. As an example of this consider (6) once more, this time in a still wider conversational context: the other addressee-oriented items are *all*, the second person pronouns, the address form *mate* and the intensifying overstatement *half killed*. The slang terms *boot* and *bollocks* can also be seen as positive politeness forms, as can the nonstandard verb form *done*:

(19) Benny: I went and grabbed him . . . he went and told him and Mike and all our other mates . . . and we all went up there and jumped on him
→ Nobby: you never . . . you you hit him with a stick then booted him and then I had to do the rest
Colin: I kicked him in the bollocks
Benny: I kicked him
Nobby: I done the most to him mate I half killed him

Similarly, *never* frequently occurs in a cluster of addressee-oriented forms at the beginning of a narrative, when the speaker needs to secure the interest of the interlocutor in order to keep the floor for an extended turn. In (20) we see *never* used in the formulaic introduction of a narrative (*I'll never forget the time when* . . .) as well as in the orientation section, together with multiple negation and the intensifier *shit*:

(20) Jacky: I . . . I'll never forget the time when I went up to bed . . . I heard a creaking sound . . . I was the only one in the house . . . my sister was with my mum and my brother was out . . . I went to bed early 'cos I never had nothing to do and I had no supper . . . and I heard a creaking upstairs and I was shit scared . . . I wouldn't stay . . . and I had all the lights on I was shit scared

Its use in the formulaic introduction of a narrative suggests that *never* can have a further role in the turn-taking system, engaging the involvement of the interlocutor and therefore allowing the current speaker to take an extended turn. It frequently occurs at locations for speaker change, when the current speaker is eliciting talk from others. In (21), for example, I was the fieldworker trying to elicit talk from a group of 13-year-old girls. My rather uninspired questions were not succeeding in eliciting more than very short utterances, but my utterance containing *never*, together with the quantifier *ever* in *whatever*, was at last followed by a longer sequence of talk, jointly constructed by two speakers:

(21) Jenny: What's your favourite food?
     Wendy: Favourite food?
     Marie: That's easy . . . chips
     Jenny: Chips
     Wendy: Roast
     Jenny: Roast dinner
     Wendy: Yes and for pudding gypsy tart
→   Jenny: Whatever's that? I've never heard of that
     Marie: Oh I can't explain 'cos . . . it's hard to explain isn't it?
     Wendy: Gypsy well it's pastry on the bottom   it's sort of
     Jenny: yes
     Marie: coffee
     Wendy: coffee on the top
     Marie: yeah coffee on the top
     Wendy: ugh

A similar example occurs in (22), where the monosyllabic Debbie finally launches into a longer turn after my reformulation of a negative with *not* into a negative clause with *never*:

(22) Jenny: Are you having fireworks this year?
     Debbie: yes
     Sharon: we have indoor fireworks as well
     Jenny: yes . . . I like them . . . sparklers
     Debbie: yes
     Sharon: not only sparklers . . . rockets
     Jenny: indoor rockets?
     Sharon: indoor rockets
     Jenny: oh I didn't know you could get those
     Debbie: yes
→   Jenny: I've never seen those
     Debbie: indoor rockets you know all the fireworks you can have outside
              you can have inside as well

Thus utterances containing *never* often have an interactional role that appears to reflect the function of *never* as an involvement strategy: speakers use *never* when they wish to take an extended turn, when they wish to show their interest in the contributions made by their interlocutor, or when they wish to attend to their interlocutor's positive face in potential face-threatening events such as arguments.

The serial effect

In all these examples speakers could equally well have chosen the alternative way of expressing negation, with *not*. Bolinger (1977) argues that variation in language always has a function: if we accept this possibility, we can explore a further dimension of English negation, that of the variable use of *not* and *never*. In particular, we can investigate what Scherre and Naro (1991; 1992) have termed the 'serial effect': a preference for similar clausal patterns to occur within a section of discourse. For example, Weiner and Labov (1983) discovered in their data a tendency for one passive form to lead to another; Schiffrin (1981), studying the use of tense in narratives, observed a general tendency for particular grammatical forms to cluster together; and several writers have identified a parallel effect for noun phrase concord, such that one plural marker tends to lead to another or, conversely, that the absence of a plural marker tends to lead to further absences within the same stretch of discourse (see Poplack 1980 on Spanish, and Scherre and Naro 1991 on Brazilian Portuguese).

In the conversations that I have analysed it is sometimes possible to observe a serial effect in the use of quantifiers. Although previous research on the serial effect has been quantitative, attempting to determine its statistical significance, it is inappropriate to apply this to *never*, since it is not always clear whether it is used as a straightforward negative or whether its temporal meaning comes into play. Problems of this kind are common when analysing syntactic variation (see Cheshire 1987 for discussion). Instead, it is revealing to analyse stretches of conversation where *never* or *ever* co-occur, and to observe the conversational outcome of this syntactic parallelism. In (23), for example, I introduce a quantifier with the question *Do girls ever have fights with each other?*. It would of course have been equally possible to have constructed an interrogative without *ever*, phrasing the question as *Do girls have fights with each other?*. The point of interest here, though, is not that *ever* is used, but that once it has been used it is repeated in the series of clauses that follow, on every occasion when it is possible to use the quantifier. Marie and Wendy cooperate in answering my question, with Wendy emphatically affirming that girls do indeed have fights; my next question again includes a quantifier, and the two girls continue to cooperate, with Marie choosing *never* for her negative clause, followed by Wendy's *ever* in her response to my small joke:

(23) Jenny: do girls ever have fights with each other?
      Marie: Yes
      Wendy: yes . . . you're telling me
→   Jenny: Have you ever been in a fight with a girl?
      Marie: yes I have I have
      Wendy: I have as well
→   Marie: but we've never fighted together
      Jenny: not yet
              (laughter)
→   Wendy: not yet you know I don't think we ever will

The sequence is unremarkable and the conversation proceeds harmoniously. In just the same way, the *not* strategy, once chosen as an expression of negation, is often continued. This is illustrated in (24), where the conversation develops from the previous discussion about gypsy tart:

(24) Jenny: Do you have dinner with her then is that where you've had it?
    Wendy: no we has it at school
    Jenny: Oh do you?
→ Marie: I has it at school but she don't
→ Wendy: No I go to home to dinner I used to stay to school dinners but I
          don't now
→ Jenny: Why don't you stay then?
→ Wendy: well they had pig's heart once and I didn't like that and they made
          me – eat it and I was sick   so my mum said I didn't have to
          stay anymore
    Jenny: yes

Syntactic harmony of this kind typically occurs when the conversation is proceeding harmoniously, with speakers cooperating to produce felicitous discourse as in the two extracts above. When the conversation takes a less harmonious turn, this can be marked by a disruption of the pattern of syntactic parallelism. Consider (25), where Nobby and Benny are teasing Ronny, first in a friendly fashion and then in a more hostile way. All three speakers use slang and much swearing, expressing positive politeness (Brown and Levinson 1987). Nobby's first teasing question rests on his professed presupposition that Ronny had stolen the carpet which was in his bag. Ronny negates the presupposition crossly, swearing and addressing Benny with the insult *you puff*. The other boys laugh, and the teasing then becomes more intense, with Nobby repeating the presupposition, despite Ronny's previous denial. Benny then insults Ronny, using *pretty* an adjective normally used to refer to girls (see Kuiper 1991 for discussion of male insults using terms that usually refer to females), and presupposing that they have succeeded in making Ronny angry. In this second part of the teasing Benny changes the syntax, choosing *never* rather than *not*, which was the negative marker that Ronny had introduced; Nobby continues the pattern of linguistic changes, using the slang expression *pinch* instead of their previous *nick* (also slang).

(25) Jenny: What's he got in there?
    Benny: A fucking carpet what else
    Nobby: Where'd you nick it?
→ Ronny: I fucking didn't nick it you puff
          (laughter)
→ Benny: You sure you never nicked it
    Nobby: Where'd you pinch it mate
    Benny: You don't half look pretty when you're angry
          (laughter)

In this case, then, the absence of syntactic parallelism mirrors the absence of conversational harmony, with the heightened teasing of the unfortunate Ronny.

In (26) there is a similar absence of syntactic parallelism. The extract is part of a conversation between a married couple, A and B, and two of their friends. Speaker B had been chastising her husband earlier for not reading enough, and she suggests that he reads the novel *Cold Comfort Farm*. A's reply is incongruous in this context, as is shown by the laughter with which it is received: not only is A male, but there had been no mention of babies in the previous discourse, and there is no obvious reason to anyone other than B why this remark is relevant. The absence of harmony in the content of A's contribution is matched by the absence of harmony in the syntax: B uses *never* whereas A responds with *not* (he could have said *I've never had a baby either*). The incongruous remark allows A and B to collaborate (after an intervening lateral sequence) in telling the story of A going to visit B in the evenings whilst B was in hospital after the birth of their baby, and A finding that B had laughed so much at the book that she had burst her stitches.

(26) B: Why darling why don't you bribe Jo to lend you her *Cold Comfort Farm*
         . . . you've never read it have you?
→   A: No but I haven't had a baby either
     { (laughter)
    B: { Oh honestly it saved my life in hospital it really did
    A: actually every evening I used to
    d: it's all right Arthur
         (approximately 6 seconds of intervening talk)
    A: anyway I used to go into the hospital in the evenings and find her . . .
         sort of in real great pain because she'd laughed so much . . . she's burnt
         a couple . . . burst a couple of stitches

                                                        (Quirk and Svartvik 1980: 626)

Thus the existence of two methods of negation allows speakers to generate discourse meanings over and above the local meaning of simple negation, by giving them the choice of following their interlocutor's selection of either *not* or of *ever* and *never*. The choice is available to all speakers of English, both 'standard' and 'nonstandard' varieties: (23), (24) and (25) are from my recordings of working-class adolescents, but (26), from the London–Lund corpus, is from the speech of educated adults.

Conclusion

As educated people, linguists are in a double bind. Try as we may, our intuitions will be influenced by norms based on standardised, written language. Analytical approaches based on intuitions, such as Klima (1964), are likely to be influenced by these norms. Even those approaches based on the empirical observation of language use are susceptible to the influence of educated norms, if they involve setting up predetermined categories within which to carry out an analysis (as in variationist analysis or in dialectology, for example). The case of *never* with reference to a single past event shows how a feature that is seen as 'incorrect' by guides to good usage has been incorrectly labelled 'nonstandard' by sociolinguists, and still more incorrectly labelled as 'nonexistent' by linguists working within a framework based on isolated sentences. I have argued that this has led us to overlook an important way of expressing negation in English, one that conforms to Jespersen's NEG First principle and that illustrates the continuation in present-day English of Jespersen's cycle. Yet in order to perform a linguistic analysis we obviously have to be educated people, trained in linguistics.

A way forward is to avoid using predetermined categories and to see instead how forms are used in discourse. This includes observing how speakers orient to the syntax that is used by their interlocutors, borrowing the methods used in conversation analysis. I hope to have shown that in the case of *never* this allows us to recognise a hitherto neglected yet important method of expressing negation in English, which involves the interlocutor in relating the negative form to the linguistic and nonlinguistic context in which it occurs, in order to determine the extent of its temporal reference. It is therefore especially well suited to the demands of face-to-face interaction, and this must surely account for the fact that throughout the history of English speakers have used it as a way of reinforcing a negative marker.

It is of course only by observing *never* in its conversational context that it is possible to observe its interactional functions and to resolve some of the questions that have perplexed linguists until now. Thus our understanding of the present-day syntax of a language can benefit from taking a more comprehensive approach than is usual, considering a syntactic form from the point of view of its history, its normative status, its syntactic relationships, its discourse functions and its occurrence in conversation.

Note

1. This can be seen clearly in different versions of some early texts. For example, Tieken-Boon van Ostade (1995: 78) points to the use of *never* with a quantifier function as an alternant to *no* in the first pair of phrases and as an alternant to *none* in the second pair:

   that there is no knyght woll fyght for hym (Winchester edn, 139. 1–2)
   that there nys neuer a knyghte wylle fyghte for hym (Caxton edn, 99. 3–4)

   that never man drew hit but he were dede or maymed (Winchester edn 987. 17–18)
   that none ne drewe it but he were dede or maymed (Caxton edn, 484. 32–3)

References

Bolinger, D. (1977) *Meaning and form*, London: Longman.
Bossuyt, A. (1983) 'Historical function grammar: an outline of an integrated theory of language change', in S. Dik (ed.), *Advances in Functional Grammar*, Dordrecht: Foris, pp. 301–25.
Brown, P. and Levinson, S. (1987) *Politeness: some universals in language usage*, Cambridge: Cambridge Univesity Press.
Chafe, W. (1982) 'Integration and involvement in speaking, writing, and oral literature', in D. Tannen (ed.), *Spoken and written language: exploring orality and literacy*, Norwood, NJ: Ablex, pp. 35–53.
Chafe, W. (1986) 'Writing in the perspective of speaking', in C.R. Cooper and S. Greenbaum (eds), *Studying writing: linguistic approaches*, Beverley Hills, CA: Sage, pp. 12–39.

Cheshire, J. (1982) *Variation in an English dialect: a sociolinguistic study*, Cambridge: Cambridge University Press.

—— (1987) 'Syntactic variation, the linguistic variable and sociolinguistic theory', *Linguistics* 25(2): pp. 257–82.

—— (1989) 'Addressee-oriented features in spoken discourse', *York Papers in Linguistics* 13: pp. 49–64.

—— (in press) 'Involvement in standard and nonstandard English', in J. Cheshire and D. Stein (eds), *Taming the vernacular: from dialect to written standard language*, Harlow: Longman.

Cheshire, J., Edwards, V. and Whittle, P. (1989) 'Urban British dialect grammar: the question of dialect levelling', *English Worldwide* 10: pp. 185–225.

Coupland, N. (1988) *Dialect in use*, Cardiff: University of Wales Press.

Fowler, (1965) *Modern English usage*, 2nd edn. London: Oxford University Press.

Gumperz, J.J. (1982) *Discourse strategies*, Cambridge: Cambridge University Press.

Holm, J. (1988) *Pidgins and creoles*, vol. i. Cambridge: Cambridge University Press.

Holmes, J. (1990) 'Hedges and boosters in men's and women's speech', *Language and Communication* 10(3): pp. 185–205.

Horn, L.R. (1989) *A natural history of negation*, Chicago: University of Chicago Press.

Hughes, G.A. and Trudgill, P. (1979) *English accents and dialects: an introduction to social and regional varieties of British English*. London: Edward Arnold.

Jeanneret, T. (1992) 'Modes de structuration en conversation', in G. Lüdi (ed.), *Approches linguistiques de l'interaction. Bulletin CILA* (Commission Interuniversitaire Suisse de Linguistique Appliquée, Neuchâtel, Switzerland) 57: pp. 59–69.

Jespersen, O. (1917) *Negation in English and other languages*, Copenhagen: Høst.

—— (1982) [1905] *Growth and structure of the English language*, London: Edward Arnold.

Klima, E. (1964) 'Negation in English', in J.A. Fodor and J.J. Katz (eds), *The structure of language*, Englewood Cliffs, NJ: Prentice-Hall, pp. 246–323.

Kuiper, K. (1991) 'Sporting formulae in New Zealand English: two models of male solidarity', in J. Cheshire (ed.), *English around the world: sociolinguistic perspectives*, Cambridge: Cambridge University Press, pp. 200–211.

Labov, W. (1973) 'Where do grammars stop'? in R. Shuy (ed.), *Sociolinguistics: current trends and prospects*, Washington, DC: Georgetown University Press, pp. 43–88.

—— (1984) 'Intensity', in D. Schiffrin (ed.), *Meaning, form and use in context*, Washington, DC: Georgetown University Press, pp. 43–70.

Orton, H., Barry, M.V., Halliday, W.J., Tilling, P.M. and Wakelin, M.F. (1963–9) *Survey of English Dialects*, 4 vols. Leeds: E.J. Arnold.

Quirk, R., Greenbaum, S., Leech, G. and Svartvik, J. (1985) *A comprehensive grammar of the English language*, London: Longman.

Poplack, S. (1980) 'The notion of the plural in Puerto Rican Spanish: Competing constraints on /s/ deletion', in W. Labov (ed.), *Locating language in time and space*, New York: Academic, pp. 55–67.

Scherre, M.M.P.S. and Naro, A.J. (1991) 'Marking in discourse: "birds of a feather"'. *Language Variation and Change* 3(1): pp. 23–32.

—— (1992) 'The serial effect on internal and external variables', *Language Variation and Change* 4(1): pp. 1–14.

Schriffin, D. (1981) 'Tense variation in narrative', *Language* 57(1): pp. 45–62.

Sundby, B., Bjørge, A.K. and Haugland, K.E. (1991) *A dictionary of English normative grammar 1700–1800*. Amsterdam: John Benjamins.

Svartvik, J. and Quirk, R. (1980) *A corpus of English conversation*, Lund: Gleerup.

Tannen, D. (1989) *Talking choices: repetition, dialogue and imagery in conversational discourse*, Cambridge: Cambridge University Press.

Tieken-Boon van Ostade, I. (1995) *The two versions of Malory's Morte Darthur*, Amsterdam: Boydell & Brewer.

Tottie, G. (1991) *Negation in English speech and writing: a study in variation*, London: Academic Press.

Trudgill, P. (1984) 'Standard English in England' in P. Trudgill (ed.), *Language in the British Isles*, Cambridge: Cambridge University Press, pp. 32–44.

Weiner, J. and Labov, W. (1983) 'Constraints on the agentless passive', *Journal of Linguistics* 19: pp. 29–58.

Wood, F.T. (1981) *Current English usage*, London: Macmillan.

9

Dialect acquisition

J.K. Chambers

Originally published in *Language*, 68(3) (1992).

Immigrants from one dialect region to another acquire features of the new dialect with varying degrees of proficiency. In modern societies regional mobility is commonplace, and for modern dialectology, involved as it is with variability, mechanisms of change, and adaptation, it is a rich source of hypotheses. This article postulates eight general principles by which immigrants adapt dialectologically to their new surroundings, based mainly on results of a developmental study of six Canadian youngsters in two families who moved to southern England in 1983 and 1984, with supporting evidence from several other studies. The principles provide a set of empirically testable hypotheses about the determinants of dialect acquisition.

Dialects in contact

One of the most common sociolinguistic situations finds people moving from one dialect region to another, and (more or less) adopting features of the new dialect. There is no reason to doubt that such situations always existed, but certainly they have multiplied and become commonplace in the last century and a half, with increased mobility of all kinds – geographical, occupational, and social.

Presumably such movements have been historically significant in linguistic developments. The first two or three centuries in the history of the English language can be viewed as waves of adaptations among the dialect-speaking Germanic invaders, and many other languages have similar geneses in the convergence of founding populations speaking mutually intelligible dialects. While language historians, especially those in the philological tradition, often attribute otherwise inexplicable developments to contact among dialects, neither dialectologists nor linguists have expended much energy on discovering the actual mechanisms of dialect acquisition. Indeed, for the first century or so of systematic dialectology, while dialect goegraphy held a dominant position, mobile populations were purposely excluded. Thus, for instance, for the Linguistic Atlas of the United States and Canada (LAUSC), Kurath prescribed a consultant who is 'a native of the community (preferably also his forebears) and [has] lived there all or most of his life' (1972: 12). Similarly, the chief fieldworker for the Survey of English dialects (Ellis 1953, quoted by Wells 1973: 45) described a consultant who is 'just the right type' as follows: 'a man of seventy or so, still mentally alert and with an excellent memory for the days of his youth, a broad speaker, with an agricultural background, born in the village of native parents, married to a wife who is herself a native of the locality . . .' Similar preferences for immobile consultants were expressed in all major dialect geography projects (see Chambers & Trudgill 1980: 33–35 et passim).

The reason for the preference is not hard to understand. Dialect geography studied regional speech patterns qualitatively, and concentrating on the speech of nonmobile, older, rural, predominantly male consultants – known acronymically as NORMs – elicited relatively stable, regionally distinctive, highly differentiated speech samples. Variability was peripheral, and only occasionally drew comment from the investigators. In an instructive exchange more than forty years ago, Davis & McDavid (1950) focused attention on the variability found among ten speakers interviewed for LAUSC in a 'transition area' in northwestern Ohio. Their purpose in doing so was to illustrate 'the problems of dialect formation in this country, where speech mixture must have been the rule from the earliest colonial times'. In a prescient response, Reed & Spicer (1952), who regularly confronted variability as LAUSC researchers in California where NORMs were harder to find, demonstrated that 'the speech patterns of transition areas grow much clearer when viewed as quantitative rather than qualitative phenomena'. They ran the data through a statistical analysis of covariance in what was perhaps the first such application in dialectology. It was also, for several years, a unique application.

In the last two decades, dialectology has been largely re-formed as a quantitative discipline, in much the terms Reed & Spicer envisaged. The turning point undoubtedly came with the importation from Labovian sociolinguistics of the linguistic variable as a structural unit. Dialect geography no longer dominates the discipline, but recent innovations from diverse sources point to its revitalization (for example, Goebl 1982, Cavalli-Sforza & Wang 1986, Kirk *et al.* 1992). Direct descendants of the LAUSC project, faced with extending the survey westward from the relatively settled Atlantic seaboard into newer, more mobile communities, are not only applying quantitative instruments but developing methods of their own (for example, Kretzschmar *et al.* 1989). Studies of isolated dialects, real or imagined, have given way to studies of dialects in contact, as linguistic variation becomes the focus of the discipline. Trudgill's 1986 book *Dialects in contact*, a synopsis of and speculation on patterns of accommodation, diffusion, mixture, and other interdialectal processes, makes a convenient landmark for the growing recognition of mobile populations at the heart of dialect studies.

My purpose in this article is to postulate some general principles which determine the acquisition of dialect features by people transplanted from one region to another. The centerpiece of the research is a developmental study I carried out with six Canadian youngsters in two families that moved to southern England in 1983 and 1984. In interviews two years apart, the youngsters discussed the social circumstances of their old and new neighborhoods, evaluated taped accents, identified various objects on picture cards, and read word lists. The methodology and data of the study have been presented in some detail in two proceedings papers (Chambers 1988, 1990), and will be repeated here as frugally as possible, with only enough detail to elucidate the general principle under discussion.

The eight principles discussed below represent generalizations extrapolated from the behavior of my six subjects as they went about eliminating features of their native Canadian English (CE) dialects and acquiring features of the Southern England English (SEE) dialects of their new home region. The subjects are not, of course, a random sample. Although they almost certainly constitute the entire population of adolescent Canadians acquiring dialect in south Oxfordshire at the time, they are a minute sample of the dialect acquirers in any place at any time. From this view point, one source of future emendations to the principles posited below should be traceable to their representativeness. Nevertheless, these six subjects, in relaxed but controlled interviews, provided considerable linguistic data as an analytic base, enough certainly to delimit if not to eliminate the dependence upon impressions or intuitions. The subjects, because they were few, may well have been subjected to closer scrutiny than would otherwise be possible, thus finding, I hope, a workable ratio between sample size and analytical returns (Milroy 1987: Ch. 2). As a further check, the existing literature was searched scrupulously for supplementary data. Direct precursors for this study of dialect acquisition are not plentiful; and they are mostly from Northern Europe, as indicated by the works cited below, except for Sibata 1958 – a pioneering study hitherto almost completely unknown outside Japan – and Payne's meticulous work (1975, 1980) on New Yorkers and others moving into a Philadelphia suburb. Such studies provide useful evidence at several points.

It is probably worthwhile at the outset to attempt a distinction between accommodation and acquisition. 'Accommodation' is widely used, since its introduction in social psychology (Giles & Smith 1979, Trudgill 1981), to characterize an individual's modifications of accent and dialect as a direct response to a particular interlocutor in a particular setting, and is transitory linguistic behavior. Trudgill distinguishes 'short-term' and 'long-term accommodation' (1986: Ch. 1), where the latter appears to be a sort of basic level of dialect adjustment maintained by the individual in all transactions in the contact area, while the former seems to be a transitory adjustment above the basic level in response to a particular social circumstance. The responses of my six subjects might possibly be construed as 'long-term accommodation', but I suspect, for reasons given in the next paragraph, that they are not accommodating at all under the circumstances, and that the dialect changes revealed in their speech are, instead, nonephemeral acquisitions. This is also a possibility mentioned by Trudgill (1986: 40), when he notes that 'if accommodation, through the adoption of a feature from an alien linguistic variety, is frequent enough, then that feature may become a permanent part of a speaker's accent or dialect, even replacing original features.'[1]

My evidence against accommodation and for the more permanent acquisition follows simply from the fact that the Canadian youngsters were interviewed individually in their Oxfordshire homes by me, in my normal, unaccommodated, middle-class CE accent. The subjects had no reason to accommodate to me in any direction whatever, and there is every indication that they did not. Although sociolinguists and, increasingly, dialectologists usually take some pains to elicit relatively unmonitored vernacular speech, for my purposes the more conventional interview segments with relatively self-conscious speech served best, because the SEE features that occurred in the subjects' CE dialects in this register could reasonably be considered irrepressible acquisitions rather than ephemeral accommodations. The lexical, pronunciation, and phonological variations analyzed and described below are based on data from picture-card elicitations and phrase-list readings, which not only provide a common database for all subjects but also a uniform style. The subjects did not guess that the multitask, discursive interview was specifically investigating their dialects – they generally guessed that I was checking their reading abilities or something similar, which I took to mean, since the actual reading they did lasted about one minute, their educational skills. At the end of the interviews, when they were asked directly about accents, every one of them stated that they sounded 'more English' when they were talking to classmates and teachers than when they were talking to me.[2] Consequently, I assume that the SEE features I recorded in their speech were those they could no longer control or suppress.

The distinction between long-term accommodation and dialect acquisition may, with further research, prove to be terminological rather than substantive. Nothing rests on it here, beyond the fact that the boundary between the two is vague in the present state of research.

Also perhaps terminological, and to that extent inconsequential, is my use of the term 'principles' to refer to the eight generalizations about dialect acquisition that follow. Although 'principles' might allow someone to infer an air of fixedness that they are not intended to have, at least that term seems more neutral than any other I could think of. Another possibility, 'strategies', lends them an air of deliberateness, in the sense of 'learning strategies', which is certainly inappropriate. By whatever blanket term, the eight principles are postulated as a set of empirically testable hypotheses about the determinants of dialect acquisition. As fine-grained sociolinguistic studies of dialect contact become more common, it is hoped that these principles will provide some reference points around which issues, evidence, and refutations may converge.

Eight principles of dialect acquisition

For each of the eight principles 2.1–2.8, the statement is first defined and then illustrated from my survey, with further illustration from other studies wherever available. Their interrelations are discussed in the final section.

Lexical replacements are acquired faster than pronunciation and phonological variants

Lexical replacements are different words for the same objects in the two dialect regions; the SEE/CE variants elicited by picture cards are listed in Table 9.1. Pronunciation variants are individual words that are the same in both dialect areas but sound different; the SEE/CE variants, elicited in the same way, are listed in Table 9.2. Phonological variants are rule-governed or systematic phonetic differences in the two dialect areas such that whole sets of lexical items are affected; several examples come up in the discussions of principles 2.3–2.5.[3]

The immediate evidence for principle 2.1 comes from the contrast between Fig. 9.1, which shows the performance of the Canadian youngsters in replacing lexical items, and Fig. 9.2, their performance in adopting SEE pronunciation variants, or Figs. 9.5–9 below, their performances in altering their phonology.

In Fig. 9.1, as in all other figures but one, the six Canadian subjects are represented by grey bars with their ages indicated underneath. In the background of Fig. 9.1, and in most of the other figures, there are black bars showing the performances of a control group of English youngsters, matched in age and gender with the Canadians. For both groups the items were elicited as responses to a set of picture cards, without prompting of any kind from the interviewer. The quantification shows the percentage of SEE items among the responses; subjects who offered both SEE and CE words, as some Canadians did, were counted as half in the tally. The purpose of the control group was, of course, to check on assumptions about the features of the SEE dialect that the Canadian youngsters were being exposed to. However, the results for the control group are occasionally interesting in their own right, and worthy of comment, albeit briefly. Their

Table 9.1 Southern England English (SEE)/Canadian English (CE) lexical variants

coach/bus	*dustbin/garbage can*	*(hand)bag/purse*
caravan/(house) trailer	*cooker/stove*	*jumper/sweater*
sledge, sled/sleigh	*spanner/wrench*	*trousers/pants*
estate care/station wagon	*chips/(french)fries*	*Wellington boots/rubber boots*
windscreen/windshield	*pushchair/stroller*	*plaster/band-aid*
bonnet/hood	*cot/crib*	*plait/braid*
boot/trunk	*pram/baby carriage*	*fringe/bangs*
queue/line-up, line	*nappy/diaper*	*(tele)phone box/phone booth*
	vest/undershirt	

Table 9.2 SEE/CE pronunciation variants

garage	[gáɹɑ́dʒ] or [[gáɹɪdʒ]/[gəɹɑ́dʒ] or [gəɹɑ́ʒ]
half	[hɑf]/[hæf]
banana	[bənɑ́nə]/[bənǽnə]
tomato	[tʰəmɑ́to] or [tʰəmáto]/[tʰəméydo] or [tʰəméyro]
yogurt	[yɒ́gɜːt]/[yówgət]

Table 9.3 Group scores for the Canadian subjects (%)

Lexical replacements	52.3
Pronunciation replacements	26.67
Phonological variants	24.9

pronunciation and phonological variants not only differ from lexical replacements but are quantitatively similar to one another. The significance of this similarity will be discussed when we get to principle 2.6.

Lexical replacements occur rapidly in the first stage of dialect acquisition and then slow down
Although lexical replacements progress rapidly in the beginning, they soon fall off. In Fig. 9.3 the individual scores of the Canadians are shown developmentally, two years apart. (Note that the 17-year-old is missing because he returned to Canada to start university just before the second round of interviews.) The increments are generally slight. The only noteworthy increase is Dan's, up by 40%; but at the time of the first interview, as noted above, Dan was lagging noticeably. Now he is perfectly aligned with his age-mate, and with the rest of the group in general. Although he started later than the others, his progress seems to have followed the same pattern.

It appears, then, that dialect acquirers make most of the lexical replacements they will make in the first two years. Words not replaced in that period might well remain unchanged, as relics of the immigrant's place of origin.

This characteristic early burst of lexical replacement can be viewed more closely in an apparent-time study of three groups of British nannies working in Toronto (based on data from Debra Anderson, personal communication, 1988). The subjects were three groups of ten nannies, all of British origin, distinguished by the length of time they had been in Toronto. One group had arrived within three months of the survey, a second group had been there 4–12 months, and the third group more than a year. As the caption of Fig. 9.4 shows, the nannies were surveyed for, among other things, their choices of certain homely objects which they would necessarily encounter working in a domestic setting (inasmuch as 'truck/lorry' is taken as a toy). The interviewer, Debra Anderson, was herself a British nanny, and so the interviewees had no reason to accommodate their speech to her.

As Fig. 9.4 clearly shows, the individual nannies progress at different rates in the very short term, much as the two 13-year-olds did in the CE/SEE study (Fig. 9.1 above). In the longer term, they end up at roughly the same point, with 50–80% of the items replaced. This apparent-time study provides an exploded view, as it were, of the developments that lie behind the progress of the Canadian youngsters in Fig. 9.1, reflecting a time similar to the most settled group (between one and two years) of the nannies.

Simple phonological rules progress faster than complex ones
Turning to phonology, it is necessary to distinguish between simple rules and complex ones. Simple rules are automatic processes that admit no

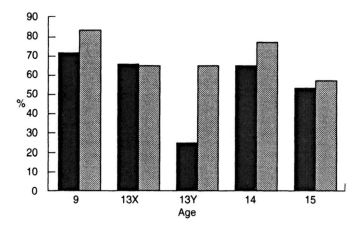

Fig. 9.3 Lexical replacement scores in interviews two years apart

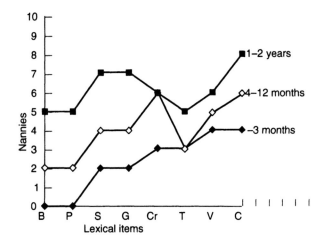

Fig. 9.4 Lexical replacements by British nannies working in Toronto

exceptions. Complex rules have opaque outputs, that is, they have exceptions or variant forms, or – a type of complexity that comes up especially in dialect acquisition, as we will see below – they have in their output a new or additional phoneme. This distinction is equivalent to Payne's 'low-level rule[s] of phonetic conditioning' and higher-level rules 'often conditioned by factors of an abstract nature; for example, boundaries, grammatical categories, and individual lexical items' (1975: 14).

A well-known example of a simple rule is T-Voicing, by which a medial /t/ is voiced to [d] when it follows a vowel or /r/ and precedes an unstressed syllable. The rule is ubiquitous in North American English, and as a result numerous pairs of words are homophones in CE, such as *putting/pudding, petal/pedal*, and *hearty/hardy*.

As Fig. 9.5 shows, the Canadian youngsters in southern England have made considerable progress in eliminating T-Voicing from their accents. The nine-year-old has no instances of it at all (= 100%), and both his brother Hal and the 14-year-old from the other family, Sam, have very few instances, at 80% and 90%. The other three score 20%. As expected, the English control subjects all score 100%.

By contrast, Vowel Backing is phonologically complex. The term refers to the contemporary SEE reflex of the lengthening and backing of ME /ă/ ('short a') before voiceless anterior fricatives, as in *plaster, bath, laughing, brass*, and *class* and before clusters of /n/ + obstruent as in *dancing, branch, France, plant*, and *tansmission*. In SEE these words have the vowel [ɑ]. The change began in London in the 18th century, too late to affect CE or most other varieties of North American English, which typically have the vowel [æ] in these words as in other words with ME /ă/.

While there seems to be no question about the complexity of Vowel Backing, there are good reasons to question its status as a rule in SEE. One reason for thinking it might be lexicalized rather than rule-governed is that its environments are never derived, and so there are no alternations between [ɑ] and [æ]. Another is that there are several words with the appropriate environments that are exceptions, that is, they invariably have the front vowel rather than the back one; examples are *cafeteria, classic*, (Roman Catholic) *Mass, ant* (as opposed to *aunt*), *pants*, and *cancer*. A plausible reason for thinking it might be rule-governed is that several words vary, even in RP ('received Pronunciation') where variation is relatively rare, such as *graph, plastic, stance*, and *transport* (for a more complete

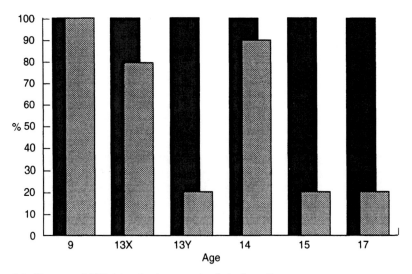

Fig. 9.5 Absence of T-Voicing in the speech of six Canadians

list, see Wells 1982: 135). Whatever its status in the phonologies of native SEE speakers, Vowel Backing occurs mainly in frequent words and offers dialect learners ample opportunity to infer a rule (spuriously or not) from the available evidence.

The complexity of Vowel Backing is suggested in Fig. 9.6 by the fact that the English control subjects did not respond categorically, as four of the six scored 90%. The difference depended upon their pronunciation of *transmission*, the only word included on the interview list that is pronounced variably in SEE. The Canadian youngsters show a very erratic response to Vowel Backing. Whereas Max has it regularly in his accent, ironically outscoring his age-mate in the control group by backing the vowel in *transmission* as well as all the others, the older subjects are making very fitful progress, if any, with respect to this complex feature. The difference here and in Fig. 9.5, the simple rule, is the basis of this principle.

Dramatic evidence of the need to distinguish complex rules from simple ones in dialect acquisition came out of Payne's work with adolescents in the highly mobile Philadelphia suburb of King of Prussia. First Payne documents the 'notable success' of the out-of-state children acquiring the 'phonetic variables' (1980: 149–56), equivalent in our terms to noncomplex rules. For example, (uw) and (ow) require the fronting of the onsets of /uw/ and /ow/, and (oy) requires the raising of the onset of /oy/ – in all cases straightforward, categorical phonetic adjustments. For more than 50 children in twelve immigrant families, Payne showed that 52–68% had fully acquired the Philadelphia system, and 30–48% had partially acquired it.

When she turned to the complex rules, the success rate indicated a different pattern. The rule called 'short-a' provides a notorious instance of complexity. Essentially, it involves the tensing and raising of /æ/ toward [eːə], but the set of conditioning factors complicates it enormously. It never occurs in 'weak' words such as *am*, *and*, or modal *can*, or before voiced

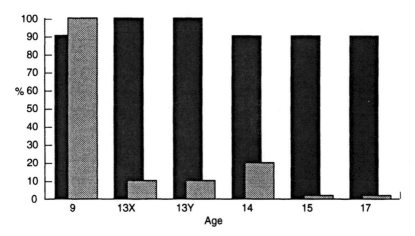

Fig. 9.6 Presence of Vowel Backing in the speech of six Canadians

obstruents except for the three words *mad, bad,* and *glad;* but it occurs invariably before final anterior voiceless fricatives, as in *laugh, path,* and *class,* though never in, say, *smash;* and also invariably before final anterior nasals as in *ham* and *man,* though never in, say, *hang.* Elsewhere it occurs variably, before liquids, as in *pal,* and before nonfinal anterior voiceless fricatives and nasals, as in *traffic* and *hammer.*[4]

Payne shows, perhaps not surprisingly, that none of the out-of-state children has mastered this Philadelphia system. What was surprising was her discovery that children of out-of-state parents failed to master it even if they were born in King of Prussia. The subjects who did master it were those who were born there of Phildelphian parents. Of the contrasting success rates, Payne says, 'The incomplete acquisition [of complex rules] indicates that children do not freely restructure and/or reorganize their grammars up to the age of 14 but that they do have the ability to add lower level rules' (1980: 175). In the early stages of dialect acquisition, as with the Canadian children in England, this difference manifests itself as simple rules progressing faster than complex ones.

Two other studies offer cogent support for principle 2.3 from very different contact situations. Vousten & Bongaerts (1990) studied the acquisition of local dialect features by people moving into Venray, Limburg, from other parts of Holland. With respect to two features, contemporary Dutch reflexes of Proto-West Germanic *î and *û, the immigrants are progressing much better with the former than with the latter, as indicated by the results summarized in Table 9.4. Phonologically, the two features differ in that the former is simple, involving a change from [ɛi] in the old accent to [i] in the Venray accent, whereas the latter is complex, in that words with [œy] in the old accent sometimes have [y] and sometimes have [u] in Venray. The word *pijp* 'pipe', for instance, pronounced [pɛip] in the old dialect area, is pronounced [pip] in Venray, without exception, and more than 60% of the immigrants have succeeded in making this change. But the word *muis* 'mouse', formerly [mœys], is sometimes [mys] and oftentimes [mus] in Venray; as a result, not only do more than 40% of the immigrants retain

Table 9.4 Acquisition of regional accents for two features in Venray, Holland (from Vousten & Bongaerts 1990)

Proto-West Germanic *î	Immigrants [ɛi]	[i]	Natives [ɛi]	[i]
strijk	31.6	68.4	2.6	97.4
pijp	36.8	63.2	0.0	100.0
rijke	28.9	71.1	0.0	100.0

Proto-West Germanic *û	Immigrants [œy]	[y]	[u]	Natives [œy]	[y]	[u]
duim	48.6	21.6	29.7	0.0	28.9	71.1
muis	42.9	22.9	34.2	0.0	32.4	67.6
duizend	40.5	40.5	18.9	0.0	81.6	18.4

their old pronunciation but a disproportionate number who make the change choose the minority Venray pronunciation, presumably because it is phonetically more similar to their old one. The difference in their competence in acquiring these two features is consistent with the simplicity and complexity of the two features.

Further evidence supporting the principle that simple phonological rules progress faster than complex ones comes from a survey by Wells (1973) of the speech of 36 emigrants from Jamaica in London, England. Wells applied the same basic methodology that I used in the CE/SEE study, recording data from his subjects and quantifying instances of old and new phonology. In interpreting his results, he too found it necessary to distinguish simple and complex phonology, separating, as he puts it, 'the variables which concern only phonetic realization, needing no phoneme split and no change in phoneme distribution or incidence', from those variables that do (1973: 118).

An example of a simple rule is the Jamaican Creole insertion of /j/ following velars and preceding low vowels in words like /kjat/ 'cat', /kjaːr/ 'car', /gjas/ 'gas', and /gjaːdn/ 'garden'. Wells notes that eliminating rules like yod-insertion is relatively easy 'since the context in which they apply can be formulated simply as a given phonetic environment' (1973: 33; also, on the same rule, 94–95).[5] In the terms used here, the rule is automatic, and admits no exceptions.

An example of a complex rule is the unmerging of Jamaican Creole (JC) /ie/ or Jamaican English (JE) /eː/ before tautosyllabic /r/. Jamaicans have homophones for *steer/stare* (JC/stier/ or JE/steːr/), whereas RP distinguishes them as 'stiə(r)/ and /stɛə(r)/. The unmerging takes in numerous items, including *fear/fair* and *fare, beer/bare* and *bear, cheer/chair, hear/hair* (1973: 34–35, 108–10). In the terms used here, the rule has opaque outputs, since not all instances of JC /ie/ become RP /iə/, and it requires acquiring a new diphthong /ɛə/, otherwise not found in JC or JE.

As principle 2.3 predicts, the London Jamaicans are progressing faster with yod-deletion than with the unmerging of /ie/, with index scores of 79% and 20% respectively. Wells's study has eight other rules that we would call simple and three other complex ones, with predictable differences in his subjects' responses to them. His conclusion (1973: 117–18) is as follows:

> The evidence gathered in this survey of the speech of Jamaicans in London thus supports the view that adolescents and adults, faced with a new linguistic environment, can adapt their speech to a certain extent by modifying the phonetic realization of their phonemes; but they do not on the whole succeed in acquiring new phonological oppositions or in altering the distributional restraints on their phonology.

Though his terms are slightly different from ours, the results are entirely consistent with principle 2.3.

Before turning to the next principle, which also appeals to the notion of phonological complexity, it is worth noting that the notion of complexity is relative, not absolute. When comparisons are carried out between dialects that are grossly different, as are CE and SEE, for instance, it may appear that complexity can be determined from the intrinsic properties of the phonological process itself. When the dialects are more closely related, or the compared features are more similar, apparent complexity may prove illusory.

Exactly this situation arises in a study of immigrants to Bergen, Norway from rural Stril (Kerswill 1985: 94–96, 149n., 153–54). The main phonological feature in the study is Bergen schwa-lowering, a variable process which lowers and fronts posttonic [ə] in utterance-final position and before other 'syntactically conditioned' pauses. Standard forms like /skúl:ə/ *skule* 'school' and /hʉ́:sə/*huset* 'the house' are sometimes pronounced utterance-finally with final [ɛ], [æ], or [a]. The feature is a marker of Bergen speech, where it increases in frequency down the social hierarchy and in lower age groups. To Kerswill's initial surprise, the Stril immigrants in Bergen proved to be very competent at acquiring schwa-lowering regardless of their age or other social factors. His closer analysis of the Stril accent then revealed that it already includes a rule merging [ə] with 'unstressed' [ɛ] in utterance-final positions. In order to acquire the Bergen phonology at this point, the Stril immigrants need only modify the phonetic output of an established feature in their speech.

As Kerswill puts it, the discovery that Stril as well as Bergen has a schwa-peripheralization process 'makes the late movers' apparent acquisition of a relatively complex phonological feature much easier to explain'. In our terms, the immigrants already had the complex rule in their phonology and needed only to adjust its phonetic output. Until Kerswill recognized this, it was the competence of the 'late movers', that is, those who moved into the new dialect region after age 17, that seemed anomalous. Implicit in this is an expectation that complex acquisitions will be age-graded, a correlation that is explicated in the next principle.

Acquisition of complex rules and new phonemes splits the population into early acquirers and later acquirers
One obvious observation about Fig. 9.6 above, charting the progress of the Canadian subjects in the complex rule of Vowel Backing, is the precipitous decline from the youngest speaker to the others. Whereas lexical replacements (Fig. 9.1) showed a gradual decline from youngest to oldest, and T-Voicing (Fig. 9.5), the simple rule, showed sustained, if erratic, progress across the age groups, Vowel Backing shows a sharp peak and a deep valley, with nothing much in between.

A similar pattern emerges for another complex rule, Low Vowel Merger. Standard CE has merged the two low back lax vowels, unlike standard SEE and United States varieties.[6] As a result, CE has homophones for word pairs like *bobble/bauble, tot/taught, offal/awful*, and so on, sometimes with the slightly rounded vowel /ɒ/ in both words (Walker 1975) but usually with unrounded /ɑ/ in both. Both columns of Table 9.5 are pronounced with the same vowel in Canada, but they have different vowels in SEE, as indicated. In order to acquire SEE, a Canadian must differentiate the two groups and learn to pronounce a new phoneme.

Fig. 9.7 shows that, as a group, the Canadians are not doing particularly well in acquiring this complex feature. Just as the Jamaican Londoners

Table 9.5 Low back lax vowels in SEE merged as CE
/ɒ/

SEE /ɒ/	SEE /ɔː/
Don	*Dawn*
hot	*water*
cot	*lawn*
jolly	*Paul*
blond	*strawberry*
tot	*naughty*
knot	*caught*
rotten	*raw*
lots	*hawks*
Scots	*slaughter*

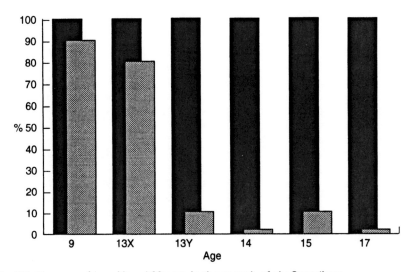

Fig. 9.7 Absence of Low Vowel Merger in the speech of six Canadians

faltered over the unmerging of /ie/, so four of the six Canadian youngsters show little or no response in the unmerging of /ɑ/. The bars measure the percentage of paired words in the phrase list, as in Table 9.5, that occurred with different vowels. The English control subjects in the background, perhaps needless to say, distinguished the vowels in all pairs. Two of the older Canadians, the 14-year-old and the 17-year-old, have made no progress whatever, with the same vowel in all pairs, and two others distinguish the vowels in only one of the ten pairs. Viewed alongside this general lack of progress, the performances of the two youngest subjects, with 90% and 80% unmerging, seem quite dramatic. The acquisition of this complex phonological feature thus splits the Canadian youngsters into early and late acquirers.

The difference between early and late acquirers is clearly age-graded. Max, who was seven years old when he emigrated, is an early acquirer for both the presence of Vowel Backing and the absence of Low Vowel Merger. His brother Hal, first interviewed at 13 after arriving in England at 11, is the other early acquirer of the absence of Low Vowel Merger. The fact that the two early acquirers are brothers might suggest that family affiliation is a relevant social factor. Note, however, that the 15-year-old, whose progress on this feature is very slight, is their sister. Although a much larger sample population would be necessary to consider family affiliation generally, it does not seem relevant in this instance or at any other point in the results for the Canadian youngsters.

The fact that age is critical in dialect acquisition will hardly be surprising in view of the well-known advantages of youth in both first-language and second-language acquisition (Long 1990). Indeed, it would be much more surprising if there were no evidence of the critical period in the results. But its effect is not uniform. While age apparently has a mild effect in the acquisition of lexical and pronunciation variants (Figs. 9.1 and 9.2), as noted earlier, it has its most telling effect in the acquisition of complex phonological features.

Although early acquirers and late acquirers correlate roughly with younger and older subjects, the age boundary between the two is indeterminate, making it prudent to resist identifying early acquirers by age group. For instance, Dan was the same age, 13, as Hal at the time of the first interview but did not join him among the early acquirers, and in fact had made no more headway with respect to ridding his accent of Low Vowel Merger two years later.

The indeterminacy of the age boundary is also evident in a pioneering study of dialect acquisition in Japan. Sibata (1958), at the conclusion of a large-scale study of dialect acquisition, postulated the GENGO-KEISEI-KI, literally 'the language-forming period', equivalent to the critical period hypothesis of Western linguistics, in the following terms: [7]

> In 1949, about 500 children were still left in Shirakawa city who were displaced directly from Tokyo and Yokohama to avoid bombardment. We interviewed every child and found that children who came there before six or seven years of age had adopted Shirakawa dialect almost perfectly in the course of five or six years, while those who came at the age of 14 or more were not affected at all by that dialect.

Sibata's evidence is based on pitch-accent features in the two dialects rather than on segmental phonology, but his age groupings are consistent with other results. A person seven or under will almost certainly acquire a new dialect perfectly, and a person 14 or over almost certainly will not. In between those ages, people will vary.

Tentative results in a study by David & Montgomery (1988) suggest that slightly older children may have an initial advantage over younger ones when both are within the age limits of the 'language-forming period'. They interviewed two sisters, aged 7 and 11, six times in their first four months in New Jersey, after the girls emigrated from southern India. The results with respect to six noncomplex phonological features show that the 11-year-old scored higher than her sister at the very beginning of the study, after five weeks in the new dialect area. Over the next twelve weeks, the duration of the study, the younger sister quickly caught up and in some cases overtook her. This rate pattern parallels the well-established finding in second-language acquisition, whereby older children have short-term advantages but younger children outperform them in the long run (Krashen *et al.* 1979, Long 1990: 260–65 et passim).

Such a pattern may hold for noncomplex rules, but fine-grained socio-linguistic studies reveal that late learners may never master complex rules of the new accent. An oft-cited example is Mr. J, who was part of a sample of middle-class subjects in a Toronto survey I conducted to investigate a change in progress in the phonetics of Canadian Raising (1984, 1989). As is well known, in standard CE /au/ has a mid onset [ʌu] before tautosyllabic voiceless obstruents, as in *lout, mouse, south*, and *couch*, and a low onset [ɑu] elsewhere, as in *loud, arouse, gouge, power, bough*, and *how*. Among younger speakers, this is changing so that a range of more fronted onsets can now be heard. Mr. J, as a 56-year-old engineer-writer from North Toronto, was expected to conform to the older pattern of Canadian Raising, along with his age-mates (46 and over) in the survey. When his interview was transcribed, however, Mr. J. proved to be out of line with his age-mates and everyone else because of a number of unraised onsets before voiceless consonants (Chambers 1984). In all other respects, he sounded like a CE speaker of his age and class. Further investigation revealed that he had moved to Toronto as an 11-year-old from upstate New York. It appears that, in his case, that was too late for him to master completely the intricacies of Canadian Raising. (For a review of this case and two other, similar ones, see Trudgill 1986: 32–37; also see Labov 1979.)

Payne 1980 supplies dramatic corroboration. None of the children in King of Prussia mastered all the intricacies of the short-*a* pattern unless they were themselves the offspring of Philadelphia natives. Among the immigrants, the native dialects influenced the specific ways in which they were likely to betray their nonindigenousness, so that those from New York City were more successful with the words in which the vowel preceded /d/ and those from the Northern Cities were more successful with the ones in which it preceded anterior fricatives.[8] Yet the effect of age is discernible. For the youngsters of three New York families, the only subjects for whom learning percentages are calculated, one family, the Morgans, shows scant learning with no sign of age-grading, but another, the Millers, shows the expected age-grading, with the younger children more proficient than the next; and the Bakers, much like the Canadian subjects in southern England, split sharply, with the youngest child partially learning the system and his older brothers learning none of it.

By contrast, with the noncomplex rules the King of Prussia subjects show no such distinction. The age of their arrival has a discernible effect, but the acquisition is much more homogeneous. Payne says (1980: 155–56):

> . . . children born and raised in King of Prussia, or those who moved to the area by the age of 4 and who have lived in King of Prussia for anywhere between 4 and 16 years, and children who have lived in King of Prussia for

8–16 years and moved between the ages of 5 and 8 have approximately the same degree of success in acquiring the Philadelphia phonetic variables. Children who moved to King of Prussia between the ages of 5 and 8 and who have lived in the area for only 4–7 years show a slightly lower degree of success of acquisition.

The split in proficiency is not evident here as it is in short-*a* acquisition. The age thresholds form a familiar pattern.

Between the ages of seven and 14, then, people who immigrate to different dialect areas will vary in their ability to acquire the more complex features of the new dialect. They may, like the people younger than themselves, become early acquirers or, like the people older than themselves, later acquirers. If the latter, they will probably never completely master the intricacies of a complex phonological rule.

In the earliest stages of acquisition, both categorical rules and variable rules of the new dialect result in variability in the acquirers
On the face of it, this principle seems obvious, amounting to no more than the observation that no features of the new dialect are acquired without initial interference from the old dialect. The converse would be a 'Minerva' theory, that changes emerge full-grown and instantaneous.[9] Nevertheless, the principle has a less than obvious application to lexical replacements, and its more obvious application to phonology will allow me to discuss a couple of processes, one categorical and the other variable, that are crucial for other principles.

This fifth principle is readily apparent in some of the data already presented. T-Voicing is a categorical rule in CE and the English control subjects lack it categorically, but the Canadian subjects are losing it variably (as shown in Fig. 9.5). Similarly, those Canadians with instances of Vowel Backing (Fig. 9.6) are acquiring them variably, and those without instances of Low Vowel Merger (Fig. 9.7) are eliminating them variably. Where the native SEE speakers have categorical forms, the Canadians who have begun acquiring them have variant forms.

A well-known categorical rule of SEE is R-lessness, the elimination of non-prevocalic /r/ in words like *summer, plaster, water, north, urban,* and *birthday*. Its categoricity is reflected in Fig. 9.8 by the performances of the control subjects in the background. The figure also shows that the Canadian youngsters, in sharp contrast, have made very little progress in acquiring R-lessness. Only three of them show any response at all. The further implications of this will be raised later, but for our immediate purposes it is enough to note that for the three youngsters who have made some progress their usage is far from categorical.

A well-known variable rule in SEE is Intrusive /r/, which inserts an [ɹ] epenthetically between vowels at a word boundary or internal juncture. The [ɹ] occurs variably in phrases such as *sofa*[ɹ] *and couch, Cuba*[ɹ] *and France, Lisa*[ɹ] *and Daniel, raw*[ɹ] *eggs,* and in words such as *draw*[ɹ]*ing*. This rule is a concomitant of R-lessness, as indicated by the fact that it is found only in accents which have a rule deleting /r/s nonprevocalically. In SEE and other nonrhotic accents, final /r/ is lost across word boundaries preceding a consonant, as in *pear tree*, but is retained preceding a vowel, as in

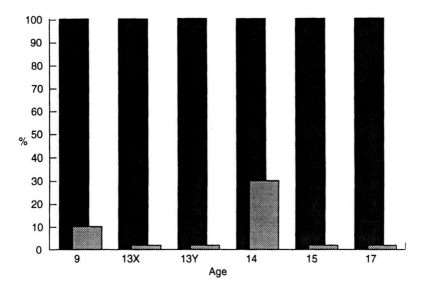

Fig. 9.8 Presence of R-lessness in the speech of six Canadians

pear and apple. The presence of the 'linking' [ɹ] in these instances, where it is organic, generalizes to other intervocalic contexts where it is 'intrusive', that is, not organic.

Though Intrusive /r/ is stigmatized, it appears to be almost impossible to suppress completely, even by the most self-conscious RP speakers. As Fig. 9.9 shows, the English control subjects varied considerably among themselves.[10] Fig. 9.9 also shows that, among the Canadian subjects, only the youngest one has made any response at all. The pattern furnishes another instance of principle 2.4, the bifurcation into early and late acquirers. The further significance of Max's response will be discussed with respect to principle 2.6 below. For now, it is enough to note that his response results in variability here as it does in the categorical rules.

Principle 2.5 has an interesting application to the acquisition of lexical replacements. Lexical items are not usually classified as variable or categorical, but the terms are clearly relevant. On the one hand, lexical items such as *car* and *auto(mobile)* co-exist in SEE just as do phonological variants such as [gɹɑːf] and [gɹæf] 'graph'. On the other hand, for a native SEE speaker, the use of the words *plaits* and *fringe* for the hairstyles that North Americans call *braids* and *bangs* is no more a matter of choice than is the nonrhoticity of [gɛːl] 'girl' or the back vowel of [bɹɑːntʃ] 'branch'.

Applying principle 2.5 to lexical acquisition by immigrants to a new dialect region would lead us to expect that replacements will occur variably in the speech of the acquirers in the earliest stages whether or not they are categorical for the native speakers. This indeed is what we find. It turns out that lexical acquisitions do not necessarily replace the old words, but often come into the vocabulary as additions or augments. When we compare the word-by-word data for each of the subjects, we discover that, for a few items, the subjects supplied the British variant in

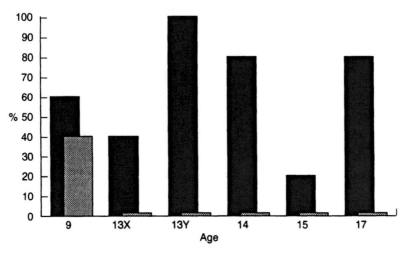

Fig. 9.9 Presence of intrusive /r/ in the speech of six Canadians

the first round of interviews and then supplied the Canadian variant in the second round, or vice versa. Such data constitute anomalies in the strictest (or perhaps just the simplest) definition of acquisition. The new lexical items do not eradicate the old ones but can co-exist beside them in the mental lexicon. In these cases, the actual use of one item or the other must be governed by a preference function, perhaps determined largely (or even exclusively) by factors in the social context. As time goes by, the old vocabulary item presumably recedes and, in some instances, may be forgotten entirely. But in the earliest stages, lexical changes, no less than phonological changes, result in variability.

Phonological innovations are actuated as pronunciation variants
With respect to the phonological acquisitions, the variability observed in the acquirers is consistent with the theory of language change known as Lexical Diffusion (Wang & Cheng 1970, Chen & Wang 1975, Chambers & Trudgill 1980: 174–80, Ogura 1990: Ch. 6). According to this theory, phonological innovations are actuated by the acquisition of particular instances of the new rule or phoneme, and they only become rule-governed or systematic (if ever, in the first generation) after a critical mass of instances has been acquired.

The archetype of a broadly-based phonological development with its roots in the pronunciation of a particular word is the diffusion of a palatalization rule through various Quichean (Mayan) dialects. Campbell (1974), in searching the earliest post-Conquest dictionaries for evidence of the spread of palatalization, made the astounding discovery that 'it always began with *ke: x* concomitantly with its shift in meaning from *deer* to *horse*'. That is, outside the Mamean region where the rule originated, the first dictionaries to record the change show it in the word *k^{y}e: x*, meaning 'horse', which occurs alongside unpalatalized *ke: x* 'deer' – the very same etymon (horse = [big] deer) – and other forms that would, in the course of time, become palatalized. Although Campbell did not state his discovery as a lexical diffusion, his reconstructed facts are entirely consistent with it, and indeed may be simply baffling for any other theory of language change. The chronology suggests that the diffusion of the horse through the Quichean region was accompanied by the Mamean dialect word for it, and from that word others with similar phonetic shapes also palatalized, until eventually the palatalization rule became established in most of the western dialects.

Principle 2.6 maintains that phonological acquisitions by immigrants begin in the same way that Quichean palatalization began, with individual words. Trudgill (1986: 58) posits the speakers' efforts at accommodation as motivation for the word-by-word diffusion of phonological innovations:

> The point is that during accommodation speakers do not modify their phonological systems, as such. . . . Rather, they modify their pronunciations of *particular words*, in the first instance, with some words being affected before others. Speakers' motivation . . . is *phonetic* rather than phonological: their purpose is to make individual words sound the same as when they are pronounced by speakers of the target variety.

In the terms we have been using, the earliest stages in the acquisition of systematic phonology will be indistinguishable from the acquisition of pronunciation variants. For instance, the acquisition of R-lessness will be initiated by the use of an SEE pronunciation such as [bɛːd] or CE [bɚd] 'bird', just as the acquisition of a pronunciation variant such as the one in *tomato* begins with the use of the SEE pronunciation [tʰəmáːto] for CE [tʰəméɪdo]. At some later stage, the two kinds of acquisition must become differentiated, when generalizations based on specific instances are appropriate for phonology but mistaken for pronunciations. As the Canadian youngsters acquire SEE pronunciations not only for *tomato* but also for *charade* with [ɑː] in place of CE [eɪ], they must at some point discern that there is no rule by which CE [eɪ] becomes SEE [ɑː], which would give the wrong result in *potato, radiator, lemonade,* and numerous other words. But having learned that *bird, Burt,* and *burr* are all pronounced without /r/, they must at some point discern that R-lessness is applicable in all similar instances.

There are two pieces of evidence in the CE/SEE study for phonological acquisition as lexical diffusion. First, the youngest subject, Max, scores higher on Intrusive /r/ with 40% (Fig. 9.9) than on R-lessness with 10% (Fig. 9.8). In terms of systematic phonology, this result would be inexplicable, perhaps ludicrous, because Intrusive /r/ is a concomitant of R-lessness, and it is a variable rule, whereas R-lessness is categorical. It would be utterly impossible for any native speaker of SEE to have higher percentages of Intrusive /r/ than of R-lessness. Evidently Max does not have these rules integrated into a phonological system. Since instances of the output of these SEE rules obviously do occur in his speech, they apparently occur as nonsystematic forms – that is, as pronunciation variants. At this stage, they are too few or too infrequent to provide the basis for inferring the rules.

Second, the responses of the Canadian youngsters to the three best-developed phonological processes conform to a pattern which is proving remarkably robust in studies of Lexical Diffusion. The typical pattern, first observed by Wang & Cheng (1970) and confirmed in numerous studies since (e.g. Bailey 1973: 77, Bickerton 1975: 65, Chambers & Trudgill 1980: 179) is the S-curve, with phonological changes occurring slowly for the first 20% or so of possible instances and then rising rapidly to about 80% before tailing off toward categoricity. The empirical basis underlying the S-curve is the sparsity of speakers caught in the middle three fifths, 20–80%, at any given time, in contrast to the clusters of speakers found at either end. These figures are taken to signify that speakers must sporadically acquire new pronunciations for about 20% of the available instances as the basis for generalizing a rule, and that, once the process becomes rule-governed, about 80% of the instances will be affected immediately, with some portion of the remaining instances, usually the less frequent ones (Phillips 1984), resisting change and perhaps remaining as residue.

The S-curve figure occurs persistently in the CE/SEE data. For absence of T-Voicing (Fig. 9.5), three speakers score 20% and the other three score 80% or more. For presence of Vowel Backing (Fig. 9.6), five score 20% or less and the other scores 100%. For absence of Low Vowel Merger (Fig. 9.7), four score under 20% and the other two score 80% or more. For none of these is any speaker caught in the middle.

If we consider Table 9.3 in the light of this evidence, it is presumably no coincidence that the group scores for pronunciation variants and phonological variants are proportionately very similar to one another, 26.67% and 24.9%, and opposed to the proportions for lexical replacements, which are about twice that. Since phonological innovations are actuated as pronunciation variants, the two are, at this early stage of dialect acquisition, one and the same.

Eliminating old rules occurs more rapidly than acquiring new ones
The process of dialect acquisition involves not only coming to sound more like the people in the new region but also coming to sound less like the people in the old region. Loosely speaking, these may amount to the same thing. Every time the Canadian immigrants fail to voice posttonic prevocalic /t/, they sound less like the CE speakers they left behind and, willy-nilly, less unlike the SEE speakers they now live among. Every time they fail to pronounce nonprevocalic [ɹ] they sound more like their SEE neighbors and less like their former CE neighbors.

Structurally, they are not the same thing at all.[11] T-Voicing is a rule of CE, and as such must be eliminated from the speakers' phonologies, R-lessness is a rule of SEE, and must be acquired in the speakers' phonologies. In the discussion to this point, this difference has been expressed by noting that the Canadians' speech is characterized by the 'absence of' a certain CE feature or by the 'presence of' a certain SEE feature. The determination of 'absence' or 'presence' follows from classic phonological axioms. T-Voicing is a rule of CE because /t/ is phonemic and [d] is derived, as indicated by pairs such as *settler: settle, heart: hearty*, with [t] and [d] alternations, in which the [d] is contextually predictable. R-lessness is a rule of SEE because

/r/ is phonemic and Ø is derived, as indicated by alternations across word boundaries before vowels or consonants as well as in pairs such as *carry: cart* and *forehead: foreplay*, where [ɹ] alternates with Ø, and the Ø form is contextually predictable. The same considerations assign Vowel Backing and Intrusive /r/ as SEE rules, therefore requiring acquisition by the Canadian youngsters, though the cases are somewhat fuzzier because exceptions and variants are involved. The splitting of the merged CE vowel [ɑ] into SEE [ɒ] and [ɔː] belongs to the phonemic inventory rather than phonological processes, so that alternations and predictability cannot be invoked. Polylectally, the CE merger is innovative. It is the absence of merged forms in the Canadians' speech that signals their accommodation to SEE, and on this basis it is considered a feature being eliminated.

Once the distinction is made, it seems intuitively obvious that eliminating old rules should come easier than acquiring new ones, and the group scores for the five phonological processes support that intuition. In Table 9.6 the features characterized by their absence, that is, the ones being eliminated, are more advanced than the ones characterized by their presence, that is, the ones being acquired.[12]

In Wells's study of Jamaicans' acquisition of London English, a number of the processes can be classified as either Jamaican features undergoing elimination or London features undergoing acquisition, although not all can be so divided by our criteria, at least from the available information. Wells himself distinguishes those 'variables [that] measure adaptation toward London speech (whether RP or cockney)' (1973: 117–18), which subsumes our category of new rules being acquired, from those 'sociolinguistic variables imported as such from Jamaica', which subsumes our category of old rules being eliminated. Insofar as the terms are comparable, they support principle 2.7 cogently, for Wells's results reveal that the Jamaican subjects are much more proficient in dealing with the latter than the former.

By way of illustration, let us look at two of the rules that clearly fit into our terms. Among the old dialect rules, Wells's subjects must eliminate yod-insertion, cited above, in JC palatalizations of /kjat/, /gjas/ and so on. Among the new dialect rules, the Jamaicans must acquire R-lessness after certain vowels, where JC is rhotic, in words such as /tʃier/, 'chair' or 'cheer', /dʒaːr/ 'jar', and /fuor/ 'four' (1973: 17–18, 100–101). Even though JC is generally nonrhotic and acquiring the new rule only entails generalizing the old one, the Jamaican subjects are relatively slow in acquiring it, with a group score of 43%, whereas in eliminating the old

Table 9.6 Group scores for five phonological processes

Phonological feature	Group score (%)
Absence of T-Voicing	55
Absence of Low Vowel Merger	31.6
Presence of Vowel Backing	23.3
Presence of R-lessness	8.3
Presence of Intrusive /r/	6.6

rule of yod-insertion their group score is 79%. These group scores are close to the median in their respective categories (44.75% and 80.2%) in Wells's study, and thus fairly represent the advantage accruing to the elimination of old rules over the acquisition of new ones.

Orthographically distinct variants are acquired faster than orthographically obscure ones

If we look again at the performances on the two noncomplex processes, T-voicing (Fig. 9.5) and R-lessness (Fig. 9.8), the discrepancy appears enormous. As Table 9.6 shows, the group scores are 55% and 8.3%, respectively. To some extent this can be accounted for by principle 2.7, for the former is being eliminated and the latter acquired. Even so, the discrepancy is considerable, and further consideration reveals that they are diametrically opposed in another respect.

The orthographic representations of the forms involved in the two processes allow different expectations, so to speak, about how they will be pronounced. Elimination of T-Voicing gives rise to pronunciations that are reinforced by the orthographical representations of the forms. Words such as *city, greetings, forty*, and the like are orthographically distinct in the sense that they are spelled with ⟨t⟩⟂, not ⟨d⟩, and are pronounced in SEE with [t], not [d]. Acquisition of R-lessness, by contrast, gives rise to pronunciations that are contradicted by the orthography. Words such as *summer, four, forty*, and the like are orthographically obscure in the sense that they are spelled with ⟨r⟩ but pronounced without [ɹ] in SEE.

In dialect acquisition, unlike first-language acquisition and, typically, second-language acquisition, the acquirers are literate. First-language acquirers are infants for whom literacy is out of the question. Second-language acquirers sometimes learn the orthography of the L2 while they are gaining competence as speakers, but even so their literacy in the language is usually not imprinted sufficiently to exert a formative influence on their speech. Dialect acquirers, as long as they are six or seven years old or older, generally know the standard orthographical representations of the pronunciations they are striving to acquire, and in fact it seems likely that those features exhibiting orthographic distinctiveness would by that very fact become more salient or obvious to them. Literacy, then, is potentially influential, and the discepancy between the Canadian youngsters' response to orthographically distinct T-Voicing and orthographically obscure R-lessness suggests its effect.

The effect is inferable in other studies as well. Taeldeman (1989) studied the dialectological consequences of another common situation resulting from urbanization, the engulfing of a formerly rural enclave in urban sprawl. Mariakerke, Belgium, was a 'peripheral village' until it became surrounded by the city of Ghent. The results of a dialect survey show that, at least for the present generation, the Mariakerke dialect persists quite hardily, with the villagers showing only about 9% overall incursions of Ghent features in their speech.

For a few features, however, the 'deviations' from Mariakerke dialect are greater. Four of these are shown in the first four rows of Table 9.7, selected from Taeldeman's larger set. For each of the features identified in the left

Table 9.7 Dialect features of Mariakerke, Belgium, and their 'deviations' toward the urban dialect of Ghent (Taeldeman 1989)

	Mariakerke	Ghent	Standard Dutch	Deviations %
Intervocalic p/t/k	voiced	voiceless	voiceless	13.4
Intervocalic g (e.g. *zwijgen*)	Ø	[ɣ]	[ɣ]	18.7
Intervocalic j/w	Ø	[j]/[w]	[j]/[w]	32.0
Intervocalic ng	Ø	[ŋ(ɣ)]	[ŋ(ɣ)]	42.5
Length of V (e.g. *rat*)	V	V:	V	0
Final en (e.g. *kloppen*)	[ən]	[ə]	[ən]	0

column, the traditional Mariakerke reflex is shown first, followed by the Ghent reflex and then by the standard Dutch reflex; the percentage in the final column indicates the frequency of the Ghent reflex in the Mariaker-kers' speech, ranging from 13.4% for the absence of voicing of intervocalic p/t/k to 42.5% for the failure to delete intervocalic velar nasals. For a few other features, such as those shown in the last two rows of Table 9.7, the traditional Mariakerke reflexes remain completely unaffected by Ghent dialect: neither the presence of long vowels in certain environments nor the reduction of final dental nasal syllables to schwa, both markers of Ghent dialect, show up in the villagers' speech.

On the basis of these results, Taeldeman concludes that 'the Mariakerke dialect is quite reluctantly moving in the direction of the Ghent dialect, but only for those aspects where the Ghent dialect resembles more the standard language' (1989: 162). Inspection of Table 9.7 reveals the justification of this conclusion: in all those features undergoing some change in the direction of Ghent dialect, the Ghent features coincide with the standard features, and in those resisting change, the Mariakerke feature, not the Ghent one, coincides with the standard feature. Another possible interpretation of these facts, not considered by Taeldeman, is that the Mariakerke dialect is not 'moving in the direction of the Ghent dialect' at all but is moving in the direction of the standard dialect.

Under either interpretation, two of our principles of dialect acquisition appear to be applicable here. For one thing, the changing features involve the elimination of two Mariakerke rules – intervocalic voicing of stops in the first row and intervocalic deletion of voiced postalveolar consonants in rows 2–4 – whereas the resistant features involve the acquisition of two Ghent rules. As principle 2.7 predicts, eliminating old rules occurs more rapidly than acquiring new ones. For another thing, those features undergoing change are orthographically distinct, whereas those resisting change are orthographically obscure. That is, Belgian spelling has ⟨p, t, k⟩ in those intervocalic positions traditionally pronounced [b, d, g] by Mariakerkers but now coming to be pronounced [p, t, k], and it has ⟨g, j, w, ng⟩ inter-vocalically where Mariakerkers traditionally deleted them but are now sometimes pronouncing them. Conversely, Mariakerkers are retaining their traditional pronunciations of short vowels in words like *rat* rather than lengthening them as the Ghentians do, as if the word were spelled *raat*, and they are persisting in pronouncing the final syllable of words like *kloppen* as [ən], as it is spelled, rather than reducing it to [ə], as the Ghentians do. As principle 2.8 predicts, orthographically distinct variants are acquired faster than orthographically obscure ones.[13]

Taeldeman's explanation in terms of standardization and mine in terms of orthographic distinctiveness may not necessarily be opposed. Standardized orthography is a prescriptivist instrument, where prescriptivism is, in Kroch & Small's epigrammatical definition, 'the ideology by which the guardians of the standard language impose their linguistic norms on people who have perfectly serviceable norms of their own' (1978: 45). Because orthography encodes most faithfully the standard accent, at least at the moment of its stipulation, rather than any other accent, acquisitions favoring orthographic distinctiveness and acquisitions favoring standard pronunciations will often amount to the same thing. However, this is certainly truer of Dutch than of English, insofar as Dutch orthography comes somewhat closer to a phonemic representation, and truer yet of many other languages in which the orthography is even more phonemic. It is also truer of Dutch and many other languages than of English because the standard dialect is more nearly definable. In our main study, the Canadian youngsters began as speakers of one standard dialect and are becoming speakers of another standard dialect; nonstandardness is not a factor for them in the same sense as for, say, the Mariakerkers. Perhaps for these reasons dialectologists working in languages other than English seem to fasten more readily on standardization (as also in n. 3) as an explanatory factor. In English, where the orthography is less reliable as an indicator of pronunciation, whether standard pronunciation or any other, and where it serves almost unchanged as the medium for several standard accents internationally, orthography is patently not coterminous with standardization, though it is clearly an important component of it. Stating principle 2.8 in terms of orthographic representation is intended to make it more specific (or less vague), and therefore more easily testable, than it would otherwise be.

Orthographic representation impinges upon dialect acquisition in another significant way. It can direct the splitting of merged phonemes in the old dialect when the split is orthographically distinct.[14] A straightforward example comes from Wells, in a discussion of the apparent difficulty Jamaican Creole speakers have in unmerging JC /t, d/ into RP /t, d/ and /θ, ð/, when he notes: 'The problem is virtually solved by an ability to spell correctly, since with a handful of exceptions (e.g. *Thames*, *Thomas*) the spelling *th* corresponds to [the latter] and the spellings *t* and *d* to [the former]' (1973: 36). Later, discussing a split of JC /uo/ into the two RP nuclei in *court* and *coat*, he observes that, 'once again, the good speller is at an advantage' because the former but not the latter involves ⟨r⟩ in the spelled form (1973: 41).

Similarly, the one merger that must be split in order for the Canadian subjects to acquire SEE is signalled by a spelling difference. CE Low Vowel Merger, with /ɒ/ in *offal: awful* and other word pairs (Table 9.5), occurs in SEE with /ɒ/ and /ɔ:, respectively, in the word pairs. In Standard English orthography, the /ɒ/-words are spelled with ⟨o⟩ in lax contexts, that is, followed by a consonant cluster as in *blond* – including orthographic geminates as in *rotten* – or by a single consonant in the absence of a tensing ⟨e⟩, as in *rot* (vs. *rote*); the /ɔː/-words, by contrast, are spelled as orthographic *a*-initial diphthongs ⟨au⟩ and ⟨aw⟩, as in *haul* and *hawk*.

Even abetted by orthographic distinctiveness, acquirers over the critical age probably never manage to split mergers like these faultlessly. One obvious reason is that splitting mergers invariably, by definition, involves complex rules, and therefore invokes the inhibitions of principles 2.3 and 2.4 (cf. n. 13). Nevertheless, orthographic distinctiveness may allow some progress in the direction of splitting old mergers, spastic though that progress may be, as Fig. 9.7 suggests. It undoubtedly plays a more significant role in reinforcing the phonetics of noncomplex changes, such as eliminating T-Voicing. Its converse, orthographic obscurity, appears to play an equally significant role in inhibiting some changes. Whatever the relative strength of principle 2.8 among the principles, the literacy of the acquirers appears to impose a limit on their responses. Literacy thus exerts a mitigating effect on dialect variation.

As such, it constitutes a minor codicil on Labov's Uniformitarian Principle (1972: 275), which holds that 'the forces operating to produce linguistic change today are of the same kind and order of magnitude as those which operated in the past five or ten thousand years.' Mass literacy is one cultural development that has taken place only in the last fraction of those five or ten millennia. Until two or three centuries ago, most ordinary folk were semiliterate or illiterate. It is surely no coincidence that accents and dialects have been most divergent in rural areas and working-class neighborhoods, where illiteracy was most pervasive.[15] It is probably no coincidence that the most competent dialect acquirers, the early acquirers of principle 2.4, are preliterate. Among literate acquirers, orthographically obscure features meet with particular resistance and probably are never completely mastered. This kind of resistance will only affect latecomers to a region, dialect-acquirers rather than first-language acquirers. It is thus a minority phenomenon, but in regions with heavy immigration its effects should be detectable ultimately in the reduction or modification of orthographically obscure dialect features. Indeed, such features may exist in dialects (and languages) only because first-language acquirers are invariably illiterate.

Overlap and relative strength

The eight principles proposed above are by no means equivalent. In the first place, they apply unequally to various linguistic levels. Lexical variants are distinguished from other types of variants in the rapidity with which they are acquired (principle 2.1). That rapidity turns out to be short-lived, with the great majority of replacements made in the first two years (principle 2.2). Like other variants, however, lexical replacements sometimes co-exist with the original dialect word, resulting in variability in lexical choices just as, in the earliest stages, there is variability in phonology (principle 2.5).

Pronunciation variants, though structurally similar to lexical elements in the sense that they are entities in the lexicon rather than processes, are nevertheless more similar to phonology in acquisition time (principle 2.1). This appears to follow from the fact that phonological changes are actuated as pronunciation variants, requiring the acquisition of a critical mass of instances as a basis for generalization (principle 2.6).

Pronunciation variants should be impeded by orthographic obscurity and encouraged by orthographic distinctiveness, as phonological processes are (principle 2.8). In the acquisition of phonology, other principles may overlap. Eliminating rules of the old dialect takes place faster than acquiring rules of the new dialect (principle 2.7), other things being equal. One of the inequalities, perhaps the most telling one inasmuch as it is supported by several studies, is that simple rules are acquired faster than complex ones (principle 2.3). It is the acquisition of complex rules that separates acquirers into early and late ones (principle 2.4), based critically on age.

The principles are not mutually exclusive, as the discussion above has already made clear. The work of unravelling their relative strengths poses a considerable challenge. A crude measure of the interrelation of principles 2.3 (simple vs. complex), 2.7 (eliminate vs. acquire), and 2.8 (orthographically distinct vs. obscure) is given in Table 9.8. The two simple rules in the CE/SEE study, T-Voicing and R-lessness, are opposed in orthographic distinctiveness and obscurity, and also in eliminability and acquisition. Not surprisingly, T-Voicing, favored by all three principles, is progressing much faster. The interaction of the principles in the rules of Low Vowel Merger and Vowel Backing is somewhat harder to evaluate: both are complex, but the former is being eliminated and is orthographically distinct whereas the latter is being acquired and is orthographically neutral (neither distinct nor obscure). Low Vowel Merger is progressing marginally faster, and a review of Figs. 9.6 and 9.7 reveals that its advantage arises solely from the fact that two of the subjects are positively involved in acquiring it whereas only one is involved with Vowel Backing. Still, it is an advantage, and the principles predict it should have one. The appositeness of this result is disturbed somewhat by looking back at R-lessness, which appears to be at least as well favored by the principles as is Vowel Backing but lags well behind it. The remaining rule, Intrusive /r/, is complex, being acquired, and orthographically obscure. With no favoring factors at all, it is lagging behind the others.

Overall, the structural properties of the acquisitions correlate reasonably

Table 9.8 Interrelation of Principles 2.3, 2.7, and 2.8 in five phonological processes

	T-Voicing	R-Lessness	Low V Merger	Vowel Backing	Intrusive /r/
Simple (+)/Complex (−)	+	+	−	−	−
Eliminate (+)/Acquire (−)	+	−	+	−	−
Distinct (+)/Obscure (−)	+	−	+	0	−
Group Scores (%)	55	8.3	31.6	23.3	6.6

well with the performances of the acquirers. The poles on the continuum, represented by T-Voicing and Intrusive /r/, are well-defined by the principles. The intermediate area is somewhat murkier, as might be expected with three principles interacting and at least one of them tern- ary-valued. The potential combinations are many-fold, and empirical studies with different combinations are required to elucidate their relative strengths.

Whether these eight principles endure in further studies of dialect acqui- sition remains to be seen. Their utility in the developmental study of Canadian youngsters in England gives them a solid basis, and their extrapolation to other studies makes them seem all the more promising. Nevertheless, I have tried to make them vulnerable to emendation by stating them as strongly as the evidence allows and illustrating them as variously as the literature permits. They are intended to be testable and, since the social situations in which they arise are so commonplace, there should be no lack of opportunities to test them. Some of those situations will surely provide tougher tests for one or another of the principles (as suggested in n. 14) or for the relative weight of overlapping principles (as suggested in n. 13).

If the principles of dialect acquisition gain empirical depth, their relation- ship to principles of first-language acquisition and second-language acqui- sition could open up a broad area of interaction among language researchers who have hitherto seldom recognized their common ground. That broadening of interests appears to be a feature of current develop- ments in dialectology. The systematic study of dialect traditionally took its own course, sometimes parallel to but more often independent of systema- tic studies of other linguistic areas. As Labov (1972: 268) put it, 'in the twentieth century, dialectology as a discipline seems to have lost any orientation towards theoretical linguistics, and dialect geographers have generally been content to collect their materials and publish them' without reference to broader linguistic issues. The shift toward contact studies potentially bridges some professional gaps. Studies of dialect acquisition inevitably involve the critical period, acquisitional order, parameters of variability, and other concerns beyond the traditional ones. In studying the efforts of displaced people to give their speech and hence themselves some semblance of indigenousness, linguists may gain a new perspective on some perennial issues.

Notes

1. The common ground shared by my research and Peter Trudgill's will be obvious at many points, and is not coincidental. Our views of the discipline overlap considerably, often strongly enough to turn us into collaborators (1980, 1991). As a Visiting Professor at the University of Reading, I was Trudgill's colleague when I conceived and organized my dialect acquisition project, and I carried out the first round of interviews around the time I was, at his request, criticizing a manuscript version of *Dialects in contact*. His acknowledgement is generous, and it is my pleasure to reciprocate it here.

2. For instance, when I asked Sam, the 14-year-old, if he thought he sounded less English talking to me than to his friends, he said, 'I think I sound less English [with you] 'cause I try harder when I'm around my friends. I try to fit in with eveyone so I don't be the odd one out or something . . . And when I'm home, like when I talk to my brothers and stuff, I don't try as hard.'

3. All the variants in this study, whether lexical, pronunciation, or phonological, are standard forms either in CE or SEE, and therefore 'standardization' is irrelevant as a factor in their acquisition. Thelander (1983) studied the speech of migrant groups in Sweden, where replacement of a nonstandard form by a standard form, or vice versa, proved influential. He discovered a strong tendency for speakers to retain the old form when it coincided with the standard form rather than replacing it with a new form that was nonstandard (1983: 28–29, 73–75; thanks to Paul Kerswill for guiding me through the Swedish text). Thelander's study extends the research on community style-shifting (Blom & Gumperz 1972, Thelander 1982) by adding immigration as an independent social variable.

4. Ferguson (1972) describes Philadelphia short *a* based on observations made in the period 1940–69. The situation was no less complex then than when Payne studied it in the mid-1970s. Ferguson argues convincingly that the Philadelphia distinction has its origins in SEE Vowel Backing, with subsequent developments in Philadelphia making it even more complex.

5. In Wells's terms of reference, Jamaicans in London acquire a rule of yod-deletion to undo the effects of the old rule of yod-insertion. In our terms, they eliminate or suppress the old rule in their phonology, without acquiring anything. The phonetic effect is the same.

6. This merger is, however, spreading rapidly in the United states (Terrell 1976), and could become a feature of the standard accent in a generation or two. Besides CE, two other standard accents have merged these low back lax vowels. In Scottish English (Hughes & Trudgill 1987: 75) and Scots-Irish (Ellen Cowie-Douglas, personal communication, 1991) the words in both columns of Table 9.5 have the vowel /ɔ/.

7. I am beholden to Motoei Sawaki and Fumio Inoue for pointing out the relevance of Sibata's work to me, and especially to Professor Sawaki for translating this excerpt of it for me.

8. Payne's results, in this respect, arguably provide evidence of transfer affecting dialect acquisition, akin to language transfer in second-language acquisition (Odlin 1989). Because of differences in their native dialects, the acquisition tasks differ. For instance, Payne notes (1980: 160, 167) that the New Yorkers face a straightforward adjustment in learning to lax short-*a* only before /d/, with three exceptions, whereas the Northern Cities speakers must also learn to lax it before all the other stops as well.

9. The reductio ad absurdum of a theory of instantaneous language change, due to James D. McCawley (personal communication, 1972), has a bewildered Londoner ordering eel the day after the Great English Vowel Shift, and being served ale.

10. At the interviews, the SEE control subjects' behavior showed an interesting response due to the stigmatization of this feature. In the readings of the phrase list, an activity where considerable self-monitoring is normal, Intrusive /r/ was most likely to occur in the first possible instance on the list, and then was decreasingly likely in each possible instance thereafter. After encountering it, the subjects were more likely to 'correct' it in the next occurrence. In the final analysis, the data formed an implicational scalogram such that if the subjects

did not pronounce Intrusive /r/ in one item on the list, then they did not pronounce it thereafter (Chambers 1988).

11. Experientially, they are also not the same thing. Dialect acquirers who immigrate after the critical age invariably discover when they revisit their old homes that their dialect is now perceived as 'foreign', yet their neighbors in their new homes also perceive their speech as 'nonnative'. Immigrants, often to their bafflement, come to sound less like the people in the old region without sounding quite like the people in the new region. The old dialect and the new one are not the converse of one another, but poles on a continuum.

12. Second-language acquisition analogously provides an apparent counterexample that illustrates the complexities interacting with this principle. English speakers learning German usually master the Final Obstruent Devoicing rule quite successfully, but German speakers learning English usually eliminate that same rule with great difficulty. Superficially, this appears to be an instance in which acquiring a new rule proves much easier than eliminating an old one. However, final obstruent devoicing is a highly natural process, to the extent that foreign-language learners may acquire it even when it is not a rule of either L1 or L2. As Odlin puts it, 'the devoicing rule has an existence somewhat independent of both the native and target languages' (1989: 121–22). If so, it is also independent of principle 2.7.

13. Principles 2.7 and 2.8 converge in the Mariakerke data, as they also do in the relevant CE/SEE data. As far as I can see, this convergence is accidental. There is no reason to expect that rules being eliminated from the old dialect will necessarily yield orthographically distinct forms, or that rules being acquired in the new dialect will necessarily produce orthographically obscure forms. Unfortunately, I have been unable to find contrary examples – not surprising, really, when the literature is so sparse. Such examples, when they do arise, should provide crucial evidence as to the relative weight of principles 2.7 and 2.8.

14. Some mergers are orthographically obscure. For instance, Northern England English (NEE) has /ʊ/ where SEE and most other varieties have /ʊ/ and /ʌ/, but the spelling system has ⟨u⟩ for both. So SEE and the other accents distinguish the vowel of *put, butcher, cushion*, etc., from that of *putt, butter, cussing*, etc., but NEE does not. It is unmarked orthographically because it is historically a split rather than a merger, with SEE unrounding ME *ŭ* in certain words (Chambers & Trudgill 1980: 127–29). The split originated in 17th-century London, too late to be incorporated into English orthography but early enough to be disseminated to the colonies. The acquisition problems of Northerners with respect to this feature, including considerable hypercorrection (for example, [bʌtʃə] for 'butcher') and residue (especially in low-frequency words such as *puttee, putty,* and *multitude*), are well known anecdotally. Presumably they are typical of orthographically obscure mergers, and presumably they differ in degree if not in kind from acquisition problems for orthographically distinct mergers. Such differences, studied under controlled circumstances, could provide significant empirical evidence of the strength of principle 2.8. If the complexity of eliminating mergers supersedes orthographic distinctiveness or obscurity, vitiating any measurable difference between them, that fact should provide significant empirical evidence for the relative weight of principle 2.8 and principle 2.3, about the inhibiting effect of complex rules.

15. Most mergers of orthographically distinct items in the standard dialect appear to have occurred before the spread of mass literacy. For example, the merger of ME *ō* and *ou* in all English dialects except a few geographically peripheral British ones (Wells 1970, Trudgill & Foxcroft 1978) took place before the 15th

century (Zachrisson 1913: 84). The merged items, such as *moan/mown, nose/ knows, toe/tow*, are for the most part orthographically distinct to this day.

References

Bailey, C-J.N. (1973) 'Variation and linguistic theory', Arlington, VA: Center for Applied Linguistics.

Bickerton, D. (1975) 'Dynamics of a creole system', Cambridge: Cambridge University Press.

Blom, J-P. and Gumperz, J.J. (1972) 'Social meaning in linguistic structure: Code-switching in Norway. Directions in sociolinguistics: The ethnography of communication', eds. J.J. Gumperz and D. Hymes, New York, NY: Holt, Rinehart & Winston, pp. 407–34.

Campbell, L. (1974) 'Quichean palatalized velars', International Journal of American Linguistics 40, pp. 132–34.

Cavalli-Sforza, L.L. and Wang, W.S-Y. (1986) 'Spatial distance and lexical replacement', Lg. 62. pp. 38–55.

Chambers J.K. (1984) 'Group and individual participation in a sound change in progress', Papers from the Fifth International Conference on Methods in Dialectology, H.J. Warkentyne ed., Victoria, BC: University of Victoria Department of Linguistics, pp. 119–36.

—— (1988) 'Acquisition of phonological variants. Methods in dialectology', ed. A.R. Thomas, Clevedon: Multilingual Matters, PP. 650–65.

—— (1989) 'Canadian Raising: Fronting, blocking', etc. American Speech 64. 75–88.

—— (1990) 'Acquisition of lexical and pronunciation variants'. Presented at the International Congress of Dialectologists, Bamberg, Germany. [To appear in the Proceedings volume, ed. Wolfgang Viereck.]

—— and Trudgill, P. (1980) 'Dialectology', Cambridge: Cambridge University Press.

Chen, M. and Wang, W.S-Y. (1975) 'Sound change: Actuation and implementation', Lg. 51. pp. 255–81.

Darwin, C. (1871) 'The descent of man', Modern Library edn. New York, NY: Random House.

David, S. and Montgomery, M. (1988) 'The acquisition of American English as a second dialect'. Paper presented at the American Dialect Society annual meeting, New Orleans.

Davis, A.L. and McDavid, R.I. Jr. (1950) 'Northwestern Ohio: A transition area', Lg. 26. pp. 186–89.

Ellis, S. (1953) 'Fieldwork for a dialect atlas of England'. Transactions of the Yorkshire Dialect Society liii. pp. 9–21.

Ferguson, C.A. (1972) 'Short *a* in Philadelphia English'. Studies in linguistics in honor of G.L. Trager, ed. E.M. Smith, The Hague: Mouton, pp. 259–74.

Giles, H. and Smith, P. (1979) 'Accommodation theory: Optimal levels of convergence'. Language and social psychology, eds. H. Giles and R. St. Clair, Oxford: Blackwell, pp. 45–65.

Goebl, H. (1982) 'Dialektometrie: Prinzipien und Methoden des Einsatzes der Numerischen Taxonomie im Bereich der Dialektgeographie', Wien: Verlag der Österreichischen Akademie der Wissenschaften.

Hughes, A. and Trudgill, P. (1987) 'English accents and dialects', 2nd edn. London: Edward Arnold.

Kerswill, P.E. (1985) 'A sociolinguistic study of rural immigrants in Bergen, Norway', Cambridge: University of Cambridge dissertation.

Kirk, J.M., Munroe, G. and O'Kane, M.J.D. (1992) 'Electronic word maps. Research in humanities computing', eds. S. Hockey and N. Ide. London: Oxford University Press, to appear.

Krashen, S., Long, M.H. and Scarcella, R.C. (1979) 'Age, rate, and eventual attainment in second language acquisition', TESOL Quarterly 13. pp. 573–82.

Kretzschmar, W.A. Jr., Schneider, E. and Johnson, E. (eds.), (1989) 'Computer methods in dialectology', Journal of English Linguistics 22, special edn.

Kroch, A. and Small, C. (1978) 'Grammatical ideology and its effect on speech. Linguistic variation: Models and methods', ed. D. Sankoff, New York, NY: Academic Press, pp. 45–69.

Kurath, H. (1972) 'Studies in area linguistics', Bloomington: Indiana University Press.

Labov, W. (1972) 'Sociolinguistic patterns', Philadelphia: University of Pennsylvania Press.

—— (1979) 'Locating the frontier between social and psychological factors in linguistic variation. Individual differences in language ability and language behavior', eds. C. Fillmore, D. Kempler, and W.S-Y. Wang, New York, NY: Academic Press, pp. 327–40.

Long, M.H. (1990) 'Maturational constraints on language development'. Studies in Second Language Acquisition 12. pp. 251–85.

Milroy, L. (1987) 'Observing and analysing natural language: A critical account of sociolinguistic method', Oxford: Blackwell.

Odlin, T. (1989) 'Language transfer: Cross-linguistic influence in language learning', Cambridge: Cambridge Univesity Press.

Ogura, M. (1990) 'Dynamic dialectology: A study of language in time and space', Tokyo: Kenkyusha.

Payne, A C. (1975) 'The re-organization of linguistic rules: A preliminary report', Pennsylvania Working Papers on Linguistic Change and Variation I–6, Philadelphia: U.S. Regional Survey.

—— (1980) 'Factors controlling the acquisition of the Philadelphia dialect by out-of-state children', Locating language in time and space, ed. W. Labov, New York, NY: Academic Press, pp. 143–78.

Phillips, B.S. (1984) 'Word frequency and the actuation of sound change', Lg. 60. pp. 320–42.

Reed, D. and Spicer, J.L. (1952) 'Correlation methods of comparing dialects in a transition area', Lg. 28. pp. 348–59.

Sibata, T. (1958) 'Conditions controlling standardization. Excerpt from Nihoñ no hōgen' [The dialects of Japan], Tōkyō: Iwanami Shotēn. Translated by Motoei Sawaki, 1990, ms.

Taeldeman, J. (1989) 'A typology of dialect transitions in Flanders. New methods in dialectology', eds. M.E.H. Schouten and P. van Reenen, Dordrecht: Foris, pp. 155–63.

Terrell, T.D. (1976) 'Some theoretical considerations on the merger of the low vowel phonemes in American English', Berkeley Linguistics Society 2. pp. 350–59.

Thelander, M. (1982) 'A qualitative approach to the quantitative data of speech variation'. Sociolinguistic variation in speech communities, ed. S. Romaine, London: Edward Arnold, pp. 65–83.

—— (1983) 'Från blåknut till brakknut: Om provinsiella drag i flyttares språk', Uppsala: Nysvenska Studier.

Thomason, S.G. and Kaufman, T. (1988) 'Language contact, creolization, and genetic linguistics', Berkeley: University of California Press.

Trudgill, P. (1981) 'Linguistic accommodation: Sociolinguistic observations on a sociopsychological theory', Parasession on Language and Behavior, Chicago Linguistic Society 17. pp. 218–37.

Trudgill, P. (1986) 'Dialects in contact', Oxford: Blackwell.

—— and Chambers, J. K. (1991) 'Dialects of English: Studies in grammatical variation', London & New York: Longman.

—— and Foxcroft, T. (1978) 'On the sociolinguistics of vocalic mergers: Transfer and approximation in East Anglia'. Sociolinguistic patterns in British English, ed. P. Trudgill. London: Edward Arnold, pp. 69–79.

Vousten, R. and Bongaerts, T. (1990) 'Acquiring a dialect as L2: The case of the dialect of Venray in the Dutch province of Limburg'. Presented at the International Congress of Dialectologists, Bamberg, Germany. [To appear in the Proceedings volume, ed. by Wolftang Viereck.]

Walker, D.C. (1975) Another Edmonton idiolect: Comments on an article by Professor Avis. Canadian English: Origins and structures, ed. J.K. Chambers, Toronto: Methuen, pp. 129–32.

Wang, W.S-Y. and Cheng, C-C. (1970) 'Implementation of phonological change: the Shûang-fêng Chinese case', Chicago Linguistic Society 6. pp. 552–57.

Wells, J.C. (1970) 'Local accents in England and Wales', Journal of Linguistics 6. pp. 231–52.

—— (1973) 'Jamaican pronunciation in London'. (Publications of the Philological Society, 25.) Oxford: Blackwell.

—— (1982) 'The accents of English: An introduction'. Vol. 1, Cambridge: Cambridge University Press.

Zachrisson, R.E. (1913) 'Pronunciation of English vowels 1400–1700', Göteborg: Wald. Zachrissons Boktryckeri A.-B.

10

Mechanisms of change in urban dialects: the role of class, social network and gender

James Milroy and Lesley Milroy

Originally published in *International Journal of Applied Linguistics*, 3(1) (1993)

Introduction

One of the most important contributions of Labov's 'quantitative paradigm' to the study of language in society has been to allow us to examine in a systematic way the relationship between language variation and 'speaker' variables such as age, gender, ethnicity, social network and social class. Language variation in cities has been revealed not as chaotic but as socially regular, and this socially patterned variation has been shown to be crucial in understanding mechanisms of linguistic change. What we want to do in this paper is discuss the way in which these extralinguistic variables are interrelated. We present some data from a number of sources to explore the relationships between the variables of class, gender, and social network in particular.

Systematic scrutiny of the way extralinguistic variables are conceptualized is rather rare in sociolinguistics, and it has been taken for granted by many investigators that socio-economic class should be treated as the most important speaker variable; i.e., it seems to be assumed without comment that social class differentiation offers a routine way of accounting for linguistic variation. We shall be rather critical of these approaches to the variable of social class, for two reasons. First, class tends to be treated as the primary variable to which other variables (particularly gender) are then related, i.e., differences according to gender are interpreted as being themselves dependent on social class differences. Yet, despite recent advances within this general framework (Labov 1990; Eckert 1989), there is a good deal of detailed evidence from a number of sources to suggest that the effect of gender on patterns of language use cannot always be accounted for primarily in terms of social class. The second objection to the way in which class is generally handled pertains to the kind of social class model which underlies modern sociolinguistic thinking, although the nature of this model is not always made explicit. We shall comment on this second, more general point before examining some data which can illuminate

179

relationships between extralinguistic variables and which are relevant to the way they affect patterns of language variation and change.

We are not the only investigators who have suggested that the social theory implicitly adopted by sociolinguists is in need of explicit formulation and critique. Woolard (1985: 738) has commented:

> . . . sociolinguists have often borrowed social concepts in an ad hoc and unreflecting fashion, not usually considering critically the implicit theoretical frameworks that are imported wholesale along with such convenient constructs as three-, four-, or nine-sector scalings of socio-economic status.

The problem is that, although social class has been shown in numerous urban dialectological studies to correlate closely with patterns of language variation, a satisfactory theoretical framework within which to interpret these correlations is still lacking, and a number of ideas based on assumptions about stratificational social class have become almost axiomatic. For example, the Labovian speech community is conceived of in terms of stratificational social class and defined in these terms; similarly, patterns of language change are interpreted as driven by class differences, and, as we have noted above, gender differences have also been interpreted as class-based.

In order to make progress towards a more satisfactory theoretical framework within which to interpret the correlations that we find, we need to do two things. First, we need to be able to link these correlations to the interactional level of analysis with some account of the interpersonal mechanisms which give rise to them. Second, we need a suitable theory of class in order to understand what these correlations mean at a broader level of social organization. A number of sociolinguists have remarked that the conception of social class underlying Labov's urban sociolinguistic work in New York City and Philadelphia is not always appropriate (Rickford 1986; Sankoff, Cedergren, Kemp, Thibault & Vincent 1989). Williams (1992) offers an extended critique of this and other issues, from a sociological rather than a sociolinguistic perspective. His general proposals are unfortunately of limited value, as they do not take account of the sociolinguist's primary (and indeed non-negotiable) focus on *language*. Thus, Williams sees sociolinguistic method as inherently flawed in that researchers take as a starting point a body of linguistic data where they inductively seek socially sensitive patterns of variation; unlike many sociologists, they do not start with a coherent social (rather than linguistic) theory as the basis for subsequent decisions on data collection, data analysis, and ultimately interpretation. Yet many sociolinguists would now agree that one of their major tasks is to find a convincing social interpretation of the substantial amount of data on variation which has been collected over the last 25 years, rather than starting *ab initio* as Williams seems to recommend. However, many of Williams' criticisms of the Labovian concept of class align with those expressed by sociolinguists.

Labov's key sociolinguistic notion of *speech community* (which is explicated in terms of social class) emphasizes shared values throughout the community, where speakers are said to agree on the evaluation of these very linguistic norms which symbolize the divisions between them. This seems to assume a consensus model of social class whereby the community is envisaged as fundamentally cohesive; yet, the vitality and persistence of non-standard vernacular communities uncovered by many researchers (including Labov) investigating both urban and rural dialects is more readily interpretable as evidence of conflict and sharp divisions in society than as evidence of consensus.

Rickford's work on Guyanese Creole has led him to conclude that conflict models of social class have been unduly neglected by sociolinguists (Rickford 1986), and despite a continuing focus on shared values, support for a conflict model of society is provided by Labov's own recent work in Philadelphia, where, with respect to a number of phonological and morphological variables, he finds progressive segregation and linguistic differentiation between black and white networks (Labov & Harris 1986). A conflict model would allow him explicitly to relate the variables of class and ethnicity to one another, whereas at the moment they have to be treated as independent of one another. Furthermore, a conflict model is essential to account for the phenomenon of linguistic change, with which social conflict is generally associated. Labov himself has acknowledged that "a thorough-going structural-functional approach to language could be applied only if linguistic systems did not undergo internal change and development" (Labov 1986: 283). In short, a social class model based on conflict, division and inequality can account better than one based on consensus for many patterns of language variation uncovered by the detailed work of sociolinguists on phonological and morphological variation.

This is particularly true of sociolinguistic studies of communities of the kind carried out in Belfast (reported in L. Milroy 1987a, J. Milroy 1992 etc). The phonological structure of Belfast vernacular can be coherently described only if it is analysed as an internally consistent (but systematically variable) vernacular, rather than as an unsuccessful approximation to educated Belfast or standard English varieties (J. Milroy 1981); yet, the latter is what a consensus model seems to require. Similarly, the new contact varieties emerging as a result of mass migrations to contemporary cities such as Stockholm, Sweden (Kotsinas 1988) and Christchurch, New Zealand (Gordon 1991) need to be analysed in their own terms rather than as poor approximations to Standard Swedish or 'cultivated' New Zealand English. The overall impression emerging from such studies is of social fragmentation and conflict rather than of cohesion.

Our own approach (which involves a critique of some aspects of Labov's practice) has been based on the perception that what are usually called low-prestige varieties can be maintained over generations as flourishing vernaculars. We have argued for many years now that strong informal social ties within communities provide the mechanisms that enable speakers to maintain non-standard dialects, rural or urban, despite intense pressure from the standard language through routes such as the educational system and the media. We have attempted to quantify these social patterns in terms of *social network*. Our analysis aligns well with the idea that language behaviour is affected by alternative linguistic markets, rather than the single, dominant market proposed by Bourdieu (Bourdieu 1977, 1984; Gal 1988). It seems, therefore, that just as a conflict model has the potential to integrate the variables of class and ethnicity, so also it could integrate the variables of class and network. This argument, to which we return shortly, is developed in some detail by Milroy & Milroy (1992). In the meantime, the relationship between the variables of class and sex, both of which have been shown to affect language behaviour, is discussed in the next section.

Social class and gender as extralinguistic variables

The chief point that we need to make here is that it is not always illuminating to explain patterns of sex differentiation in language primarily with reference to (and as dependent on) social class in the way Labov and many of those following him have tended to do. Aside from our own inner-city Belfast study, which explicitly avoided the variable of social class in the first place, most quantitative sociolinguistic studies in western societies have followed Labov (1966) in initially setting out to examine the relationship between language and class (or to a lesser extent, language and ethnicity). The evidence of linguistic gender-marking that has emerged is therefore a kind of by-product, the surveys not having been designed in the first place with this dimension of variation in mind. The form which linguistic gender-marking has commonly been interpreted as taking is for women to approximate more commonly than men of similar status to the (so-called) prestige norm. But as Coates (1986) has pointed out, no satisfactory explanation has emerged of why women should be more oriented than men to a prestige norm. Moreover, such an interpretation of the very salient and theoretically important gender differences which plainly do exist relies on the analyst's capacity to assign a comparable social class index score to both males and females. In fact, women are seen as problematic and are classified in a somewhat arbitrary manner, sometimes being assigned the class of their husbands or fathers, while at other times their class is determined by their own occupations.

Horvath's (1985) regraphing of some of Labov's data in accordance with the linguistic groupings into which speakers seem to cluster, rather than initially in terms of social class, suggests quite strongly that the variable (dh) in New York City is more clearly stratified by gender than by class. Fasold's alternative graphic representation, adapted as Fig. 10.1, shows the considerable influence of the sex of the speaker on variation particularly clearly (Fasold 1990: 101). The same point emerges even more clearly in Fig. 10.2, where variation between glottalized and non-glottalized realizations of (p) in Newcastle upon Tyne, England are shown in relation to the sex and social class of 16 speakers (Rigg 1987; see L. Milroy 1992 for details). Although realizations of (p) certainly show some effect of class, this effect is dwarfed beside that of sex of speaker. The glottalization which is so characteristic of Tyneside vernacular (see Wells 1982: 374) is better described as a male norm than a working class norm.

Glottalization is a complex and interesting case, and we return to it below. Here we note also that the examples above are by no means isolated or idiosyncratic. Coates (1986) has regraphed a substantial amount of data

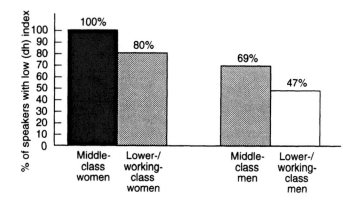

Fig. 10.1 Percentage of speakers with high (dh) index, by sex and social class

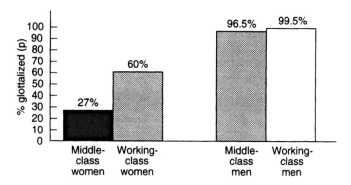

Fig. 10.2. Use of glottalized (p) in Newcastle upon Tyne, by sex and social class

from a number of well-known sociolinguistic surveys which shows that sex of speaker quite commonly accounts for patterns of variation at least as well as, and on some cases better than, social class. In a study of the dialect of Amsterdam, Schatz (1986: 102) provides a spectacular example of the problems created by the standard practice of conceptualizing sex differences in terms of social class. Sex-related differences in the distribution of variants of the (a) variable emerge in low-status speakers only, rather than the expected pattern of women approximating to the norms of a higher social group. The problem faced by Schatz and others who encounter such 'anomalous' patterns is that current sociolinguistic thinking does not provide a framework for interpreting patterns of this kind. Mees (1990: 185 and notes) reports difficulties in interpreting patterns of variation in respect of several phonological variables in Cardiff English which are affected in different ways by the sex and social class of speakers. One of these is glottalization (including the glottal stop), to which we now return.

The glottal stop variant of /t/ in British English (in intervocalic and word-final position) has a male, working-class image and has been traditionally heavily stigmatized (see, for example, Romaine & Reid 1976;

Macaulay 1977). Despite this, however, it has recently been observed to be spreading quite rapidly and is now a salient characteristic of the speech of young speakers of the 'prestige' accent, Received Pronunciation (Wells 1982: 106). Gender differences appear to be involved in quite a complex way in its spread, and the relation of gender to social class and to prestige patterns is by no means consistent or predictable from the usual assumptions about females preferring higher social-class norms. Mees in Cardiff finds that the glottal stop is most advanced in middle-class, rather than working-class, speech and that the change towards it is being led by young females. So much for the male, working-class image! In Coleraine, Northern Ireland, as reported by Kingsmore (forthcoming), it is again females who favour the glottal stop. Fig. 10.3 shows a fascinating pattern of alternation between flapped /t/ and the glottal stop (in final position in words of the type *not, what*), with males favouring the flap and females the glottal stop in several different age-groups. Again, this seems to be contrary to what we might expect.

A recent study of Newcastle upon Tyne school-children by Hartley (1992), which is a pilot study for a more extensive investigation of phonological change, complicates the picture further. Fig. 10.4 shows general agreement with Rigg (1987) in that males make more use of glottalized variants than females. However, when we distinguish glottal replacement (the glottal stop) from glottal reinforcement (a traditional feature of Tyneside English affecting /p, t, k/), we find again that the females are leading in the spread of the glottal stop, whereas the males are favouring glottal reinforcement (see Figs. 10.5 and 10.6).

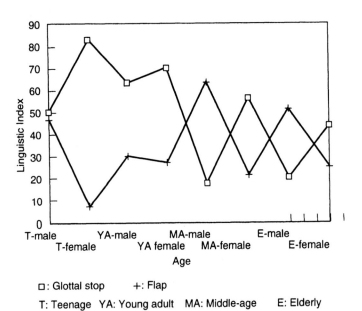

Fig. 10.3 Variation between glottal stop and flap (for /t/) in word-final position in Coleraine, Northern Ireland, by age and sex

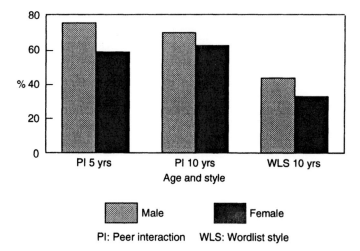

Fig. 10.4 Percentage of all glottal variants in 5-year-old and 10-year-old children, by age and style, in Newcastle upon Tyne

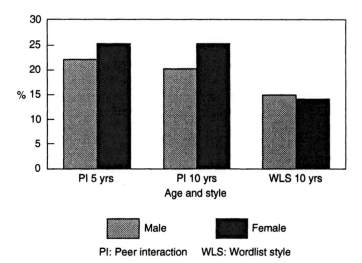

Fig. 10.5 Percentage of use of glottal replacement in 5-year-old and 10-year-old children, by age and style, in Newcastle upon Tyne

The explanations for varying patterns of glottalization (which we have presented here in a simplified form) are extremely complicated and to some extent reflect difficulties in phonetic description and analysis of segments described as 'glottal' or 'glottalized' (see Wells 1982: 260–1). Such explanations must also take into account the embedding of the change in the localized speech patterns of the different areas investigated and the historical origins of the patterns. However, these examples suggest quite strongly that gender difference may well override social class as a mechanism

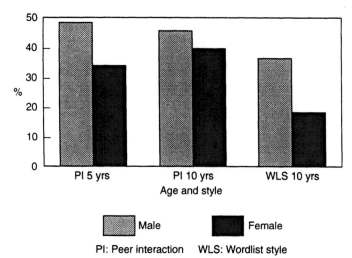

Fig. 10.6 Percentage use of glottal reinforcement in 5-year-old and 10-year-old children, by age and style, in Newcastle upon Tyne

whereby linguistic change is implemented. One possible interpretation here is that females lead in the change, and that the establishment of the glottal stop as a middle-class form is dependent on and secondary to the gender pattern. In this interpretation, female usage is instrumental in bringing about a reversal of the traditional low evaluation of the glottal stop. The generalization suggested is not that females favour prestige forms, but that they create them; i.e., if females favour certain forms, they become prestige forms. In these developments, both class and gender are implicated, but gender is prior to class.

Further observations may be made with respect to the patterns evident in Figs. 10.3–6. In both Tyneside and Coleraine, it is strictly localized variants which are most frequently used by males, while the high frequency variant favoured by females – the glottal stop – has become supra-local and apparently quite generalized in its distribution in contemporary British English (cf. the comments of Wells 1982). This has implications (which we cannot explore here) for theories of linguistic change based on the 'change from above'/'change from below' dichotomy, which seek to associate these patterns with different social subgroups and their respective configurations of 'prestige'. A more fruitful future line of enquiry may emerge from the apparently gender-related local/supra-local dichotomy suggested by the data reported here.

Social class and social network as extralinguistic variables

We noted earlier that analysis of the relationship between language variation and personal network structure in three Belfast inner-city communities suggested that a close-knit network functions as a conservative force, resisting pressures for change originating from outside the network. By close-knit we mean relatively dense and multiplex, these two concepts being of critical importance in a comparative analysis of social networks. In a maximally dense and multiplex network, everyone would know every-one else (density), and the actors would know one another in a range of capacities (multiplexity). Close-knit networks, which will of course vary in actual levels of density and multiplexity, are assumed to have the capacity to maintain and even enforce local conventions and norms – including linguistic norms. It is, after all, remarkable that stigmatized linguistic forms and low-status vernaculars can persist over centuries in the face of power-ful national policies for diffusing and imposing standard languages, and network analysis gives us a good basis for understanding the mechanisms that underlie this process of language maintenance.

Fig. 10.7 illustrates the link between network strength and high values of the non-standard variant (deletion of the intervocalic fricative) in Ballyma-carrett, Belfast. The highest network scores cluster towards the right of the scattergram (high scores for the 'vernacular' variant) and the lowest towards the left (low 'vernacular' scores). There is also a clear effect of gender difference here, with no overlap between male and female linguistic scores; i.e., females are always lower than males in usage of the vernacular variant. Furthermore, where females and males have the same network strength scores (two females and two males all have a score of 3), females are still differentiated from males by lower scores for the vernacular var-iant. Thus, the difference here is not accounted for by network strength alone: gender difference is also implicated in accounting for the variation.

We have suggested that a close-knit network structure is associated with language maintenance; the corollary to this is that a loose-knit network structure is associated with language change. We have argued in detail elsewhere that where ties are relatively loose-knit, communities will be susceptible to change originating from outside localized networks. These changes are not necessarily in the direction of the standard (see Milroy & Milroy 1985). We have also suggested that linguistic innovators are likely to be individuals who are in a position to contract many weak ties, and that

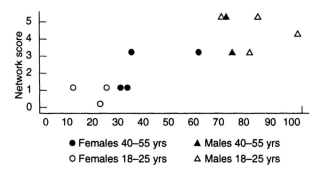

Fig. 10.7 Scores for deletion of intervocalic voiced dental fricative for Ballymacarrett, Belfast, by age, sex and social network strength

one consequence of successful innovation is the weakening of stable, local-ized community norms.

Before looking at some evidence from our Northern Ireland research to support this argument, let us consider briefly the implications of this link between loose-knit network ties and linguistic change in terms of the relationship between the variables of social class and social network. It is clear in a general way that the two variables are linked, in that different types of network structure are associated with different social classes: loose-knit structures with socially and geographically mobile middle class speakers, and close-knit ties with lower and upper class speakers. Fischer (1982) and Cochran et al. (1990) offer extensive analyses of the relationship between class and network, chiefly in cities. This relationship is not random or arbitrary, but springs from the operation of large-scale social, political and economic factors. The development of a class structure in small com-munities has been linked by the anthropologist Mewett (1982) to a decline in multiplex relationships. This is probably because a close-knit localized network of strong ties is a necessary prerequisite for a focused set of distinctive vernacular norms (see Le Page & Tabouret Keller 1985 for a discussion of the notion of 'focusing'). The evidence from such extensive empirical work in the sociological and anthropological literature does not support Guy's (1988) analysis of class as a macro-level concept, unrelated to network, which pertains to the micro-level; specifically, if we consider weak as well as strong ties, we see that the two variables are linked. Furthermore, the network variable, which operates at the level of inter-personal relationships, has some potential for explaining how the lan-guage/class correlations which are such a prominent part of the sociolinguistic literature actually come about (see further Milroy & Milroy 1992).

In view of the norm-enforcing capacities of groups built up mainly of strong ties, it is easy to see why innovators are likely to be persons weakly linked to such a group. Susceptibility to outside influence is likely to increase in inverse proportion to the strength of the tie with the group (measured in the Belfast communities by a network strength scale). Where groups are loose-knit – i.e., linked mainly by weak ties – they are likely to be generally more susceptible to innovation. This is consistent with Labov's principle that innovating groups are located centrally in the social hierar-chy, characterized by him as upper-working or lower-middle class (Labov 1980: 254; Kroch 1978). For it is likely that in what we used to call 'Western' societies, close-knit networks are located primarily at the highest and low-est strata, with a majority of socially and geographically mobile speakers falling between these two points.

This 'weak tie' model accounts for a number of observations which have been made about patterns of change, and we will discuss just two exam-ples. First, changes have often been observed to skip from city to city, missing out the intervening terrain. The merger apparently adopted from London English between /v/:/ð/ and /f/:/θ/ reported in Norwich teen-age speech (Trudgill 1986: 54ff) is an example of such a change. It is hard to explain in terms of close contact between London and Norwich speakers, since teenagers tend to contract their close ties near to home. But the change could plausibly be transmitted through a great many weak links, and Trudgill suggests tourists and football supporters as individuals who might contract such links. We must assume, however, that before a change like this stands any chance of becoming established in a network, the links through which it is transmitted are numerous (cf. Granovetter 1973: 1367).

Second, such a model illuminates a very puzzling pattern of variation with respect to the alternating phonolexical variable (u) (as in *pull, push, foot*) in inner-city Belfast. There is strong evidence of clear cross-community consensus on the social values associated with two alternative realizations, not (as we might expect) amongst older speakers who had contracted close cross-community ties prior to the current civil disorders, but amongst the younger speakers who had been prevented from contracting such strong cross-community ties. The contrast between the patterns associated with the two generations is clearly shown in Fig. 10.8. However, the paradox is resolved if we assume that innovations are transmitted via the multiple weak ties of everyday urban interaction in the neutral areas outside close-knit community territories (Milroy & Milroy 1985). A 'weak tie' model of change thus seems able to account for some instances of variation and change which are difficult to explain in terms of the usual unqualified assumption that linguistic change is encouraged by frequency of contact and relatively open channels of communication, and discouraged by boundaries of one sort or another, or weaknesses in lines of communication.

Interestingly, our argument here aligns well with the traditional assumption of historians of language that the emergent, mobile merchant class were largely responsible for the appearance of Midland and Northern dialectal innovations in late Middle and Early Modern ('Standard') English

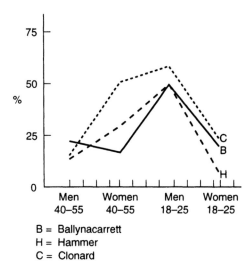

B = Ballynacarrett
H = Hammer
C = Clonard

Fig. 10.8 Percentage use of unrounded variant in words of the type *pull, push, foot* in inner-city Belfast (see, for example, Strang 1970: 214f; Ekwall 1956; Baugh & Cable 1978: 194). One of the purposes of undertaking empirical research in Belfast in the first place was to cast light on historical cases of this kind (J. Milroy 1992: viii–x), and it is not surprising, therefore, that there are a number of other patterns in the history of English and in the development of the Indo-European languages which might be usefully restated in terms of strong- and weak-tie patterns rather than solely in terms of geographical splits. Further afield, Grace (1992) has used a network-based argument to explain some puzzling developments among the Austronesian languages, which show widely differing patterns of susceptibility to change that cannot be explained using traditional assumptions (see also Grace 1990).

Relationships between the variables of class, gender and network: some evidence from Northern Ireland

Thus far we have considered two-way relationships between speaker variables: first, class and gender; second, class and network. Here we consider a three-way pattern involving gender, class and network. The manner in which these three variables may interact in either inhibiting or enabling linguistic change can be demonstrated by the history and social distribution of variants of the Belfast variables (a) and (e). These vowels were studied very intensively, both in the inner-city communities of Ballymacarrett, Clonard and Hammer and the slightly higher-status communities of Andersonstown and Braniel (see, for example, Harris 1985; J. Milroy 1992; Milroy & Milroy 1985). Their broad social-class distribution was established by means of a doorstep survey carried out in Belfast (see Milroy 1987b: 82 for details). Both variables are strongly affected by the sex, network struture and social class of speakers. Raised, lengthened variants of (e) are associated principally with women and middle-class speakers, and backed variants of (a) with men. Tables 10.1 and 10.2 describe the range of realizations associated with the two vowels, together with some complex phonetic constraints, some of which are categorical and some variable.

Table 10.1 Simplified representation of phonetic range of /a/ in Belfast vernacular, using key words

[ɛː]	[æ]	[a]	[ɑ]	[ɔ]
bag	*bat*	*bad*	*bad*	
bang	*back*	*snap*	*grass*	*grass*
		ant	*hand*	*hand*
		back	*snap*	

Front only:	velar environments
Back only:	fricative and voiced consonant environments (excluding velars)
Front/Back:	fricative and voiced consonant environments (excluding velars): back variants attested only among East Belfast youths.

Table 10.2 Simplified representation of phonetic range of [e] in Belfast vernacular, using key words

Mid e.g., [eː]	Low e.g., [a]
bed, bend, best (fricative and voiced consonant environments	wet, went (voiceless stop) and (sonorant + voiceless stop environments)

From a historical and geographical survey, we can get evidence of the direction of shift in these two variables and the gradual spread of innovatory forms. It is clear from the historical and dialectological data presented by Patterson (1860), Staples (1898), Williams (1903) and Gregg (1972) that /a/-backing and /e/-raising are both relatively recent phenomena in Belfast but are characteristic of modern Scots and originate in the Ulster-Scots speaking dialect area of Down and Antrim (as distinct from the Mid- and West-Ulster non-Scots hinterland). As we have pointed out elsewhere (Milroy & Milroy 1985), East Belfast adjoins the Ulster-Scots region of North Down, whereas West Belfast points south-west down the Lagan Valley, the dialect of which is Mid-Ulster, with less Scots influence. Furthermore, immigration to West Belfast is recent and is largely from a Mid- and West-Ulster hinterland. Present-day sociolinguistic evidence suggests that the incoming variants of (e) and (a) are diffusing from the East to the West of the city; scores for /a/-backing are higher for Ballymacarrett men than for any other group studied, while Ballymacarett women use the incoming mid variants of (e) more than any other group (see Tables 10.3 and 10.4).

As might be predicted from this pattern of gender-differentiation in the inner city, the higher-status Andersonstown and Braniel speakers exhibit a similar pattern of gender-differentiation but use the incoming variants of (e) more frequently and the incoming variants of (a) less frequently than Ballymacarrett and Clonard speakers (for details, see J. Milroy 1992, Milroy & Milroy 1985).

In summary, raised variants of (e) are in the inner city associated particularly with women and with slightly more prestigious outer-city speech; data collected by survey methods from a large and more heterogeneous sample of the Belfast population confirms that the higher the status of the speaker, the more likely he or she is to use raised variants. Incoming variants of (a) show an almost perfectly converse pattern of social distribution, being associated with male, vernacular inner-city speech. Taking this evidence together with the historical and geographical data outlined above, we may conclude that although incoming variants of both vowels appear to have originated in the same hinterland Scots dialect, each has assumed a diametrically opposed social value in its new urban setting.

The relationship between speaker choice of variant and individual network structure adds a further complexity to this pattern. Detailed quantitative analysis shows that the choice of variant correlates with network structure amongst some inner-city subgroups, but the social patterns are

Table 10.3 Incidence of retraction and backing of /a/ by age, sex and conversational style in two Belfast communities, calculated by an index score ranging from 0 (minimum) to 4 (maximum)

Style	Men 40–55	Women 40–55	Men 18–25	Women 18–25
East Belfast (Ballymacarrett)				
Interview	3.03	1.75	2.89	1.89
Spontaneous	3.58	2.58	3.43	2.10
West Belfast (Clonard)				
Interview	2.79	1.77	2.36	2.36
Spontaneous	2.79	1.85	2.33	2.61

Table 10.4 Percentage of mid realizations of /e/ in typically 'short' phonetic environments in two working-class Belfast communities

	Men 40–55	Women 40–55	Men 18–25	Women 18–25
Ballymacarrett	13	38	11	47
Clonard	11	26	21	31

quite different for each vowel. Although (a) is generally sensitive to network structure, the choice of variant is more closely correlated with network structure for women than for men, despite the fact that on average they use incoming backed variants much less frequently than men. The converse is true of (e); while men use incoming raised variants on average much less than women, the correlation between choice of variant and network structure is higher for men. These results were subjected to confirmatory statistical analyses, details of which are reported in L. Milroy (1987a) and elsewhere. We can thus argue that (e) functions particularly clearly for men and (a) for women as a network marker, and note that in each case *it is the group for whom the vowel has less significance as a network marker which seems to be leading the linguistic change*. This complex relationship between sex of speaker, network structure and language use is summarized in Table 10.5 and of course, as we have seen, social class is also implicated.

Conclusion

Using evidence from a number of places in the sociolinguistic literature, we have argued that contemporary quantitative sociolinguistics needs to develop more sophisticated procedures for dealing with the extralinguistic variables which have been shown in numerous empirical studies to affect patterns of linguistic variation and change in a powerful and systematic fashion. In particular, we need to develop a more reflective approach to the

Table 10.5 Contrasting patterns of distribution of two vowels involved in change, according to sex of speaker, relative frequency of innovatory variants, and level of correlation with network strength

Variable	Change led by	High correlation with network strength
(a)	men	women
(e)	women	men

concept of social class. While it is reasonable to suggest that both social conflict and social consensus underlie systematic patterns of variation, the contribution of conflict models of class to our understanding of these patterns has been unduly neglected.

There has sometimes been misunderstanding of the role that a variable such as social network (which attempts to measure closeness of ties within communities) might play in models of linguistic variation and change. Some linguists have apparently assumed that 'social network' is concerned only with strong ties and is roughly synonymous with 'peer-group', whereas we have emphasized the relativity of this intrinsically structural concept, comparing individuals and groups in terms of the relative strength or weakness of the social ties that bind them. Similarly, some linguists have seemed to believe that individuals may or may not possess a 'social network', when in fact all individuals are embedded in networks. However, these differ greatly in structure and content, and some may meaningfully be characterized as 'weaker' than others. Li, Milroy & Pong (1992) outline various procedures for modelling and measuring network 'strength'. The most important misunderstanding, however, is the belief that network and class are opposing variables which cannot be reconciled in a sociolinguistic analysis. We have argued that the form that social networks assume in particular societies is dependent on the broader social and economic structure of the societies in question: they constitute themselves in response to the needs of particular groups – needs that are themselves largely brought about by the position of these groups within the socio-economic structure. In Milroy & Milroy (1992) and in the present paper, we have attempted to clarify the network/class relationship.

We have also attempted to show that the variable of gender is closely implicated in patterns of change and closely related to class and network. However, although the three variables are interrelated, current interpretative frameworks do not help us to understand how they work together in structuring the patterns of linguistic variation which have been repeatedly observed in empirical studies of speech communities. Sociolinguistics urgently requires a more accountable and integrated approach to the social variables which provide a means of understanding patterns of linguistic variation and the mechanisms of linguistic change. We have made some suggestions here as to how we can make progress towards this.

References

Baugh, A.C. and Cable, T. (1978) *History of the English Language* (3rd edition), London: Routledge and Kegan Paul.

Bourdieu, P. (1977) 'The economics of linguistic exchanges', *Social Science Information* 16(6): pp. 645–68.

Bourdieu, P. (1984) 'Capital et marché linguistique', *Linguistische Berichte* 90: pp. 3–24.

Coates, J. (1986) *Women, men, and language*, London: Longman.

Cochran, M., Larner, M., Riley, D., Gunnarsson, L. and Henderson, C.R. Jr. (1990) *Extending families: the social networks of parents and their children*, Cambridge: Cambridge University Press.

Cohen, A. (ed.), (1982) *Belonging*, Manchester: Manchester University Press.

Eckert, P. (1989) 'The whole woman: sex and gender differences in variation', *Language Variation and Change* 1: pp. 245–68.

Ekwall, E. (1956) *Studies in the population of mediaeval London*, Lund: Lund Studies in English.

Fasold, R. (1990) *The sociolinguistics of language*, Oxford: Blackwell.

Fischer, C. (1982) *To dwell among friends: personal networks in town and city*, Chicago: University of Chicago Press.

Gal, S. (1988) 'The political economy of code choice', in M. Heller (ed.), *Code-switching*, Berlin: Mouton de Gruyter, pp. 245–63.

Gordon, E. (1991) 'The development of spoken English in New Zealand', in G. McGregor and W. Williams (eds.), *Dirty silence: aspects of language and literature in New Zealand*, Auckland: Oxford University Press, pp. 19–29.

Grace, G. (1990) 'The "aberrant" (vs. "exemplary") Melanesian languages', in P. Baldi (ed.), *Linguistic change and reconstruction methodology*, Berlin: Mouton de Gruyter, pp. 155–73.

—— (1992) 'How do languages change'? (More on 'aberrant' languages), *Oceanic Linguistics* 31.1: pp. 115–30.

Granovetter, M. (1973) 'The strength of weak ties', *American Journal of Sociology* 78: pp. 1360–80.

Gregg, R.J. (1972) 'The Scotch-Irish dialect boundaries of Ulster', in M. Wakelin (ed.), *Patterns in the folk speech of the British Isles*, pp. 109–39.

Guy, G. R. (1988) 'Language and social class', in F. Newmeyer (ed.), *Linguistics: the Cambridge Survey*, pp. 37–63.

Harris, J. (1985) *Phonological variation and change*, Cambridge: Cambridge University Press.

Hartley, S. (1992) *A study of the effects of sex and age on glottalisation patterns in the speech of Tyneside schoolchildren*, Undergraduate dissertation: University of Newcastle upon Tyne.

Horvath, B. (1985) *Variation in Australian English*, Cambridge: Cambridge University Press.

Kotsinas, U-B. (1988) Immigrant children's Swedish: a new variety? *Journal of Multilingual and Multicultural Development* 9: 129–40.

Kroch, A.S. (1978) 'Towards a theory of social dialect variation', *Language in Society* 7: pp. 17–36.

Kingsmore, R. (forthcoming) *Variation in an Ulster Scots dialect: a sociolinguistic study*, Birmingham: University of Alabama Press.

Labov, W. (1966) *The social stratification of English in New York City*, Washington DC: Center for Applied Linguistics.

—— (ed.), (1980) *Locating language in time and space*, New York: Academic Press.

—— (1986) 'Language structure and social structure', in S. Lindenberg et al., *Approaches to social theory*, NY: Russell Sage.

—— (1990) The intersection of sex and social class in the course of linguistic change, *Language Variation and Change* 2: pp. 205–54.

—— and Harris, W. (1986) 'De facto segregation of black and white vernaculars', in Sankoff (ed.), *Diversity and diachrony*. Amsterdam: John Benjamins, pp. 1–24.

Le Page, R.B. and Tabouret-Keller, A. (1985) *Acts of identity*, Cambridge: Cambridge University Press.

Li Wei, Milroy, L. and Pong Sin Ching (1992) 'A two-step sociolinguistic analysis of code-switching and language choice: the example of a bilingual Chinese community in Britain', *International Journal of Applied Linguistics* 2.1: pp. 63–86.

Macaulay, R.K.S. (1977) *Language, social class and education*, Edinburgh: Edinburgh University Press.

Mees, I. (1990) 'Patterns of sociophonetic variation in the speech of Cardiff schoolchildren', in N. Coupland (ed.), *English in Wales: diversity, conflict and change*, Avon: Multilingual Matters, pp. 167–94.

Mewett, P. (1982) 'Associational categories and the social location of relationships in a Lewis crofting community', in A. Cohen (ed.), *Belonging*, Manchester: Manchester University Press, pp. 101–30.

Milroy, J. (1981) *Regional accents of English: Belfast*, Belfast: Blackstaff.

—— (1992) *Linguistic variation and change*, Oxford: Blackwell.

—— and Milroy, L. (1978) 'Belfast: change and variation in an urban vernacular', in P. Trudgill (ed.), *Sociolinguistic patterns in British English*, London: Edward Arnold.

—— and Milroy, L. (1985) 'Linguistic change, social network and speaker innovation', *Journal of Linguistics* 21: pp. 339–84.

Milroy, L. (1987a) *Language and social networks* (2nd edition), Oxford: Blackwell.

—— (1987b) *Observing and analysing natural language*, Oxford: Blackwell.

—— (1991) 'New perspectives on the analysis of sex differentiation in language', in K. Bolton (ed.), *Sociolinguistics today: international perspectives*, London: Routledge, pp. 163–79.

—— and Milroy, J. (1992) 'Social network and social class: towards an integrated sociolinguistic model', *Language in Society* 21: pp. 1–26.

Patterson, D. (1860) *Provincialisms of Belfast*, Belfast: Mayne Boyd.

Rickford, J. (1986) 'The need for new approaches to social class analysis in linguistics', *Language and Communication* 6.3: pp. 215–21.

Rigg, L. (1987) *A quantitative study of sociolinguistic patterns of variation in adult Tyneside speakers*, Undergraduate dissertation: University of Newcastle upon Tyne.

Romaine, S. and Reid, E. (1976) 'Glottal sloppiness: a sociolinguistic view of urban speech in Scotland', *Teaching English* 9.3. Edinburgh: C.I.T.E.

Sankoff, D., Cedergren, H., Kemp, W., Thibault, P., and Vincent, D. (1989) 'Montreal French: language, class and ideology', in R. Fasold and D. Schiffrin (eds.), *Language change and variation*, Amsterdam: Benjamins, pp. 107–18.

Schatz, H. (1986) *Plat Amsterdams in its social context*, Amsterdam: P. J. Meertens institut voor dialectologie., Volkskunde en Naamkunde.

Staples, J.H. (1898) 'Notes on Ulster English dialect', *Transactions of the Philological Society*: pp. 357–87.

Strang, B.M.H. (1970) *A history of English*, London: Methuen.

Trudgill, P. (1986) *Dialects in contact*, Oxford: Blackwell.

Wells, J.C. (1982) *Accents of English: an introduction*, Cambridge: Cambridge University Press.

Williams, G. (1992) *Sociolinguistics: a sociological critique*, London: Routledge.

Williams, R.A. (1903) 'Remarks on Northern Irish pronunciation of English', *Modern English Quarterly* 6: pp. 129–35.

Woolard, K. (1985) Language variation and cultural hegemony: toward an integration of linguistic and sociolinguistic theory, *American Ethnologist* 12: pp. 738–48.

11

The development of a morphological class

Gregory R. Guy and Sally Boyd

Originally published in *Language Variation and Change*, 2 (1990).

One problem that must be confronted in studying child language development is that of describing a system that is rapidly changing but that retains structure and systematicity in the midst of the change. This is similar to the problem that has arisen in studies of language change in society. In the sociolinguistic arena, two basic concepts that have facilitated successful approaches to the study of changing structure are *orderly heterogeneity* (Weinreich, Labov, & Herzog, 1968), which highlights the systematic nature of linguistic differences between individuals or social groups, and the *variable rule* (Cedergren & Sankoff, 1973; Labov, 1969), which makes it possible to model quantitatively the alterations that a changing system passes through. These concepts from the phylogenetic approach can also be fruitfully applied to the ontogenetic problem, the study of language development within the lifetime of an individual.

One such application is Labov and Labov (1977), a study of the development of *wh-* questions by the authors' daughter. They followed the classic case-study approach: an extended study of the language development of a single individual. Whereas such a study may reveal a lot about the rapidly changing grammar of one child, there is always a question about the extent to which the observations are generalizable to the speech community. Also, longitudinal approaches are less useful in studying changes that occur more slowly. The answer to both problems is a cross-sectional population study, which samples a number of speakers at different ages. This allows us to establish simultaneously the generality of linguistic processes in the population and the course of ontogenetic development.

This is the approach taken in the present study. Our object of interest is the development of morphological categories in the English verbal system. This is a topic much discussed in the acquisition literature (see, e.g., Bybee & Slobin, 1982; Marchman, 1988). Our focus here is specifically on the closed class of "semiweak" verbs, listed in Table 11.1. These are unique in English because they combine morphological characteristics of both the strong class and the weak. In the past tense, they have a root-vowel change (/slip-slɛpt, luz-lɔst/) like strong verbs *and* an apical stop suffix like the

Table 11.1 English semiweak verbs

Ablaut pattern	Present	Past
u–ɔ	lose	lost
ɛ–ow	sell	sold
	tell	told
i–ɛ	sleep	slept
	keep	kept
	weep	wept
	creep	crept
	sweep	swept*
	leap	leapt*
	leave	left
	feel	felt
	deal	dealt
	kneel	knelt*
	mean	meant
	lean	leant*
	dream	dreamt*

weak verbs, a reflex of the -ed past tense marker. However, this class cannot be treated as simply an overlap of the other two classes, because some of its members show unique properties: absence of voicing assimilation in the suffix (compare *dreamt* with *creamed*) or regressive assimilation (*lost, left*). Rather, they constitute a separate verbal class, which is unproductive and appears to be losing members.[1] Table 11.1 notes certain of these verbs that in our experience tend to be dialectally or idiosyncratically regularized (i.e., inflected as weak verbs).[2]

For the child language learner this class presents a developmental challenge. As one learns semantic and formal oppositions like {PRESENT} versus {PAST} and attempts to implement these in the lexicon, a few salient generalizations should rapidly emerge. One is the "regular" lexical rule of -ed suffixation. Another, salient by reason of the high frequency of many of its exemplars, is root-vowel ablaut. As learners begin to partition the lexicon along these lines, how will they treat the semiweak class? Are they initially subsumed under one of the two larger classes? When do they begin to be treated as a distinct morphological group? Do all speakers treat them in a similar fashion? These were some of the questions we set out to address.

Of course, direct evidence about a speaker's morphological category system is hard to obtain. Our approach to the data problem was to examine a variable phonological process that interacts with, and is sensitive to, morphological structure. This is the one referred to in the literature as -t, d deletion:[3] the variable omission in natural speech of /t/ and /d/ from word-final consonant clusters, yielding pronunciations such as *wes' side* and *bes' frien'*. We treat it as a variable rule because it only occurs some of the time, even on successive repetitions of the same phrase by the same speaker in a single speech style. Nevertheless, it is extremely widespread in English; we know of no dialect where the process *never* occurs. It has evidently been operative since the Middle English period, and similar processes are reported for other Germanic languages (Romaine, 1986). Its relevance to the question at hand lies in the fact that the past tense forms of the semiweak verbs are subject to this rule since they all terminate in consonant clusters with final -*t* or -*d*.

Deletion of -*t,d* is one of the most thoroughly studied variable processes in English. Studies such as Labov, Cohen, Robins, and Lewis (1968), Labov (1972a, 1972b, 1989), Wolfram (1969, 1974), Fasold (1972), Guy (1977, 1980), Neu (1980), Baugh (1983), and Nesbitt (1984) revealed several contextual constraints that affect its rate of application. For example, more deletion occurs when a following word begins with a consonant (e.g., *wes' side*) than with a vowel (*west end*). Most such constraints have been found to be remarkably uniform in effect across all dialects and all speakers.

One constraint on -*t,d* deletion that appears to be pan-English concerns the morphological status of the deletable segment. This is where the rule becomes relevant to the issues at hand. All these studies have found that the rule has a lower rate of application in the past tense forms of weak verbs, where the -*t,d* represents the past tense marker (e.g., *missed, packed*), than in uninflected words where the -*t,d* is part of the root morpheme (e.g., *mist, pact*). This constraint is arguably functional in origin (deleting past tense markers would cause surface identity with present tense forms), but this issue is not pursued here.

Any adequate analysis of English phonology will, of course, require some representation of the distinction between inflected and uninflected words, since this contrast is crucial for many phonological processes. In the formalism of Chomsky and Halle (1968), boundaries are the device used to represent morphological structure. Thus, a regular past tense verb form is represented as having a "word" boundary (#) separating root from affix, whereas the uninflected words have no internal boundaries, as illustrated in (1). The semiweak verbs are distinguished by a different boundary type – a "formative" boundary (+), as in (2). Following this approach, the morphological condition on *t,d* deletion can be characterized as a boundary constraint (i.e., the rule is inhibited after a boundary).

(1)   a.   Uninflected words: *mist, pact* /mɪst, pækt/
     b.   Past tense verbs (weak): *missed, packed* /mɪs#t, pæk#t/
(2)   Past tense verbs (semiweak): *lost, left, told* /lɔs+t, lɛf+t, tol+d/

We are now in a position to state our research questions in a formal framework. First, if the morphological constraint on -*t,d* deletion is a boundary condition, do the different types of boundaries have different effects? Second, when do English-speaking children develop distinctive morphological analyses of the semiweak verbs, represented here as in (2)? What analysis of these forms do they have before this? Do all speakers eventually converge on an analysis like (2)?

The strategy we adopted to answer these questions was to use the variable rule of -*t,d* deletion as a probe of the speaker's mental morphological structures. Comparing rates of deletion in uninflected words, semi-weak past tense forms, and weak past tense forms, we should be able to infer whether an individual assigned them different morphological analyses or not and whether one, two, or three different analyses were used. We reasoned that if speakers deleted, say, semiweak verbs at the same rate as uninflected words, they probably assigned them the same morphological structure. If there were only a small number of such deletion patterns in the community, and they were ordered with respect to speaker's age, then we would have evidence bearing on the acquisition of this particular morphological distinction.

Some of the prior studies of -t,d deletion mentioned earlier investigated the semiweak verbs, with a variety of results. Although most constraints on the rule (especially the inhibition in past tense forms) are quite uniform across English dialects, the semiweak class was sometimes found to inhibit deletion, whereas other studies found it undergoing deletion at a high rate. Some studies even reported contrasting treatments of this class by different members of the same family. These patterns are strikingly confirmed in the recent study by Labov (1989), which showed a child closely matching his parents' rates of -t,d deletion in most environments but diverging from them in precisely the semiweak verbs.

Earlier investigations by one of us (Guy, 1977, 1980) suggested that two different grammatical lects existed in the population. One group of speakers treats the final -t or -d of semiweak verbs as noninflectional, not demarcated from the root by an internal boundary. Thus, they undergo deletion at the same high rate as *west* and *wind*. Another group analyzes these words as containing some kind of boundary and deletes them at a lower rate, although usually not as low a rate as the weak verbs. This implies that these speakers have a distinctive analysis for these forms, involving a formative boundary, which inhibits deletion but not as strongly as a full # boundary. It was also noted by Guy (1980) that the two lects showed age grading, and it was conjectured that they might be developmental stages.

The present work seeks to test these earlier proposals, via a more detailed examination of the age grading in a larger and dialectally more cohesive sample, using improved analytical procedures. The sample population has been greatly expanded by Boyd; the results reported here include data from 42 speakers from Philadelphia and two of its adjoining suburbs (King of Prussia, PA, and Cherry Hill, NJ), ranging in age from 4 to 65.

Procedures

The corpus from which we drew our sample is that collected by William Labov and his associates at the University of Pennsylvania in connection with the Linguistic Change and Variation (LCV) project (Labov, 1984; Payne, 1980). It consists of tape-recordings of sociolinguistic interviews, collected by trained fieldworkers using standard sociolinguistic survey methods. All speakers were recorded in a familiar setting (usually their own home or a familiar site in their neighborhood, such as a park or a friend's home). The interviews were structured to be as naturalistic and as close to informal conversation as possible, to yield the maximum amount of spontaneous speech.

From the LCV corpus we selected a sample designed to give a broad overall age range coupled with more intensive coverage of the childhood years. Both male and female speakers are included, and the social class range of consultants was restricted to the interior of the class scale, excluding both extremes. All our data were drawn exclusively from spontaneous speech styles; no formal elicitation devices were used. Speakers therefore span the styles that Labov (1972a: 79) characterized as casual and careful. Previous studies (e.g., Guy, 1980) have shown only modest style sensitivity for -*t,d*- deletion across this stylistic range. For each speaker, a complete study was done of all relevant tokens (i.e., all words terminating in a consonant cluster whose final segment is -*t* or -*d*, other than the word *and*) encountered in one full interview; interviews averaged about 1 hour in duration for adults, but appreciably less for small children.

As we have noted, the rate of -*t,d* deletion is significantly affected by other factors besides morphological structure, especially the following phonetic environment. Our results for these effects replicated those in studies already cited and hence are not examined here. Nevertheless, such factors must be controlled for in order to obtain meaningful comparisons of deletion rates in different speakers. Therefore, we conducted a multivariate variable rule analysis of the data, using the VARBRUL2 program (Rousseau & Sankoff, 1978), coding the data according to the analysis used in Guy (1980). Thus, we distinguished the following three factor groups: preceding phonetic environment (sibilants, fricatives, nasals, stops, and laterals), following phonetic environment (obstruents, liquids, glides, vowels, or pause), and morphological class (uninflected words [i.e., those without a boundary before the final stop], past tense forms of semiweak verbs, and past tense forms of regular verbs). In coding morphological class, we treated *went* as uninflected, as well as cases like *found* and *held*. However, *sent*, *bent* and so forth, were included in the semiweak class along with the words in Table 1, despite lacking a vowel change, because we concluded that in terms of the boundary formalism, they should be analyzed with the + boundary. The results to be reported are the parameter values obtained from the VARBRUL2 analysis, representing the probability of stop deletion occurring in the semiweak verbs, as contrasted with the other two morphological classes examined. These values range from 0 (no deletion) to 1 (total deletion).

Results

Analysis of the complete data pool for all speakers yielded the results shown in Table 11.2. As expected, uninflected words show a high rate of deletion, and past tense forms of weak verbs a low rate. (Furthermore, this ordering of these two categories held for every speaker in the sample for whom enough data were obtained to do a reliable individual analysis.) In the pooled data, the semiweak verbs occupy an intermediate position, undergoing deletion less often than uninflected words but more often

Table 11.2 /-t,d/ deletion: effect of morphological class (pooled data – all speakers)

Class	Probability of Deletion
Uninflected words (e.g. *mist*)	.65
Past tense of semiweak verbs (e.g. *lost*)	.55
Past tense of regular verbs (e.g. *missed*)	.31

than the weak verbs (although they are closer to the former than to the latter).

However, these pooled values obscure the considerable individual variability in the treatment of semiweak verbs that is our point of focus here. To obtain a finer picture of the acquisition of this class, we needed to break the data down as finely as possible. Ideally, this would mean a separate analysis for each individual in the corpus, but achieving this goal depends on the quantity of data available. Meaningful analytical results cannot be obtained if there are fewer than 10–15 tokens of the target category in a data set (Guy, 1980: 20). Speakers for whom we have less than this number of tokens cannot be analyzed individually.

In our corpus, the numbers of past tense semiweak verbs obtained were sufficient to undertake individual analyses for 25 of 27 adult consultants, but only 2 of the 15 children (aged 10 and 14). The remaining consultants, including all children under the age of 10, had to be combined in speaker groups for quantitative analysis. The children were combined according to neighborhood peer groups: children of approximately the same age (±1 year), who lived close to one another, played together regularly, and named one another as friends. Six such groups were thus obtained (five pairs and one group of three). In view of the linguistic uniformity of children's peer groups demonstrated by Labov et al. (1968) and Labov (1972b), this procedure should introduce minimal distortion to the analysis. The two adult consultants who were combined for analytical purposes were a married couple, both in their late 50s. The total number of data points obtained is therefore 34, consisting of 27 individual speakers and 7 speaker groups.

The probabilities of -t,d deletion in the semiweak verbs for the 34 data points are plotted in Figure 1 against the speaker's age. (For speaker groups, an average age of members of the group is used.) The data clearly show orderly heterogeneity in the age dimension: the probability of deletion declines with increasing age. We have included in the figure a regression line fitted to the dispersion; it has a negative slope equivalent to a decline in deletion probability of .052 for each decade increase in age. The correlation between age and deletion probability is $r = -.72$, which is highly significant. By way of contrast, the phonological constraints on this rule correlate with age only to an insignificant extent ($|r| < .2$); regression lines for these are essentially flat, with slopes of about .01 or less per decade.[5] Thus, it appears that only the treatment of semiweak verbs changes significantly with age. How can we account for this?

One point that must be dealt with at the outset is the question of change in progress. Fig. 11.1 represents a distribution in apparent time (Labov,

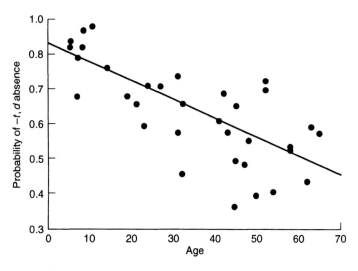

Fig. 11.1 Probability of -t,d absence in semiweak less verbs, by age

1966: 318–322), not different points in real time. It could therefore represent either a developmental process, through which all speakers of English pass as they age, or a change in progress in which a shift in community norms is occurring, and each successive generation of speakers behaves differently from their predecessors. Which of these two cases obtains here? Is the Philadelphia dialect undergoing a change in progress, involving increased deletion of -t,d semiweak verbs, and possibly the eventual loss of affixes in this verb class?

To answer these questions, we first note that we have no evidence that the whole process of -t,d deletion is involved in change or even in age grading. On the contrary, previous studies characterized it as stable and uniform.[6] Our results show age grading just for this one class of words; the other parameter values (including the input probabilities that track the overall rate of deletion per speaker) were not significantly correlated with age. So whatever process is going on, it is affecting just this verbal class. This alone may lead us to suspect acquisition is involved, since diachronic reorganizations of morphological classes tend to be associated with other changes in phonology and syntax. They also tend to be fairly slow, whereas this one, if it is a change in progress, looks to be heading to completion in a single lifetime.

The best kind of evidence for deciding whether change in progress is occurring is historical evidence from real time showing how the items in question were treated in the dialect at an earlier time. In the present case, we have no such evidence (other than the fact that semiweak verbs have existed in English with final affixes for many centuries). Therefore, we must rely on other types of evidence, principally the social distribution of the variable. Previous studies of known changes in progress revealed certain characteristic distributions of innovative forms across a speech community (see Guy, Horvath, Vonwiller, Daisley, & Rogers, 1986; Labov, 1981). Innovations are generally led by the working and middle classes, and by women. They are often differentially acquired by different ethnic groups and geographic areas. They frequently acquire some social evaluation and become subject to style shifting. In the present case, these characteristics are not observed. We found no significant correlation between the rate of deletion in semiweak verbs and other social characteristics of the speaker, such as sex, social class, geographic background, or ethnicity.[7] There is very little social awareness of the different treatments of this verb class, and no style shifting.

Thus, although the absence of real time data means we cannot completely rule out change in progress, the other evidence suggests it is unlikely. Since the characteristic social distributions of change in progress are completely lacking, we conclude that the age grading in Fig. 11.1 represents, in all probability, a developmental sequence reflecting the acquisition of this morphological class.

Viewed in this light, it seems possible to give a more refined analysis of this process of acquisition. The distribution of data points in Fig. 11.1 allows a more discrete interpretation than is suggested by the continuous regression line. In the upper left corner, the children are all tightly clustered with very high probabilities of deletion in semiweak verbs, generally above .75. Next, the younger adults tend to cluster around an approximate mean of .65. Finally, adults 45 years and older, although not as tightly grouped as the others, tend to fall at or below a value of .60. These values are suggestive. Recall that the probability of deletion in uninflected words shown in Table 11.2 for the pooled data was .65. Therefore, the values in Fig. 11.1 that are appreciably above .65 are showing *preferential* absence of -t,d in semiweaks verbs; that is, this is the most favored morphological class for deletion. Values that approximate .65, however, represent essential equivalence between this class and the uninflected words. Finally, only those values that are appreciably lower than .65 are displaying an inhibitory morphological constraint on deletion.

We can formalize these observations in terms of three deletion patterns. What we will call Pattern I is high deletion in semiweak verbs, defined as a probability greater that .75. This pattern characterizes most of the children. Pattern II is defined as a probability value between .60 and .75 and characterizes most of the young adults. Pattern III is defined as a deletion probability below .60; most adults over 45 have this pattern. The distribution of speakers across these three patterns is shown in Table 11.3.

The sharpest division is between the children and all the adults. Not a single adult uses Pattern I, and only one of the data points for children crosses into Pattern II. Thus, a very high rate of -t,d absence in semiweak verbs is a feature strictly characteristic of the speech of children. The division between older and younger adults is somewhat less sharp. Whereas each adult group has a distinctive, strongly modal distribution in Table 11.3, about a quarter of the individuals in each group have the nonmodal pattern. The data suggest that the cohesiveness of cohorts declines with age.

Table 11.3 Distribution of speakers by age and pattern of deletion in semiweak verbs[a]

Deletion pattern	Age of Speaker		
	0–18	19–44	45+
I (probability of deletion > .75)	7	0	0
II (.75 > probability of deletion > .60)	1	9	4
III (probability of deletion < .60)	0	3	10

[a] $\chi^2 = 40.83$, $p < .001$.

The development within the adult group merits further attention. Fig. 11.1 shows the adult values for deletion in the semiweak verbs trending toward the average value for deletion in the regular verbs (.31). But is this confirmed by the values for each individual? Fig. 11.2 provides such a comparison, plotting the difference between the factor values for the semi-weak class and the regular past tense forms for each speaker. (There are fewer data points in this graph because not all speakers had comparable factor values for the past tense forms, either because data were insufficient or because this factor proved to be a knockout.) The general trend of Fig. 11.1 is still apparent, and the division between the younger and older adults is perhaps even more pronounced. But note that for most older adults, the value for semiweak verbs remains above that for regular verbs; crossover occurs for only three speakers.

What is the significance of the three patterns and their age distribution? We propose an explanation in terms of morphological acquisition. First, consider the children's pattern. They exhibit nearly categorical absence of -t,d in semiweak verbs. (In fact, several individuals in the peer groups did show complete absence.) We interpret this to mean that children simply do not have a final apical stop in the underlying forms of these words. They treat such words as ordinary strong verbs, marking past tense only by means of the stem-vowel change. The underlying forms would be as shown in the first two columns of Table 11.4. The /i-ε/ vowel alternation that characterizes many of them parallels the ablauting pattern of several strong verbs, for example, *feed-fed, read-read, meet-met.*

In this hypothesis, the child's mental lexicon (by age 5) admits just two basic verb classes: weak verbs, which take the apical suffix, and strong verbs, which ablaut. The semiweak class does not exist, and its members are consigned to the strong class.[8] Such final -t,ds as do occur in children's speech are considered as sporadic borrowings from adult models.

The second stage of acquisition is represented by Pattern II, where the initial differentiation of the semiweak class from the broader strong class begins. At this point, speakers have recognized that such words do have a -t,d in the underlying form, but they are morphologically analyzed an uninflected, according no special status to the final apical stop. The vowel change is still the unique representation of past tense, and the alterations at the end of the word are lexically entered idiosyncrasies analogous to *teach-*

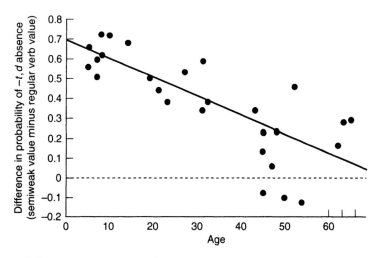

Fig. 11.2 Difference in probability of -t/d absence between semiweak forms and regular past tense forms, by age

Table 11.4

Semiweak verbs					
Present tense	Past tense				
	Pattern I	Pattern II	Pattern III	Regular verbs	Uninflected words
tɛl	tol	told	tol+d	rol#d	fold
slip	slɛp	slɛpt	slɛp+t	stɛp#t	æpt
liv	lɛf	lɛft	lɛf+t	pəf#t	lɪft
luz	lɔs	lɔst	lɔs+t	tɔs#t	kɔst

taught and *stand-stood*. The underlying forms contain no internal boundaries, as shown in the third column of Table 11.4.

In the final stage, represented by Pattern III, speakers take a further step in their analysis of verbal morphology, They connect the apical stops in semiweak verbs with those found in regular weak verbs (the orthographic *-ed* suffix). Hence, these *-t,d*s begin to partake of the resistance to deletion that characterizes the *-ed* suffix in weak verbs. But rarely do deletion rates in semiweak verbs drop as low as in regular preterites. The semiweak verbs are, of course, still distinguished by several characteristics, such as the stem-vowel change, regressive voicing assimilation, and nonproductivity. If it is functional considerations that inhibit *-t,d* deletion in regular verbs, they would not operate as strongly here because the {PAST TENSE} meaning is still recoverable after deletion.

These facts can be captured in our formalism by postulating that Pattern

III speakers have arrived at some mental treatment of such forms analogous to our representation of them in the fourth column in Table 11.4,
which delimits the affix by a + boundary.[9] It is only at this stage that a
distinctive third class of verbs is developed, and the final -*t,d*s are accorded
some resistance to deletion because of their morphological status.

Movement from the holistic analysis of Pattern II to the atomic analysis
of Pattern III is not a step that speakers take early in life. Of the speakers in
the sample who show Pattern III, the youngest are 31 and 32 years old, and
the average age is 49. This clearly implies that language acquisition is not a
process confined to childhood. Fig. 11.1 shows speakers continuing to
reanalyze their language well into adult life. But the data also show that
mature native speakers of a single dialect may still entertain different
mental grammars. Not everyone, evidently, arrives at a Pattern III analysis,
it coexists in the adult population with Pattern II.

The difference between the two reanalyses (the childhood shift from
Pattern I to II and the adult shift from Pattern II to III) is striking. The
earlier shift seems to occur in the entire population at a specific age, but the
later one occurs in only part of the population over a much wider age
range. What might account for the difference?

The first reanalysis, which involves inserting the final stops in the underlying forms of past tense semiweak verbs, is most plausibly driven by the
basic imperative of language acquisition: accommodation to the production
of other speakers. The nearly categorical absence of these stops in the
speech of children using Pattern I is a qualitative difference from the adult
patterns; this should provide sufficient evidence for all speakers to undertake the first reanalysis, when they reach an appropriate developmental
level. The surface outputs of Pattern II and Pattern III speakers, however,
differ only quantitatively, by relatively small amounts in the frequency of -
t,d deletion in this small class of verbs. We hypothesize that, in this case, the
difference does not provide sufficient evidence to prompt the reanalysis
that leads to Pattern III.

Another potential facilitating factor to be considered in the development
of Pattern III is the economy and generality of the competing analyses (cf.
Fodor & Crain, 1987). The reanalysis involves a changed derivation for the
forms in Table 11.1. Pattern II treats them as strong verbs and uses lexically
specific rules to generate the past tense forms, whereas Pattern III presumably makes use of more general inflectional rules, although some lexically
specific rules are still required. If linguistic development favors more general rules and more economical grammars, the Pattern III analysis might be
slightly favored. But the magnitude of any such effect should be small in
this case. Given that only about a dozen lexical entries are involved, and
that some lexically specific rules are required in either case, little grammatical economy is gained by this reanalysis, whereas the cost includes for-
mulating a new verb class with an inflectional pattern differing from both
the strong and weak classes. Hence, this is also unlikely to constitute a
sufficient factor for provoking the adult reanalysis.

We conclude, therefore, that the adult shift to Pattern III is probably the
result of spontaneous linguistic insight by individuals and is neither socially
motivated nor developmentally required. As Bates and MacWhinney (1987:

171) noted, "form-form . . . and form-function connections can be observed and pondered in their own right, whether or not the organism is currently being driven to meet some primary need." For some individuals, the eventual result is, evidently, a new analysis.

Phonological form classes

Since the developments we postulate involve the reclassification of words in the mental lexicon, it is worth examining the semiweak verbs more closely to see how uniform this process is. The most interesting question to address would be whether the reanalyses proceed word-by-word – a developmental "lexical diffusion." We suspect that this is the case, but to demonstrate it at a statistically significant level would require appreciably more data than were available to us, as it would involve tracking each word separately in the speech of each individual and obtaining sufficient tokens of each to control for the other factors influencing -*t,d* deletion. Our data are, however, sufficient to investigate differentiation between phonological form classes. As we noted, one of the factors affecting -*t,d* deletion is the preceding phonological environment. The main direction of this effect is that preceding /s/, stops, and nasals favor deletion, whereas /l/ and non-sibilant fricatives disfavor (Guy, 1980). Since, fortuitously, all of these environments are represented in the semiweak verbs, we may examine the data to see if such classes are differentiated and whether they are significant for morphological reanalysis.

Since very fine partitioning of the data set unavoidably worsens the obscuring effect of statistical noise, sampling error, and so on, we confine our attention to the most robust aspect of the pattern. In the present case, that is the shift from categorical absence of final -*t,d* in Pattern I to underlying presence in Pattern II. We therefore focus on the children's data in this section.

When the shift to Pattern II has occurred for a particular set of words, surface absence of -*t,d* in that set should be due entirely to the effect of the phonological deletion process. This effect can be minimized by examining those following phonological environments in which -*t,d* deletion is least likely to occur: nonconsonantal ones (i.e., following pause, liquid, glide, or vowel). If the various phonological form classes of semiweak verbs then show only minor differences in -*t,d* absence, they are probably undifferentiated in the reanalysis process. But if they show substantial differences, then those form classes that show unusual absence of -*t,d* should be lagging in reanalysis. Relevant figures are given in Table 11.5.

The nearly categorical absence of -*t* in the *kept, slept* group, even in these phonologically conservative contexts, implies that such segments are not present underlyingly; they contrast starkly with comparable uninflected words (e.g., *act,apt*) where the deletion rate is only 44% in the same environments. Therefore, these words must lag in the reclassification from Pattern I to Pattern II. The words with preceding nasals also appear to be lagging in this process. Compare a deletion rate in comparable uninflected words (e.g., *tent*) of 22%. On the other hand, the categorical presence of -*t* in

Table 11.5 Semiweak verbs in phonologically conservative contexts: /-t,d/ absence by preceding segment (all children under age 14)

Preceding segment	N	% -t,d absent
/f/ (*left*)	10	0
/l/ (*told, sold, felt,*etc.)	20	0
nasal (*meant, sent, dreamt,* etc.)	46	78
/s/ (*lost*)	3	33
/p/ (*kept, slept,* etc.)	35	97

left, and in *told, sold,* and so on, indicates that these words are reclassified early and treated equivalently with comparable uninflected forms (which for these speakers in the same following contexts show a deletion rate of 10% on 20 tokens; given the Ns, this is not significantly different). Concerning *lost,* with only 3 tokens, there is little to be said.

The data may also be taken to indicate that the presence or absence of regressive assimilation could affect the reanalysis. The words that are lagging in this process – those with preceding nasal or /p/ – become fairly typical strong verbs without their final stops. They then have only a vowel change. But *lef'* and *los',* without final stops, are anomalous in the strong class. Only a few such words have stem-final alterations in the past (aside from the addition of *-t,d*), and none have devoicing of a segment other than /d/. Possibly the presence of this stem-final voicing anomaly focuses learners' attention on the end of the word, facilitating insertion of the final stops. (But this does not explain early reanalysis of *told, felt,* etc., unless it has to do with the dearth of strong verbs ending in liquids.)

These data are thus consistent with a view of morphological reanalysis that is granular rather than uniform. The relevant phonological form classes defined by the *-t,d* deletion rule are differentiated in the reanalysis process. Future investigations should examine whether the individual lexical items within these form classes are also differentiated and whether other factors such as frequency (cf. Phillips, 1984) affect the process.

Conclusion

The data we have examined clearly indicate that the semiweak verb class of English is treated differently by speakers at different ages, at least with respect to the occurrence or nonoccurrence of final /t,d/. We propose that the observed quantitative differences reflect different stages in the ontogenetic course of development of the speakers' verbal morphological systems. Initially, the semiweak class does not exist, and children assign these verbs to the strong class on the basis of their most salient feature: root-vowel ablaut. Hence, they follow the dominant pattern of the strong class: no alteration at the end of the word. Final apical stops are therefore categorically absent.

At the next stage, these verbs are differentiated from the rest of the strong class as lexical exceptions that undergo stem-final alterations in the past tense. These alterations, we hypothesize, are treated holistically and are not related to the productive pattern of *-ed* affixation in the weak verbs. Quantitatively this means that final apical stops are variably present. All speakers proceed to this stage by late adolescence.

Lastly, some speakers go on to formulate the semiweak verbs as a separate morphological class, which undergoes both ablaut and affixation. This leads to a low rate of final apical stop deletion, as occurs in weak verbs.

This pattern is broadly similar to the stages in morphological acquisition identified by MacWhinney (1976) in his study of Hungarian. In his Stage II, "amalgams are analysed semantically, but not morphologically" (p. 400). Our Pattern II speakers have the correct past tense semantics for the semiweak forms but do not analyze them with any internal morphology. In MacWhinney's Stage III, complex forms begin to be analyzed morphologically, which is what occurs among our Pattern III speakers.[10] Of course, MacWhinney's data refer just to child language and to morphological classes that are more regular than the one we have examined, but the developmental parallels are evident.

This sequence may reflect a general principle of language acquisition. Forms are first acquired holistically; analyses of their internal morphology come later. For example, the process of pidginization (a special case of adult L2 acquisition) classically involves completely holistic acquisition. All forms are free morphemes devoid of inflection or other internal morphology. It seems that the word – a linguistic sign binding sound to meaning – has a cognitive primacy over formal linguistic processes of morphology and syntax.

Finally, we also conclude that language development does not end with puberty or majority but goes on into adult life. If the empirical facts that one confronts every day in one's language allow multiple interpretations, at least some speakers may arrive over time at a new mental analysis. In this case, the cognitive pressure to do so is fairly slight. The accommodation imperative that drives language development – the motivation to make one's output resemble the corpus of data that one perceives others to be producing – will not exert much influence in a community with the internal diversity evident in Fig. 11.1. But this very age-graded diversity also demonstrates that the ontogeny of language must continue through a speaker's lifetime.

Notes

1. Certain other groups of verbs share some characteristics of those in Table 1 but with other differences. Verbs such as *taught, thought, caught* have the root-vowel change and final *-t* in the past tense but also have additional irregularities at the end of the root. They are also unaffected by *-t,d* deletion since they lack a final cluster in the past tense. Cases like *found* and *held* have a final stop that is straightforwardly analyzed as part of the root. The *sent, spent* group lack a root-vowel change, and *went* is suppletive. This list is restricted to vowel-

changing verbs whose past tense forms terminate in a consonant cluster that can be unambiguously segmented into a root-final consonant and an apical stop affix.

2. Regularizations by adults were rare in our corpus; for the treatment of children's regularizations, see note 8.

3. Referring to this process as a "deletion" implies that the segments in question are underlyingly present. As we shall see, for our youngest speakers this is probably not the case. However, the quantitative analysis reported here does not depend on this assumption; the results may be consistently interpreted in terms of probability of the absence of -*t,d*, regardless of how that absence comes about.

4. These issues are discussed in Guy and Bisol (1988), but the field awaits a more comprehensive treatment of the implications of variation data for phonological theory.

5. Within the morphological factor group we cannot make independent comparisons because VARBRUL normalizes factor values within a group around the .5 value. Therefore, if one factor in a group is trending down with age, some other value(s) in the group must trend reciprocally upward. In our data, the deletion rates in the uninflected words and regular verbs show the consequent positive correlations with age (r = .164 and .675, respectively). One might therefore consider the possibility that these rises are the primary (even if weaker) effects, and the fall in semiweak verbs the consequence of normalization. However, this hypothesis is not confirmed by the unnormalized raw frequencies.

6. Comparatively high overall rates of -*t,d* deletion have been noted for Black English Vernacular speakers (Labov 1972b; Wolfram, 1969), and there are dialectal differences in the effect of a following pause (Guy, 1980), but otherwise no major differences have appeared in the populations studied to date.

7. Guy (1980) conjectured that working-class adult speakers might show higher deletion rates in semiweak verbs, but the present study did not find this to be significant. Sex differences were small and inconsistent in our data. Higher deletion rates were found in male children but in female adults.

8. Many children, aged 2–6, go through a stage of regularization, where strong and semiweak verbs are variably treated as weak, forming past tense forms with the -*ed* suffix and no vowel ablaut (e.g., *drinked, leaved*). Such cases were treated as weak verbs in our analysis. Our discussion deals with developments after forms have been correctly identified as exceptions to the their Class III (our semiweak class, plus cases like *said, did*) are regularized less often than most other vowel-changing verbs. They attributed this to the redundant cue to past tense provided by the presence of the final stop. However, they did not discuss the rate of final stop *absence* in their data.

9. In a multilevel morphology, this would be represented as replacing a lexical entry for the past tense that includes the final segment by a derived form involving level 1 affixation.

10. MacWhinney's Stage I addresses the early childhood phenomenon of using inflected forms in semantically inappropriate ways; an analogous situation in English would be the use of *came* or *went* as present tense forms. Our study begins with age groups that already possess the correct semantic analysis of the forms in question.

References

Bates, E., and MacWhinney, B. (1987) 'Competition, variation, and language learning' in B. MacWhinney (1987) pp. 157–193.

Baugh, J. (1983) *Black street speech*, Austin: University of Texas Press.

Boyd, S., and Guy, G.R. (1979) *The acquisition of a morphological category*. Paper presented at the Linguistic Society of America annual meeting; also presented at the Australian Linguistic Society annual meeting, 1980.

Bybee, J. L., and Slobin, D. I. (1982) 'Rules and schemas in the development and use of the English past tense', *Language* 58: pp. 265–289.

Cedergren, H., and Sankoff, D. (1973) 'Variable rules: Performance as a statistical reflection of competence', *Language* 50: pp. 333–355.

Chomsky, N., and Halle, M. (1968) *The sound pattern of English*, New York: Harper & Row.

Fasold, R.W. (1972) *Tense marking in Black English*, Arlington, VA: Center for Applied Linguistics.

Fodor, J.D., and Crain, S. (1987) 'Simplicity and generality of rules in language acquisition', in B. MacWhinney (1987) pp. 35–63.

Guy, G.R. (1977) 'A new look at -t,d deletion', in R.W. Fasold and R.W. Shuy (eds.), *Studies in language variation*, Washington, DC: Georgetown University Press, pp. 1–11.

—— (1980) 'Variation in the group and the individual: The case of final stop deletion', in Labov (1980), pp. 1–36.

Guy, G.R., and Bisol, L. (1988) *Phonological theory and variable data*. Paper presented at NWAV-XVII, Université de Montréal. [To appear in Portuguese in *Organon*.]

Guy, G.R., Horvath, B., Vonwiller, J., Daisley, E., and Rogers, I. (1986) 'An intonational change in progress in Australian English', *Language in Society* 15(1): pp. 23–51.

Kiparsky, P. (1985) 'Some consequences of lexical phonology', *Phonology Yearbook* 2: pp. 85–138.

Labov, W. (1966) *The social stratification of English in New York City*, Arlington, VA: Center for Applied Linguistics.

—— (1969) 'Contraction, deletion, and inherent variability of the English copula', *Language* 45: pp. 715–762.

—— (1972a) *Sociolinguistic patterns*, Philadelphia: University of Pennsylvania Press.

—— (1972b) 'Where do grammars stop?', in R.W. Shuy (ed.), *Sociolinguistics: Current trends and prospects* (GURT 23), Washington, DC: Georgetown University Press. pp. 43–88.

—— (ed.) (1980) *Locating language in time and space*, New York: Academic.

—— (1981) 'What can be learned about change in progress from synchronic description?', in D. Sankoff and H. Cedergren (eds.), *Variation omnibus*, Edmonton: Linguistic Research, pp. 177–200.

—— (1984) 'Field methods used by the project on linguistic change and variation', in J. Baugh and J. Sherzer (eds.), *Language in use: Readings in sociolinguistics*, Englewood Cliffs, NJ: Prentice-Hall.

—— (1989) 'The child as linguistic historian', *Language Variation and Change* 1: pp. 85–97.

Labov, W., Cohen, P., Robins, C., and Lewis, J. (1968) *A study of the non-standard English of Negro and Puerto Rican speakers in New York City*. Report on Co-operative Research Project 3288, New York: Columbia University Press.

Labov, W., and Labov, T. (1977) 'Learning the syntax of questions', in R. Campbell and P. Smith.

MacWhinney, B. (1976) 'Hungarian research on the acquisition of morphology and syntax', *Journal of Child Language* 3: pp. 397–410.

—— (ed.) (1987) *Mechanisms of language acquisition*, Hillsdale, NJ: Erlbaum.

Marchman, V. (1988) 'Rules and regularities in the acquisition of the English past tense', *Center for Research in Language Newsletter* Vol. 2, No. 4 (April).

Mohanan, K.P. (1986) *The theory of lexical phonology,* Dordrecht: Reidel.

Nesbitt, C. (1984) *The linguistic constraints on a variable process: /t, d/ deletion in Sydney speech,* BA Honours thesis, University of Sydney.

Neu, H. (1980) 'Ranking of constraints on /t, d/ deletion in American English: A statistical analysis', in Labov (1980) pp. 37–54.

Payne, A. (1980) 'Factors controlling the acquisition of the Philadelphia dialect by out-of-state children', in Labov (1980) pp. 143–178.

Phillips, B.S. (1984) 'Word frequency and the actuation of sound change', *Language* 60: pp. 320–342.

Romaine, S. (1986) 'The effects of language standardization on deletion rules: Some comparative Germanic evidence from *t/d* deletion', in D. Kastovsky and A. Szwedek (eds.), *Linguistic across historical and geographic boundaries* (Vol. 1), Amsterdam: Mouton de Gruyter, pp. 605–620.

Rousseau, P. and Sankoff, D. (1978) 'Advances in variable rule methodology', in D. Sankoff (ed.), *Linguistic variation: Models and methods,* New York: Academic, pp. 57–69.

Sankoff, D. and Labov, W. (1979) 'On the uses of variable rules', *Language in Society* 8: pp. 189–222.

Weinreich, U., Labov, W. and Herzog, M. (1968) 'Empirical foundations for a theory of language change', in W.P. Lehmann and Y. Malkiel (eds.), *Directions for historical linguistics,* Austin: University of Texas Press, pp. 95–189.

Wolfram, W. (1969) *A sociolinguistic description of Detroit Negro speech,* Washington, DC: Center for Applied Linguistics.

—— (1974) *Sociolinguistic aspects of assimilation,* Arlington, VA: Center for Applied Linguistics.

12

Linguistic change in intonation: the use of high-rising terminals in New Zealand English

David Britain

Originally published in *Language Variation and Change*, 4 (1992).

Whereas most Labovian sociolinguistic research has analyzed phonological variation, very little work has been undertaken in this paradigm into examples of prosodic variability. This is not altogether surprising. An almost total lack of historical evidence with which to support research findings, combined with the lack, until relatively recently, of widely available user-friendly spectrographic software have no doubt served as deterrents to would-be investigators. Perhaps a far greater barrier, however, has been of a theoretical nature, namely, whether linguistic change that affects a shift in both form and function can be analyzed using the concept of "linguistic variable." As readers of this journal are aware, there has been considerable discussion about the acceptability of quantifying syntactic and discourse variables for well over a decade (see Hasan, 1989; Lavandera, 1978; Sankoff, 1988). As the perceived illocutionary force of an utterance is often dependent on suprasegmental features (Ching, 1982; Selting, 1988), it follows that these same issues of variable analyzability are of relevance in the study of intonational variation. A careful line therefore has to be drawn between the quantitative investigation of such features, on the one hand, and the implication, on the other, that the variants in question can be regarded as alternative realizations of the same structural entity in the same way, for example, that (r) was analyzed in New York (Labov, 1966).

This article reports sociolinguistic research into a particularly salient intonation contour used in New Zealand English, the high rising terminal contour (HRT) in declarative clauses, a feature also found in Australia (Guy, Horvath, Vonwiller, Daisley, & Rogers, 1986; Guy & Vonwiller, 1984), Canada (James, Mahut, & Latkiewicz, 1989), and the United States (Ching, 1982) (see Appendix). Classified as Tone 2 by Halliday (1967), it is similar in many respects to the contour often used in English polar questions ("Do you want lasagne for dinner?") and in so-called queclaratives (Geluyken, 1987), which turn statements into questions (such as "You want lasagne for dinner?"). The HRTs under investigation here do not have the interrogative function of polar questions. Example (1) highlights how HRTs

are used in discourse. Italicized clauses terminate with a high rising terminal, marked ↑, + marks a pause.

(1)   Pam: and um he just stood there + *and I I've got a fear of a real phobia for*
big moths↑ *I hate them flying around me and that*↑ *and I as I was sort of*
nodding off to sleep I could hear a um + *like what I thought was a moth*↑
banging on the window↑ and I just remember thinking ooh yuck you
know and my cat was on the bed *and it growled and jumped off the bed*↑
and I turned around and there- um there was a guy standing there by
my bed and it was a water bed and it was sort of shoved up right
against the wall so he was + *he'd got down between the wall and the*
water bed↑ *so he was in an awkward position*↑ and I just jumped up out
the bed when I got to the door he was still just standing there.

What do HRTs mean?

Research into the communicative function of HRTs both in New Zealand (S.
Allan, 1990; Britain, forthcoming) and elsewhere (Guy & Vonwiller, 1984;
Guy et al., 1986) has conclusively rejected the social inequality hypothesis
put forward by Lakoff (1975: 16). She claimed that the use of HRTs, stereo-
typically by women and young people, marks a lack of both commitment
and confidence in what is being said and displays the speaker's deference
and social powerlessness to the listener. As we shall see, such an interpretation of the function of HRTs cannot explain the way in which their use is
socially stratified, nor, in particular, can it account for their occurrence in
differing frequencies in a wide variety of discourse text types, such as in
descriptions, explanations, and narratives such as that in (1).

Based on research carried out in Australia, Guy and Vonwiller suggested
a more positive, interactional role for HRTs, namely, "TO SEEK VERIFICATION OF
THE LISTENER'S COMPREHENSION" (Guy & Vonwiller, 1984: 4; emphasis theirs).
By using an HRT, they claimed, a speaker may wish to obtain feedback
about the listener's reaction to an utterance, negotiate a longer turn, secure
listener empathy, or simply ensure that the hearer has grasped the meaning
of the utterance in question. We can distinguish two distinct speaker motivations implicit in their argument. Their claim for HRT function combines
affective goals, which aim to secure common ground between speaker and
hearer, and *instrumental* goals, which seek to overcome practical obstacles
in the mutual construction of talk (see Meyerhoff, 1991). Later discussions
of HRT function by the Sydney researchers (Guy et al., 1986; Horvath, 1985)
have tended to emphasize the instrumental, rather than affective, motives
behind HRT use. In particular, they pointed to the regulation of turn taking
in which HRTs have a dual role (Guy et al., 1986: 26; Horvath, 1985: 131).
On the one hand, they form the first part of an adjacency pair and thus
signal that a response is required from the hearer. On the other, however,
they mark the speaker's desire to continue the turn at talk. HRTs, then, like
you know and *right?*, allow only a minimal response from the listener.

Horvath's (1985) discussion looked at another instrumental function of
HRTs, namely, as a way of maintaining the engagement of conversational

partners. She explained how the success of such text types as narratives and descriptions can be measured by the extent to which the message of the text is understood and the listener(s) are actively engaged in the conversation (Horvath, 1985: 130). Similar explanations to those proposed by the Australian research team are given by S. Allan, who conducted the only previously published work carried out in New Zealand (S. Allan, 1990). Allan's study showed that HRTs are used by the speaker to demand both a minimal response from the listener and a continued and extended turn at talk.

These claims made for HRT function seem valid enough and are clearly supported by the evidence available. However, the discussions up until now have failed to give adequate attention to the affective goals behind HRT use, namely, the establishment of solidary common ground between the speaker and the hearer, a point that was raised, but not fully developed by the Australian researchers. Having established the "other-oriented" nature of HRT use, our further analysis of its function requires a socio-linguistic model sensitive to the interactive and mutually constructive nature of talk. Brown and Levinson's theory of politeness provides such a framework, based as it is on the conversational needs and wants of both speaker and hearer (Brown & Levinson, 1987). Extending Goffman's notion of "face," Brown and Levinson distinguished between people's *negative* face wants (the desire for freedom of action and unimpeded attention [1987: 129]) and their *positive* face wants (the desire that the addressee's wants be thought of as desirable [1987: 101]). I argue that rather than marking negative politeness, by hedging and showing deference, as linguists such as Lakoff have implied, high rising tones in declarative clauses are markers of positive politeness toward the addressee, inviting him or her to participate vicariously and empathetically in the production of the talk and emphasizing the in-group nature of the relationship between speaker and hearer. Brown and Levinson proposed three classes of strategies by which conversationalists can address the hearer's positive face wants. Several of these strategies can be accomplished by the use of HRTs.

Their first class of strategies is to claim common ground (1987: 103–125). One way a speaker can attempt to achieve this is to "intensify the interest of his own contribution to the conversation, by 'making a good story'" and hence "pull [the hearer] right into the middle of the events being discussed . . . thereby increasing their intrinsic interest to him" (1987: 106–107). But how do speakers "make a good story"? Schiffrin's research on conversational management devices contrasted both opinion and narrative texts to demonstrate how these two distinct types of talk achieve particular speaker goals. Opinions, on the one hand, are *self*-management devices that allow speakers to shield themselves from the truthfulness of the facts by focusing on their own stance toward what is being said. Narratives, on the other hand, which involve the sharing of personal, often intimate experiences, are much more other-oriented, allowing the speaker "to transform the person who is listening into an audience that vicariously participates in the narrator's experience" and inviting "the listener to join in an interactional allegiance and endorse the speaker's position" (Schiffrin, 1990: 252–253). Certain units of narrative structure, namely, orientations and, in particular,

evaluations (Labov & Waletzky, 1967), play an important role in the creation of heightened interest. The following extract is from Pam, a young
middle-class Pakeha woman recounting an incident when a man followed
her through a park. The speaker uses a great number of HRTs, particularly
in evaluative positions. One very plausible interpretation is that the HRTs
intensify and dramatize the message of the story, thereby heightening the
hearer's vicarious participation in the development of the experience,
ensuring she comprehends her anxiety and guaranteeing her sympathetic
alignment. Hence, Pam is using HRTs to make a good story.

> (2) Pam: I had another incident of someone in Porirua following me followed
> me home from the railway station *and tried to cut me off in the park*↑ I
> was walking home about half past seven at night and I knew he was
> following me fr- *and I stopped in at the chicken shack*↑ *and bought some
> chips*↑
>
> Int: mmm
>   and everything
> Pam: and m- mucked around *and um when I got out the shop I couldn't
> seen him around*↑ and I w- crossed the cr- road at the crossing walked
> up to where the bridge is to go over the park
> Int: yeah
> Pam: and started to walk up the path *well just out of the
> corner of my eye I saw him across the road*↑ *in the bushes*↑ *across the road*↑
> and he crossed the road *and started to come up the road behind me*↑ and
> I ran across the park back down to the shops *and he tried to cut me off
> the other way*↑ *so I was going like this and he was going like that*↑ and we
> just sort of met + there and he said don't be scared of me + huh and
> said F off [laughs] and then I phoned up my father and he came
> down and got me

Another positive politeness strategy that can be realized through the use
of an HRT is called a "point of view operation" (Brown & Levinson, 1987:
118–122; see Schiffrin's [1990] "deictic shifts"). These shifts can involve
personal center switches, where the speaker talks as if the hearer's understanding is equal to the speaker's own, or alternatively shifts in spatial
and/or temporal reference. In example (3), the interviewer, Boyd, is talking
to Joe, a young Maori man, about why he likes living in Porirua.

> (3) Boyd: what's what say + what do you find about it what's good about it?
> Joe: oh I like the um + I like the closeknitness of the en- of um + of the
> locals, you know? um i- it- it's a real secure sort of feeling + just
> knowing everybody I think eh↓ and *and the fact that i- you know
> your kids can pretty much walk around here and feel fairly safe*↑

Here, Joe uses common ground raising pragmatic markers at the end of
each clause. At the end of the first clause he uses "you know," in the
second, "eh↓," and in the third, an HRT. All such techniques are commonly
used to reduce the distance between the points of view of the speaker and
hearer (see Holmes [1986] for an analysis of *you know* and Meyerhoff [1990]
for *eh↓*).

In example (4), Boyd is talking to Glen, another young Maori man, who
is comparing life in Porirua with life in Australia.

(4) Glen: when I went to Australia um found out that there was more to offer
than just what I knew in Porirua ++ like um you'd never get bored I
used- here I always get bored you know I got fr- *if I've done everything
I wanted to do in that day or that week I've got nowhere else to go↑ or
nothing else to do↑*

Boyd: yeah

Glen: *your options are sort of limited↑*

HRTs are often used in clauses that follow initiating opinions. In example
(4), Glen uses HRT clauses in his explanation of why he is bored in Porirua
and in this way is signaling that he feels Boyd, too, can understand his
dilemma.

The second major class of positive politeness strategies in Brown and
Levinson's (1987) framework is based on the desire that both speaker and
hearer convey to each other that they are conversational *co-operators* (125–
129). To a certain extent, this strategy overlaps with the establishment of
common ground discussed earlier. Furthermore, it includes some of the
functions of HRTs put forward by the Sydney researchers: the mutual
adherence to turn taking rules (namely, the request for minimal affirmation
and extended turn length) (Guy et al., 1986: 26–27; Horvath, 1985: 131) and
the heightening of listener engagement in the conversation (Horvath, 1985:
130). These strategies address the hearer's positive face wants by demon-
strating the speaker's willingness to overcome any obstacles that may
potentially hinder their successful engagement in talk.

HRTs play an important role in the conversational development of closer
relationships between the speaker and the hearer, who can establish shared
knowledge, claim reciprocity of wants and obligations, and vicariously
participate in the exchange of personal experiences. "Positive politeness
marker" is therefore an umbrella term sheltering a number of their distinct
functions.

The quantitative analysis of discourse variables

Quantitative analyses of linguistic variables have previously depended on
a number of factors, including: (1) the semantic equivalence of the variants
of the variable and (2) the ability to establish a list of all but only those parts
of speech where the variable could potentially occur.

For a phonological variable, these two factors have caused few methodological difficulties. Taking (r) as an example, we can establish that [kɑː r] is
semantically equivalent to [kɑː], and that it is possible to define a closed set
of instances in which (r) occurs and then to calculate the percentage of
realizations of [r] from the total number occurring in the selected recording.
It is then relatively straightforward to index a person's use of (r) and
measure the variable's sensitivity to differing contexts and audiences
(Bell, 1984; Coupland, 1988; Labov, 1966; Trudgill, 1986).

To what extent, however, can we study the variable use of discourse
features such as HRTs and maintain our adherence to these two working
rules of quantitative analysis? Clearly, a clause with an HRT carries a

meaning that a clause with falling intonation does not. But is this meaning *instead of* or *additional to* the meaning usually associated with falling tone declarative clauses? If we decide that HRTs replace the "statementhood" of the falling tone declarative with a positive politeness marking rising tone declarative, then we cannot claim that the two variants hold any semantic equivalence. Factor 1 would have been violated. Consider the following, however: [2]

No HRT:	Form:	falling tone + declarative clause	
	Function:	statement + statement	
With HRT:	Form:	rising tone + declarative clause	
	Function:	Positive politeness + statement	

Does the adoption of the HRT change the meaning?
Affective meaning: Yes
Referential meaning: No

Statements can be seen to be doubly marked, by the intonation and by the declarative syntax. Even with rising intonation, one of the functions of the clause remains that of a statement. HRT clauses have an *additional* function, namely, marking positive politeness toward the interlocutor. A quantitative measure of HRT use can be established by calculating the number of HRT clauses as a percentage of the total number of declaratives. Such a measure can then guide our qualitative interpretations of the rates of HRT adoption among different sections of the community. So far so good.

However, the establishment of a closed set of the potential locations of discourse features such as HRTs proves to be a more complicated task. In a similar methodological discussion on the adaptability of quantitative techniques, Dines (1980) sought ways of defining a taxonomy of variants of set-marking tags such as *and that, and stuff like that,* and *or anything,* which function to "cue the listener to interpret the preceding element as an illustrative example of some more general case" (p. 22). Her analysis of such features found that they were used much more often by the working-class speakers in her sample. She argued that because "in comparable discourse situations . . . there will be comparable needs to satisfy certain discourse functions . . . the present set of tags constitutes an incomplete taxonomy of variants because it does not indicate what alternatives are available to speakers who tend not to use the putative ill-favoured forms" (p. 18). In other words, we do not know which forms middle-class speakers use to fulfill the same function as set-marking tags for working-class speakers. We are confronted with a similar problem in the analysis of HRTs. The Australian researchers (Guy et al., 1986: 43–44) determined that there are textual and turn-length constraints on HRTs, but that these were just constraints and not total barriers. Their data showed that HRTs are more likely to occur in narratives than in opinions and in multiclause speaker turns more than in one-word turns. There have been no reports, however, of contexts in which HRTs *cannot* occur. Further research is underway on our New Zealand data to enable a more refined analysis of textual constraints on HRT use (Britain, forthcoming), but as yet there have been few positive indications that such textual contexts exist.

However, we must not conclude from this that we would be likely to find an individual who had 100% use of HRTs in declarative clauses. Although we may be many research hours away from finding textual bars to the use of rising tones in declaratives, it seems certain that there must be total constraints of some kind. I have discussed the role of HRTs in the creation of common ground between speakers. Common ground, as several authors have made clear (see, e.g., Clark & Wilkes-Gibbs, 1986; Meyerhoff, 1991), is not a conversational constant, but fluctuates throughout the duration of talk as speakers continually negotiate, consolidate, and adjust their inter-personal relations. We would expect HRT use and the sociopsychological construction and maintenance of solidarity between speakers to go hand-in-hand. The use of rising tones is likely to reflect both the fluidity of the speaker-hearer relationship and, as the Sydney researchers have shown, any instrumental barriers that threaten to jeopardize that relationship. Our inability to measure such fluctuations in the speaker-hearer dyad in an objective way means that we cannot precisely define the outer envelope of variation for this feature. This envelope would include all (and only) those clauses in which the speaker wishes to signal a desire to establish or confirm or maintain common ground with the listener. Common ground can be realized in a number of ways, however. In addition to the use of HRTs, speakers could use other positive politeness markers such as *you know* (Holmes, 1986) or *eh↓* (Meyerhoff, 1990). Features such as these have a similar, but probably not identical, affective meaning to HRTs.

Evidently we are not in a position to claim that our analysis can adhere to Factor 2, given earlier. It is therefore difficult to see how a study of HRT use can proceed within the theoretical framework of the linguistic variable. Although we can still use quantitative analyses of nonphonological varia-tion in language to guide our interpretations of our findings, we cannot claim that the use or non-use of such features as HRTs are different ways of saying the same thing. This investigation of HRT use in New Zealand English uses quantitative techniques to measure the degree and rate of adoption of the tone. Our interpretations of the results, however, must be sensitive to the fact that the interactive functions of an HRT clause have consequences for the sociolinguistic patterning of its use.

Quantitative research on the use of HRTs

The Sydney research mentioned earlier was the first published quantita-tive survey of the use of HRTs in English (see Guy & Vonwiller, 1984; and esp. Guy et al., 1986; Horvath, 1985). The speech of 130 speakers – divided into cells according to sex, ethnicity (Italian, Greek, and Anglo-Celtic), age group (for Anglo-Celtic speakers, years 11–14, 15–19, 20–39, 40+; for Italian and Greek speakers: teenager, adult), and socioeconomic class (lower working, upper working, and middle) – was analyzed for the frequency of HRT use in declarative sentences. The researchers found that over the whole sample, 1.6% of all tone groups had HRTs, but that this figure hid quite marked social stratification (see Table 12.1). Age, they found proved to be a statistically significant variable in the pattern of HRT use, as did the class and sex of the informants. By contrasting their

Table 12.1 HRT use in Sydney according to age, sex, and class

	% Use of HRTs	Varbrul probability
Age		
(Whole sample)		
Teenagers	2.29	.74
Adults	0.23	.26
(Anglo-Celtic only)		
11–14 years	1.60	.64
15–19 years	2.00	.67
20–39 years	0.50	.51
40+ years	0.20	.21
Class		
Lower working	2.50	.59
Upper working	1.70	.51
Middle	0.70	.40
Sex		
Female	2.20	.59
Male	1.00	.41

Source: Guy *et al.* (1986: 36–39).

data with the results of an analysis of recordings made in Sydney in the early 1960s (Mitchell & Delbridge, 1965), which showed a 0.3% use of HRTs, the researchers had real-time evidence with which to conclude that linguistic change favoring the use of HRTs for certain interactive functions was in progress.

S. Allan's (1990) research on HRT use in New Zealand English (NZE) was a pilot study analyzing the speech of nine working-class women (four Maori, five Pakeha), aged 25–35 years, from Levin, a town approximately 60 miles north of Wellington. The principal aim of his study was to compare ethnic differences in the frequency of HRT use in New Zealand. As can be seen in Table 12.2, S. Allan found that the use of HRTs was higher among young Maori women.

The Porirua survey of HRT use has a number of aims. Primarily, as this research forms only one part of an ongoing project analyzing a number of variables in NZE (see Holmes, Bell, & Boyce, 1991), this article is an investigation into social, gender, and ethnic variation in the use of the English language in the small New Zealand city of Porirua. Second, it was hoped that by "using the present to explain the past," the data from Porirua would enable not only an analysis of change in the use of HRTs in New Zealand, but would also facilitate comparisons with the Sydney research and hence shed some light on the geographical origins of the feature (see Bauer, in press). Finally, the research attempts to broaden our knowledge not only of the function of HRTs as positive politeness markers, but also of the textual constraints on their use that may exist (Britain, forthcoming).

Table 12.2 HRT use among young working-class women in Levin, New Zealand, according to ethnicity

Ethnicity	% Use of HRTs	No. of PDUs[a]
Maori	3.58	2201
Pakeha	2.33	1887

[a] PDU = pause-defined unit (see Brown, Currie, & Kenworthy, 1980).
Source: S. Allan (1990: 120).

The speech community

As English is spoken as a first language by around 95% of the population of 3.4 million, New Zealand must count as one of the world's most monolingual countries.[3] Speakers of Maori account for roughly 3% of the population, around 70,000 people (Benton, 1991: 187).[4] Yet, despite its dominance in New Zealand society, until recently very little sociolinguistic research had been carried out on a speech variety that had often been treated in the literature as a side branch of Australian English.[5] In the past 5 years, however, a number of linguists have made valuable contributions to place NZE quite clearly on the map of world Englishes (Bauer, 1986, in press; Bayard, 1987, 1991; Bell & Holmes, 1990, 1991; Gordon & Deverson, 1985). The present investigation into the use of HRTs is drawn from recorded data collected during New Zealand's largest social dialect survey to date, the Porirua Project (Holmes et al., 1991).

Porirua is a small city of around 45,000 people, located approximately 12 miles north of Wellington, the nation's capital. Once a small, quite isolated farming settlement, the city has expanded rapidly since World War II, when it was designated a residential and industrial overspill zone for Wellington. Its socioeconomic profile is of an ethnically mixed, predominantly working-class community, with relatively higher than average unemployment and a predominantly secondary and tertiary employment structure.

Methodology

Our informant sample consisted for 60 working-class speakers, each classified according to years of age (20–29, 40–49. 70–79), sex, and ethnicity (Maori and Pakeha). A small control group of 15 middle-class Pakeha women from each of the three age groups was included to enable class comparisons (see Table 12.3). Informants were located using the "friend of a friend" technique successfully adopted by Milroy (1980) in Belfast. We made contact with a number of local Porirua community advisers who identified people that fitted our predetermined social criteria. These advisers contacted the people they had identified to obtain their agreement to be interviewed. The interviewers, who all lived or had lived in Porirua, only recorded interviews with people of the same gender and ethnicity.

Table 12.3 The demographic structure of the Porirua sample

		Working class		Middle-class Pakeha
		Pakeha	Maori	
Women	20–29	5	5	5
	40–49	5	5	5
	70–79	5	5	5
Men	20–29	5	5	–
	40–49	5	5	–

During the recordings, the informants were asked to suggest other people who might be willing to be interviewed. In this way, our interviewers obtained data from a total of 75 people through such second-order network contacts.

As well as eliciting detailed demographic and network information, the interview format comprised a number of reading passages and word lists, questions on the informants' competence in and attitudes toward the Maori language, and a number of topics likely to elicit casual speech, including the "danger-of-death" question (Labov, 1966), experiences of fights and accidents, and attitudes toward the local community. The average length of each recording was approximately 60 minutes.

The analysis of HRT frequency was carried out on 20-minute sections of the recordings that were designed to elicit narrative and opinion texts as well as free speech between the interviewer and informant that was not part of the interview format. These 20-minute sections were orthographically transcribed. Following Guy et al. (1986), the text was divided into tone groups as the unit for identifying HRTs. Tone groups are used by speakers to organize utterances into meaningful units of information with a syntactically and semantically coherent structure. The "size" of a tone group depends on the way the speaker decided to segment the utterance. One tone group can span two or more clauses, or a single clause may be subdivided into two or more tone groups. As they always encompass meaningful blocks of information in discourse, tone groups were better suited to an analysis of HRT use than the rival notion of pause-defined units (PDU) (Brown, Currie, & Kenworthy, 1980), which divide text into units situated between pauses that are not necessarily semantically coherent. The decision to use tone group instead of PDU also enabled clearer comparisons with the Sydney results.[6] At this stage, certain tone groups were excluded from analysis because they were not considered potential sites for the occurrence of HRTs. These were questions, both direct and tagged, queclaratives, imperatives, and *yes* and *no*. A Varbrul analysis of the data was carried out using the Goldvarb Macintosh package.[7] Each tone group was coded according to presence or absence of HRT; the age, sex, class, and ethnicity of the speaker; and the type of text in which the tone group was found.

The designation of text types (narrative, description, explanation, and opinion), chosen once again to enable comparisons with previous research in Australia and New Zealand, proved to be quite difficult. Rather than allocate tone groups to a particular text type according to the question asked by the interviewer, as Guy et al. (1986) had, they were classified according to the pragmatic development and schematic structure of each informant speech turn. Narrative texts were defined in terms of Labov and Waletzky's (1967) structure of narratives, which Labov defined as "a method of recapitulating past experience by matching a verbal sequence of clauses to the sequence of events which actually occurred" (1972: 359–360). Opinion texts were analyzed along the lines of Horvath and Eggins's (1988) schematic structure model (see also Rohany, 1991). According to Horvath and Eggins, an opinion text has the purpose of "proposing, elaborating, defending and exchanging opinions about people, things or events" (1988: 5) and comprises an initiating opinion, followed by a reaction, and, optionally, evidence in favor of or against the initiating opinion and a resolution. Explanations were defined as accounts, clarifications, or justifications of previously mentioned concepts, locations, people, situations, and so on. Descriptions, on the other hand, were designated according to their literal meaning of "a picture in words."

Although the HRT analysis was designed to match the Australian study as closely as possible, there were a few other distinctions between the two studies that must be borne in mind when we later look at the results from Porirua:

The number of tokens selected
The Australian researchers analyzed all the declarative clauses throughout each interview which lasted an average of 45 minutes (Horvath, 1985: 50). Their analysis of 130 speakers provided 107,685 tokens, an average of approximately 830 per speaker. The Porirua interviews, excluding reading passages and word lists, were roughly of the same length. In order to make the coding of the HRTs more manageable for one researcher, it was decided to limit the analysis, as mentioned previously, to a 20-minute section of the recording that included the danger-of-death question, other narrative- and opinion-inducing questions, and the spontaneous casual speech toward the end of the interviews. I obtained 14,844 tokens from 75 speakers, an average of approximately 200 per speaker.

The analysis of text types
Guy et al. (1986: 43) found that narratives favor the use of HRTs. The sections chosen from the Porirua data for HRT analysis deliberately elicited more narrative texts, the effect of which was to create a much more even distribution of tokens across text types (see later discussion of textual constraints and Table 6).[8] The major implication of these differences, however, is that the New Zealand data are biased in favor of HRT-laden contexts. We therefore need to be particularly careful when we compare the *overall* rates of HRT use in Sydney and Porirua.

The "factual" text type
The Australian researchers and S. Allan (1990) in his Levin study both
included a fifth text type category, "factual," to cover generally short
factual answers to questions such as "What is your name?" "Where do
you live?" (Guy & Vonwiller, 1984: 13). The sections of recordings chosen
for our analysis contained too few such question/answers to enable
adequate comparisons.

Results

The analysis of the speech of the 75 Porirua residents unearthed 612 HRT
tone groups out of a total of 14,844, or 4.12%. The stereotypical users of
HRTs in New Zealand are young women. The pattern shown in Table 12.4
mostly confirms this. The young in our survey are over five times more
likely to use HRTs than the oldest age group. The difference between
women and men, however, is not as sharp as perhaps the stereotype would
have us believe. The use of HRTs is favored among women, but only by a
relatively small, albeit statistically significant ($p = .01$), margin. S. Allan
(1990: 120) found that Maori tended to favor HRT use slightly more than
Pakeha; this finding is confirmed in our study.

We also found that HRT use among the middle classes (female Pakeha
only) was *higher* than among the working-class informants. Our Varbrul
analysis showed that this difference was not at all significant ($p = .44$).
However, this apparent lack of a class distinction contrasts strongly with
the findings of the Sydney research team, who found that working-class

Table 12.4 The use of HRTs in Porirua according to age, ethnicity, sex and class

Group	No. of HRTs	Total No. of tone groups	% Use of HRTs	Goldvarb probability
*Age***				
Young	374	4,715	7.9	.683
Middle-aged	165	5,254	3.1	.477
Old	73	4,875	1.5	.344
Total	612	14,844	4.1	
*Ethnicity***				
Pakeha	320	9,095	3.5	.445
Maori	292	5,749	5.1	.586
*Sex**				
Female	418	9,428	4.4	.521
Male	194	5,416	3.6	.464
Class (Pakeha, females only)[a]				
Working	126	3,198	3.9	.486
Middle	147	3,346	4.4	.543

* $p < .01$; ** $p < .001$.
[a] The statistical significance of the class figures is very low ($p = .440$).

speaker use of HRTs outnumbered middle-class speaker use by 3 to 1 (Guy et al., 1986: 37).[9]

Fig. 12.1 shows the results of a cross-tabulation by age, ethnicity, sex, and class. Young Maori speakers appear to be most advanced in the use of this innovative feature, with on average over 9% of all tone groups carrying a high rising tone, with little consistent variation between Maori men and women in the three age groups we studied. Among young Pakeha, in contrast with the Maori informants, there is a striking sex differentiation. Pakeha women use three times more HRTs than the Pakeha men in that age group. The same sharp distinction is true for the middle-aged Pakeha, with overall lower frequencies.

Fig. 12.2 is a graphic representation of the Varbrul scores for these cross-tabulations. There are a number of points to note. As one might expect, the older age groups all disfavor HRT use in comparison with the younger age cohorts. The middle-aged group shows more variation in factor weightings, from .278 (Pakeha men) to .668 (Maori women). Of particular interest is the fact that *all* age groups of Pakeha men disfavor the use of HRTs.

Linguistic change in progress?

The social stratification of HRT use shown in Figs 12.1 and 12.2 poses the question of whether a linguistic change is in progress, or whether this is a case of age grading. In order to answer this, we need to find convincing real-time evidence that HRTs were not used in previous generations. The first published report of HRT use in New Zealand was attributed to Maori school-children. In a report on their English language-learning difficulties, Benton (1966: 56) noted that:

> A distinctive rising intonation, especially marked in the speech of 5 to 8 year old children, but present in a modified form in the speech of older children too was encountered in one Bay of Islands area, and in Hawkes Bay and

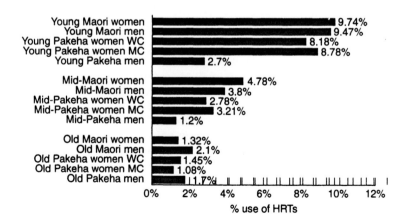

Fig. 12.1 Percentage use of HRTs in Porirua according to ethnicity, age, sex and class

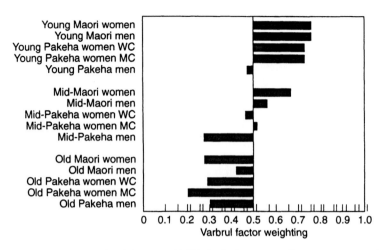

Fig. 12.2 A Varbrul analysis of the use of HRTs in Porirua according to age, sex, ethnicity and class

Whanganui, as well as in one Tuhoe settlement.[10] All but the latter were areas where the children's knowledge of Maori is negligible and any European children attending the schools seemed to follow the Maori children's speech pattern.

Tentatively, then, we would claim that a linguistic change is in progress favoring the use of HRTs, and that the change was initiated by Maori. We would not be able to claim this more convincingly, however, until real-time research in the future confirms our findings.

Gender, ethnicity, and positive politeness

What can we say about the apparently "deviant" behavior of Pakeha men in using so few HRTs? One partial explanation concerns the reaction of some of the Pakeha men to the interview itself.[11] Two informants from the young male group were particularly unresponsive to the interviewer, apparently perceiving the event as a task to be completed as swiftly and efficiently as possible, rather than as an opportunity to engage in prolonged conversation. Since previous research (S. Allan, 1990; Guy et al., 1986) has found that HRTs are most common in multiple-clause responses and particularly in narratives, one would expect perhaps that an absence of such structures would tend to have an inhibiting effect on HRT use. In the speech of some of the young Pakeha men, narratives in particular were either nonexistent or stripped bare to the most essential evaluative details.

(5) Interviewer: right + ah have you ever seen a really bad accident?
     David: oh yeah + an- oh nah I've been in one but it wasn't bad just rolled
     Interviewer: tell us about it?

David: oh we just rolled that's all
Interviewer: whereabouts?
David: up by the National Park
Interviewer: oh yeah on that straight road
David: swing round the corner and lost it r- rolled
Interviewer: car damaged?
David: car was damaged yeah [laughs]

This said, however, as Table 12.5 shows, perceived uncooperativeness on the part of the speaker does not necessarily equate to lack of HRTs.

The popular image of HRTs in New Zealand among the more standard-speaking middle classes is of young females who use HRTs to show deference to the hearer or alternatively hesitation about the validity of what they are saying. Based on this stereotype, and following Lakoff's (1975) argument, it might be argued that the low use of HRTs by Pakeha men is symbolic of masculinity and assertiveness. Eckert (1989: 253) put forward what in many ways can be seen as a similar argument to this: that the use of HRTs is associated with subordination and lack of power. She claimed that, "gender differentiation is greatest in those segments of society where power is the scarcest – at the lower end of the socioeconomic hierarchy where women's access to power is the greatest threat to men" (p. 256). Using Guy et al.'s (1986) results, Eckert claimed that the low use of HRTs by men in Sydney is, therefore, "an avoidance of the linguistic expression of subordination by men in the socioeconomic group that can least afford to sound subordinate" (p. 257). Of course, there are a number of problems with this argument in relation to HRT use. First, it assumes that lower working-class men perceive its use as the expression of subordination. We have no evidence to suggest this is the case. Second, it is questionable whether Guy et al.'s (1986) social class scale, with three subdivisions, is finely detailed enough to be able to make such strong claims.[12] In addition, the weight of evidence cited to support her argument is outbalanced by the number of counterexamples.

In a recent discussion of sound changes in Philadelphia, Labov (1990) showed that the degree of differentiation between men and women is dependent to a large extent on the progress of the change through time.

Table 12.5 Percentage use of HRTs by the five young Pakeha male speakers

Name	% Use of HRTs	Goldvarb probability (if applicable)
Less responsive		
David	0.00	–
Eric	5.33	.626
More responsive		
George	0.00	–
Henry	1.51	.315
Frank	6.39	.677

$p = 0.187$.

Sex differences were found to be smaller in both incipient and old and completed changes, but much greater in new and vigorous changes (1990: 240). Evidence from the Philadelphia data (1990: 234–235) disconfirms Eckert's claim that it is among the lower working classes that linguistic sex differentiation is at its peak.

However, neither Eckert's nor Labov's hypotheses can satisfactorily explain the HRT findings from our Porirua research. If Eckert's arguments were valid, we would expect a particularly sharp gender difference in HRT use among Maori, who, in comparison to Pakeha, are socioeconomically disadvantaged in New Zealand society.[13] As it is, there is no difference at all in the likelihood of young Maori men and women using HRTs (Varbrul factor weightings .765; see Fig. 12.2). Labov's claims are clearly supported by the 6% differential between the HRT scores of the young Pakeha men and women (see Fig. 12.1). However, his hypothesis can only be totally vindicated if we can accept that among young Maori, where there is minimal sex differentiation, the change to HRT use is approaching completion. As mentioned earlier, however, the concept of "completion" in the adoption of HRTs is incompatible with its interactive function. Constantly fluctuating interactive constraints are more likely to determine HRT use once the change is underway. Clearly, an explanation for the low use of HRTs by Pakeha men and high use by Pakeha women and Maori men and women lies elsewhere.

In recent years, one of the more conclusive findings of research into the issue of language and gender in Western cultures has been that "women put more emphasis than men on the importance of talk in establishing and maintaining relationships, whereas men more often regard talk as a means of communicating information" (Holmes, 1990: 260–261; see also Graddol & Swann, 1989). Authors such as Coates (1986, 1988), Holmes, and others (e.g., Stubbe, 1991) have provided ample empirical evidence that women's frequent use of supportive minimal responses, epistemic modal forms, simultaneous speech (Coates, 1988: 120), tag questions, and other pragmatic tags such as *you know* (Holmes, 1984, 1986, 1990) is indicative that women, more than men, pursue speech styles based on solidarity and support. In other words, women's conversational behavior is more positively polite (Brown & Levinson, 1987: 251) than that of men. It is not surprising, therefore, that high rising terminals are used more extensively by Pakeha women than Pakeha men. Meyerhoff's (1990) research into the use of the particle tag *eh↓* in NZE revealed a similar pattern to that of HRT use. She found that Pakeha women used *eh↓* over three times more often than the Pakeha men in the study. Of course, this is not to say that men do not tend to display positive politeness in their speech, but simply that they do so less, relative to women, and in different ways.[14]

As we saw earlier, the use of HRTs among Maori is consistently high for both women *and men*. A cross-cultural analysis of conversational strategies in maintaining interspeaker relations can show, however, that this is not inconsistent with our hypothesis of HRT function. A growing body of evidence from non-Western cultures has shown that a number of such societies place great emphasis on the "creation of involvement" in informal discourse. Tannen (1989: 128) cited examples from Greece and Brazil;

Sweeney (1987) from Malaysia and Indonesia; Billings (1987) from the Melanesian islands of Tikana and Larongai; and the articles in Brenneis and Myers (1984), White and Kirkpatrick (1985), and Watson-Gegeo and White (1990) from a range of other communities in the Pacific.

These societies appear to share a more sociocentric perception of self than most Western cultures. Greater emphasis is placed on interpersonal rather than individualistic constructions of personality and identity. Commenting on Hawaiian society, Ito (1985: 301) stated that, "the conceptualization of self is a highly interpersonal one; it is based on the reflexive relationship of Self and Other, and on the dynamic bonds of emotional exchange and reciprocity." The establishment of shared knowledge and understanding is a critical process in such societies. The linguistic creation of affect is therefore an essential aspect in the development of an individual's communicative competence. For example, Edwards and Sienkewicz (1990) claimed that, "members [of oral cultures] share a common set of expectations, emphasizing the importance of interaction between speaker and audience" (p. 195) and "place more emphasis on personal topics, binding together speaker and audience in a single referential web" (p. 197). In contrast, "literate societies place greater stress on decontextualized content . . . the importance of speaker-audience interaction is minimized" (p. 195). The affective value of talk to speakers from oral communities is so great that it is often considered just as important as the content of the discourse itself (see, e.g., Atkinson, 1984; Ito, 1985; Lutz, 1985; White & Watson-Gegeo, 1990).

One of the most extensive sociolinguistic investigations of the conversational strategies in a Polynesian society is Besnier's (1988, 1989) research on Nukulaelae Tuvaluan. Once again,we find evidence of the importance of common ground seeking in informal discourse. For example, Besnier (1989) stated that, "Interpersonal harmony is in fact more than desirable in Nukulaelae gossip; it is essential for its success. In order to create a successful gossip session, gossips must ensure that their audience shares their own feelings and attitudes towards the topic of the gossip" (p. 320). Nukulaelae speakers create conversational affect to these ends in a number of ways, such as the creation of collusion between speakers, the use of contrapuntal co-constructed narratives as allusions to common knowledge, the strategic use of information withholding sequences, and even the use of HRTs in declarative clauses in narrative evaluations.[15] A number of studies from the Pacific have mentioned other similar features: the use of hedges, intensifiers, and first person nonsingular inclusive pronouns (see Besnier, 1988; Ito, 1985; Lutz, 1985).[16] The use of positive politeness markers such as these "enable a group to maintain and underscore its internal cohesion" (Besnier, 1989: 336), an essential process in their construction of personal identity. This evidence, then, points convincingly to a recognition that *members of Pacific cultures, both male and female, share with women in Western societies a more cooperative conversational style.*

The limited research into the conversational strategies employed by Maori speakers supports this claim. Metge and Kinloch (1978), in their research on cross-cultural communication among Maori, Samoans, and Pakeha, constantly emphasized the existence among Maori of a view of talk based on shared knowledge and consensus. In formal Maori contexts, people are actively encouraged to participate in public decision-making processes, which will continue, if possible, until total agreement is reached among those present. This cooperative style of negotiation is also carried over into more private domains, where once more the affective meaning of conversation is seen to be as important as the referential.

> Both Maoris and Samoans consider that meeting itself is the primary purpose of meeting. Once gathered together, they are perfectly prepared to discuss any matter that is raised, so that discussion can range widely, including much that is "irrelevant" (in the Pakeha view) to the ostensible reason for the gathering. (Metge & Kinloch, 1978: 32)

This discussion has shown that conversational solidarity is a particularly important goal for speakers in Pacific societies and is expressed in a number of ways that linguists class as markers of positive politeness. We have found that in their conversational English, young Maori of both sexes use high levels of HRTs, which similarly express a desire to establish inter-speaker common ground. Evidence suggests a very plausible link between these two findings. For example, in her research on the use of the pragmatic particle *eh↓*, Meyerhoff (1990) discovered that Maori speakers used the feature almost five times more than Pakeha in their conversational English, and, in particular, that Maori men used it 13 times more than Pakeha men. The origins of *eh↓* in NZE are not totally clear, but one very plausible explanation is that it is a borrowing of the similarly functioning Maori particle *ne*. As explained earlier, HRTs were first noted in New Zealand among Maori in the early 1960s, and, as a new feature, we would expect younger age groups to be in advance of older speakers in the change.

Differences do exist, of course, in the English spoken by Maori men and women. The analysis of a number of *phonological* features of Maori English has shown that Maori *men* seem to be more innovative than the women. For example, they appear to be more advanced in the merger of /iə/ and /eə/ in NZE (Holmes et al., 1991: 71). It seems quite plausible, however, that by maintaining a cultural consensus on the need to mark positive politeness in conversation, HRTs serve a function of particular importance to both male and female members of a Polynesian culture for whom the expression of shared knowledge and understanding is a fundamental social characteristic.

The use of HRTs and text type

Finally, in this discussion of HRT use in NZE, we can take a look at the effects of textual constraints. Table 12.6 displays the results from our Porirua analysis and compares them with the Sydney data. Although the figures reveal only a small difference between the two studies in the use of HRTs in description texts, they are used in New Zealand four times more often in opinion texts, over three times more often in explanation texts, and over two and one-half times more often in narrative texts. We should again be cautious in our interpretations of these results. Our state of knowledge

Table 12.6 The use of HRTs according to text type: a comparison between Sydney, Australia (Guy et al., 1986), and Porirua, New Zealand

Text type	Australia			New Zealand ($p < .001$)		
	% Use of HRTs	No. of tokens	Varbrul	% Use of HRTs	No. of tokens	Varbrul
Opinion	0.6	28,067	.33	2.6	4,296	.403
Description	2.8	45,988	.67	3.1	2,454	.454
Explanation	1.1	5,792	.50	4.0	5,070	.514
Narrative	2.7	3,752	.70	7.4	3,024	.649

about the identification of text types is such that we cannot be completely sure of the comparability of the text types. However, following the work by Labov and Waletzky (1967) on narratives and Horvath and Eggins (1988) on opinions, we can probably be confident that these text types were defined in similar ways. It is therefore very reassuring that both studies came to the same conclusion that opinion texts tend to disfavor HRT use and narrative texts tend to favor them. Our next task is to go further than this in our analysis of the textual constraints placed by narrative and opinion texts. Which particular aspects of narrative and opinion structure, if any, favor HRT use? This is the topic of research presently underway (Britain, forthcoming).

Conclusion

The results of our analysis of the Porirua data suggest that linguistic change is in progress in New Zealand English favoring the declarative use of high rising terminal intonation contours. We can draw this conclusion from the very much higher rates of HRT use among the young in our survey, similar findings elsewhere in New Zealand (S. Allan, 1990), and from the fact that the first reports of HRT use come from the early 1960s. We must await a more extensive real-time survey to be able to show conclusively whether this innovation is a permanent change or an age-graded feature. Will people in their 20s today still be using such high levels of HRTs in 40 years' time? The adoption of HRTs appears to be led by Maori speakers, but Pakeha women also use the feature to a similar extent. The lack of a class distinction in our results suggest that HRTs are not as stigmatized as in Australia.

A comparison of the use of HRTs in New Zealand and Australia raises the question of the geographic origins of the feature, and, considering the very close relationship between the two countries, of whether one country was responsible for its diffusion to the other. Although the results of the New Zealand studies show higher levels of use than the Sydney research, methodological differences, and the 10-year gap between the collection of the data in the two countries, mean that we cannot conclude with any certainty that HRTs are a New Zealandism that has crossed the Tasman Sea to Australia. Particularly as HRTs are also found in Canada and the United States, HRTs may well be an independent innovation in each country.

In their discussion of the possible social origins of HRTs, Guy et al. (1986: 49) reminded us of Labov's (1980: 263) suggestion that much linguistic change appears to be set in motion following the arrival of new racial and ethnic groups into the speech community. Such an influx can, it is claimed, provoke a renewed assertion of group identity by the existing established communities. This led Guy et al. (1986) to speculate whether the adoption of HRTs in Australia could have been motivated by the large-scale immigration there from southern Europe following World War II. In a New Zealand context, this hypothesis is less convincing because immigration has been much less extensive. However, a steady number of Pacific Islanders, Asians, and southern Europeans have arrived in the past 40 years. An investigation of HRT use in New Zealand Samoan English, for example, would provide a fascinating check for the hypothesis forwarded in this article.

I have argued here that HRTs are positive politeness markers used to emphasize speaker-hearer solidarity and to assist in the cooperative management of talk. As Horvath (1985: 132) concluded, "the underlying meaning of rising tones . . . is that by using such tones a speaker *requests the heightened participation of the listener*" (emphasis in the original) They are most used as such by those members of New Zealand society for whom the affective meaning of conversation is an important cultural characteristic, namely, Pakeha women and Maori.

Notes

1. "Pakeha" is the Maori term for a New Zealander of European descent.
2. I am grateful to one of the reviewers for *Language Variation and Change* for this point.
3. Apart from English and Maori, some of the other languages spoken in New Zealand include Samoan, Cook Island Maori, Niuean, Tongan, Tokelauan, Dutch, Greek, Cantonese, Gujerati, Italian, among others (see Bell & Holmes [1991: 153–154] for more details).
4. Benton (1991: 187) claimed that around 18% of the Maori population speak fluent Maori.
5. For example, Turner (1970: 87) stated that, "since Bennett made his brief comments on New Zealand pronunciation in 1943 . . . the chief advantage the observer [of NZE] of today has . . . is access to accurate and detailed accounts of the pronunciation of Australian English which help greatly in drawing attention to details in the similar New Zealand pronunciation."
6. See S. Allan (1990) for a discussion of the merits of pause-defined units in the analysis of HRTs.
7. Whereas Varbrul analyses are almost the norm in quantitative sociolinguistics in North America, they are less common in Australasia and virtually never used in Europe. Therefore, a brief sketch of the workings of the program in relation to the analysis of HRT use is necessary here. For a more detailed description of the program, see Rand and Sankoff (1988). The Goldvarb analysis used for our Porirua data has four stages:
   1. *The creation of a token file.* Each token of the linguistic feature under investiga-

tion is coded according to the realization or nonrealization of the dependent variable and according to the chosen independent variables, such as age, sex, and so forth. In the case of the HRT analysis, my coding categories were as follows: the use of HRT, the dependent variable (1 = HRT clause, 0 = clause without an HRT), speaker number within each cell (2–8), age (Y = young, M = middle-aged, O = old), ethnicity (M = Maori, P = Pakeha), sex (F = female, M = male), class (W = working class, M = middle class), and the text type in which the clause occurred (N = narrative, O = opinion, E = explanation, D = description). The coding string (12YMMWE therefore means that the clause in question was realized with an HRT (1), by speaker number 2 in the cell (2), who was young (Y), Maori (M), male (M), and working class (W), with the clause occurring in an explanation text (E). (Each coding string begins with "(" to differentiate information that the program should process from comments and other information that it should ignore.)

2. *The creation of a condition file.* The program operator can decide which independent variables to correlate with the dependent variable. By specifying particular independent variables (known as factor groups) or combinations of them, the operator can create more detailed categorizations without changing the token file. For example, in the case of HRT analysis we may wish to cross-tabulate both sex and ethnicity and see how this correlates to HRT use. In the condition file, we can combine the factors "male" (M) with "Pakeha" (P) to make a new factor group "X" = male Pakeha, and so on.

3. *The cell file.* The cell file, created by Goldvarb from the token and condition files, displays the raw token numbers and percentages for the presence (HRT use) or absence (no HRT use) of the feature under investigation, correlated with the sociological and linguistic factors chosen in the condition file.

4. *The Varbrul analysis.* The output of a Varbrul analysis is a list of numbers, one for each factor that the operator has chosen to create in the condition file. These numbers are called factor weights, which indicate the degree to which the factor in question favors or disfavors use of the dependent variable in comparison with the other factors in that factor group. The factor weights all fall between 0 and 1. A score of 0.200 shows that the factor quite strongly disfavors the application of the dependent variable. A score of, say, 0.750 displays quite strong favoring of the application. A score of 0.500 shows that the factor neither favors nor disfavors the application of the dependent variable. The Varbrul analysis can also provide the statistical significance of the results of a factor group.

8. In Guy et al. (1986), 3.5% of all tone groups analyzed were narratives. In our data, 20.4% were in narratives.

9. Closer inspection of our middle-class data revealed that one young woman, Pam, with an individual HRT score of 23.9%, accounted for over 40% of all middle-class HRTs. Her overall HRT score was the highest in the 75-speaker sample, the next highest being a young Maori man, with 18.5%. However, her demographic and network profile provide no clues as to why her pattern of HRT use should differ so dramatically from other young, middle-class women. One possible partial explanation is that part of her recording consisted of two long and extremely dramatic and emotive narratives, which appear to favor HRT use. Despite this, though, Pam has higher than average HRT scores for *all* the different text types (opinions: 14.0%, explanations: 11.0%, descriptions: 13.0%, narratives: 41.2%).

10. All these areas are in the Northern half of New Zealand's North Island.

11. A number of studies have found that men's behavior in sociolinguistic

interviews, oral examinations, and the like, tends to be more task oriented than that of women (see Jenkins & Cheshire, 1990; Stubbe 1991).

12. Thanks for this point to a *Language Variation and Change* reviewer. Labov (1990: 220) suggested that an adequate social class scale for such purposes needs at least four subdivisions.

13. Benton (1991: 197) cited two findings of the 1981 Census to highlight this fact. (i) In 1981, 75% of Maori aged 15 or over had incomes *below* NZ$10,000 per annum (cf. 66% of the rest of the population). (ii) Less than 5% of Maori full-time workers are in employment classified as "professional and technical" or "administrative and managerial" (cf. over 18% of the rest of the workforce).

14. Kuiper (1991) recently showed that one way men express positive politeness in all-male groups is by the use of face-threatening acts, such as sexually humiliating terms of address.

15. For example, Besnier (1989: 326) included the following narrative by one of his Nukulaelae informants. The speaker is exchanging stories about people's lack of familiarity with Western life on trips away from the atoll (boldface added).

S: [very high pitch] *Kae aa laa aka ttou fafinee,* [mid high pitch] *ulu ki loto i te: meaa, tiko. "e aa koee na?"* au e kilo atu nei **koo ggalo ana vae i loto i te poo::** ↑ [laughs]
(Besnier's translation [1989: 326], boldface added)

S: What 'bout our friend, (she) walks into the thing [i.e., the toilet], she shits. [I say to her,] "What are you doin'?" I look at her, **she's got both her feet deep inside the toilet bowl.**↑

HRTs in declaratives are also common in Samoan narratives (Duranti, 1981).

16. Ito (1985) cited further such features for Hawaiian, such as the use of kinship terms as forms of address for nonkin and the use of *ho'oponopono*, a Hawaiian method of conflict resolution. Lutz (1985: 33–34) implied that on the Micronesian atoll of Ifaluk, the use of first person singular pronouns is almost a face-threatening act on the part of the speaker.

References

Allan, K. (1984) 'The component functions of the high rise terminal contour in Australian declarative sentences', *Australian Journal of Linguistics* 4: pp. 19–32.

Allan, S. (1990) 'The rise of New Zealand intonation', in A. Bell and J. Holmes (eds.), *New Zealand ways of speaking English,* Clevedon: Multilingual Matters. pp. 115–128.

Atkinson, J. (1984) 'Wrapped words: Poetry and politics among the Wana of Central Sulawesi, Indonesia', in D. Brenneis and F. Myers (eds.), *Dangerous words: Language and politics in the Pacific,* New York: New York University Press, pp. 33–68.

Bauer, L. (1986) 'Notes on New Zealand English phonetics and phonology', *English World-Wide* 7: pp. 225–258.

—— '(in press) 'The history of English in New Zealand', in R. Burchfield (ed.), *The Cambridge history of the English language: Volume 5,* Cambridge: Cambridge University Press.

Bayard, D. (1987) 'Class and change in New Zealand English: A summary report', *Te Reo* 30: pp. 3–36.

—— (1991) 'Social constraints on the phonology of New Zealand English', in J. Cheshire (ed.), *English around the world: Sociolinguistic perspectives,* Cambridge: Cambridge University Press, pp. 169–186.

Bell, A. (1984) 'Language style as audience design', *Language in Society* 13: pp. 145–204.

Bell, A. and Holmes, J. (eds.) (1990) *New Zealand ways of speaking English*, Clevedon: Multilingual Matters.

—— (1991) 'New Zealand', in J. Cheshire (ed.), *English around the world: Sociolinguistic perspectives*, Cambridge: Cambridge University Press, pp. 153–168.

Benton, R. (1966) *Research into the English language difficulties of Maori schoolchildren: 1963–64*, Wellington: Maori Education Foundation.

—— (1991) 'Maori English: A New Zealand myth?', in J. Cheshire (ed.), *English around the world: Sociolinguistic perspectives*, Cambridge: Cambridge University Press, pp. 187–199.

Besnier, N. (1988) 'The linguistic relationships of spoken and written Nukulaelae registers', *Language* 64: pp. 707–736.

—— (1989) 'Information withholding as a manipulative and collusive strategy in Nukulaelae gossip', *Language in Society* 18: pp. 315–341.

Billings, D. (1987) 'Expressive style and culture: Individualism and group orientation contrasted', *Language in Society* 16: pp. 475–497.

Brenneis, D. and Myers, F. (eds.) (1984) *Dangerous words: Language and politics in the Pacific*, New York: New York University Press.

Britain, D. (forthcoming) 'A pragmatic analysis of the use of high rising terminals in New Zealand English'.

Brown, G., Currie, K. and Kenworthy, J. (1980) *Questions of intonation*, London: Croom Helm.

Brown, P., and Levinson, S. (1987) *Politeness: Some universals in language use*, Cambridge: Cambridge University Press.

Cheshire, J. (1987) 'Syntactic variation, the linguistic variable and sociolinguistic theory', *Linguistics* 25: pp. 257–282.

Ching, M. (1982) 'The question intonation in assertions', *American Speech* 57: pp. 95–107.

Clark, H. and Wilkes-Gibbs, D. (1986) 'Referring as a collaborative process', *Cognition* 22: pp. 1–39.

Coates, J. (1986) *Women, men and language*, London: Longman.

—— (1988) 'Gossip revisited: Language in all female groups', in J. Coates and D. Cameron (eds.), *Women in their speech communities*, London: Longman, pp. 94–121.

Coupland, N. (1988) *Dialect in use*, Cardiff: University of Wales Press.

Cruttenden, A. (1986) *Intonation*, Cambridge: Cambridge University Press.

Dines, E. (1980) 'Variation in discourse – "and stuff like that"', *Language in Society* 9: pp. 13–31.

Duranti, A. (1981) *The Samoan fono: A sociolinguistic study*, Canberra: Australian National University, Department of Linguistics.

Eckert, P. (1989) 'The whole woman: Sex and gender differences in variation', *Language Variation and Change* 1: pp. 245–268.

Edwards, V. and Sienkewicz, T. (1990) *Oral cultures past and present: Rappin' and Homer*, Oxford: Blackwell.

Finnegan, R. (1988) *Literacy and orality*, Oxford: Blackwell.

Geluyken, R.(1987) 'Intonation and speech act type', *Journal of Pragmatics* 11: pp. 483–494.

Gordon, E. and Deverson, A. (1985) *New Zealand English: An introduction to New Zealand speech and usage*, Auckland: Heinemann.

Graddol, D. and Swann, J. (1989) *Gender voices* Oxford: Blackwell.

Guy, G., Horvath, B., Vonwiller, J., Daisley, E. and Rogers, I. (1986) 'An intonation change in progress in Australian English', *Language in Society* 15: pp. 23–52.

Guy, G. and Vonwiller, J. (1984) 'The meaning of an intonation in Australian English', *Australian Journal of Linguistics* 4: pp. 1–17.

Halliday, M. (1967) *Intonation and grammar in British English*, The Hague, Mouton.

Hasan, R. (1989) 'Semantic variation and sociolinguistics', *Australian Journal of Linguistics* 9: pp. 221–275.

Holmes, J. (1984) 'Hedging your bets and sitting on the fence: Some evidence for hedges as support structures', *Te Reo* 27: pp. 47–62.

—— (1986) 'Functions of *you know* in women's and men's speech', *Language in Society* 15: pp. 1–21.

—— (1990) 'Politeness strategies in New Zealand women's speech', in A. Bell and J. Holmes (eds.), *New Zealand ways of speaking English*, Clevedon: Multilingual Matters, pp. 252–275.

Holmes, J., Bell, A. and Boyce, M. (1991) *Variation and change in New Zealand English: A social dialect investigation*, Project Report to the Social Sciences Committee of the Foundation for Research, Science and Technology, Wellington: Victoria University of Wellington, Department of Linguistics.

Horvath, B. (1985) *Variation in Australian English: The sociolects of Sydney*, Cambridge: Cambridge University Press.

Horvath, B. and Eggins, S. (1988) *Opinion texts in conversation*. Unpublished manuscript.

Ito, K. (1985) 'Affective bonds: Hawaiian interrelationships of self', in G. White and J. Kirkpatrick (eds.), *Person, self and experience: Exploring Pacific ethnopsychologies*, Berkeley: University of California Press, pp. 301–327.

James, E., Mahut, C. and Latkiewicz, G. (1989) 'The investigation of an apparently new intonation pattern in Toronto English', *Information Communication* 10: pp. 11–17.

Jenkins, N., and Cheshire, J. (1990) 'Gender issues in the GCSE oral English examination: Part 1', *Language and Education* 4: pp. 1–27.

Kuiper, K. (1991) 'Sporting formulae in New Zealand English: Two models of male solidarity', in J. Cheshire (ed.), *English around the world: Sociolinguistic perspectives*, Cambridge, Cambridge University Press, pp. 200–212.

Labov, W. (1966) *The social stratification of English in New York City*, Washington DC: Center for Applied Linguistics.

—— (1972) *Language in the inner city*, Philadelphia: University of Pennsylvania Press.

—— (1980) 'The social origins of sound change', in W. Labov (ed.), *Locating language in time and space*, New York: Academic, pp. 251–265.

—— (1990) 'The intersection of sex and social class in the course of linguistic change', *Language Variation and Change* 2: pp. 205–254.

Labov, W. and Waletzky, J. (1967) 'Narrative analysis. Oral versions of personal experience', in J. Helms (ed.), *Essays in the verbal and visual arts*, Seattle: University of Washington Press, pp. 12–44.

Lakoff, R. (1975) *Language and woman's place*, New York: Harper & Row.

Lavandera, B. (1978) 'Where does the sociolinguistic variable stop?', *Language in Society* 7: pp. 171–183.

Linde, C. and Labov, W. (1975) 'Spatial networks as a site of language and thought', *Language* 51: pp. 924–939.

Lutz, C. (1985) 'Ethnopsychology compared to what? Explaining behaviour and consciousness among the Ifaluk', in G. White & J. Kirkpatrick (eds.), *Person, self and experience: Exploring Pacific ethnopsychologies*, Berkeley: University of California Press, pp. 35–79.

Metge, J. and Kinloch, P. (1978) *Talking past each other – Problems of cross-cultural communication*, Wellington: Victoria University Press.

Meyerhoff, M. (1990) *"Sounds pretty ethnic eh?"*: *A pragmatic particle in Porirua speech.* Paper presented to the new Zealand Seminar on Language and Society, Victoria University, Wellington.

—— (1991) *Grounding and overcoming obstacles: The positive politeness motivations of high rise terminals.* Unpublished manuscript.

Milroy, L. (1980) *Language and social networks*, Oxford: Blackwell.

Mitchell, A. and Delbridge, A. (1965) *The speech of Australian adolescents*, Sydney: Angus Robertson.

Rand, D. and Sankoff, D. (1988) *Goldvarb: A variable rule application for the Macintosh*, Montreal: Université de Montréal, Centre de Recherches Mathématiques.

Rohany, H. (1991) *A comparative study of opinion giving strategies in British and Malaysian English*, Ph.D. dissertation, University of Essex.

Salmond, A. (1975) *Hui – A study of Maori ceremonial gatherings*, Wellington: Reed.

Sankoff, D. (1988) 'Sociolinguistics and syntactic variation', in F. Newmeyer (ed.), *Linguistics: The Cambridge survey: Volume 4. Language: The socio-cultural context*, Cambridge: Cambridge University Press, pp. 241–259.

Schiffrin, D. (1990) 'The management of a co-operative self during argument: The role of opinions and stories', in A. Grimshaw (ed.), *Conflict talk*, Cambridge: Cambridge University Press, pp. 241–259.

Selting, M. (1988) 'The role of intonation in the organization of repair and problem handling sequences in conversation', *Journal of Pragmatics* 12: pp. 293–322.

Stubbe, M. (1991) *Talking at cross purposes? The effect of gender on New Zealand primary schoolchildren's interaction strategies in pair discussions*, M.A. thesis, Victoria University of Wellington.

Sweeney, A. (1978) *A full hearing: Orality and literacy in the Malay world*, Berkeley, University of California Press.

Tannen, D. (1989) *Talking voices: Repetition, dialogue and imagery in conversational discourse*, Cambridge: Cambridge University Press.

Trudgill, P. (1986) *Dialects in contact*, Oxford: Blackwell.

Turner, G. (1970) 'New Zealand English today', in W. Ramson (ed.), *English transported: Essays on Australasian English*, Canberra: Australian National University Press, pp. 84–101.

Watson-Gegeo, K. and White, G. (eds.) (1990) *Disentangling: Conflict discourse in Pacific societies*, Stanford: Stanford University Press.

White, G. and Kirkpatrick, J. (eds.) (1985) *Person, self and experience: Exploring Pacific ethnopsychologies*, Berkeley: University of California Press.

White, G. and Watson-Gegeo, K (1990) 'Disentangling discourse', in K. Watson-Gegeo & G. White (eds.), *Disentangling: Conflict discourse in Pacific societies*, Stanford: Stanford University Press, pp. 3–52.

Appendix

The following are three F0 plots of HRTs (or strings of HRTs) from the Porirua data. The speech was digitized using a MacAdios digitizer, sampling at the rate of 10 kHz. The F0 plots were calculated from 21ms or 42ms time segments using MacSpeechLab 2.0 software on a Macintosh Plus. I am particularly grateful to John Newman of Massey University, Palmerston North, both for allowing me to use the MacSpeechLab software and for assisting me with the F0 analysis.

The HRT in Fig. 12A.1 is from Pam, a young, middle-class Pakeha

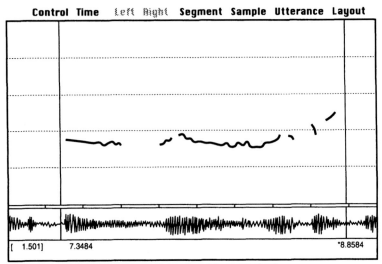

between the wall and the water bed

Fig. 12A.1 Between the wall and the waterbed

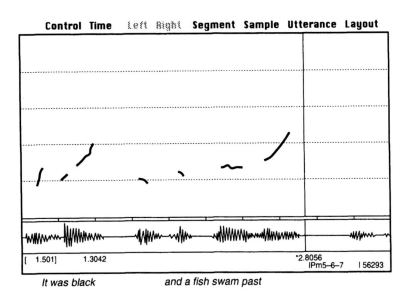

It was black   and a fish swam past

Fig. 12A.2 It was black and a fish swam past

woman. The F0 plot shows a pitch of between 160 and 190 Hz rising to 249 Hz at the end of the clause.

The HRT in Fig. 12A.2 is from Glen, a young, working-class Pakeha man. In this case, the rises begin from between 95 and 115 Hz and climb to 201 Hz on *black* and 224 Hz on *past*.

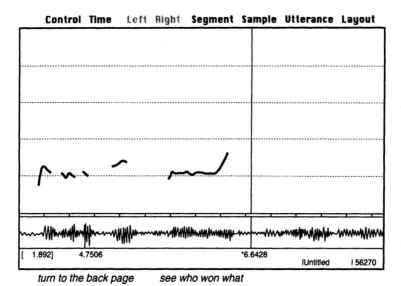

Fig. 12A.3 Turn to the back page and see who won what

The final example, Fig. 12A.3, is from Matt, a young, working-class Maori man. The first rise to *page* is from around 100 Hz up to 136 Hz; the second rise to *what* begins again from around 100 Hz and climbs to 159 Hz.

13

Decreolization?

Guy Bailey and Natalie Maynor

Originally published in *Language in Society*, 16 (1987).

In a recent discussion of the Black English Trial in Ann Arbor, Michigan, William Labov points out that in the aftermath of sharp polemics and bitter debate, linguists have reached a consensus on the nature and origin of the Black English Vernacular (BEV.)[1] He lists four generalizations which form the basis of this consensus:

1. The Black English Vernacular is a subsystem of English with a distinct set of phonological and syntactic rules that are now aligned in many ways with the rules of other dialects.

2. It incorporates many features of Southern phonology, morphology and syntax; blacks in turn have exerted influence on the dialects of Southern whites where they have lived.

3. It shows evidence of derivation from an earlier Creole that was closer to the present-day Creoles of the Caribbean.

4. It has a highly developed aspect system, quite different from other dialects of English, which shows a continuing development of its semantic structure (Labov 1982: 192).

While the consensus leaves considerable room for disagreement – for example, about the exact relationship between black and white speech in the South, about the origins of the creole ancestor, and about the source of particular features – Labov is surely right in claiming that general agreement about the structure and history of black speech does exist. Most scholars are now convinced that BEV had its origins in an earlier creole, although is has been decreolizing for some time, and that many of the differences between BEV and "standard English" are due to the persistence of creole features.

The linguistic evidence for this consensus, however, is puzzling. Initially, two types of evidence formed the basis for the hypothesis that BEV is a development of an earlier creole – evidence from the social history of blacks in the New World and attestations of creolelike forms in literary representations of black speech (see Stewart 1967, 1968; Dillard 1972). The data later used to confirm the creole hypothesis and to describe the structure of BEV come primarily from the speech of children (e.g., Labov et al., 1968; Baugh 1980), as do the most important data on black and white speech in the South (Dunlap 1974; Wolfram 1974). Only Rickford's work in Philadelphia (1975, 1977) explicitly examines the speech of adults in relation to creole languages. Even those studies which include adults (e.g., Fasold 1972; Baugh 1983) make no attempt to determine the actual directions of linguistic changes in progress. They simply assume that the grammars of adults and children are essentially alike; that BEV is decreolizing, its grammar becoming "aligned in many ways" with the grammars of whites; and that difference between black and white speech reflect the persistence of creole features.

In the absence of comparative studies of the speech of children and adults and, more generally, of any attempt to determine the directions of language change in BEV, these assumptions are simply unwarranted. In fact, our research on the development of the present tense of *be* in BEV suggests that all three of these assumptions are false. The grammars of adults and children are structurally, not just quantitatively, different; BEV is becoming less like, not more like, white varieties of English; and some of the most significant differences between black and white speech are the result of grammatical changes in progress, not the persistence of creole features.

Methods

The primary data for our research come from tape-recorded conversational interviews with seven black adults and twenty black children, all of them natives of the Brazos Valley in East-Central Texas. Despite the discrepancy in the number of informants, we have about the same amount of data from each group (see Table 13.1). The choice of informants is crucial in any attempt to determine the direction of language change in BEV since some scholars claim that the most creolelike features are age-graded, with the consistent use of basilectal patterns (that is, basilectal in terms of black speech in the United States) restricted to children under the ages of seven or eight.[2] In order to minimize the possible effects of this kind of age-grading, we restricted our sample in the following manner. All of the adults are over seventy years old, are members of the lower class with less than a grade school education, have restricted social contacts, and have not traveled extensively. Most of them are tenant farmers or the wives of tenants. The speech of these adults, which we described in more detail in an earlier paper on black folk speech (Bailey & Maynor 1985a), serves as a baseline for determining the directions of grammatical change. The children in our sample are all twelve or thirteen years old and are lower-class sixth graders whose formal education and insularity approximate that of the folk speakers. Their education in integrated schools over the last seven years compensates for the greater social experience of the adults.

In order to sample as broad a stylistic range as possible, we interviewed the children both individually and in peer groups. While we were unable to interview the adults in peer group sessions, we did interview several in family groups, and two were interviewed a number of times over a period of several years by Joe Graham, a folklorist studying the system of tenantry. From these interviews we took each instance of every form of the present tense of *be: am, is, are, ain't, ø,* and invariant *be.* In order to insure accuracy in retrieving and transcribing the data, both authors audited all of the tapes. In instances of disagreement about transcriptions, we classified the forms as ambiguous and eliminated them from the analysis.[3]

In classifying the transcribed forms for analysis, we follow Labov et al. (1968) and Fasold (1972) in distinguishing instances of invariant *be* that derive from *will* and *would* deletion from those which have no underlying modal and take *do-* support. Thus we clearly distinguish examples like (1) and (2) from those like (3), (4), and (5).

(1) I *be* 82 on the 29th.
(2) It *be* green. It would be just like peas.
(3) I see them children [who] sometimes *be* down yonder.
(4) There don't *be* nothing in church now but sinners.
(5) The cabbage *bees* the kind they have now.

We follow Labov in calling this second type *be₂*, and we consider only these in our analysis.[4] We differ from Labov, though, in our treatment of the realization of *t's* sequences in *it's, that's,* and *what's* as [s] (e.g., *its* realized as [ɪs]). Labov notes that the status of these forms is unclear, and he eliminates them from his calculations. However, he points out that they may in fact be instances of copula deletion rather than contraction, with the [s] actually representing "the assibilated [t] of *it*: the verb *is* [would have] entirely disappeared, leaving behind its footprint on the preceding pronoun in the following fashion:

It ## IZ
It ## əZ   vowel reduction
It ## Z   contraction
Is ## Z   assibilation
. . .
IS ## deletion" (Labov 1972: 116).

Thus according to this analysis, both [ðæs ðə truθ] and [ðæt ðə truθ] would contain instances of deletion. While such an analysis is well motivated by the interrelationships among contraction, deletion, and other phonological rules, it poses a number of problems. First, it violates the intuitions of native speakers, as Dunlap (1974) points out and as our experiments with Texas A&M students show. When taped samples were played for them, these students maintained that the copula was present in forms like [ɪs]. Second, it means that copula deletion is standard in some cases but nonstandard in others, because reduced forms like [ðæs], [hwas], and [ɪs] are quite common in standard Southern speech. Third, the analysis ignores parallels with consonant reductions where the penultimate consonant is deleted: In our data, *let's* is usually [lɛs], *egrets* is often [igrɪs], and *moths* is almost always [mɔs]. Fourth, it also ignores instances of [ɪs] that are reductions of *it has,* as in

(6) Now *i's* [ɪs] done got to be a big junior college.

Finally, the analysis fails to account for the fact that syntactic constraints on the occurrence of these forms are not like those on the occurrence of zero copula; rather, the constraints are the same as those on *is*. Thus [ɪs], [ðæs], and [hwas], like *is*, occur most often before noun phrases, somewhat less often before adjectives and locatives, and least often before verbs and *gonna*. In light of these problems, we have classified realizations of *t's* sequences as [s] as contracted forms.

Distribution of the present tense forms

Our data from Texas, excluding *ain't* (which we have treated as a single negating morpheme), include 2,264 unambiguous instances of the present tense of *be*, 1,147 tokens from folk speech, and 1,117 tokens from the speech of children. These forms comprise the same ones that occur in other studies of black speech: *am, is, are, ø,* and *be₂*. Table 13.1 summarizes their person/number distribution. The same pattern of distribution emerges for both varieties, but the frequency with which some forms occur differs remarkably. In both groups the standard forms dominate in the first and third singular, although they are slightly less common in the speech of children. Most of the variation in this subsystem occurs in the plural and second singular, a pattern which seems to be consistent for all varieties of BEV and for white speech as well (see Bailey & Maynor 1985a, 1985b).

The nonstandard forms which have elicited the most comment – *be₂* and zero copula – are also distributed in much the same fashion in both varieties. As Fig. 13.1 shows, *be₂* occurs most often in the plural and second singular, less often in the first singular, and rarely in the third singular. The greater frequency of *be₂* in the speech of adolescents is a major quantitative difference between the two varieties, with *be₂* occurring about three times as often in all three environments in their speech. For these speakers, the frequency of *be₂* in all environments is quite similar to what Labov found among teenagers in New York City, as Table 13.2 indicates.

As Fig. 13.2 demonstrates, similar patterns of distribution also emerge for ø. In both varieties, the zero copula is the most common realization of the plural and second singular, is less common in the third singular, and is extremely rare in the first singular. In addition, the frequency of occurrence

Table 13.1 Person/number distribution of forms of the present tense of *be*

Environment	1st sing.			3rd sing.			Pl. and 2nd sing.				Total
Form	*am*	*be₂*	*ø*	*is*	*be₂*	*ø*	*are*	*be₂*	*ø*	*is*	
Folk	129	8	1	679	9	46	41	22	159	52	
speakers	(92%)	(6%)	(1%)	(93%)	(1%)	(6%)	(15%)	(8%)	(58%)	(19%)	1147
Children	110	23	1	610	33	115	26	63	117	19	
	(82%)	(17%)	(1%)	(81%)	(4%)	(15%)	(12%)	(28%)	(52%)	(8%)	1117

[a] Omitting one instance of *is* in the 1st sing.

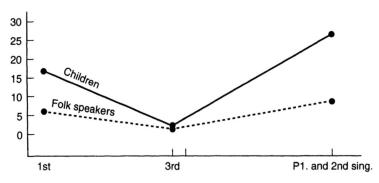

Fig. 13.1 Percentage of *be₂* in environments where Standard English requires *am, is* and *are*

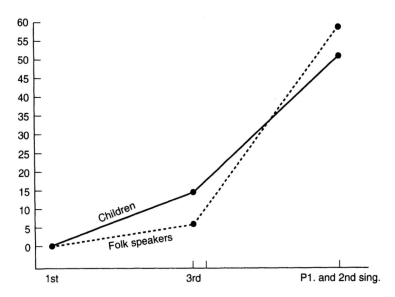

Fig. 13.2 Percentage of zero forms in environments where Standard English requires *am, is,* and *are*

Table 13.2 Percentage of *be₂* in Labov's New York City data

	1st sing.	3rd sing.	Pl. and 2nd sing.
Thunderbirds	14	7	37
Jets	13	6	29
Cobras	16	15	32
Oscar Brothers	24	0	16

Source: Labov (1972).

of ø where standard English has *am* and *are* is quite similar in both groups. In the third singular, however, ø occurs more than twice as often in the speech of children. Even though zero forms comprise 15 percent of the third singular tokens in the speech of children, that total seems small in comparison to zero forms in the figures from Labov's New York City data, which account for over 40 percent of the tokens in casual speech and about a third of them in careful speech. The discrepancy between our data and that from New York City, though, is only apparent. As we indicated above, we classified instances of *tha's, wha's* and *i's* as contractions, while Labov eliminated them from his calculations. Had we followed his procedure, zero forms would comprise about 25 percent of our data from the third singular, a figure not unlike Labov's findings for formal speech.

One other feature of the present tense paradigm, subject-verb disagreement, is also remarkable. In folk speech, *is* accounts for almost a fifth of the tokens in the plural and second singular and is more common there than *are*, which does not occur at all in our data for one of the adults. While *is* accounts for only 8 percent of the tokens in this environment in the speech of adolescents, the pattern of subject-verb disagreement is the same: *is* occurs where standard English requires *are*, but *are* never occurs for *is*.

As we have suggested elsewhere, the paradigmatic structure outlined here seems to be consistent throughout BEV, although the frequency of occurrence of be_2, ø and *is* for *are* varies considerably (Bailey & Maynor 1985a). If the differences between folk speech and the speech of children were only differences of frequency, not of meaning and structure, then surely we would have to concur with those scholars who maintain that the creolelike features of BEV are age-graded, occurring most often in the speech of young children. After all, it is the two features usually associated with creole origins, be_2 and ø, which are more frequent in the speech of children here; the other nonstandard feature, the use of *is* where standard English requires *are*, occurs more than twice as often in the speech of adults. These differences are not mere differences in frequency, however. In fact, the paradigmatic similarities between folk speech and the speech of children obscure remarkable structural differences between the two varieties.

Syntactic constraints on present tense forms

Both Baugh (1980) and Holm (1980, 1984) have pointed out that Caribbean creoles preserve an African pattern wherein the following predicate determines which form of the "copula" (or more properly, which copula) is used, and that BEV seems to preserve the creole pattern.[5] A reanalysis of Labov's New York City data confirms this position (Baugh 1980). In Caribbean creoles and to some extent in BEV, then, dependency relations are between the copula and its predicate rather than between the copula and its subject, as in other varieties of English. Decreolization would involve a shift from one type of dependency relationship to another.

Since these syntactic constraints are crucial in any analysis of the direction of grammatical change in BEV, we have classified every instance of a present tense form of *be* in the data according to its following predicate. Tables 13.3 and 13.4 and Figs. 13.3 and 13.4 summarize the results of our analysis, with first person forms separated from the others because ø is not a productive variant in that environment. In the plural and in the second and third singular, zero copula is by far the dominant form before progressives and before the intentional future *gonna* in both folk speech and the speech of children. Before predicate adjectives, predicate locatives, and noun phrases, ø is less common, with *is/are* predominant in all three environments, especially before noun phrases. The high frequencey of ø before verbs and *gonna* is not surprising since it parallels the situation in Caribbean creoles. The relatively low frequency of ø before adjectives in folk speech, however, is surprising because, as Holm points out, "in the protocreole . . . adjectives were a subclass of verbs requiring no copula" (1984: 298), and because Baugh (1980) found that a following adjective favored copula deletion in Labov's New York City data. In the speech of

Table 13.3 Syntactic constraints on present tense forms in the plural and 3rd and 2nd singular

Folk speakers	Vb + *ing*		gonna		Predicate adjective		Predicate locative		NP		Misc.	Total
is/are	21	(23%)	23	(32%)	174	(83%)	62	(73%)	398	(90%)	94	772
ø	67	(73%)	50	(68%)	29	(14%)	13	(15%)	38	(9%)	9	206
be_2	4	(4%)	0		6	(3%)	10	(12%)	7	(1.5%)	4	31
Total	92		73		209		85		443		107	1009

Children	Vb + *ing*		gonna		Predicate adjective		Predicate locative		NP		Misc.	Total
is/are	20	(14%)	6	(11%)	149	(73%)	76	(67%)	328	(86%)	76	655
ø	58	(41%)	47	(89%)	51	(25%)	22	(19%)	45	(12%)	9	232
be_2	62	(44%)	0		5	(2%)	15	(13%)	8	(2%)	6	96
Total	140		53		205		113		381		91	983

Table 13.4 Syntactic constraints on present tense forms in the first person singular

Folk speakers	Vb + *ing*		gonna		Predicate adjective		Predicate locative		NP		Misc.	Total
am[a]	36	(90%)	39	(100%)	27	(93%)	6	(86%)	14	(93%)	7	129
be_2	4	(10%)	0		2	(7%)	1	(14%)	1	(7%)	0	8
Total	40		39		29		7		15		7	137

Children	Vb + *ing*		gonna		Predicate adjective		Predicate locative		NP		Misc.	Total
am[a]	31	(66%)	58	(100%)	13	(100%)	4	(57%)	3	(100%)	1	110
be_2	18	(34%)	0		0		3	(43%)	0		2	23
Total	49		58		13		7		3		3	133

[a] Excludes one instance of ø for *am*

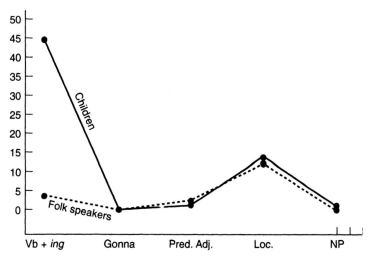

Fig. 13.3 Syntactic constraints on be_2 (be_2 as a percentage of present tense forms in the plural and second and third singular)

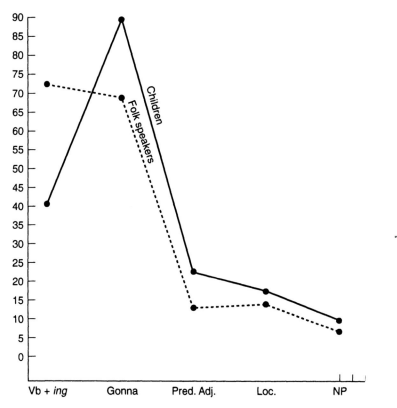

Fig. 13.4 Syntactic constraints on ø (zero as a percentage of copula froms in the plural and second and third singular)

the fifth and sixth graders, though, the constraints on ø are more like what Baugh and Holm predicted for BEV, with deletion more likely before predicate adjectives than before predicate locatives. With this exception, then, the pattern of syntactic constraints on ø is similar among both children and adults, although the incidence of ø is greater among the former.

The syntactic constraints on be_2, however, provide a remarkable contrast and suggest a major structural difference between the grammars of the two groups. In our data from folk speech, be_2 never occurs before *gonna* and occurs rarely before verbs, predicate adjectives, and noun phrases. Only predicate locatives seem to favor be_2 at all, and even in that environment it is the least common variant. Before *gonna*, predicate adjectives, predicate locatives, and noun phrases, the constraints are identical in the speech of children, but before verb + *ing*, be_2 accounts for 44 percent of the data and is the most common variant there – a striking contrast to the situation among folk speakers. The constraints operating in the first person suggest that this difference is not an anomaly. There, be_2 accounts for over a third of the data before verbs in the speech of children but only a tenth of the tokens in folk speech. (See Appendix for sample tokens of be_2 in the children's data.)

At first glance, the discrepancy seems odd. Why should there be a dramatic increase of be_2 in only one environment? Age-grading, which might explain the greater frequency of ø in the speech of children, can hardly be the explanation here. Zero forms are more common in the speech of children in all environments except before verbs, and the high frequency of be_2 accounts for the lower frequency of ø there. However, both the actual numbers of be_2 and its frequency of occurrence are almost identical in both varieties before all predicates except for verbs: The difference is not just one of frequency, then, but of structure, of syntactic constraints. The nature of the constraint becomes clearer when we recognize that previous work on the BEV copula actually collapses two distinct grammatical categories: the auxiliary *be*, used with a following present participle in forming the progressive; and copula *be*, which links its subject to predicate nouns, adjectives, and locatives. It is the greater use of be_2 as an auxiliary, not as a copula, that distinguishes the speech of children from that of adults. In the speech of children, progressive constructions have come to favor the occurrence of be_2.

While the recognition that be_2 occurs frequently as an auxiliary but rarely as a copula provides an accurate account of the form's distribution in the speech of children, it does not explain why be_2 has become so common in that environment. The explanation may well lie in the semantics of the English progressive. As Comrie (1976), Palmer (1974), and Leech (1971) all point out, the English progressive has "an unusually wide range" (Comrie 1976: 33) and can signal a number of meanings that are not "progressive" at all. Thus, progressives can be used to refer to future, habitual, and continuous activities, as in:

(7)   I'm leaving Monday.
(8)   I'm jogging every day this winter.
(9)   I'm getting older.

Comrie's classification of typical aspectual oppositions (see Table 13.5) is enlightening here. In examples (7) and (8), according to his system, the English progressive is actually subsuming a more general set of oppositions, habitual and continuous. The latter is a category that semantically incorporates the progressive, which usually refers to "single temporary happenings" (Leech 1971: 27).

An analysis of all the progressives in our corpus suggests that the more frequent use of be_2 in that environment by adolescents is largely a response to these anomalies in the English progressive. As Table 13.6 indicates, folk speakers make no semantic distinctions among *be* forms in the progressive, although three of the four uses of be_2 refer to activities that occur either habitually or for an extended period of time. Among children, the situation is quite different. Zero and conjugated forms are used to signal limited duration, the meaning typically associated with the progressive, or to refer to future events.[6] The only three instances of be_2 in these contexts refer to actions that took place in the past. For habitual actions and events of

Table 13.5 Comrie's (1976) classification of aspectual oppositions

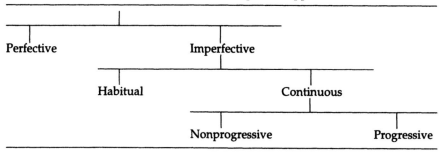

Table 13.6 Meaning of present tense forms before verb +*ing*

Folk speakers

	Limited duration/ future	Extended duration/ habitual		Ambiguous	Total
is/are	7 (21%)	10	(20%)	4	21
ø	26 (79%)	36	(73%)	5	67
be_2	0	3	(6%)	1	4
Total	33	49		10	92

Children

	Limited duration/ future	Extended duration/ habitual		Ambiguous	Total
is/are	16 (29%)	2	(3%)	2	20
ø	36 (65%)	14	(20%)	8	58
be_2	3[a] (5%)	54	(77%)	5	62
Total	55	70		15	140

[a] All three instances refer to actions in the past.

extended duration, however, be_2 is clearly the dominant form, accounting for over three-fourths of the tokens in those contexts. The following examples from adolescents illustrate the contrast in the use of *is/are* as opposed to be_2.

(10) What you getting for Christmas?
(11) They having left-overs this week . . .
(12) In health, we talking about the eye . . .
(13) FW: What's he doing?
     Inf: He trying to scare [us].
(14) He big, and he always be fighting.
(15) Sometimes them big boys be throwing [the ball].
(16) You know———, I be messing with her [i.e., she's my girlfriend].

Sentence (10) is clearly future, while sentences (11) through (13) all refer to activities of limited duration, with (11), uttered on a Monday, possibly carrying future meaning as well. Sentences (14) and (15), on the other hand, refer to iterative events, while (16) refers to an event of extended duration. This contrast, of course, also provides a solid explanation for absence of be_2 before *gonna*, the form of the progressive used as an intentional future. We should caution, however, that the contrast is not yet absolute, as the following sentences illustrate.

(17) We racing all the time
(18) They chasing other people all the time; they got a four-wheel drive and sometimes they be jumping in.

Nevertheless, a distinction between be_2 on the one hand and ø and *is/are* on the other clearly is developing within the progressive in BEV.

To summarize, then, be_2 occurs in folk speech as an occasional variant both for the copula and for auxiliary *be*. In the speech of adolescents, be_2 persists as an occasional variant for the copula, but as an auxiliary it has come to contrast systematically with ø and the conjugated forms. While be_2 is used for extended duration and habitual meaning, ø and *is/are* refer to activities of limited duration and future events.

Although this explanation accounts nicely for our data, we still are left with two important questions: How general is this contrast within the progressive, and how did that contrast arise? Since other scholars have not studied black folk speech and have not analyzed the syntactic constraints on be_2, we have no firm evidence on the extent of the patterns we have described here, but scattered comments and data in other studies suggest that these patterns may be wide-spread. For example, in a study of the speech of black fifth graders in Atlanta, Sommer (1986) notes that be_2 occurs far more often in the progressive than elsewhere. Among middle-class children, progressives account for a third of the instances of be_2, while among lower-class children they account for half. Likewise, Fasold says that "in particular, [be_2] can occur as the auxiliary in the progressive construction *be* + VERB + *ing* . . . " (1972: 151), and half of the examples of be_2 cited by Labov et al. (1968) are used in progressives. Data from the *Linguistic Atlas of the Gulf States* (LAGS) suggest that the pattern we found in folk speech is also widespread. Of the thiry-eight instances of be_2 in LAGS data from East Louisiana and Lower Mississippi, analyzed in detail by Bailey and Bassett (1986), only two are in progressives. The same pattern holds for LAGS data from Lower Alabama (three of twenty-two examples are auxiliaries) and West Louisiana (four of forty-four tokens are auxiliaries). Brewer's (1979) work with Rawick's edition of the Work Projects Administration (WPA) slave narratives provides some evidence for an even earlier period of BEV. Of the twenty-four instances of be_2 that she cites, only one occurs in a progressive construction. If her data are representative, then our folk speakers are merely preserving an older pattern, with the extensive use of be_2 in progressives a recent innovation.

One other source of evidence, Loman's *Conversations in a Negro American Dialect* (1967), provides additional confirmation of this hypothesis. About 80 percent of Loman's corpus, gathered in the mid-1960s in Washington, D.C., is from children and is roughly comparable to our data from adolescents.[7] As Table 13.7 shows, the syntactic constraints on the present tense forms in Loman's data are much like those for the Texas children, although significant quantitative differences in the occurrence of some forms do exist (e.g., be_2 is about three times as frequent in the Texas corpus, while ø is more common in the Washington data.) As in the Texas corpus, ø is most common before *gonna* verbs, somewhat less frequent before predicate adjectives and locatives, and least common before noun phrases. Likewise, be_2 is a common variant in the progressive, never occurs before *gonna*, and is rare in other environments. More importantly, as Table 13.8 suggests, the same semantic contrast between be_2 and other forms seems to be emerging within the progressive in the Washington corpus, although the contrast is not as fully developed as in Texas. This last difference, however, may be misleading since Loman's data were gathered some twenty years earlier

Table 13.7 Syntactic constraints on present tense forms in Loman (1967)

	Vb + *ing*	gonna	Predicate adjective	Predicate locative	NP	Misc.	Total
is/are	1 (4%)	2 (11%)	11 (50%)	11 (48%)	74 (76%)	30	129
ø	20 (77%)	17 (89%)	10 (45%)	11 (48%)	22 (23%)	15	95
be_2	5 (19%)	0	1 (5%)	1 (4%)	1 (1%)	0	8
Total	26	19	22	23	97	45	232

Table 13.8 Meaning of present tense forms before verb + *ing* in Loman (1967)

	Limited duration/ future	Extended duration/ habitual	Ambiguous	Total
is/are	0	0	1	1
ø	12 (100%)	8 (62%)	0	20
be_2	0	5 (38%)	0	5
Total	12	13	1	26

than ours. What his data seem to suggest is an intermediate stage between the folk speakers and the Texas adolescents, and they provide some evidence as to when the distinctive use of be_2 in the progressive developed. The semantic contrast within the progressive, which apparently did not exist in the early decades of this century, must have begun to emerge by the middle of the century and by 1970 was close to completion. While absolute confirmation of this hypothesis requires far more extensive data than are currently available, the hypothesis does account nicely for the evidence that we do have.

Syntactic reanalysis of be_2

The second question – how the contrast within the progressive between be_2 and the other present tense forms arose – is more complicated and actually includes two related problems: the linguistic mechanism that motivated the distinction and the social mechanism that triggered its propagation. The mechanism most often used to explain current developments in BEV is decreolization, the claim being that BEV is realigning its rules in the direction of the target language, Standard English, as its speakers achieve greater social mobility and have more contact with whites.[8] The development of be_2 as a habitual/durative marker in the auxiliary, though, can hardly be the result of decreolization because the direction of change is away from, not toward, other varieties of English and involves the development of a grammatical distinction not in the "target language." Our earlier work on the relationship between black and white folk speech in the South (Bailey & Maynor 1985a, 1985b) has demonstrated that those two varieties are only quantitatively different: The same forms occur in both dialects, distributed in the same ways and operating under similar syntactic constraints.[9] The direction of grammatical change in the speech of black adolescents, however, makes their speech less like both white varieties and black folk speech. The increase in the frequency of ø in the third singular in the speech of children provides additional evidence that BEV is not simply decreolizing. Rather, the developments in black speech described here seem to be the consequence of an independent syntactic reanalysis.[10]

Langacker (1977) describes syntactic reanalysis as

> change in the structure of an expression or class of expressions that does not involve any immediate or intrinsic modification of its surface manifestation. Reanalysis may lead to changes at the surface level . . ., but these surface changes can be viewed as the natural and expected result of functionally prior modifications in rules and underlying representations (1977: 58).

Thus, while reanalysis itself is unobservable, its effects can be observed and can provide the clearest evidence that reanalysis has taken place. According to Langacker, radically new uses of existing forms and changes in the distribution of forms are among the most important of these effects, which "interact in . . . interesting way[s] with substantive language universals" (94). Finally, Langacker points out that reanalysis often has its motivation in tendencies toward signal simplicity and perceptual optimality and usually is a response to specific structural pressures.

The development of be_2 in adolescent speech clearly parallels the cases of syntactic reanalysis which Langacker has observed. As the distinction between folk speech and the speech of children demonstrates, the use of be_2 in the auxiliary as a habitual/durative marker, contrasting with ø and conjugated forms, represents a new use of an existing form and dramatically alters that form's distribution. Originally just an occasional variant of both auxiliary and copula *be*, be_2 was reanalyzed as an aspectual marker, a marker of habituality and duration. As a result, the form is now increasingly restricted so that it occurs primarily as an auxiliary. As we pointed out above, this semantic/syntactic reformulation is probably a response to structural pressures within the English progressive, which includes a number of meanings (e.g., habitual, durative, and future) that are not progressive at all. The establishment of the opposition between habitual/durative forms on the one hand and progressive/future forms on the other suggests both the interaction of universal grammar with syntactic reanalysis and a movement toward perceptual optimality. The separation of habitual/durative forms from progressives, as we suggested above, is a movement toward a more typical set of aspectual oppositions. The type of optimality involved here is what Langacker calls

> transparency . . ., the notion that the ideal or optimal linguistic code, other things being equal, will be one in which every surface unit . . . will have associated with it a clear, salient, and reasonably consistent meaning or function, and every semantic element in a sentence will be associated with a distinct and recognizable surface form (1977: 110).

He further suggests that languages become more transparent as they eliminate meaningless morphemes or assign them new meanings. The latter process, of course, accounts for the development of be_2 as a habitual/durative marker in the auxiliary.

While black folk speech shows none of these effects of reanalysis, one characteristic of be_2 in that variety suggests a reason why be_2, rather than some other form, was reanalyzed. As Fasold (1969, 1972) has indicated, frequency-of-occurrence adverbials (e.g. *often*, *sometimes*, and *when* clauses) are used with be_2 far more often than with other present tense forms. In our corpus, this relationship holds not only in the speech of children, but also in folk speech, as Table 13.9 shows. In the latter variety, frequency adverbials occur almost three times as often with be_2 as with ø and almost ten times as often as with conjugated forms.

On the basis of this evidence alone, one might be tempted to claim that be_2 had already begun to function as a marker of habitual/durative aspect in folk speech, but several factors mitigate against such an analysis. First, a simple tally of adverb cooccurrence is misleading because not all present tense forms can be used in the same way. For example, almost a fourth of the zero forms in folk speech occur before *gonna*, where be_2 never occurs and where frequency adverbials are unlikely (they never occur there in our corpus). While the elimination of these tokens from the analysis of adverb cooccurrence would not alter the pattern of cooccurrence dramatically

Table 13.9 Cooccurrence of forms with frequency-of-occurrence adverbs and *when* clauses

	Folk speakers		Children	
	Frequency adverbial	No frequency adverbials	Frequency adverbial	No frequency adverbials
am/is/are	18 (2%)	884 (98%)	7 (1%)	758 (99%)
ø	15 (7%)	191 (93%)	15 (6%)	218 (94%)
be₂	9 (19%)	39 (81%)	35 (29%)	84 (71%)

Table 13.10 Cooccurrence of instances of infinitive *be* with frequency-of-occurrence adverbs and *when* clauses in folk speech

	Frequency adverbial	No frequency adverbial
Deleted *will/would*	10 (21%)	38 (79%)
No deletion	20 (6%)	323 (94%)

Source: Bailey & Maynor (1985a).

(increasing the percentage from seven to ten with ø), the change does suggest that we need to account for variations in the use of the present tense forms. Second, in our data from folk speech, far more habitual/durative contexts are not marked by be_2 than are marked by the form: No systematic contrast exists (see Bailey & Maynor 1985a).

Third, the same pattern of cooccurrence with frequency adverbials exists in white folk speech, with these adverbials accompanying 45 percent of the be_2 tokens, 8 percent of the ø forms, and only 2 percent of the conjugated forms (see Bailey & Maynor 1985b). Whatever the explanation for the patterning of frequency adverbials, that patterning is not unique to BEV. The patterning is also not unique to present tense forms; it operates with certain instances of infinitive *be*, too. As Table 13.10 indicates, in black folk speech frequency adverbials are used with tokens of invariant *be* derived from *will/would* deletion about four times as often as with other infinitives. The reason for this parallel between the two kinds of invariant *be* is not at all clear, although we have suggested elsewhere (Bailey & Maynor 1985a) that the "invariantness" of the two forms (i.e., the lack of any overt structural cues) may account for their tendency to occur with frequency adverbials. What is clear, however, is that the pattern of adverb cooccurrence is not unique to be_2.

Finally, Brewer's evidence from the WPA slave narratives suggests that the tendency for be_2 to occur with frequency adverbials is not a current development but probably dates back at least to the mid-nineteenth century. The use of be_2 as a habitual/durative marker, then, emerges only in the speech of children in our corpus and seems to be a recent innovation. That does not mean that the syntactic reanalysis has not begun earlier, in folk speech, but its effects are not apparent there, and thus we have no evidence for determining whether it had begun. Nevertheless, the tendency for be_2 to occur with frequency adverbials must have been important in triggering its reanalysis.

While the anomalies of the English progressive and the tendency for be_2 to occur with frequency adverbials probably motivated the syntactic reanalysis of be_2, they do not account for the propagation of that reanalysis. If these internal linguistic factors were the only ones involved, be_2 should also have been reanalyzed in white speech. The spread of the reanalysis in BEV, then, must be the result of social factors which did not affect the white population. The age differences between our two groups of informants provide an immediate cue to these social factors. The folk speakers range in age from seventy to eighty-nine and acquired their language by the beginning of the third decade of this century, while the children, all of whom are twelve or thirteen years old, acquired theirs about seventy years later. This seventy-year period, of course, coincides exactly with the "Great Migration," the process that one demographer has called "the most significant sociological event in our country's recent history" (Hamilton 1972: 80). The Great Migration, a dual movement of blacks from the South to the North and from rural to urban areas, "represents by far the most rapid redistribution of any major group in America" (Lee 1972: 62) and brought about massive changes in social relations between blacks and whites in the Unites States.[11]

In 1890, 90 percent of the black population lived in the South, and 80 percent lived in rural areas. Twenty years later, 89 percent was still in the South and less than 25 percent was in cities. With the advent of World War I, however, blacks began moving in large numbers to cities and to the North, responding to increasing economic opportunity there, decreasing economic opportunity in the South (the consequences of the boll weevil, fluctuation in cotton prices, and technological innovation), and the desire to escape racial discrimination. By 1970, the results of this massive shift in the population were clear: 47 percent of the black population lived outside the South, while 77 percent lived in cities, with 34 percent of the black population concentrated in seven major urban centers: New York, Chicago, Detroit, Philadelphia, Washington, D.C., Los Angeles, and Baltimore.

As striking as these figures are, they actually understate the social effects of the Great Migration. The migration of blacks was not just to cities but to inner city areas. As Jones (1980) points out, the settlement of blacks in inner cities extended from the earliest years of the Great Migration to the present. By 1960, over half of the black population lived in inner cities; in 1976, that figure had risen to nearly 60 percent. The movement of blacks into inner cities, of course, parallels a movement of whites away from those areas so that the two streams of migration have produced cities within cities, islands where blacks often have little contact with whites. The increasing spatial isolation has been accompanied by a declining labor market after World War II as industries have followed the white population away from inner cities. The consequent economic stagnation has, in turn, led to increasing unemployment and poverty in urban areas (see Jones [1980] for a full account of this). The effects of the Great Migration, then, are a drastic relocation of the black population into homogeneous and relatively permanent ghettoes characterized by spatial segregation and economic stagnation, "areas where

all the long-standing urban problems of crime, poverty, and disease exist
. . . in aggravated form" (Glaab & Brown 1967: 287) and where there is
limited hope for entry into the larger society.[12]

The linguistic consequences of these social developments, of course, are
the formation of separate black speech communities which have only
marginal interaction with white communities and which operate with distinct speech acts and events and with distinct linguistic norms, as Labov et
al. (1968) and Kochman (1970) have demonstrated. The emergence of such
speech communities is precisely the kind of sociolinguistic situation which
might favor the propagation of syntactic reanalysis. As these speech communities emerge, BEV becomes a vehicle for reaffirming "bonds of solidarity" (Rickford 1983: 305), of establishing cultural identity, with these new
motives taking precedence over the motivation for a shift to standard
English so that the process of decreolization is halted (cf. Rickford's
[1983] discussion of a similar situation in Guyanese creole). Without the
constraining effects of standard English and influence of white varieties,
BEV would be free to respond to the structural pressure created by anomalies in the English progressive and to the lack of transparency created by
linguistic variants with similar meanings and functions.

The two groups of informants in our corpus clearly seem to represent
two different periods in the emergence of a distinct BEV speech community.
The folk speakers are probably representative of the social and linguistic
situation before the Great Migration. Primarily rural (one speaker is a
native of Bryan, the rest are from rural areas), these informants have never
lived in spatial segregation, even though they have lived most of their lives
under legal and institutional segregation. In spite of their politically and
socially subordinate positions, they have always lived in close proximity to
whites and have had day-to-day contact with them. As a result, their
speech is much like that of the whites with whom they have been in contact
(Bailey & Maynor, 1985a).

The children, on the other hand, all live in Bryan, the major urban area in
the Brazos Valley. In fact, it is quite difficult to find comparable black
children outside of cities and towns in the area. In spite of the fact that
these children live in an institutionally integrated society, they are actually
more segregated spatially and more isolated culturally from whites than
the folk speakers ever were. All of these children, like most blacks in Bryan,
live in the northwest quadrant of town, and their contact with whites is
generally limited to contact at school. More importantly, the adolescents in
this sample are part of a close-knit sociolinguistic network, a network
generally limited to speakers of BEV and to a few bilingual Spanish speakers.[13] The network revolves primarily around four centers of activity: the
local Boys' and Girls' Clubs, an arcade with video games, a dance hall
where breakdancing is performed, and school. Whites are present only at
school, and even there the interaction is superficial.[14]

Given these differences between the sociolinguistic situations of the folk
speakers and the children, it is not surprising that the adolescents are part
of a distinct BEV speech community whose language is diverging from
white dialects and that forms such as *be₂* are being reanalyzed and are
acquiring new functions. As Lambert (1979) has pointed out, the recent

tendency of ethnolinguistic groups is toward linguistic distinctiveness, not convergence.

The sociolinguistic analysis presented here, however, still leaves an important question unanswered. How did the same syntactic reanalysis of be_2 and the same consequences spread to a number of widely separated areas? The answer probably lies in the population movements that preceded the Great Migration and that are occurring now. The Great Migration itself included three broad streams of movement: movements from the South Atlantic states to Northeastern cities, from the East South Central states to North Central cities, and from the West South Central states to Western and Midwestern cities (Rose 1969). These migrations, however, followed an earlier movement during Reconstruction from the South Atlantic and East South Central states to the West South Central region, a pattern of westward movement that had begun well before the Civil War. Ultimately, then, all three streams of migration have the same source and more than likely carried similar dialects with them.

In addition, since World War II a new migration pattern had been developing, one that involves movement from city to city. Taeuber and Taeuber note that after 1950 the migratory pattern that emerges is one of intermetropolitan movement, "both from Southern metropolitan areas to Northern metropolitan areas, and between Northern metropolitan areas" (1969: 128). Both Rose (1971) and Jones (1980) point to this new intermetropolitan migration as a "major path of movement" (Jones 1980: 102), and Rose suggests that the primary sources of new migration to urban ghettoes in recent times have been other urban ghettoes. Thus, black urban areas throughout the United States have a common cultural hearth, but more importantly, they are linked by intermetropolitan migration that provides continual interchanges of populations. Black urban areas, then, form a kind of "mega speech community," as the term BEV suggests: one not correlated with either region or class but with the racially distinct, though interconnected, cultural islands that resulted from the Great Migration. In this context, similarities in the development of be_2 are not at all surprising.

To summarize, the syntactic reanalysis of be_2 and its resulting effects are probably the consequences of internal linguistic factors – the anomalies in the English progressive, the lack of tansparency among the various forms of the present tense of *be*, and the tendency of be_2 to occur with frequency adverbials. The propagation of the reanalysis and its effects, however, are the consequences of social factors that have helped create a distinct BEV speech community: the Great Migration, which led to homogeneity and to spatial and cultural isolation, and the intermetropolitan migrations, which linked black inner cities together demographically and culturally. Either of these factors alone is not sufficient to explain the differences between folk speech and the speech of children, but together they provide the linguistic and social mechanisms which are causing BEV to diverge from white varieties, developing new distinctions which result neither from contact with Standard English nor from developments of an earlier creole.

Conclusions

Our evidence clearly challenges many of the assumptions that underlie the consensus on BEV. First, it demonstrates that the grammars of elderly adults and young children are not alike. Paradigmatic similarities in the present tense of *be*, the subsystem most often discussed in the literature, actually mask significant structural differences. Although both folk speakers and children use be_2 as an occasional variant of the copula, the children also use it as a systematic variant of auxiliary *be*, contrasting with ø, *is*, and *are* to mark a habitual/durative aspect. This distinction, in turn, suggests that black speech is diverging from, not converging toward, white speech. Black and white folk speech differ only quantitatively: both varieties use the same forms, distributed in the same ways and operating under the same syntactic constraints. The children's use of be_2 as a habitual/durative auxiliary, however, suggests a movement away from both black and white folk speech. Finally, the development of be_2 as a habitual/durative auxiliary indicates that some of the most significant differences between black and white speech are the consequences of recent grammatical changes that result from independent syntactic reanalysis, not of the persistence of creole forms or of decreolization.

Our evidence for grammatical changes that do not result from decreolization and for the divergence of the black and white vernaculars becomes even more compelling when taken in conjunction with the findings of Labov and his associates. The work of Myhill and Harris (1986) shows that verbal -*s* is being reanalyzed in much the same way as be_2 while the work of Labov (1980), Ash and Myhill (1986), and Graff, Labov, and Harris (1986) suggests that the phonological systems of the black and white vernaculars may also be diverging. As Labov has pointed out, "many observers find it surprising that white and black vernaculars are growing more different. They feel that the forces of convergence and assimilation are greater than the forces of divergence" (1986: 20). In light of the increasing spatial segregation of blacks and whites over the last seventy-five years, however, divergence in their speech is really not surprising. Because language is deeply embedded in social structure, a drastic change in that structure – especially one of the magnitude of the Great Migration – will surely have significant linguistic consequences. As these consequences work themselves out in present-day BEV, they suggest that what is really remarkable about that variety is not its past but its present.

Notes

1. The research for this paper was supported by a series of grants from the College of Liberal Arts at Texas A&M University; the interviews with the children were done in conjunction with the Multi-Ethnic Reading/Language Arts Program in the Bryan Independent School District, a project funded by the Meadows Foundation. We wish to thank the staff of that project, especially Donna Norton, Principal Investigator, Sue Morhman, and Avlyn Speck, for their help in setting up and conducting the interviews. We also wish to thank Joe Graham for

contributing fieldwork, and Crawford Feagin, Ian Hancock, Michael Montgomery, Salikoko Mufwene, and John Rickford for comments on an earlier draft of the paper. Finally, we would like to thank William Labov for his encouragement and for providing a detailed critique of that earlier draft. The strengths of this essay clearly reflect that critique; its weaknesses, however, remain our own.

2. See Dillard (1972) for a fuller discussion of this concept, first advanced by William Stewart. The emphasis on adolescent speech in the literature on BEV is largely a response to this claim.

3. See Bailey and Maynor (1985a) for a more detailed treatment of our methods, including a discussion of some of the sources of ambiguity.

4. In spite of these differences with regard to *do*-support, there are striking parallels between the two types of invariant *be*. As we point out below, frequency-of-occurrence adverbs pattern similarly with both forms. Sommer (1986) points out additional similarities. These parallels deserve close consideration. Because of the controversial nature of be_2, representative samples of that form in the speech of the children are presented in the Appendix. Instances of be_2 in folk speech can be found in Bailey and Maynor (1985a).

5. As Holm (1984) and Labov (1982) point out, the term *copula* here is inaccurate, in spite of its conventional use in this way. As we point out below, however, the failure to distinguish copula from auxiliary *be* has been a critical mistake in the study of BEV.

6. One example of be_2 in folk speech seems close to conveying future meaning: "if I *be* living that long, I'll move there" – that is, if I am living at Christmas, I'll move to Houston.

7. See Loman's introduction for a fuller discussion of his sample and Bailey and Maynor (1985a) for an analysis of the present tense of *be* in his corpus.

8. The concept of decreolization as an explanatory mechanism is something of a problem. As Hancock (1985, 1986) points out, decreolization has been used as a catch-all mechanism to explain varying proximities of creoles to each other and to English, as well as to explain variation within creoles. He suggests, instead, that "the reason for this variation is to be sought in the componential matrix at the time of the formation of the individual creoles" (1986: 12). Further, he notes that the "very term *decreolization* may be called into question since it implies the reversal of the same process as that which initially produced the creole, whereas progression toward the lexifier is change that moves ahead, not backward" (1986: 9). Mufwene (1984, 1985) points to other problems in decreolization; Rickford (1983) is an explicit attempt to explain what happens in the process. The evidence that we present below demonstrates some of the problems with decreolization as a generalized explanatory device. We are not questioning the creole origins of BEV here, nor are we claiming that decreolization has never affected BEV and is not at work now in some subsystems of the dialect. Decreolization is not, however, the most important process at work now.

9. We are not suggesting here that black folk speech is simply a derivative of white folk speech – only that the two varieties are fundamentally alike. We recognize that these similarities may result, at least in part, from the influence of BEV on white varieties.

10. Compare Bickerton's (1980) concept of spontaneous change.

11. Scholars have produced a massive literature on the Great Migration. Our discussion relies heavily on Davis and Donaldson (1975), Groh (1972), Hamilton (1972), Jones (1980), Meier and Rudwick (1966), Rose (1969, 1971), and Smith (1966). For a discussion of the importance of the Great Migration to the sociohistorical context of Southern speech, see Bailey (1985).

12. To use Hancock's term, there has been a change in the componential matrix

within which BEV exists. We believe that his concept is useful in explaining current developments in BEV, as well as its origins.
13. See Milroy (1980) for a discussion of the importance of sociolinguistic networks.
14. Informal visits to the schools and interviews with black and white children confirm this observation. Blacks and whites tend to organize themselves into separate groups both within and outside the classroom. While there seems to be no overt hostility between the two groups, neither is there any real interaction. We are not claiming that social relations between blacks and whites were somehow better in the past; we are simply claiming that the dynamics of interaction were different.

References

Ash, S. and Myhill, J. (1986) 'Linguistic correlates of inner ethnic contact', in D. Sankoff (ed.), *Diachrony and diversity*, Amsterdam: John Benjamins, pp. 33–45.

Bailey, G. (1985) *A social history of the Gulf states. LAGS Working Papers* (2nd Series) No. 1. Ann Arbor: University Microfilms.

Bailey, G. and Bassett, M. (1986) 'Invariant *be* in the lower South', in M. Montgomery and G. Bailey (eds.), *Language variety in the South: Perspectives in black and white*, Tuscaloosa: University of Alabama Press, pp. 158–79.

Bailey, G. and Maynor, N. (1985a) 'The present tense of *be* in southern black folk speech', *American Speech* 60: pp. 195–213.

—— (1985b) 'The present tense of *be* in white folk speech of the southern United States', *English World-Wide* 6: pp. 199–216.

Baugh, J. (1980) 'A re-examination of the black English copula', in W. Labov (ed.), *Locating language in time and space*, New York: Academic. pp, 83–106.

—— (1983) *Black street speech: Its history, structure, and survival*, Austin: University of Texas Press.

Bickerton, D. (1980) 'Decreolization and the creole continuum', in A. Valdman and A,. Highfield (eds.), *Theoretical orientations in creole studies*, New York: Academic, pp. 109–29.

Brewer, J. (1979) 'Nonagreeing *am* and invariant *be* in early black English', *The SECOL Bulletin* 3: pp. 81–100.

Comrie, B. (1976) *Aspect*, Cambridge: Cambridge University Press.

Davis, G.A. and Donaldson, F.C. (1975) *Blacks in the United States: A geographic perspective*, Boston: Houghton Mifflin.

Dillard, J.L. (1972) *Black English: Its history and usage in the United States*, New York: Random House.

Dunlap, H.G. (1974) 'Social aspects of a verb frame: Native Atlanta fifth-grade speech – The present tense of *be*', *PADS* pp. 61–62.

Fasold, R.W. (1969) 'Tense and the form *be* in black English', *Language* 45: pp. 763–76.

—— (1972) *Tense marking in black English: A linguistic and social analysis*, Washington, D.C.: Center for Applied Linguistics.

Glaab, C.N. and Brown, A.T. (1967) *A history of urban America*, New York: Macmillan.

Graff, D., Labov, W. and Harris, W. (1986) 'Testing listeners' reactions to phonological markers of ethnic identity: A new method for sociolinguistic research', in D. Sankoff (ed.), *Diachrony and diversity*, Amsterdam: John Benjamins, pp. 46–58.

Groh, G. (1972) *The black migration: The journey to urban America*, New York: Weybright and Talley.

Hamilton, H. (1972) 'The Negro leaves the South', in H. M. Hughes (ed.), *Population growth and the complex society*, Boston: Allyn and Bacon, pp. 79–90.

Hancock, I. (1985) 'The domestic hypothesis, diffusion, and componentiality: An account of Atlantic anglophone creole origins'. Paper presented at the Workshop on Universals vs. Substrata in Creole Genesis, University of Amsterdam.

—— (1986) 'A preliminary classification of the anglophone Atlantic creoles', in G. Gilbert (ed.), *Pidgin and creole languages: Essays in memory of John E. Reinecke*. Honolulu: University of Hawaii Press, pp. 264–333.

Holm, J. (1980) 'The creole "copula" that highlighted the world', in J.L. Dillard (ed.), *Perspectives on American English*, The Hague, Mouton, pp. 367–75.

—— (1984) 'Variability of the copula in black English and its creole kin', *American Speech* 59: pp. 291–309.

Jones, M.E. (1980) *Black migration in the United States with emphasis on selected central cities*, Saratoga, Calif.: Century Twenty One.

Kochman, T. (1970) 'Towards an ethnography of black speech behavior', in N.E. Whitten, Jr. and J.F. Szwed (eds.), *Afro-American anthropology*, New York: Free Press, pp. 145–62.

Labov, W. (1972) *Language in the inner city: Studies in the black English vernacular*, Philadelphia: University of Pennsylvania Press.

—— (1980) 'The social origins of sound change', in *Locating Language in Time and Space*, New York: Academic, pp. 251–65.

—— (1982) 'Objectivity and commitment in linguistic science: The case of the black English trial' in Ann Arbor, *Language in Society* 11: pp. 165–202.

—— (1985) 'The increasing divergence of black and white vernaculars'. Manuscript.

Labov, W., et al. (1968) *A study of the non-standard English of Negro and Puerto Rican speakers in New York City*, USOE Final Report, Research Project 3288.

Labov, W. and Harris, W.A. (1986) 'De Facto segregation of black and white vernaculars', in D. Sankoff (ed.), *Diachrony and diversity*, Amsterdam: John Benjamins, pp. 1–24.

Lambert, W.E. (1979) 'Language as a factor in inter-group relations', in H. Giles and R.N. St. Clair (eds.), *Language and social psychology*, Oxford: Basil Blackwell, pp. 186–92.

Langacker, R.W. (1977) 'Syntactic reanalysis', in C.N. Li (ed.), *Mechanisms of syntactic change*, Austin: University of Texas Press, pp. 57–139.

Lee, E.S. (1972) 'People on the move', in H.M. Hughes (ed.), *Populaton growth and the complex society*, Boston: Allyn and Bacon, pp. 61–78.

Leech, G.N. (1971) *Meaning and the English verb*, London: Longman.

Loman, B. (1967) *Conversations in a Negro American dialect*, Washington, D.C.: Center for Applied Linguistics.

Meier, A., and Rudwick, E. (1966) *From plantation to ghetto*, New York: Hill & Wang.

Milroy, L. (1980) *Language and social networks*, Oxford: Basil Blackwell.

Montgomery, M. and Bailey, G. (1986) 'Introduction', in M. Montgomery and G. Bailey (eds.), *Language variety in the South: Perspectives in black and white*, Tuscaloosa: University of Alabama Press pp. 1–29.

Mufwene, S.S. (1984) 'Gullah and Jamaican creole: An issue on decreolization'. Paper presented at the Fifth Biennial Meeting of the Society for Caribbean Linguistics, University of the West Indies at Mona, Kingston, Jamaica.

—— (1985) 'Misinterpreting linguistic continuity charitability'. Paper presented at the Ninth Annual Language and Culture in South Carolina Symposium, University of South Carolina.

Myhill, J., and Harris, W.A. (1986) 'The use of the verbal -s inflection in BEV', in D. Sankoff (ed.), *Diachrony and diversity*, Amsterdam: John Benjamins, pp. 25–31.

Palmer, F.R. (1974) *The English verb*, London: Longman.

Pederson, L., et al. (1981) *LAGS: The basic materials*, 4 Parts, Ann Arbor: University Microfilms.

Rickford, J.R. (1975) 'Carrying the new wave into syntax. The case of black English BIN', in R.W. Fasold and R.W. Shuy (eds.), *Analyzing variation in language*, Washington, D.C.: Georgetown University Press, pp. 162–83.

—— (1977) 'The question of prior creolization in black English', in A. Valdman (ed.), *Pidgin and creole linguistics*, Bloomington: Indiana University Press, pp. 190–221.

—— (1983) 'What happens in decreolization', in R. Andersen (ed.), *Pidginization and creolization as language acquisition*, Rowley, Mass.: Newbury House, pp. 248–319.

Rose, H. (1969) 'Social processes in the city: Race and urban residential choice', *Commission on College Geography* (Resource Paper No. 6) Washington, D.C.: Association of American Geographers.

—— (1971) *The black ghetto: A spatial behavioral perspective*, New York: McGraw–Hill.

Smith, L.T. (1966) 'The redistribution of the Negro population of the United States, 1910–1960', *Journal of Negro History* 51: pp. 155–73.

Sommer, E. (1986) 'Variation in southern urban English', in M. Montgomery and G. Bailey (eds.), *Language variety in the South: Perspectives in black and white*, Tuscaloosa: University of Alabama Press, pp. 180–201.

Stewart, W. (1967) 'Sociolinguistic factors in the history of American Negro dialects', *Florida FL Reporter* 5(2): pp. 1–4.

—— (1968) 'Continuity and change in American Negro dialects', *Florida FL Reporter* 6(1): pp. 3–4, 14–16, 18.

Taeuber, K.E. and Taeuber, A.F. (1969) *Negroes in cities: Residential and neighborhood change*, New York: Atheneum.

Wolfram, W. (1974) 'The relationship of white southern speech to vernacular black English', *Language* 50: pp. 498–527.

Appendix: Sample instances of *be₂* in the speech of children:

I.   Before verb + *ing* (62 tokens)
   a.   Yesterday we went to Sommerville, where all the people *be* swimming.
   b.   Sometimes them big boys *be* throwing [the ball].
   c.   They *be* doing the breaking in PE and during class time.

II.   Before adjectives (5 tokens)
   a.   He [5th grade teacher] *be* mean.
   b.   You know, when it *be* sunny like today.

III.   Before locatives (15 tokens)
   a.   When I was at the race track there, we *be* at the race track [he had a wreck].
   b.   One team *be* over here and another team *be* over there . . .

IV.   Before noun phrases (8 tokens)
   a.   It *be* two wide receivers [on a football team].
   b.   It *be* some logs going down . . .

V.   Miscellaneous (6 tokens)
   a.   Tha's the only way I *be* played [sic] Donkey Kong.
   b.   They *be* – over here they break too much.

14

Language planning and language change

Ernst Håkon Jahr

Originally published in L.E. Breivik and E.H. Jahr, eds, *Language Change: Contributions to the Study of Its Causes* (Mouton de Gruyter, 1989).

Deliberately planned changes

Linguistic changes discussed in the literature are almost without exception unconscious and unintended changes, changes that have occurred without deliberate actions or motivations on the part of the speakers/users to change the language or part(s) of the language. Here, I want to draw attention to some changes that are consciously and deliberately initiated by language users, or rather, by the speech community through planning. Language planning can be said to be the only activity in which a language community takes action actively and intentionally in order to obtain a linguistic change.

In earlier periods language planning did not play any part in linguistic change, since, of course, language planning was non-existent. Only from the time of the founding of the first language academies, as in France in 1635 and in Sweden in 1786, can we begin to discuss the possibility of influence of language planning on language change. Up till the present century, however, the academies had very limited possibilities for directing language development.

With the development of a compulsory school system in most European countries over the last two centuries, and with a school period of up to 9 or even 12 years in some countries, the political authorities now have a powerful instrument which enables them – in principle – to reach the whole population with language planning.

In this paper, then, I will focus on the role of language planning in language change. By 'language planning' I understand 'a deliberate effort by political authorities, some institution or prescriptive linguists to change a spoken language or a spoken variety of a language in a certain defined direction'. Adopting this definition I exclude, of course, that type of language planning which deals with the relationships between different languages within an area or country, e.g. the relationship between English and indigenous languages in former British colonies, or the relationship between the two Norwegian written standards *Bokmål* and *Nynorsk*. I also exclude examples of the reviving of entire languages, such as modern Hebrew in Israel, as well as languages of communities with very few speakers, where it is possible for a small group or even individuals to bring about major linguistic changes. Melanesia has many such communities with less than 500 speakers.

What I want to look at are cases where (small) parts of actual languages have been changed through means controlled by political or administrative bodies, mainly, it turns out, through the compulsory school system and broadcasting. Actions taken by individual schoolteachers to correct the speech of their pupils are also excluded, unless such corrections are motivated by and are part of a wider language planning policy.

Most of the language planning around the world is concerned with functional, legal, or other relationships between different languages within a region – or with cultivation of or changes in written languages. Language planning concerning speech is much rarer, and, it seems, most often unsuccessful. However, it can be and has been done, and I will present three examples, from Norwegian and Icelandic, which will illustrate different effects of language planning on Norwegian and Icelandic speech.

There are at least three possible ways in which language planning can cause changes in speech in a given language:

1. *By introducing a new feature into the language in question.* A feature not previously found in the language is either just added, or – and this is, I think, in most cases the objective of the language planners – this new feature replaces an old one, which then disappears. To obtain a complete substitution in this way seems to be extremely difficult. But I will give one rather surprising example from Norwegian which shows how language planning has added an important feature to the core lexicon of practically every Norwegian, and thereby created an area of linguistic variation which did not exist before and which can be studied and described within a sociolinguistic framework.

2. *By removing a feature from the language in question, most often by halting and reversing an ongoing (and spreading) change.* This is, then, a type of anti-change, where language planning engages in maintaining the linguistic state prior to a change that is not favoured by the language planners. I shall report on one successful and illustrative example of this type, from Icelandic, where a phonological feature found in almost 40% of the capital's inhabitants in the early 1940s was removed and today is almost non-existent in Reykjavik.

3. *By changing the written standard of a language and through this, as a side effect, influencing the speech variety most closely connected with this written standard.* This third type is, obviously, of a somewhat different kind than the first two. Here, there is no conscious wish on the part of the language planners to actually change the spoken language. But if a change nevertheless occcurs as a result of a conscious change in the written standard, language planning is of course responsible, and, consequently, the cause of the change. I will discuss some changes in upper-class Oslo speech from about 1880 onwards as a possible example of this type.

Counting two-digit numbers over 20 in Norwegian

In 1950–51, the Norwegian Government as well as Parliament set out to change the pronunciation of every two-digit number over 20 in Norwegian. Although Norway has a long history of language planning, this was the first, and up till now, the only time that the spoken language has been dealt with specifically. Language planning in Norway has otherwise been exclusively preoccupied with the written language.

The modern Germanic languages have two distinct methods of compounding numbers from 21 to 99, including cases where these are expressed as part of a higher number, as in 243 for example. Modern German, Dutch, Danish, and Faeroese place the units before the tens, as in German 'einundzwanzig'. Modern English, Swedish, and Icelandic, however, put the tens first, as in English 'tweny-one'.

Before 1951, Norwegians – without exception – counted with the units before the tens, as in German, Dutch, Danish and Faeroese. The reform of 1951 introduced the English, Swedish, and Icelandic method, with tens before units. This new method was made compulsory in schools and broadcasting, and the Norwegian population was urged to change to the new method.

The language planners were quite optimistic about the reform, expecting the new method of counting to replace the old one completely after a few years. Those in favour of the change claimed that the new method was more logical and more international (!) than the old method. In this context, then, 'international' means in line with English and Swedish, departing however from Danish and German.

Today every Norwegian uses both methods, units before tens as well as tens before units. A recent sociolinguistic study of 30 informants from Northern Norway yielded the results shown in Table 14.1 (Mercer 1986). These results are set out in Fig. 14.1. It turns out that age and formality are important factors: the younger the informant and the more formal the situation, the higher the frequency of the new forms. The variation ranges from the youngest group (11–12 year-olds) who had no occurrences of old forms in the reading tests, to the oldest group (above 55 years old) who had 90.2% occurrences of the old forms in informal conversation. There seems

Table 14.1 Percentage usage of old and new method of counting: age and formality

Age group	Reading				Informal interview, conversation	
	Formal text		Informal text			
	Unit-tens	Tens-units	Unit-tens	Tens-unit	Unit-tens	Tens-unit
11–12	0.0	100.0	0.0	100.0	14.3	85.7
17–18	0.9	99.1	1.8	98.2	85.7	14.3
19–35	0.9	99.1	0.0	100.0	51.2	48.8
36–55	55.6	44.4	52.1	47.9	73.5	26.5
> 55	60.2	39.8	50.0	50.0	90.2	9.8

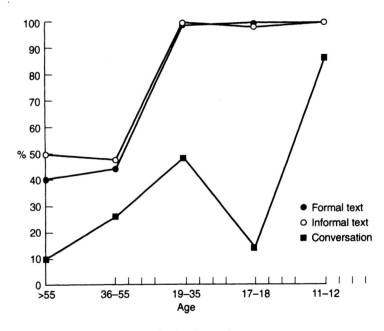

Fig. 14.1 Usage of old and new methods of counting

Table 14.2 Percentage usage of tens-unit counting (48 informants: 24 males, 24 females, aged 11, 14, and 17)

	11-year-olds		14-year-olds		17-year-olds	
	Reading	Informal interview	Reading	Informal interview	Reading	Informal interview
West	85.6	52.8	66.7	32.4	60.7	35.7
East	68.9	41.1	34.5	20.6	29.8	10.7

to be a clear difference between those born before and those born after the introduction of the new forms in 1951. (The exceptionally low proportion of new forms used in conversation by the age group 17–18 may be a result of few occurrences of compound forms – only 14 were recorded.)

These results – from 1986 – can be compared with a study done in Oslo ten years ago (Kvifte 1978); see Table 14.2, *West* is a middle and upper-class area, *East* is a working class area. The figures in this table correspond to the columns shown in Fig. 14.2. Here, we observe a fall in frequency of new forms from the youngest to the oldest group, both in the reading test and in the informal interview, but in this study the oldest informants were only 17 years old. Especially low was the frequency in the informal interview in the 17 year-olds from the eastern part of Oslo (10.7%).

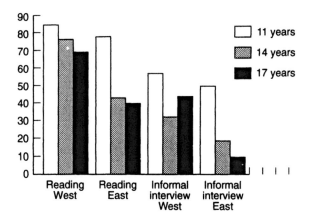

Fig. 14.2 Usage of ten-unit counting

These results from young Oslo speakers can be interpreted in two very different ways: (1) the use of new forms seems to be increasing since they are more frequent among the very young than in the groups of teenagers, or (2) young speakers tend to decrease the use of new forms when they become teenagers.

Without a new study today, it is impossible to decide which one of these interpretations is correct. However, when the figures from the Oslo study are compared with the results reports in Table 14.1, it seems most plausible that the use of new forms is increasing.

Furthermore, if we can apply the usage by youngsters in Kvifte's 1978 study to the population in Oslo in general, it seems that social class is also a factor involved in variation between new and old forms. New forms were more frequently used by the young informants from the middle and upper-class West area than from the working class East area.

Table 14.1 and 14.2 show that the language planning reform of 1951 has created an area of variation within Norwegian today which did not exist before, and the frequency of occurrence of units-ten forms now seems to depend on such sociolinguistic factors as social class, age, and formality of context.

The reform of 1951 has not, however, succeeded completely, since the old method of counting is still very much alive, especially in casual everyday speech. I will mention only one important linguistic factor that could be claimed to work against the reform.

The new forms which were introduced by the reform were in conflict with a trochaic stress pattern which is usual in Norwegian. The trochaic Norwegian stress pattern has been referred to in order to explain why Norwegian developed units-ten counting in the first place (Liestøl 1910: 23). The new forms with tens first mostly had a strong stress on the final syllable, since only two of the nine Norwegian words for the units have two syllables – *fire* 'four' and *åtte* 'eight'. This strong word-final stress often produced a clash with the word-initial stress of the following word. If, however, units are used first – as in the pre-1951 method of counting – this problem does not arise, since all the words for tens have the stress-pattern strong-weak. The problem of having two strong stresses within the compound number is then resolved by insertion of a stressless *og* 'and' between the unit and tens numbers. This important prosodic factor was not fully appreciated in the debate prior to the reform.

This stress pattern must also be the reason why Mercer in his study (1986) found more occurrences of units-ten forms when the number was followed by a noun (with first syllable stress) than when it occurred alone; thus they were more likely in phrases such as 25-*watts pære* '25 Watt bulb' or 25 *prosent* '25 percent' than in the year '1925' or a telephone number '253525'.

What we have seen here, then, is a change in the *core lexicon* of a spoken language. When we take that into account, I think it is fair to conclude that the result of the 1951 reform is quite remarkable. Most, perhaps all, Norwegians use both tens-unit and units-ten forms in their speech. The occurrence of a units-ten form as opposed to a tens-unit form depends on several factors, such as age, style, and context: the less formal the style, the more likely is the use of a units-ten form, and the older the speaker, the more likely the occurrence of units-ten forms. In addition, social class also seems to play a part.

The 1951 reform has had an effect on everybody's speech, though only in the most formal style of the older generation. Before 1951, nobody used tens-unit counting and now everybody does to a certain degree. And the reform can be the only and exclusive reason for the change.

Flámæli: The merging of /ɪ/ with /e/, and /ʏ/ with /ø/ in Icelandic

In his paper 'The vowel system of Icelandic' (1959), Hreinn Benediktsson showed how the Icelandic vowel system has developed and has been reduced in terms of distinctive features from Old to Modern Icelandic (Benediktsson 1959). The last step in this long historical development of the vowel system (see Fig. 14.3) is the merging of /ɪ/ with /e/, and /ʏ/ with /ø/, which is manifested by a lower of /ɪ/ and /ʏ/ and a raising of /e/ and /ø/, yielding a vowel of intermediate quality, or a concomitant diphthong. This process makes homophones out of words like *viður* 'wood' and *veður* 'weather', and *flugur* (plur. of *fluga* 'fly') and *flögur* (plur. of *flaga* 'slab, flake'). This last step in the development of Icelandic vowels origi-

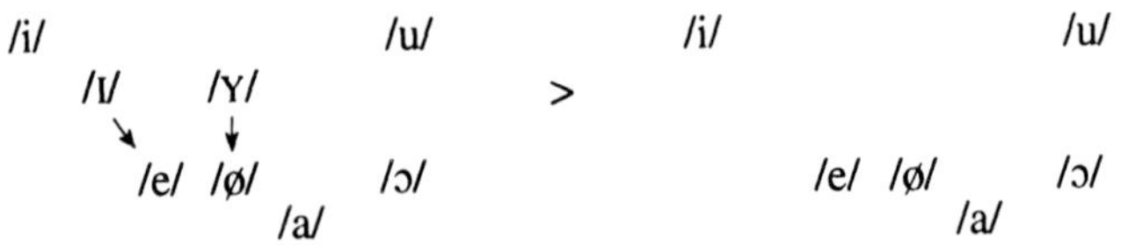

Fig. 14.3 *Flámæli*: the merging of /ɪ/ with /e/, and /ʏ/ with /ø/ in Icelandic

nated among the common fisherman in the 19th century, and spread rapidly in the west, east, and north of the country.

There are no dialects in the traditional sense in Iceland. But speakers of Icelandic have different linguistic features to a variable degree. There is also no sharp contrast between a standard spoken language and other varieties of Icelandic. Most variable features are considered equally 'good' and 'correct' socially. But there is one important exception to this: the vowel merging just mentioned. The Icelandic name given to this feature suggests a low social reputation. In Iceland it is called *flámæli* 'slack-jawed speech'. (The opposite of *flámæli* is *réttmæli* 'correct speech'.) Its origin among common fishermen, who were the first proletarians in Iceland, may account for the low social status of this specific feature.

Around the time of World War II, Björn Guðfinnsson conducted the largest dialect survey investigation ever in Iceland. He interviewed about 10,000 subjects, mostly school children. The purpose of the project was to map recent phonological innovations in order to establish a basis of knowledge for intensive planning of the spoken language through the school system.

In his investigation in the early 1940s Björn Guðfinnsson found *flámæli* present in 38.55% of all his informants in the capital Reykjavik (Guðfinnsson 1964: 84). He also claimed that it was spreading rapidly (Guðfinnsson 1947: 27). After that, however, *flámæli* was systematically opposed on all levels of instruction and education. Guðfinnsson himself published a normative guide in pronunciation where several pages were dedicated to the fight against the 'slack-jawed speech' (Guðfinnsson 1947: 41–48).

The scenario we have here, then, is a conflict between a sound change that is the last step of a long historical development of the Icelandic vowel system, a change that is clearly in line with the preceding development, and, on the other hand, the extra-linguistic factor of social evaluation. The language planners of Iceland found the outcome of this particular sound change unacceptable and took action against it.

Twenty years after Guðfinnsson's survey investigation, Hreinn Benediktsson (1961–62: 95) reported that as a result of the intensive campaign against *flámæli* it was said to be losing ground among the youngest generation. According to Benediktsson, however, the outcome was still not certain at that time.

Then, after another twenty years, in the early 1980s, Höskuldur Þráinsson and Kristján Árnason did a new survey investigation in Reykjavik in order to compare it with Guðfinnsson's of the early 1940s. Their results show a quite dramatic change in the use of the *flámæli* feature. While Guðfinnsson found – as already mentioned – that 38.55% of the Reykjavik speakers in his investigation had this feature in their speech, Þráinsson and Árnason (1984: 123, cf. also Árnason 1987: 89) found the same feature in only 2.6% of their informants. Among the younger generation they did not find it at all. Linguistically speaking the Icelanders had reversed the last step in the historical development of their vowel system.

Since the campaign for the eradication of *flámæli* in Icelandic could draw to a considerable extent on the low social value of this particular phonological feature, one important question arises. Is it the low social status that is responsible for the result now reported from Reykjavik by Þráinsson and Árnason, or is the action taken by normative linguists and the schools responsible?

In Jahr 1988, I have tried to show how the parameter *urban–rural* plays a decisive part in the halting of a sound change in Oslo Norwegian. A recent change in the system of laterals in Oslo Norwegian, where an alveolar or retroflex *l*-allophone replaced a dental allophone, has been stopped before reaching completion, i.e. after the vowels /a/ and /ɔ/ we still find a dental allophone. The reason for this linguistically uneconomical situation is that a pronunciation of alveolar or retroflex *l* after /a/ or /ɔ/ sounds extremely rural to the inhabitants of Oslo.

Now, could this also apply to the Icelandic example, and perhaps explain why *flámæli* is non-existent among the younger generation of the capital Reykjavik? I believe not. The main difference here is that *flámæli* was well established among young people in Reykjavik 50 years ago, while alveolar/retroflex *l* after /a/ or /ɔ/ never entered Oslo speech. It seems that the parameter urban – rural is not as important in Iceland as it is in Norway.

Another possible explanation for the eradication of *flámæli* could perhaps be this: the vowel phonemes that were the outcome of the lowering of /ɪ/ and /ʏ/ and the merger with /e/ and /ø/ became functionally overloaded. This functional overload then created a reaction, yielding again the older system.

This system-internal explanation is, however, contradicted by the fact that Þráinsson and Árnason in their study (1984: 125) found a slight tendency among young people in the direction of a new merging process, i.e. the merging of /ø/ with /ʏ/ by a *raising* of the /ø/. This tendency has also been observed by Blöndal (1984). This indicates that instead of reacting against simplification, the vowel system seeks new ways of obtaining reduction (by raising the /ø/), since the first attempt (starting with the lowering of /ɪ/ and /ʏ/) has been stopped.

Language planning, then, with steps taken against the *flámæli* feature from the late 1940s onwards is responsible for the decline of *flámæli* in Icelandic.[1]

The changes voiced > unvoiced stops after long vowels in some words in upper-class Oslo Norwegian

Around 1880, the spoken language of the upper classes in Norway was greatly influenced by the written standard of the 19th century, which was predominantly Danish. When Norway got her political independence from Denmark in 1814, after a 400-year union, the Norwegians continued to use the Danish standard which had been the common written medium during the period of the union. Upper-class speech in the 19th century was strongly influenced by this written standard, often reflecting a near spelling pronunciation.

In an attempt to nationalize the written standard the Norwegian authorities have engaged heavily in language planning and have succeeded in changing the written standard from being Danish to being predominantly

Norwegian. The transformation from Danish to Norwegian has been completed through a step-by-step Norwegianization. By including more and more elements from spoken Norwegian in the written standard and at the same time removing salient Danish features, the language planners have been able to change the written standard quite dramatically.

By means of three language reforms in this century (1907, 1917, 1938), the orthography and word forms of the written standard changed from the Danish forms to a way of spelling which, to the language planners, reflected a more 'Norwegian' pronunciation. But since upper-class speech to a considerable degree was influenced by Danish spelling, several important features of this spoken variety were not regarded as sufficiently national. Thus, the language planners turned to other spoken varieties, considering them to be more genuinely Norwegian. To the language planners this followed logically from and was merely a consequence of the desire to nationalize the written standard. But members of the upper classes regarded this as an impairment and vulgarization of the written standard. Being upper class they were used to considering their own spoken variety 'correct', 'nice', and 'educated', and why, they asked, should not the written standard reflect this?

Thus, the upper classes have on the whole been extremely negative to the official planning of the written language. Generally speaking, we may say that as long as changes in the standard were made within, and could be motivated by, upper-class pronunciation, they were reluctantly accepted after a few years. This applies especially to the 1907 changes. However, when popular and dialectal pronunciation was taken account of in the reforms of 1917 and 1938, this initiated a most active and organized resistance. Nevertheless, upper-class speech has not been unaffected by the changes made in the written standard.

The changes in upper-class speech which I want to focus on here is the development of /b/, /d/, /g/ to /p/, /t/, /k/ after long vowels in words like

Danish *skaber* – Norwegian *skaper* 'creator'
Danish *vide* – Norwegian *vite* 'know'
Danish *rige* – Norwegian *rike* 'realm'

A major aim of language planning in Norway was to replace *b, d, g* by *p, t, k* in all words having the Danish form.

Upper-class speech, however, had long ago adopted a pronunciation with voiced stops after long vowels in many of these words, in line with the Danish orthographic system. But with the orthographic changes in these words in the written standard, upper-class speech also changed, as can be seen in Table 14.3. The use of /p/, /t/, and /k/ after long vowels has increased in the words in question and is now predominant even in this high prestige spoken variety of Norwegian. In terms of Norwegian language planning, we may say that upper-class speech, too – along with the written standard – has been 'Norwegianized'. Subsequently, the fierce opposition to the official spelling with *p, t* and *k* has declined.

Table 14.3 The changes from *b, d, g* to *p, t, k* in spelling and upper-class pronunciation. (from Jahr 1986)

Written form 1880 Dano-Norwegian	Pronunciation 1880	Written form 1907 ('–' means no change)	Pronunciation 1910	Written form 1917	Pronunciation 1925	Written form 1938 Bokmål	Pronunciation today
sæbe 'soap'	se:bə	sápe	se:pə/sɔ:pə	–	se:pə/sɔ:pə	–	sɔ:pə/se:pə
råbe 'call'	rɔ:bə/ru:pə	rope	ru:pə	dáp/dáb	ru: pə	dáp	ru: pə
dåb 'baptism'	dɔ:b	–	dɔ:b		dɔ:p/dɔ:b		dɔ: p
skaber 'creator'	ska:bər	–	ska:bər	skaper	ska:pər/ska:bər		ska:pər
håbe 'hope'	hɔ:bə	–	hɔ:bə	hápe/hábe	hɔ:bə	hápe	hɔ:bə/hɔ:pə
læbe 'lip'	le:bə	–	le:bə	lepe/lebe/leppe	le:bə/lepə	leppe/lepe	lepe/le:bə
skib 'ship'	ʃi:b	–	ʃi:b	skib/skib	ʃi:b	skip	ʃi:b/ʃi:p
våben 'weapon'	vɔ:bən	–	vɔ:bən	vápen/vében	vɔ:ben	vápen	vɔ:bən/vɔ:pen
-hed (suffix)	-he:d/-he:t	-het	-he:t	–	-he:t	–	-he:t
båden 'the boat'	bɔ:dn̩	båten	bɔ:tn̩	–	bɔ:tn̩	–	bɔ:tn̩
foruden 'without'	fɔrʉ:dn̩	foruten	fɔrʉ:tn̩	–	fɔrʉ:tn̩	–	fɔrʉ:tn̩
udgjøre 'constitute'	ʉdgjøre/-t-	utgjøre	ʉ:tjøre	–	ʉ:tjøre	–	ʉ:tjøre
vide 'know'	vi:də/vi:tə	vite	vi:tə	–	vi:tə	–	vi:tə
ved 'know' pres.	ve:d/ve:t	vet	ve:t	vet/veit	ve:t	–	ve:t
vidende 'knowing'	vi:dn̩e	–	vi:tn̩e/vi:tn̩	vitende/vidende	vi:tn̩e/vi:tn̩	vitende	vi:tn̩e/vi:tn̩
viden 'knowledge'	vi:dn̩	–	vi:dn̩	–	vi:dn̩	viten	vi:dn̩/vi:tn̩
pigen 'the maid'	pi:gən	piken	pi:kən	–	pi:kən	–	pi:ken
tilbage 'back' adv.	tilbɑ:gə/-k-	tilbake	tilbɑ:ke	–	tilbɑ:ke	–	tilbɑ:ke
rige 'realm'	rige/ri:ke	rike	ri:ke	–	ri:ke	–	ri:ke
sprog 'language'	sprɔ:g	–	sprɔ:g	språk/sprog	sprɔ:g	språk	sprɔ:g

The question is, then, whether we can count these changes in upper-class Oslo speech as an example of language change caused by language planning.

In the upper-class speech of 1880 there were in fact some tendencies to move away from the use of voiced plosives after long vowels in some of the words in question (see Table 14.3). It is therefore legitimate to ask whether this 'Norwegianization' of upper-class speech would not have taken place anyway, without the reforms of the written language. It is not easy to reject this objection totally, since – of course – there is no possible way of finding out whether the observable development in upper-class speech would have occurred regardless of the language reforms.

A cautious conclusion about the influence of the language planning on upper-class Oslo speech would be that the changes in the written standard have at least *stimulated tendencies* within upper-class speech itself, and that they have caused an acceleration of the general shift to unvoiced plosives after long vowels.

Conclusion

The three examples of language change discussed above are all caused by language planning, but to a varying degree. The first change is the only one about which we can say with absolute certainty that without language planning this change would not have taken place. A decision was made by Parliament stating that a language change was to be implemented, and the political authorities acted accordingly using the means at their disposal: the school system and the radio (there was no television in Norway in the early 1950s). The outcome can be studied today: Norwegians use both the old and the new method of counting, and the variation can be studied and described in well-known sociolinguistic terms, taking into account, among other things, age, social class, formality, and linguistic context. It is reasonable to assume that level of education may be an important factor here as well.

The *flámæli* example is also fairly certain, although it is different from the first one in many respects. First, it concerns the eradication of a phonological feature, not the establishment of something new. The objective was to preserve the state of development of the Icelandic vowel system referred to by the Icelanders as *réttmæli* 'correct speech'. But there was no vote in the Icelandic Allting or a decision by the Icelandic government behind the action taken against *flámæli* from the 1940s onwards. It was a tacit decision made by everyone who had to do with the study and cultivation of Icelandic, based on the view that it was important to preserve the opposition in the phonological system between the vowels involved in *flámæli*. The low social reputation of this feature in Icelandic society helped support this decision. There was a consensus among linguists, school teachers, and the cultural establishment in general that the *flámæli* feature ought to be obliterated, and they worked together to reach that objective. I have, however, no hesitation in calling this also 'language planning', in line with the first Norwegian example. Although there was no decision made by a language planning body, or Parliament, as in the Norwegian example, a clear goal was defined that meant a linguistic change for a large part of the Icelandic population. A phonological feature that was already well established in the speech of nearly half the population first had to be stopped from spreading any further, and then done away with.

The third example, from upper-class Oslo speech, is of course more dubious, since the changes, on the basis of tendencies within upper-class speech itself, might have occurred regardless of the planning of the written standard. It is, however, difficult to imagine that the changes would have happened as rapidly as they have without the support of the changes made in the written standard. Around 1880, pronunciation with unvoiced stops in many words in question was considered utterly vulgar by the upper classes. However, when codified in the written standard with *p*, *t*, or *k*, some of these words lost the vulgar stigma that was associated with a pronunciation with unvoiced stops, and could then be more easily accepted also in upper-class speech. Therefore, we may conclude, language planning has also played a role in these changes in upper-class Oslo speech, although the effect of language planning in this example is more indirect than in the first two.[2]

Notes

1. The fate of *h*-dropping around the English speaking world provides a possible parallel example to the Icelandic *flámæli*-example. There is a lot of documentary evidence to suggest that, just as in England and Wales, *h*-dropping was very common in the U.S. and in Australia and New Zealand in the 19th century. Certainly in the U.S. and in New Zealand it has died out altogether. Elizabeth Gordon (1983) quotes an interesting report from a school inspector of the 19th century in New Zealand complaining about *h*-dropping in the speech of the school children. But in the 100–150 years which have elapsed since then, *h*-dropping has disappeared; even in very colloquial speech in New Zealand today we do not find it. It seems to have been a joint effort on the part of school inspectors and presumably also of other people in the cultural establishment to get rid of it. However, in this process in New Zealand – contrary to what was the case in Iceland – the influence of Standard English and the influence of immigrants from Scotland and Ireland, which did not have *h*-dropping, probably combined with the efforts by the school inspectors to get rid of the *h*-dropping. In Iceland there is no single speech variety with an influence comparable to that of Standard English in the English speaking world, and there was, of course, no immigration like that in New Zealand. Still, the fact of *h*-dropping in New Zealand provides a case rather similar to the Icelandic example described in this paper. (I thank Peter Trudgill for informing me about *h*-dropping in New Zealand, cf. Trudgill 1986: 138–139.)
2. I thank Leiv Egil Breivik and Toril Swan for correcting my English.

References

Árnason, Kristján (1987) 'Icelandic dialects forty years later: the (non)survival of some northern and south-eastern features', in: *The Nordic languages and modern linguistics 6*, edited by Pirkko Lilius – Mirja Saari, (Helsinki), pp. 79–92.

Benediktsson, Hreinn (1959) 'The vowel system of Icelandic: a survey of its history', *Word* 15: pp. 282–312.

—— (1961–62) 'Icelandic dialectology: methods and results', *Islenzk Tunga/Lingua Islandica* 3: pp. 72–113.

Blöndal, Þórunn, (1984) 'Flámæli. Nokkrar athuganir á framburði Reykvikinga fyrr og nú'. Unpublished thesis, Háskóla Íslands, Reykjavik.

Gordon, Elizabeth (1983) 'New Zealand English pronunciation: an investigation into some early written records', *Te Reo* 26: pp. 29–42.

Guðfinnsson, Björn (1947) *Breytingar á frambuði og stafsetningu* (Reykjavik: Ísafoldarprentsmiðja H.F.).

—— (1964) *Mállyzkur II Um islenzkan framburð* (= Studia Islandica 23). Reykjavik.

Jahr, Ernst Håkon (1986) 'The influence of a century's language planning on upper-class speech in Oslo', in: *Linguistics across historical and geographical boundaries. Vol I: Linguistic theory and historical linguistics*, edited by Dieter Kastovsky – Aleksander Szwedek, (Berlin: Mouton de Gruyter) pp. 397–408.

—— (1988) 'Social dialect influence in language change: the halting of a sound change in Oslo Norwegian', in: *Historical dialectology, regional and social*, edited by Jacek Fisiak, (Berlin: Mouton de Gruyter), pp. 329–337.

Kvifte, Bjørn Harald (1978) 'Den nye tellemåten – departementalt påfunn eller språkforbedring? Søkelys på tallreformen av 1951'. Unpublished thesis, University of Oslo.

Liestøl, Knut (1910) 'Nynorsk maalføring i tale og skrift samanlikna med gamalnorsk', in: *Maal og Minne* 2, (Kristiania (Oslo): Bymaalslaget), pp. 18–36.

Mercer, David (1986) 'Can Norwegians count? An investigation into the conflict in the Modern Norwegian counting system'. Unpublished paper, University of Tromsø / University of Reading.

Þráinsson, Höskuldur – Kristján Arnason (1984) 'Um reykvisku', in: *Íslenskt mál og almenn málfrœði* 6, (Reykjavik), pp. 113–134.

Trudgill, Peter (1986) *Dialects in contact* (= Language in Society 10). (Oxford: Blackwell).

Index